Note from the General Editors

Each volume in this series brings together a selection of important contributions on a particular theme, comprising excerpts from books and previously published journal articles. The need for publishing these *Readers* arises from the fact that over the years economic journals have become both numerous and expensive. Most of the journals and a good many of the books have gone beyond the reach of scholars and students in developing countries. It is for them that these volumes are primarily meant. The topics selected for these volumes are also those which are of particular interest to them.

The present series of *Readers* is a companion to the series on *Themes in Economics*, which is already being brought out by Oxford University Press. While the two series have the common objective of providing easy access to research in particular areas to students and teachers in developing countries, their contents are different. The *Themes* volumes carry freshly written survey articles while the *Readers* put together already published work which has stood the test of time.

KAUSHIK BASU
PRABHAT PATNAIK

MEASU...
INEQU... ...POVERTY

OXFORD IN INDIA READINGS

Readers in Economics
(Themes in Economics Series)

GENERAL EDITORS

- Kaushik Basu
- Prabhat Patnaik

MEASUREMENT OF
INEQUALITY AND POVERTY

Edited by

S. SUBRAMANIAN

OXFORD
UNIVERSITY PRESS

OXFORD

UNIVERSITY PRESS

YMCA Library Building, Jai Singh Road, New Delhi 110001

Oxford University Press is a department of the University of Oxford. It
furthers the University's objective of excellence in research, scholarship, and
education by publishing worldwide in

Oxford   New York

Athens   Auckland   Bangkok   Bogota   Buenos Aires   Cape Town
Chennai   Dar es Salaam   Delhi   Florence   Hong Kong   Istanbul Karachi
Kolkata   Kuala Lumpur   Madrid   Melbourne   Mexico City   Mumbai Nairobi
Paris   Sao Paulo   Shanghai   Singapore   Taipei   Tokyo   Toronto   Warsaw

with associated companies in   Berlin   Ibadan

Oxford is a registered trade mark of Oxford University Press
in the UK and in certain other countries

Published in India
By Oxford University Press, New Delhi

© Oxford University Press1997

ISBN   019 565551 6

Typeset by Rastrixi, New Delhi 110 070
Printed in India at Rashtriya Printers, Delhi 110 032
Published by Manzar Khan, Oxford University Press
YMCA Library Building, Jai Singh Road, New Delhi 110 001

Acknowledgements

The publishers wish to thank the following for permission to include the following articles in this volume:

Penguin Books, London, for Henry Mayhew, 'Of the Dustmen of London', excerpts from Henry Mayhew, *London Labour and the London Poor*, 1985 (1851), pp. 218–49, selections made and introduced by Victor Neuberg.

Journal of the American Statistical Association for M.O. Lorenz, 'Methods of Measuring the Concentration of Wealth', new series, 70, June 1905, pp. 209–19.

Oxford University Press, New York, for S. Anand, 'The Measurement of Income Inequality', excerpts from Appendices A, B and D of S. Anand, *Inequality and Poverty in Malaysia: Measurement and Decomposition*, 1983, and S. Anand, 'The Definition and Measurement of Poverty', in S. Anand, *Inequality and Poverty in Malaysia: Measurement and Decomposition*, 1983, chapter 4. Reprinted by permission of Oxford University Press.

Blackwell Publishers, U.K., for Lawrence Haddad, and Ravi Kanbur, 'How Serious is the Neglect of Intra-household Inequality?', *Economic Journal*, 100, 1990, pp. 866–81.

Elsevier Science for S. Anand and S.M.R. Kanbur, 'Inequality and Development: A Critique', reprinted from *Journal of Development Economics*, 41, 1993, pp. 19–43, and for M. Ravallion, 'On the Coverage of Public Employment Schemes for Poverty Alleviation', *Journal of Development Economics*, 1990, 34, pp. 57–79. With kind permission from Elsevier Science – NL Sara Burgerhartstraat 25, 1055, KV Amsterdam, The Netherlands.

Oxford University Press, U.K. for A.K. Sen, 'Poor, Relatively Speaking', *Oxford Economic Papers*, 35, July 1983, pp. 153–69, and for C. Gopalan, 'Undernutrition: Measurement and Implications', in S. Osmani (ed.), *Nutrition and Poverty*, Clarendon Press, 1992. Reprinted by permission of Oxford University Press.

The Econometric Society for A.K. Sen, 'Poverty: An Ordinal Approach to Measurement', *Econometrica*, 44, March 1976, pp. 219–31, and for

J. Foster, J. Greer, and E. Thorbecke, 'A Class of Decomposable Poverty Measures', *Econometrica*, 52, May 1984, pp. 761–6.

International Labour Review for S. Guhan, 'Social Security Options for Developing Countries', *ILR*, 133, 1994, pp. 35–53.

Indian Statistical Institute, Delhi Centre, for Bhaskar Dutta, Manoj Panda and Wilima Wadhwa, 'Human Development in India', *Discussion Papers in Economics Series*, No. 95–01, 1994.

Contents

x *Contents*

Introduction:
The Measurement of Inequality and Poverty

S. SUBRAMANIAN

The subject of this book, considered on its own, is vast enough: when considered in association with related fields of enquiry, its dimensions become impossibly large. To keep the task of selection and discussion within reasonably manageable bounds, the essays in this volume have been chosen with an eye mainly to issues on *measurement* from the perspective of *economics*.

The approach in this book has been to introduce the student to certain relevant themes in the measurement of inequality and poverty, so that these might serve as samples of, and pointers to, a larger arena of enquiry. Both conceptual and technical issues of measurement are sought to be addressed; and the relevance of these concerns to aspects of developing country experience are also explored in some of the essays in this volume. The intended outcome of the collection, thus, is to familiarize the scholar with some mix of concepts, theory and applications that might be expected to convey a flavour of the concerns that typically inform the work of analysts confronted with the task of measuring inequality and poverty.

In the ensuing introduction, I shall make an effort to cover certain parts of the territory under investigation, with as little resort to cumbersome technicalities as possible. Even so, the treatment — due to inevitable constraints of space — is likely to be terse. Partly as a compensation for such a compressed review, a fairly large list of references has been appended to this introduction (as a supplement to a much smaller, separate, annotated bibliography).

THE NOTION OF INEQUALITY
It is easier to characterize the notion of inequality — as being

essentially complex, not to say messy — than it is to define it. Not the least of the reasons for this is the multiplicity of places in the general scheme of things assigned to equality by a multiplicity of ethical theories.[1] *Utilitarianism* is an ethical theory which assesses the 'goodness' of a state of affairs in terms of the sum total of the utilities accruing from that state to individuals in a society. What implications does utilitarianism have for the distribution of incomes? It is conventional to assume that each person's utility function, defined on his income, is increasing, concave,[2] and indefinitely differentiable. Maximization of a utilitarian social welfare function — which is simply the sum of individual utilities — implies that the optimal distribution of income is one in which each person's marginal utility is equal to each other person's marginal utility. Utilitarianism will, thus, prescribe *the equality of marginal utilities*, which will translate to equality of *incomes* only in the special instance of all persons sharing the same utility function (see Sen 1973). Clearly, utilitarianism will tend to reward differentially those persons who are more efficient 'pleasure machines' than others.[3]

There are other ethical theories which are not concerned with the utility calculus at all (see Sen 1992). Thus, for example, in Nozick's 'entitlement theory',[4] the appropriate form of a theory of distributive justice is one in which the legitimacy of holdings is viewed with reference to three broad principles: (a) principles of acquisition; (b) principles of transfer; and (c) principles of rectification of past injustice. Nozick would require that the rules governing acquisition, transfer and rectification should be such that they are not violative of anybody's rights, which place prior constraints on the actions of others, including, in particular, the state. The emphasis here is thus on 'equal rights'

---

[1] Much of my appreciation of these issues is due to Sen (1973, 1980, 1992).

[2] Concavity is a technical restriction which guarantees that the marginal utility of income is non-increasing. Strict concavity ensures strictly diminishing marginal utility of income.

[3] See Sen (1973) for an example revolving around a two-person society in which one person, by virtue of being disabled, derives a utility level which is less than the other's for every level of income. Both the income and the total utility distributions that are recommended by utilitarianism would be tilted *against* the disabled person, which one's moral intuition — prompted, perhaps, by considerations of *need* — might find odd.

[4] See Nozick (1973). For a lucid exposition and critique of Nozick's thesis, see Varian (1975), which I have found very useful as a basis for the brief summary provided in the text.

For Dworkin (1977), it is a moot point whether people have any generalized 'right to liberty', as such. Liberty, in Dworkin's view, is compromised by equality only when liberty is interpreted as licence: it is one's generalized 'right' to liberty (as licence) that Dworkin questions. He believes that what 'political morality' should demand is the 'liberal conception of equality': this is a conception of equality, not of liberty, and requires that all citizens are entitled to being treated with the *same concern and respect* as all others. What is being emphasized here is the 'right to being treated as an equal', which Dworkin takes to be fundamental.

In the Rawlsian theory of justice (see Rawls 1971), we again have a clean break from utilitarianism. Rawls reckons advantage in terms of an index of *primary goods*, a notion which encompasses such things as rights, liberties, incomes, opportunities and the social bases of self-respect. Rawls' first principle of justice demands that each person is to have an equal right to the most extensive basic liberty compatible with a similar liberty for all. The second principle — the celebrated Difference Principle (also often referred to as the maximin principle) — requires that priority be given to maximizing the advantage (in terms of an index of primary goods) of the worst-off person. A complication of the Difference Principle which Rawls allows is what he calls the 'Lexical Difference Principle', which is essentially a lexicographic extension of the maximin principle.

Yet another ethical theory whose focus moves away from the space of utilities is Sen's theory of *capabilities* (Sen 1980, 1984, 1985a, 1992). For Sen, the appropriate domain of concern for a moral theory is one focusing on the capability of people to function. A functioning is a state of being or doing (a state of being in good health, or a state of being able to move about freely, for example). A functioning n-tuple is a list of various states of being and doing, and a *capability set* is a collection of functioning n-tuples which together define the *freedom* available to a person.[5] Sen is concerned to argue for *equality on the space of capabilities*. A capability-based approach to ethical evaluation is exempt from certain embarrassments to which utilitarianism is prone, such as the latter's propensity to differentially favour relatively more efficient 'pleasure machines' in judgments on the optimal inter-personal distribution of resources.

[5] The comparison of capability sets in terms of the freedom they offer is an extremely complex affair. For examples of exercises in this endeavour, see Pattanaik and Xu (1990) and Bossert, Pattanaik and Xu (1994).

The preceding, brief review of alternative ethical theories, each of which is concerned with a demand for equality on a different 'space' or 'domain', invites attention to each theory's respective appeal to our moral intuition, to its overall 'moral plausibility'. My job, fortunately, is not that of an arbitrator. So without quite changing the subject, I shall now move on to a consideration of aspects of inequality in the field of welfare economics.

To make inequality comparisons one needs to be able to make interpersonal comparisons. Welfare economics has been traditionally concerned to evaluate the goodness of any state of affairs solely in terms of the information provided by n-tuples of *ordinal, interpersonally noncomparable utilities*, which makes for a system of evaluation that would be subsumed under what Sen (1979) has called 'welfarism'. Welfarism, clearly, is not a fertile ground for breeding inequality judgments. One way of relaxing the informational tightness of welfarism is to effect interpersonal comparisons of welfare — without, however, moving away from 'ordinalism' — through the device of what Arrow (1977) has called 'extended sympathy'. This consists in making judgments of the form: 'it is no worse to be person j in state x than to be person k in state y'. (We shall proceed here on the assumption that it is possible to make such judgments with coherence: Basu [1995] questions this view by pointing to the possibility that such judgments could be vitiated by certain problems of trivialness or ambiguity attending them). Using the 'extended sympathy' approach, Hammond (1976) has presented a social choice-theoretic axiom of *Equity* (a generalization of Sen's [1973] 'weak equity axiom'), which essentially demands that, given a pair of social states x and y and a pair of individuals j and k, if k is worse off than j in both states x and y and if k prefers y to x while j prefers x to y with the rest of society being indifferent as between x and y, then society should defer to the relatively disadvantaged person k's preference between x and y in ranking the two alternatives. Now it can be demonstrated that, under well-specified conditions, the equity axiom just defined can conflict with a social choice-theoretic formulation of the right to liberty in purely personal matters — called 'minimal liberalism' — due to Sen (1970). Somewhat more worrying is the fact that under appropriately defined conditions, the equity axiom could run into problems of internal consistency.[6]

A further matter deserving consideration has been put in the following fashion by Sen (1992, p. 136):

[6] Typically, in societies with at least three individuals.

No matter which space is chosen for the assessment of equality, a conflict can arise between *aggregative* considerations (e.g. enhancing individual advantages, no matter how distributed) and *distributive* ones (e.g. reducing disparities in the distribution of advantages). Considerations of 'efficiency' — much discussed in economics — reflect a common element in aggregative concerns.

The reader interested in exploring the nature and implications of the conflict between equity and efficiency considerations, alluded to by Sen, should consult Rae (1975) and Weale (1980).

In the preceding brief discussion of the notion of inequality we have seen that a student of the subject must contend with several domains in which the requirement of equality has been urged by different ethical theories; that the pursuit of equality in one space may well promote inequality in some other space (Sen 1992); that the informational framework exploited by traditional welfare economics is barely adequate to perform inequality comparisons, which need to be predicated on the interpersonal comparability of welfares; that one particular (social choice-theoretic) method of formulating a principle of equity, which makes use of 'extended sympathy' as a means to this end, could run into problems of both coherent interpretation and internal consistency; that equity is only one among many social virtues, such as the right to liberty in purely private matters, and that principles of equity and liberty could clash; and that there can also be severe conflicts between 'aggregative' and 'distributional' considerations in any ethical theory. This very broad-based smattering of issues should be a sufficient preliminary introduction to the promised complexity of the notion of inequality. Further attention will be confined to the restricted field of measuring economic inequality.

MEASURING INCOME INEQUALITY

Quantification and the Assessment of Inequality

Inequalities in the distribution of income and wealth in a society can often be inferred by mere inspection. An understanding of the nature and sources of inequality and how the latter affects the lives of people is greatly advanced by good descriptions of social arrangements — descriptions that are not overly loaded by the minutiae of statistics. Chapter 1 of this volume — Henry Mayhew's (1985) pen-picture of the dustman in Dickens' London — is an example in this genre of a microcosmic view of both poverty and inequality. Readers will note though that the immediacy of Mayhew's descriptive account is only heightened by the considerable recourse he has to numbers and quantification. We shall proceed on the understanding that measurement is important for — without amounting to a whole account of — the appraisal of the phenomena of poverty and inequality.

Preliminary Concepts

We shall be concerned specifically with inequality in the space of *incomes*. An *income distribution* is a vector of incomes $x = (x_1, \ldots, x_i, \ldots x_n)$ where x_i is the income of the ith person in a society of n individuals. The mean of the distribution x will be written as $\mu(x)$, and the dimensionality of x as $n(x)$. What we have just discussed is a *discrete* distribution. On occasion we shall have reason to employ a *continuous* distribution. Here income is a random variable with a lower bound of x_o (≥ 0) and an upper bound of $\bar{x}$. The density function of x (viz. the proportion of the population with income x) is $f(x)$, $F(x)$ is the cumulative density function (viz. the proportion of the population with incomes not exceeding x), and $F_1(x)$ is the first-moment distribution function (viz. the cumulative share in income of units with incomes not exceeding x). Note that, by definition, $F(x) = \int_{x_o}^{x} f(y)dy$ and $F_1(x) = 1/\mu \int_{x_o}^{x} yf(y)dy$, where μ is the mean of the distribution. (For a clear statement of preliminary concepts and definitions, see Kakwani 1980a).

The Lorenz Curve

A visually appealing way of representing the inequality of an income distribution is obtained by plotting the cumulative share in total income against the cumulative proportion of the population with incomes not exceeding a given level, for every level of income. (In the context of a continuous distribution the relevant graph is obtained as a plot of $F_1(x)$ against $F(x)$). This curve, discovered by Lorenz (1905; see Chapter 2 in this volume), will typically look like any one of the curves drawn for three hypothetical (unequal) distributions, x, y and z in Figure 0.1.[7]

Now, given any two distributions x and y, x will be said to *Lorenz-dominate* y — written xLy — if the Lorenz curve of x lies somewhere inside and nowhere outside the Lorenz curve of y. The

---

[7] Readers will note that, as it happens, Lorenz drew his curve 'upside down', that is he plotted the curve obtained by inverting the axes in Figure 0.1.

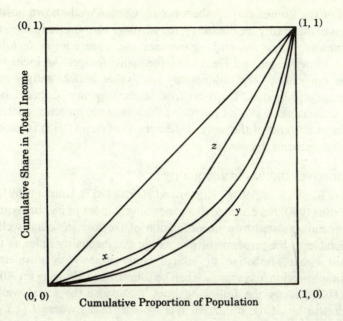

Figure 0.1

binary relation L is *reflexive* (that is, xLx for any distribution x) and *transitive* (that is, for any three distributions x, y and z, xLy and yLz imply xLz), but is not *complete* (that is, it is not necessarily true that for every pair of distributions x and y either xLy or yLx must hold: neither statement would be true if the Lorenz curves for the two distributions intersected). In Figure 0.1, we have a situation in which xLy and zLy but neither xLz nor zLx. Typically, the binary relation L is a *partial ordering*. A real-valued index of inequality, by contrast, will induce a 'regular' ordering of distributions since any pair of real numbers can be compared with each other in terms of the '$\geq$' relation. By a real-valued index of inequality, we mean an index I which assigns a real number to every distribution x, where the real number is intended to signify the extent of inequality in the distribution.

'Positive' Indices of Inequality

A large class of real-valued inequality indices is one that is constituted by the so-called 'positive' or 'descriptive' indices, which are essentially statistical measures of dispersion. Many of these indices are directly based on the Lorenz curve, others not so. Certain well-known positive indices of inequality are the *range*, the *variance*, the *squared coefficient of variation*, the *variance of log incomes*, the *relative mean deviation*, the *Gini Coefficient*, and Theil's two inequality indices. An index such as the range is a very rudimentary one; other indices satisfy more demanding properties. I forbear from discussing any of these issues here, since Anand (1983: Chapter 3 in this volume) presents a detailed and lucid account of the subject. Chapter 3 of Sen (1973) is another valuable guide to the reader.

'Normative' Indices of Inequality

Writers like Dalton (1920), Aigner and Heins (1967), Kolm (1969) and Atkinson (1970) have argued that a meaningful index of inequality must be somehow related to a quantification of the loss in social welfare attributable to the presence of inequality: the inequality index is thus imbued with a 'normative' or 'ethical' connotation. With considerable oversimplification, the approach can be summarized, drawing on Atkinson (1970), along the following lines.[8] Suppose the social welfare function to be of the utilitarian type: $W = \Sigma_i \, U\,(x_i)$ where $U(\,.\,)$ is a utility function — assumed identical for all individuals — which is non-decreasing and concave. Let $\hat{\mu}(x)$ be that level of income such that its equal distribution leads to a level of welfare which is the same as the welfare level at the actual distribution under consideration. The egalitarian tilt secured by concavity of the utility function will ensure that $\hat{\mu}$ does not exceed μ. Atkinson refers to $\hat{\mu}$ as the 'equally distributed equivalent income'. The difference between μ and $\hat{\mu}$, expressed as a proportion of μ, can now be interpreted as a measure of inequality: it measures the welfare loss, occasioned by inequality, in equivalent income units. In deriving his inequality index, Atkinson specializes the utility function to the so-called 'constant-elasticity-of-marginal-utility' form, given by $U(x_i) = 1/1 - \in x_i^{\,1-\in}$ (for $\in \neq 1$) and $U(x_i) = \log x_i$ (for $\in = 1$); to ensure concavity of $U(\,.\,)$, $\in$ is confined to non-negative values, and the parameter $\in$ is interpreted as measuring a degree of 'aversion' to inequality.

[8] This is essentially the approach of Atkinson. It should be clarified that writers like Aigner and Heins (1967), for example, have specified social welfare to be a function directly of the income levels in the distribution, without the mediation of individual utility functions, and they measure equality in terms of the ratio of the actual level of welfare to its maximum value (which is attained through a redistribution of incomes in which each person receives the mean income).

While this approach to inequality measurement is strikingly interesting, it has its own problems, which have been carefully discussed by Sen (1978). Sen points out that inequality indices must measure inequality and not the loss in social welfare occasioned by inequality: conflating the two notions could do violence to the independent descriptive role which an inequality index has. Further, as Shorrocks (1988) points out, standard 'positive' measures of inequality can themselves be absorbed within the 'ethical' fold: the implicit social welfare functions underlying these descriptive measures can always be 'uncovered'. The argument — which is not likely to be always conclusive — will then have to be about the relative appeals of the SWFs underlying the different indices.

The Welfare Basis of Inequality Comparisons

Recall that the 'ethical' approach to inequality measurement espoused by Atkinson is based on postulating an SWF given by $W = \Sigma_i\ U(x_i)$, where the $U(.)$ function is non-decreasing and concave. Now there are any number of $U(.)$ functions which will answer to the description of non-decreasingness and concavity. The question arises: under what conditions can two distributions x and y with the same mean and population be ranked without particularizing any further the form of the $U(.)$ function? Atkinson (1970) has presented a remarkable equivalence theorem which accords a central place to the Lorenz dominance relation L, discussed above. His theorem states that given any two distributions x and y with a common mean and a common population, if xLy then welfare from x will be judged to be no less than welfare from y no matter which $U(.)$ function is used (so long as it is non-decreasing and concave); and conversely, if welfare from x is no less than welfare from y no matter which $U(.)$ function is used (so long as it is non-decreasing and concave), it must be the case that xLy. Atkinson's theorem, and related results, are very elegantly discussed in Anand's essay in this volume.[9] Strengthened and generalized versions of Atkinson's result are available in a number of other contributions (among others, see Rothschild and Stiglitz 1973 and Dasgupta, Sen and Starrett 1973).

[9] Partly in order to avoid duplication, and partly in view of the fact that Atkinson's essay — which has been widely anthologized — is easily accessible, this modern classic has, with genuine regret, been excluded from the present collection.

Properties of Inequality Measures

A number of properties that may be regarded as being desirable for an inequality index to satisfy have been proposed in the literature (see Foster 1985 and Shorrocks 1988). Some of these properties — often presented in the form of axioms — are briefly described below. *Symmetry* requires that an inequality index should be invariant with respect to a permutation of incomes across individuals; the *Pigou–Dalton* or *transfer* axiom requires that, *ceteris paribus*, a rank-preserving transfer of income from one person to a poorer person should cause the extent of measured inequality to decline; *transfer-sensitivity* requires that an inequality index should be more sensitive to transfers at the lower end of a distribution than at its upper end;[10] *normalization* requires the inequality index to assume a value of zero for a perfectly equal distribution of incomes; *continuity* requires the inequality index to be continuous in the domain of income distributions; *scale-invariance* (or *mean-independence*) requires the extent of inequality to remain unchanged if every income in a distribution is multiplied by a positive real number;[11] *replication-invariance* (or *population-invariance*) requires that if each income in a distribution is replicated m times over (where m is any positive integer), the extent of inequality for the 'replicated' distribution should be the same as for the original distribution; and *subgroup consistency* requires that, *ceteris paribus*, an increase in inequality in every subgroup within a population should lead to an increase in overall inequality.

The usefulness of an inequality index must often be judged in relation to the purpose on hand. For example if one's object is to assess the contribution of different subgroups (constituted on the basis of say, age, caste or gender) to overall inequality, then passing the test of subgroup consistency becomes an important criterion for eligibility of an inequality index: indeed, in one fell swoop, the set of admissible indices shrinks to the class of 'Generalized Entropy Measures', of which Theil's two indices and the squared coefficient of variation are special cases.[12]

[10] For alternative versions of the transfer-sensitivity property, see the formulations in Kakwani (1980b, 1984), Shorrocks and Foster (1987) and Foster and Shorrocks (1988c).

[11] The class of inequality indices which satisfies this property is *'relative'* inequality measures. Scale-invariance is not an uncontroversial property (for example Kolm 1976a, 1976b has argued that an inequality index should be sensitive to the absolute sizes of the incomes, too).

[12] For a precise statement of the relevant result and associated discussion, see Shorrocks (1988).

Haddad and Kanbur (1990, Chapter 4 in this volume) provide an example of the usefulness of being able to 'decompose' overall inequality into its 'within-group' and 'between-group' components. They address the specific problem of reckoning the contribution to overall inequality of within-household inequality in the distribution of the calorific adequacy of food consumption (an assessment that is often rendered difficult by the non-availability of data). Using sample survey data for the Philippines, Haddad and Kanbur find that the neglect of within-household inequality can lead to a significant reduction in the estimate of overall inequality. (This particular issue is of both methodological and substantive importance, especially in the context of assessing gender-related biases in the intra-family distribution of food [on which see, among others, Kynch and Sen 1983 and Harriss 1990]).

Inequality Comparisons and Unambiguous Rankings

Another reason for being sensitive to the properties of an inequality index arises from the fact that with several indices jostling for space, we may fail to obtain an 'unambiguous'[13] ranking of distributions, unless the set of admissible indices is constrained to a manageable size by requiring the indices to share certain desirable properties. The conditions under which members of an admissible set of indices, sharing certain specified properties, can be expected to yield identical rankings of distributions, have been studied: some of the relevant results are discussed in Anand (see also Foster and Shorrocks 1988c for further insights into this problem).

INEQUALITY AND DEVELOPMENT

The Kuznets Hypothesis

A classic thesis on how inequality in the distribution of income responds to an economy's development has been formulated by Kuznets (1955). In his celebrated paper, Kuznets advanced, with a great deal of circumspection and tentativeness, the hypothesis that as a country's average per capita income increases over time, there would probably be a tendency for inequality to first rise and subsequently decline: this is the famous 'inverted- *U*' hypothesis — which as it happens — was predicated on the fulfilment of certain well-defined conditions. Empirical

---

[13] The presence of ambiguity has led some analysts to view inequality measurement as being a particularly apposite field for the application of *fuzzy* logic: see, in this connection, Basu (1987) and Ok (1995).

verification (or rejection) of Kuznets' hypothesis is obviously a matter of considerable importance — one in which economists of different ideological persuasions have profound stake.[14] It is, therefore, hardly surprising that the empirical literature seeking confirmation of Kuznets' thesis is shot through with disagreement and controversy (for references, see the papers cited in Anand and Kanbur 1993b, Chapter 5 in this volume).

The most influential support for Kuznets' hypothesis has come from the work of Ahluwalia (1974, 1976a, 1976b) and Ahluwalia et al. (1979). In two companion pieces, Anand and Kanbur (1993a and 1993b [Chapter 5]) have undertaken a detailed critical scrutiny of the Ahluwalia findings. Readers are advised to study both pieces together. A quick summary of the Anand–Kanbur critique would boil down to the judgment that there is much that is wrong and little that is right with the Ahluwalia (1976b) exercise. First, a cross-section study (such as the one Ahluwalia conducted) is not apposite to the purpose on hand. Second, the functional form of the relation between (in)equality and income, which Ahluwalia specifies, is in no way dictated by the 'mechanics' of the Kuznets process, which is claimed to have spawned the relationship being tested. Third, there is a whole host of inequality indices to choose from, and the privileged position accorded by Ahluwalia to the income share of the poorest 40 per cent is, at least, arbitrary. Fourth, in Anand and Kanbur (1993b), the regression of I (the income-share of the poorest 40 per cent) against μ (average per capita income) for the cross-section of countries considered by Ahluwalia yields, for alternative functional forms, wide variations with respect to goodness-of-fit and turning points; nor is each functional form dominated by the Ahluwalia specification in an appropriately conducted econometric test of dominance. Fifth, country-specific projections of the income-share of the poorest 40 per cent are found to be extremely sensitive to the precise functional form employed. Sixth, the data set employed by Ahluwalia is found to be inconsistent in respect of aspects on which Kuznets himself (1955;

[14] Of relevance here is the familiar 'growth versus redistribution' debate. For an analysis of the 'trade-off' between growth and poverty eradication through redistribution, with specific reference to the economy of Fiji, see Kanbur (1985); Kanbur suggests that the growth costs of redistributive poverty eradication could be exaggerated, at least in terms of the numbers as they work out for Fiji, and that there is a case for examining the issue more closely on a country-specific basis. See also in this connection — for an application to India — Jayaraj and Subramanian (1995a).

p. 3) urged great caution: 'income concept, unit of observation, and proportion of the total universe covered'. Chapter 5 is a sombre, cautionary tale which upholds the moral of that old English proverb: 'he that forsakes measure, measure forsakes'.

Inequality between and within Countries

Given inadequate, unreliable and often non-comparable data sets, cross-country comparisons of inequality are very difficult to achieve. A painstaking effort at such comparisons, subject to these constraints, is to be found in Grilli (1994). The reader is referred particularly to Table 3.8 of Grilli's paper, which presents a summary picture of the unequally skewed distribution of global GDP; and to Table 3.9, which carries information on within-country inequality (relating to the distribution of total household income, the data on which are of national coverage) for a set of 32 countries in the 1980s.

Inequality in India

Despite such data as have been collected by the National Council of Applied Economic Research, information on the distribution of *income* is not available on a systematic basis for India. What we do have are data on the distribution of *consumer expenditure*. These data are available from the 1950s, and after the mid-1970s, the National Sample Survey (NSS) data are available quinquennially.

The Planning Commission's (1969) *Report of the Committee on Distribution of Income and Levels of Living* (Part II: *Changes in Levels of Living*) is an example of a remarkably detailed analysis of certain early rounds of the NSS data. A particularly noteworthy feature of the analysis is its sensitivity to the impact of inflation on the relative and absolute levels of living of the poorer sections of the population, with specific reference to the quantity and quality of food consumed by them. Such studies have great relevance for certain contemporary trends of rising food prices which are being observed in a time of structural adjustment and economic 'reform'. Situated a little less than half-way between Independence and now, the Planning Commission's 1969 study still has lessons for us — a fact which is both instructive and disheartening.

Secular trends in the behaviour of the Gini coefficient of inequality in the distribution of consumption expenditure have been studied by, among others, Ahluwalia (1978), Dutta (1980) and Sundrum (1987). Vaidyanathan (1974) takes note of the possibility that since consumers in different size-classes typically consume different commodity-bundles, they would be confronted with differential rates of inflation: both methodologically and substantively, his effort at reckoning inequality after deflating nominal expenditure levels with fractile-specific price indices is an important contribution. Suryanarayana (1991) alerts the user of NSS data to the possibility that a combination of secular inflation and the relatively infrequent NSS reclassification of the expenditure size-classes in nominal terms could — by understating the convexity of the Lorenz curve — make for a built-in bias toward progressively understating inequality over time. A review of various studies would suggest that, by and large, the Gini coefficient of inequality in the distribution of consumption expenditure has been of the order of 0.3 or more during the last four decades. Considering that we are dealing with consumer expenditure rather than income, and given the generally low levels of consumer expenditure that have obtained, a Gini coefficient of 0.3 must be judged to signal substantial inequality. It seems, on the whole, fair to suggest that there has been no dramatic secular decline of inequality in the distribution of consumption expenditure in the country (for more detailed considerations of these issues, see Srinivasan and Bardhan 1974, 1988).

Asset-concentration is again a pronounced feature of the Indian economy. In a useful survey of the evidence, Vaidyanathan (1990), basing himself on the Reserve Bank's *All India Debt and Investment Surveys* of 1971–2 and 1981–2, indicates that there has been some slight decline in a high level of concentration in the distribution of assets across households over the decadal period under consideration. (The Gini coefficient has been in excess of 0.6 in both years.) Altogether, the orders of magnitude we have reviewed suggest that in terms of the distribution of both endowments and entitlements to final goods, India is a country of large inequalities.[15] Policy performance in the matter of redressing this circumstance — whether in the field of land reform (see Bandopadhyay 1988), or of curtailing tax evasion and the burgeoning of a 'parallel economy' (see National Institute of Public Finance and Policy 1984), or of raising revenues for redistribution by taxation of a largely untaxed agricultural sector (see Raj 1973) — has remained disappointingly unprogressive.

[15] For a micro-level study of how inequality in access to productive resources can affect the functioning of markets and determine patterns of surplus extraction in a rural setting, see Janakarajan (1992).

MEASURING POVERTY:
THE IDENTIFICATION EXERCISE

'Relativist' versus 'Absolutist' Conceptualizations of Poverty

In the measurement of poverty, two issues come to the fore: those of 'identification' (who are the poor?) and 'aggregation' (how to construct a real-valued index of poverty on the basis of information about the poor?). If, as is usually the case, it is income-poverty one is concerned with, the identification exercise would consist in specifying a level of income, called the *poverty line*, which separates the poor from the non-poor. A widely used procedure for specifying the poverty line, especially in developing countries which are a long way away from a generalized state of having met most citizens' basic needs, is subsumed in the 'biological' approach (Sen 1981a), in terms of which the poverty line is fixed with reference to the income needed to achieve a calorifically adequate diet (on which more later).

At a general level, the question needs to be addressed of whether the notion of poverty should be assessed in 'relative' or 'absolute' terms. Sen (1983; Chapter 6 in this volume), who rejects (a certain sort of) relativism and claims that there is an irreducible 'absolutist core' to poverty, offers an important clarificatory statement on the subject, which should be of considerable assistance in sorting out certain confusions that are pervasive in one's attempts at conceptualizing the notion of poverty. Sen's rejection of 'relativism' is not to be confounded as amounting to an endorsement of the view that needs are fixed and unchanging across space and over time, and that therefore resort should be had to an unvarying poverty line (subject only to correction for price variations) in cross-sectional and inter-temporal comparisons. (Such a construction of Sen's thesis by Townsend seems to be at the heart of the exchanges between Townsend [1985] and Sen [1985].) For Sen, it is most profitable to regard poverty in an absolute light in the domain of capabilities (including, for example, the capability to 'live without shame'), and this might entail regarding poverty in a relative light in the domain of incomes or resources. Where Sen resists 'relativism' is when such relativism renders poverty indistinguishable from inequality. To define poverty in terms, for example, of the income share of the poorest x per cent of the population is problematic: a doubling of incomes would leave the value of this quantity, and therefore one's assessment of the extent of inequality, unaltered; but to claim that there has been no change in poverty under these circumstances is certainly dubious.

Measuring Undernutrition

One approach to the identification exercise — alluded to in the previous section — revolves around the notion of counting the poor as those who do not (have the means to) escape undernourishment. Nutritional status is conventionally measured in terms of either nutrient intake or anthropometric criteria. The measurement issues involved here are complex in the extreme, and the literature (as contributed to by both development economists and biological scientists) is saturated with claims, counterclaims and a fair amount of bad blood. Gopalan (1992; Chapter 7 in this volume) provides a lucid account of the issues and controversies involved, with specific emphasis on certain India-related concerns.

In measuring undernutrition in relation to calorific adequacy, the conventional practice has been to specify a cut-off level of calorific requirement as an average of the requirements of 'reference-type' individuals, with due regard for age, sex, body weight and activity status. Various norms of requirements in kilocalories per day have been suggested (see, for example, FAO 1973, cited in Dasgupta and Ray 1990; Dandekar and Rath 1971; Planning Commission, Government of India 1981, and so on). In a number of influential writings, Sukhatme and his associates[16] have argued that it is misleading to classify persons as being undernourished if their calorific intake, averaged over a short reference period, is found to fall short of the requirement norm, which is a long-term average.

Sukhatme advances two hypotheses to support his view: the 'auto-regulatory hypothesis' and the 'adaptation hypothesis'. The efficiency with which energy is utilized in the conversion of food into work plays an important part in both hypotheses. Under the first hypothesis, the efficiency of energy utilization is viewed as a variable that is amenable to modelling as an auto-correlated variable which 'induces' a corresponding auto-correlation in intake: when efficiency is 'high', the

---

[16] See Sukhatme (1978, 1981, 1982) and Sukhatme and Margen (1980). In a spirit of candid confession, I must admit to not having found Sukhatme at all easy to penetrate. Two quite brilliant expositions which are indispensable aids to achieving a measure of comprehension of the issues at stake are those by Osmani (1992) and Dasgupta and Ray (1990). For other responses to Sukhatme, see Dandekar (1981), Krishnaji (1981) and Zubrigg (1983). The collection of papers in Osmani (1992) is an important one for readers interested in pursuing these matters further.

body regulates intake to a 'low' level, and *vice versa*. For a reference period of a week or so, Sukhatme estimates the coefficient of variation in intra-individual requirement to be of the order of 15–20 per cent. Letting μ stand for the long-run requirement of energy and σ for the standard deviation, it is clear that there is a 95 per cent probability that a healthy, unconstrained individual will have an intake in time t, I_t, which is in the range $[\mu - 2\sigma, \mu + 2\sigma]$. Arising from this, Sukhatme suggests that persons need be considered undernourished only if their observed intake is less than $\mu - 2\sigma$. On this basis, he estimates nutritional deprivation in India, using NSS data for 1971–2, to be considerably less than the estimate of the population in deficit obtained by Dandekar and Rath (1971).[17]

In Sukhatme's *adaptation* hypothesis, the direction of causality is reversed: it is no longer intake which adjusts itself to efficiency of energy utilization, but the other way around. In this view, the body has a capacity to organize the efficiency with which energy is utilized in such a way that (within bounds), efficiency is raised when intake is low, and lowered when intake is high. By drawing on the auto-regulatory hypothesis, Sukhatme again justifies $\mu - 2\sigma$, now considered as the lower bound yielded by *adaptation*, as an appropriate requirement norm.

A few points must be noted here. First, the clinical evidence for Sukhatme's hypotheses is dubious (Dasgupta and Ray 1990, Osmani 1992 and Gopalan, Chapter 7 of this volume). Second, as Osmani (1992) points out, under the autoregulatory hypothesis, an observed intake of less than $\mu - 2\sigma$ is only a sufficient condition for undernourishment, not a necessary condition. Third, again as Osmani (1992) argues, Sukhatme's justification of the lower cut-off point of $\mu - 2\sigma$ under the adaptation hypothesis is based on the logic of the autoregulatory hypothesis, which is unacceptable since the one hypothesis reverses the direction of causation between intake and efficiency as postulated by the other. Fourth, it is at least questionable if Sukhatme's use of the $\mu - 2\sigma$ formula is applicable in the context of NSS data in which the reference period is a full thirty days: Sukhatme is nowhere

[17] It is important to note that Sukhatme's estimates are not directly comparable to the Dandekar–Rath estimates. Sukhatme was measuring the incidence of undernutrition proper, while Dandekar and Rath were concerned to estimate the proportion of the population with per capita consumption expenditure levels in deficit of what was required to gain command over food items that could meet the given norms of calorific adequacy.

explicit on how long the period of observation must be for the observed mean intake to converge on the long-term mean requirement (see Krishnaji 1981 and Dasgupta and Ray 1990).

Clearly, the measurement of undernutrition is an activity from which normative evaluation cannot be divorced; at the least, one has to be clear about one's attitude toward which of two types of risks one wishes to minimize: the risk of classifying an undernourished person as well nourished, and the risk of classifying a well-nourished person as undernourished. Gopalan's values, in this sense, are clearly in evidence in his rejection of Sukhatme's hypotheses as also of Seckler's (1982) 'small but healthy' hypothesis which postulates that stunting as an adaptive response to reduced intake may not necessarily spell severe functional impairment if the weight-for-height measure is at an acceptable level.

MEASURING POVERTY:
THE AGGREGATION EXERCISE

Counting Heads and Gaps: A Prelude to Sen's Index

The identification exercise, as we have seen in the previous section, is a vexed business. We shall now consider the aggregation problem on the assumption that the identification problem has been somehow solved, so that we can proceed to treat the poverty line as 'given'. It is this issue with which Sen (1976a; Chapter 8 of this volume) and Foster, Greer and Thorbecke (1984; Chapter 9 in this volume) are directly concerned.[18] We begin by letting $x = (x_1, \ldots, x_i \ldots, x_n)$ stand for an ordered n-vector of incomes, with $x_i \leq x_{i+1}$ for all $i = 1, \ldots, n-1$.

A real-valued index of poverty $P(x; z)$ is a function which, for every income-vector x and positive poverty line z, specifies a unique real number which is intended to signify the extent of poverty associated with the regime $(x; z)$. The simplest index of poverty one can think of — called the *headcount ratio* — is the proportion of the population in poverty, and is given by $H = q/n$, where q is the number of poor persons[19] and n is the total population. H clearly measures the *incidence*

---

[18] For an excellent survey of aggregation issues, see Foster (1984); also Kakwani (1984) and Atkinson (1987).

[19] A 'poor' person is defined as one whose income does not exceed the poverty line z. This is the strong definition of the poor; the weak definition identifies the poor as those with incomes strictly less than the poverty line. The difference can be of crucial significance in a variety of contexts (see Donaldson and Weymark 1986).

of poverty in a population. If we are interested in the *depth* of poverty, that is, in how poor the poor are on average, we might use an index called the *income-gap ratio* which measures the proportionate shortfall of the average income μ^p of the poor from the poverty line, and is given by $I = 1 - \mu^p/z$.

A seemingly mild requirement for a poverty index is that it should satisfy the *focus* axiom which requires the poverty measure to be insensitive (other things equal) to an increase in the income of a non-poor person. A second desirable property is that, other things equal, a reduction in a poor person's income should increase the value of the poverty measure: this is called the *monotonicity* axiom. A third desirable property is the *transfer* axiom: this axiom demands that, other things equal, a transfer of income from a poor person to a richer poor person should raise the value of the poverty index. A weakened version of this axiom — the *weak transfer* axiom — would require that a regressive transfer of the type just described should increase the value of the poverty index, provided the beneficiary of the transfer continues to remain poor after the transfer. It is easy to see that both H and I satisfy the focus axiom; that H violates both monotonicity and weak transfer; and that I satisfies monotonicity while violating weak transfer.

Sen (Chapter 8) seeks to derive an index of poverty which is capable of satisfying weak transfer as well as the other axioms just discussed.[20] Pursuing a persuasively axiomatic approach,[21] Sen demonstrates that the only index capable of satisfying a set of plausible properties he advances is given, in the asymptotic case where the number of poor persons is 'large', by

$$P^s(x; z) = H[I + (1 - I)G^p], \qquad (1)$$

where G^p is the Gini coefficient of inequality in the distribution of poor incomes. Sen's index is a *distribution-sensitive* index: it satisfies the weak transfer axiom (though not necessarily the transfer axiom), as well as the focus and monotonicity axioms, and presents a comprehensive picture of poverty by utilizing data on the *incidence* of poverty (H), the *depth* of poverty (I), and the *extent of inequality* in the distribution of poor incomes (via G^p). Sen's index also satisfies *symmetry*, which requires that the value of the poverty index should be invariant with respect to a permutation of incomes across individuals.

---

[20] For a remarkable early effort which in many ways anticipates Sen's work, but without the use of an explicitly axiomatic framework, see Watts (1968).

[21] For a further axiomatization of Sen's 'normalization axiom', see Basu (1984).

Some Additional Real-Value Poverty Indices

Sen's work has triggered off a number of contributions to the poverty measurement literature. An early critical response to Sen's approach is to be found in Takayama (1979). Thon (1979) has advanced a variant of the Sen index which satisfies not only the weak transfer but also the transfer axiom, which could be violated by Sen's index. An aspect of distributional interest resides in the requirement that a poverty index be more sensitive to transfers at the lower than at the upper end of the income distribution of the poor. Concretely, one could require the index to satisfy a property which one may call *transfer-sensitivity*-1 (TS-1), according to which the increase in poverty attendant upon a regressive transfer of given size between two poor individuals a fixed number of individuals apart should be greater the poorer is the pair of persons involved in the transfer (see Foster 1984). In the quest for indices with the potential for satisfying TS-1, Kakwani (1980b, 1984) has offered a generalization of Sen's index by advancing a whole family of (suitably parametrized) indices. Anand (1977) has an interesting poverty index which lends itself to interpretation more as a measure of the redistributive effort that would be required to eradicate poverty in a society than as a measure of poverty *per se* (see Anand 1977 and Sen 1981a).

Atkinson (1987) and Keen (1992) have pointed out that one approach to formulating a poverty index is to write it as an arithmetical average of the 'deprivation functions' $\pi(x_i; z)$ of all persons in a society.

$$P(x; z) = (1/n) \sum_{i=1}^{n} \pi(x_i; z). \tag{2}$$

If the deprivation function $\pi(x_i; z)$ is of the form $\emptyset(x_i/z)$, we obtain a relative measure of poverty.[22] (A relative measure satisfies the property that $P[x; z] = P[\lambda x; \lambda z]$ for any $\lambda > 0$.) For given z, the function $\emptyset(.)$ (see Keen 1992) might reasonably be expected to display the following properties: (a) $\emptyset$ should be non-increasing in x_i/z (which would correspond to a weakened version of the monotonicity condition); (b) if $\emptyset$ declines with x_i/z, it should do so at a non-decreasing rate (which is a weak convexity requirement that would correspond to a weakened version of the weak transfer axiom); and (c) $\emptyset(x_i/z) = 0$ for $x_i/z \geq 1$ (that is, deprivation vanishes when a person's income hits the poverty line).

---

[22] On the distinction between relative and absolute measures of poverty, see Blackorby and Donaldson (1980). Here we shall not be concerned with absolute measures (P); x; z; $\Pi(x_i; z)$; and (6.2.1); and $\Omega[x_i - z]$.

Foster, Greer ánd Thorbecke (Chapter 9 in this volume) present an entire class of relative poverty indices, parametrized in terms of the quantity α, which can be interpreted as a measure of 'poverty aversion' and given by

$$P_\alpha(x; z) = \frac{1}{n} \Sigma_{i=1}^q \, \varnothing(x_i/z) \text{ where } \varnothing(x_i/z) = [(z-x_i)/z]^\alpha, \, \alpha \geq 0 \quad (3)$$

Two properties of poverty indices addressed by the P_α class merit mention. The first is a property which one may call *transfer-sensitivity-2* (TS-2), which requires that the increase in poverty arising from a given regressive transfer between two poor persons a fixed income apart should be greater the poorer is the pair of persons involved in the transfer (see Foster 1984). (P_α becomes more and more distributionally sensitive as α increases, and satisfies TS-2 for $\alpha > 2$). The second property of interest is that of *decomposability*, which requires that the poverty index be amenable to being expressed as a weighted sum of subgroup poverty indices, the weights being the subgroup population shares. P_α satisfies decomposability for all $\alpha \geq 0$. A weaker condition than decomposability is that of *subgroup consistency* which requires only that overall poverty should increase when, *ceteris paribus*, poverty in any subgroup increases. (For a characterization of the class of subgroup consistent poverty indices, see Foster and Shorrocks 1991). Sen's index fails subgroup consistency (and therefore decomposability), whereas the headcount ratio does satisfy decomposability, despite its other shortcomings.

Various other poverty indices can be obtained through alternative specifications of the 'deprivation function' $\varnothing(x_i/z)$: an indicative — but not exhaustive — list of important contributions to the stock of poverty indices would include those due to Watts (1968), Clark, Hemming and Ulph (1981) and Chakravarty (1983a and 1983b). In addition to these, mention must be made of the class of so-called 'ethical' poverty indices discussed by Blackorby and Donaldson (1980) (see also Hagenaars 1987): these indices are analogous to the 'ethical' indices of inequality. Each index in this class can be written as a distinguished per capita income gap ratio $H\hat{I}$, where $\hat{I}$ measures the proportionate shortfall of Atkinson 'equally distributed equivalent income' $\hat{\mu}^p$ (computed for the distribution of poor incomes) from the poverty line. Depending on what specific 'social evaluation function' we employ, we will obtain different expressions for $\hat{\mu}^p$ (and therefore for $\hat{I}$ and the corresponding 'ethical' poverty index).

Properties of Poverty Measures

As we have seen, several criteria have been advanced as being desirable ones for a poverty measure to satisfy: focus, symmetry, monotonicity, weak transfer, transfer, transfer-sensitivity, subgroup consistency, decomposability. From the preceding brief review, it is clear that not all poverty indices satisfy all these properties. Further, many axioms for the measurement of poverty are individually appealing, but it can happen that our effort at characterizing the class of poverty indices satisfying a given set of axioms terminates in a discovery of non-existence. (A celebrated 'impossibility theorem' for poverty indices is one due to Kundu and Smith [1983]; for a whole host of other impossibility results, see Donaldson and Weymark [1986].) The measurement of poverty is thus attended by problems of pluralism — necessitating choice among competing contenders — logical inconsistency, and ambiguity of interpretation. There can be no prior assumption as to freedom from confusion in this field of enquiry, but presumably the area of confusion can be narrowed down with some clarity of thought regarding purpose and context.

Poverty Measures and Unambiguous Rankings

Unambiguous poverty rankings could be hard to come by for two reasons: (a) not all poverty indices may yield the same ranking of two given distributions x and y for a given poverty line z; and (b) the same poverty index may rank x over y for some poverty line z_1 and y over x for some other poverty line z_2. Problem (a) is analogous to the one we have encountered in the context of inequality rankings, and a stratagem to cope with it would be to restrict the set of 'admissible' indices by requiring these to satisfy a set of 'reasonable' axioms and seek conditions under which all the indices in the admissible set coincide in their rankings of distributions (see Foster and Shorrocks 1988c). Problem (b) has been lucidly addressed in Foster and Shorrocks (1988a, 1988b) in the context of the P_α family of poverty indices, and the relevant results suggest that the prospect of obtaining unambiguous poverty rankings is linked in a specific way to the fulfilment of various stochastic dominance conditions.[23] Although this issue will not be

---

23 On stochastic dominance, see Hadar and Russell (1969).

pursued here, it is important to note that it is a crucial one: applied work on data sets suggests that one's estimate of poverty can be critically sensitive to *where* one pitches the poverty line, and reversals .of poverty rankings for variations in the poverty line within reasonable bounds could make one's estimate very non-robust.

The Poverty of Nations

The vast literature on the conceptual and technical issues underlying the measurement of poverty has sought application in a number of country-specific studies of poverty over the years. It is very difficult to provide a synoptic view of magnitudes and trends in the developing world, but a painstaking compilation of available evidence for the decades of the 1970s and 1980s can be found in Grilli (1994). The reader is particularly referred to Table 3.11 in Grilli, which furnishes estimates of the headcount ratio — drawn from various sources — for a sample of thirty-four developing countries. Anand's (1983) study of Malaysia is an example of a concrete application of measurement issues to an assessment of poverty in a country. (Chapter 10 in this volume is an extract from his book.) The reader will note that Anand's analysis covers many of the issues in measurement that have been reviewed here. His piece carries a careful analysis of the identification problem in the Malaysian context, and considers both relative and absolute approaches to the specification of a suitable poverty line; alternative poverty measures, and their meaning and appropriateness in alternative contextual trappings, are discussed; estimates of poverty are obtained at an aggregative level, employing various relatively sophisticated measures of poverty; recourse is had to the headcount ratio, by virtue of its decomposability property, in order to present a detailed profile of poverty in Malaysia, through a classification of the population into various groupings based on race, location, employment status, occupation and education: this is particularly important for the formulation of policy and the efficient targeting of anti-poverty measures, which is greatly facilitated by the establishment of correlates between poverty and various other characteristics that may be more readily inferred then income can be; and the robustness of the poverty estimate with respect to the poverty line selected is assessed by sensitivity analysis.

Since there is no reading specifically devoted to a consideration of trends and magnitudes of poverty in India, I present a very quick review of some salient features in this regard in the following section.

POVERTY IN INDIA

Norms for the Estimation of Poverty

The literature on poverty in India is comparable in magnitude to India's own poverty. I shall have to resort here to providing a ruthlessly encapsulated version of the evidence from this literature. For an extremely useful review of the methodologies and findings of various poverty studies in the country, the reader is referred to the *Economic and Political Weekly's* Research Foundation Survey (1993); the two volumes of essays edited by Srinivasan and Bardhan (1974 and 1988) and the volume edited by Krishnaswamy (1990) are also indispensable guides. For three other excellent surveys — of recent vintage — on poverty in India, the reader should consult Tendulkar, Sundaram and Jain (1993), Dutta (1994) and Suryanarayana (1995).

In a paper entitled 'Perspective of Development: 1961–1976',[24] put out by the Perspective Planning Division of the Indian Planning Commission (1962), there is a frank admission of the extent of poverty the country could 'afford' at the time. The balanced diet recommended by the Nutrition Advisory Committee, together with a modest allowance for consumption of other items, yielded a poverty line of Rs 35 per capita per month at 1961–2 prices — a poverty line that would have precipitated 80 per cent of the population into poverty. A Working Group set up by the Planning Commission, taking a more sober view of things, recommended in July 1962 that the poverty line should be pegged at Rs 20 per capita per month at 1961–2 prices. Subsequently, Dandekar and Rath (1971), by relating the poverty line to the consumption expenditure that corresponded to a food intake whose calorific value was of the order of 2250 kcals per person per day, arrived at a rural (urban) poverty line of Rs 15 (Rs 22.50) per person per month at 1960–1 prices. By the time Ahluwalia (1978) was estimating trends in rural poverty, he was able to note that the Rs 15 poverty line had acquired ' . . . a well-established pedigree in the Indian literature' (Ahluwalia 1978, p. 279).[25] More recently, the Planning Commission (1981) has postulated that an appropriate calorific norm would be 2400 kcals (2100 kcals) per person per day in the rural (urban) areas; using 1973–4 NSS data on the distribution of consumption, both by value

[24] Reprinted in Srinivasan and Bardhan (1974).

[25] For other (pre-1975) contributions to the identification (and also aggregation) exercise in the Indian context, see, *inter alia*, Ojha (1970), Minhas (1971), Bardhan (1973), Bhatty (1974) and Rudra (1974).

and quantity, the expenditure levels at which the calorific content of food items corresponded to these norms were worked out: these yielded poverty lines of Rs 49.09 (Rs 56.54) per capita per month at 1973–4 prices for the rural (urban) areas of the country. In 1993, an Expert Group appointed by the Planning Commission (see Planning Commission 1993) endorsed these poverty lines.

Different studies on the estimation of poverty in India have differed with respect to: (a) the poverty line employed; (b) the price deflator used to express the base-year poverty line at current prices; (c) the methodology employed for computing the value of the poverty index from grouped data available in the NSS surveys;[26] and (d) the poverty index used. In respect of (d), the Bhatty (1974) and Ahluwalia (1978) studies were among the first to move away from the standard headcount measure and to consider more sophisticated poverty indices such as Sen's index; more recent papers which have also employed the P_{α} family of indices include those by Tendulkar et al. (1993) and Suryanarayana and Geetha (1994). Even restricting oneself to the headcount ratio, it is clear that the acute sensitivity of the estimated extent of poverty to the precise assumptions one makes regarding the poverty line, the price deflator and the computing technique employed, should guard one against ad hoc and hasty judgments on the choice of these variables.

The methodology recommended by the Planning Commission (1981) is a case in point. Of particular significance was the Commission's decision to estimate the headcount ratio on the basis of the Lorenz curve for consumption expenditure yielded by the NSS distribution data, while scaling the NSS estimate of mean consumption up by a factor equal to the ratio of the Central Statistical Organisation's (National Accounts Statistics) estimate of mean consumption to the NSS (weighted-average) estimate of mean consumption. Such strange 'hybrid' procedures of marrying estimates from alternative data sources are extremely questionable to adopt in the context of inferring intertemporal poverty trends — a project that (presumably) should be informed by some seriousness. Such ad hoc procedures eventually end up verifying the consistency of arithmetic, without necessarily verifying much about what is actually happening to poverty on the ground. This procedure seems to continue to be in vogue in the 'official' poverty estimates put out by the Government of India, despite the fact that the

[26] See Kakwani (1980a) for an excellent discussion of computational techniques and estimation problems.

Report of the Expert Group (Planning Commission 1993) has criticized this aspect of the Planning Commission's methodology.[27]

Broad Trends and Magnitudes

In this welter of confusion occasioned by different estimates put out by different studies, it would appear that by and large there is some consensus on the view that there has been a sharp increase in poverty from 1960–1 to 1968–9, followed by a gradual decline up to the late 1970s and a more accelerated decline over the decade of the 1980s. There is some indication (see Tendulkar and Jain 1995) that there may have been an increase in poverty again in the early 1990s following the initiation of the 'reform' process in the Indian economy. It also appears that it might have taken up to the early 1980s for poverty to be restored to its 1960–1 level. Going by the Expert Group's (Planning Commission 1993) estimates, about two–fifths of the population must be deemed to have been in poverty in India as recently as 1987–8. It is to be noted that all these estimates of poverty have been based on the extremely conservative assumption of an intertemporally unvarying (in real terms) poverty line. This performance on the poverty front must be contrasted with the sentiments expressed in the Planning Commission's 1962 'Perspective of Development — 1961–1976' (see Srinivasan and Bardhan 1974, p. 10):

The central concern of our planning has to be the removal of poverty as early as possible. The stage has now come when we should sharply focus our efforts on providing an assured minimum income to every citizen of the country within a reasonable period. Progressively the minimum itself should be raised as development grows apace.

Against this background of vast generalized deprivation, one must also note that there are substantial inter-group variations in the extent of poverty. At the *regional* level, states like Punjab and Haryana at one extreme are relatively better off than states like Bihar and Orissa at the other extreme: according to the estimates of Tendulkar et al. (1993), the headcount ratios (in per cent terms) for Punjab, Haryana, Orissa and Bihar in 1987–8 were, respectively, 21.83, 23.17, 65.64 and 66.26. *Occupational groupings* also reflect disparities in the distribution of poverty. Tendulkar et al. (1993) estimate that in rural India in 1987–8, the P_α measure of poverty for agricultural labourer/wage earner

---

[27] For another important criticism, which takes account of problems relating to the appropriate choice of price deflators, see Minhas et al. (1987).

households, at .0697, was over twice as large as the P_α measure, at .0317, for self-employed households. Another significant basis of grouping is that of *caste*. On the basis of NSS data for 1983, Jayaraj and Subramanian (1995b) estimate that at the all-India (rural) level, the P_α measure for the Scheduled Castes and Tribes (taken as one group), at .0535, was again over twice as large as the P_α measure, at .0250, for the rest of the population.[28] The *feminization* of poverty has also been increasingly noted. In an environment of generalized disadvantage, the relative disadvantage suffered by certain identifiable subgroups of the population adds a bitter twist to the nature of poverty in India.

Determinants of Poverty[29]

I shall here attempt to very briefly review some of the literature dealing with the determinants of poverty. For the most part, attempts at inferring causation have been confined to the phenomenon of rural poverty; and Ahluwalia's (1978) study — which presents a time-series on rural poverty levels over the period 1956–7 to 1973–4 — is one of the earliest systematic efforts in this direction. At the all-India level, Ahluwalia noted that there was a significant negative relationship between agricultural performance (captured, *inter alia*, by the net domestic product in agriculture at 1960–1 prices per head of rural population) and the extent of poverty (captured by the headcount ratio and also by the Sen index). In the absence, however, of a significant time trend in both agricultural performance *and* rural poverty, it is clearly difficult to make any assessment of the possible impact of a 'trickle-down' effect on poverty. It is similarly difficult to infer, from Ahluwalia's study, any possible beneficent effects of 'trickle-down' on poverty at the level of individual states.

In recent times a great deal of interest has been generated by Dharm Narain's discovery that poverty and nominal prices are positively correlated;[30] more precisely, he estimated, in logarithmic form, a linear regression of the headcount ratio on three variables: net domestic product in agriculture per head of rural population, an index of prices, and time. And his estimated regression equation yielded statistically significant negative slope coefficients for the first and third variables,

[28] Poverty magnitudes estimated by different studies may not be directly comparable because of differing assumptions regarding the poverty line, etc.

[29] This subsection is heavily dependent on Subramanian (1990).

[30] Dharm Narain's work on this topic is contained in unfinished, unpublished notes.

and a statistically significant positive slope coefficient for the second variable. The use of a nominal price index as an explanatory variable, together with an index of real per capita income, is somewhat intriguing; and several papers in a recent book (Mellor and Desai 1986) have been devoted to analysing the Dharm Narain equations. Amartya Sen's chapter in this book (Sen 1986) is particularly helpful in enabling one to come to grips with the possible import of Dharm Narain's equations. The explanatory value of the price variable probably resides in its reflecting alterations in the 'real' command over goods of specific sections of the population; as such, the price index serves as a sort of surrogate variable which captures the effect of changes in the distribution of purchasing power wrought by inflation. Briefly, then, the observed relationship points to the possibility that inflation is accompanied by a redistribution of purchasing power; and that there are particularly vulnerable sections of the population for whom price rises are not quite compensated by corresponding increases in nominal income.

An exhaustive cross-sectional analysis of the determinants of interregional variations in poverty has recently been attempted by Jain, Sundaram and Tendulkar (1989). Using NSS data for 1971–2, the authors have attempted to explain variations in poverty (as measured both by the headcount ratio and the Sen index) and in levels of living (as measured both by the mean consumer expenditure level and the median consumer expenditure level) across fifty-six regions of the country. In effect, interregional variations in poverty have been sought to be explained indirectly (i.e. through the mediation of the level of living, the rate of unemployment, and the extent of wage dependancy) by five exogenous variables of which three variables (GINIC:[31] the Gini coefficient of inequality in the distribution of consumer expenditure; GINIA: the Gini coefficient of inequality in the distribution of the value of household assets; and DENHA: the density of population per hectare of operated area) are 'distributional' in character, and two variables (AHH: the value of assets per household; and AGHA: the value of agricultural output per hectare of gross cropped area) are 'structural' in character. As might be expected, poverty is found to be

[31] It should, I think, be noted carefully that the relationship between poverty (P) on the one hand, and GINIC and the level of living (LLI) on the other hand, does not so much uncover causation as it reflects a sort of imperfect decomposition: the mean and dispersion of a distribution do not so much causally 'explain' poverty as they are constitutive of it in a definitional, non-stochastic sense. The regression of P on LLI and GINIC does, therefore, present some interpretational difficulty.

positively associated with the distributional variables and negatively with the structural variables; the five exogeneous variables together are found to substantially explain the interregional variations in poverty; and the matrix of point partial elasticities derived from the reduced-form equations of the model suggest that (a) at the margin, agricultural performance (as measured by AGHA) has less of an impact on poverty than mean asset security (as measured by AHH), and (b) the marginal impact on poverty of each of the five exogenous variables is higher (in absolute terms) when poverty is measured by the relatively more comprehensive Sen index than when it is measured by the headcount ratio. This has been an unavoidably hurried account of the Jain–Sundaram–Tendulkar model, but one can see that the explanatory framework employed by the authors is certainly suggestive. In particular, we are pushed from a consideration of the causation to a consideration of the mitigation of poverty. To this issue I now turn.

POVERTY MEASUREMENT AND POVERTY REDRESSAL

Poverty Measures and Optimal Budgetary Rules

A commonly deployed anti-poverty measure is that of *direct income transfers*, whereby income, in cash or in kind, is transferred by the state to the poor. The question arises: given a budget of fixed size available for transfers, how should the budget be allocated among the poor so as to minimize poverty?[32] This problem has been addressed by, among others, Bourguignon and Fields (1990), and Gangopadhyay and Subramanian (1992). The solution to the problem would presumably depend on how we choose to measure poverty. Here I shall take a quick look at the solutions which emerge from a consideration of the Foster–Greer–Thorbecke P_α family of indices.[33]

For $\alpha = 0$, i.e. when poverty is measured by the headcount ratio, it turns out that the optimal transfer schedule is of the type in which the least poor members of the population lay claim to the entire budget such that, starting with the richest of the poor and working one's way downward, each person's income-gap is bridged till the budget is exhausted. This is what Bourguignon and Fields call a 'type-r policy', whereby it is only the richest among the poor that benefit from

---

[32] It is typically assumed that the budget is not large enough to eradicate poverty, and that transfers are non-negative (that is no person is taxed).

[33] The ensuing discussion draws on Gangopadhyay and Subramanian (1992).

intervention. When $\alpha = 1$, i.e. poverty is measured by the per capita income-gap ratio, it turns out that any feasible transfer schedule that exhausts the budget is also an optimal one: this is not particularly helpful as a guide to policy. When α exceeds unity, so that P_α is now a distributionally sensitive measure, the optimal solution requires the implementation of a sort of 'lexicographic maximin principle', whereby one starts with the poorest person and, via a schedule of progressive and income-equalizing transfers, one works one's way upward till the budget is exhausted.[34] This corresponds to what Bourguignon and Fields call a 'p-type' policy, whereby it is only the poorest among the poor that benefit from intervention.

The budgetary exercises outlined above clearly share a certain resonance with the 'lifeboat dilemma' propounded by utilitarian philosophers: if three sailors on board a lifeboat have among themselves rations that will suffice only for two, should one of the sailors be thrown overboard, or should the rations be shared equally, in which case none of the sailors is likely to survive? In effect, P_o and $P_{\alpha>1}$ recommend a 'man overboard' solution: P_o would 'throw overboard' the 'neediest',[35] while $P_{\alpha>1}$ would jettison the 'ablest'; and P_1 is oddly compatible with both the 'equal rations' and the 'man-overboard' solutions.

The foregoing considerations focus on the fact that how we choose to measure poverty clearly has implications for the way in which budgetary allocations for the minimization of poverty are undertaken. It could be the case that our choice of a poverty measure is not prior but posterior in the sense that the *outcomes* dictated by the budgetary rules for different indices may themselves serve to clarify our intuition regarding the import of these indices. In fact, Bourguignon and Fields (1990, p. 424) observe that ' . . . an alternative approach to the axiomatics of poverty would be to start from assumptions about the optimal allocation of an anti-poverty budget'.

---

[34] This is what Anand (1983) calls 'The Redressal of Poverty Rule'.

[35] It should be noted that 'needs' can sometimes figure in optimal budgetary policy in a peculiar way, as has been exemplified in what Keen (1992) calls 'the paradox of targeting'. This paradox revolves around the possibility that a formal exercise of poverty minimization subject to a budgetary constraint can sometimes yield the intuition-defying conclusion that a subgroup of the population whose needs increase ought to have the resources allocated to it reduced, rather than enhanced. Keen (1992) offers a careful analysis of the circumstances under which this sort of paradox can arise, and of the restrictions needed to be imposed on poverty measures in order to guard against its occurrence.

Some Complications: Targeting,[36] Information Gaps, Administrative Costs and Incentive Effects

In the optimization exercises reviewed in the previous section, we have adopted a particularly simplistic approach to the redressal of poverty, by assuming that targeting — by which is meant the directing of benefits to the desired segment of the population, namely (a subset of) the poor — can be costlessly achieved. In practice, though, means-testing — which is the use of an income criterion to identify the target population, each member of which is guaranteed a minimum level of income not exceeding the poverty line — is not costless. Typically, while at best information may be available on the shape of the cumulative distribution function $F(x)$, the agency engaged in the alleviation of poverty will not have information on who has what income. This fact of 'hidden information' could potentially lead to a problem of 'adverse selection', with scarce resources being mis-directed to undeserving (i.e. typically non-poor) sections of the population. Administrative costs on collecting the required information for effective targeting are unavoidable; administrative costs incurred on logistical and infrastructural components of a programme are also likely to be non-negligible. Incentives effects could, further, impose costs on the claimants of benefits; these costs could be in the form of 'hassle' (time lost in queuing up for benefits, filling out forms, etc.) or of 'stigma' (the psychic disbenefit of being identified, under means-testing, as a recipient of public charity[37]). Incentive problems in terms of 'moral hazard' must also be reckoned with: the guaranteed income implied by means-tested schemes could adversely affect a potential beneficiary's incentive to work for his income. In view of these costs, the question arises as to whether universal provisioning — the transfer of benefits without restrictions imposed in terms of an income criterion for eligibility — may not have something to commend it. This question has been explicitly addressed by Besley (1990) in a well-defined poverty measurement setting. While the specific simulation exercises undertaken by Besley for the P_α class of poverty indices indicate that universal provisioning does not easily dominate means-testing, his work, at a general level, suggests that complications in the form of administrative costs and incentive effects must be explicitly

---

[36] For a superb non-technical discussion of the crucial issues involved in targeting, see Besley and Kanbur (1993).

[37] The terms 'hassle' and 'stigma' are due to Cowell (1986, cited in Besley 1990).

accommodated into the calculus of poverty minimization before targeting can be confidently taken to represent a superior alternative to unrestricted universalism.

Imperfect Targeting

To see the options available as being confined to either means-testing or universalism is a needlessly restrictive dichotomization: intermediate cases of 'imperfect targeting' may well be indicated in several situations. A case in point is that of food subsidies (Kanbur 1987, Besley and Kanbur 1988). In analysing 'infra-marginal' subsidies, Besley and Kanbur (1988) make the point that while 'unrestricted universalism' may entail large leakages to the non-poor, a switch to a completely means-tested scheme may prove prohibitively costly. The case for 'imperfect targeting', entailing the 'optimal' location of ration shops on the basis of information on the distribution of the poor population across different locations, comes to the fore here. Kanbur (1987) and Besley and Kanbur (1988) provide yet another example of the utility of imperfect targeting, in the context of 'marginal' commodity subsidies. It can be shown, for example, that in order to minimize poverty as measured by the per capita income-gap ratio, only that commodity should be subsidized which accounts for the largest share in the consumption of the poor. This is an instance of a situation in which while provisioning is universal, a measure of targeting can be achieved without resort to means-testing.

At a more general level, Ravallion and Chao (1989) have examined the question of the gains that are to be had from exploiting information — which is often available from national sample surveys — on region-specific distributions of income, with a view to optimally allocating a budget of given size across regions. They demonstrate that even if the best that can be done is to transfer the same income to each person within a given region, this is a superior alternative to a scheme of unrestricted universalism in which each person in the entire country receives the same transfer. (The authors supply empirical applications of this principle for Bangladesh, the Philippines, Sri Lanka and Indonesia.)

The broad principle of imperfect targeting is to direct resources to the target population by exploiting such information as is available on variables that might be expected to be correlated with income, and which are easier to observe and verify than is income. (Recall, in this connection, the discussion of the targeting-related utility of Anand's detailed group-wise analysis of the characteristics of the poor in Malaysia.) These issues are addressed by, among others, Glewwe (1992) and Kumar and Stewart (1992). These and other contributions to what is by now a large corpus of literature, suggest that — depending on the context at hand — there are potential benefits to be had from targeting on the basis of regional location; race; ethnicity; caste; gender of household head; the quality and size of housing owned or rented; access to amenities such as drinking water; possession of consumer durables; occupation; employment status; and landholding status.

Self-Targeting: The Case of Employment Programmes

There are certain forms of anti-poverty intervention which impose costs on the claimants that do not make it worthwhile for the non-poor to seek participation: such forms of intervention, by inducing 'self-selection', avoid the need for costly targeting. The most widely discussed of such poverty alleviation schemes are those constituted by *public works programmes* (examples include Bangladesh's Food For Work Programme, the Employment Guarantee Scheme in the state of Maharashtra, and other centrally sponsored Indian schemes such as the Jawahar Rozgar Yojana). The underlying principle of 'self-targeting' is as follows: if the wage on offer in a works programme does not exceed the poverty line, then those whose incomes exceed the poverty line (namely the non-poor) will simply select themselves out of the programme.

It can be shown that if we seek to minimize poverty as measured by the P_α family of indices, then the optimal wage rate would be the poverty line z when $\alpha = 0$; as α increases, the optimal wage declines and coverage increases until, in the limit as α approaches infinity, the optimal budgetary rule coincides with a prescription of Basu's (1981, 1990): the wage is set as low as is compatible with creating the maximum number of jobs for which there are takers, given the size of the budget.[38] While the non-poor are excluded by self-selection, for finite values of α the optimal solution presumes the capacity for precise targeting *among* the poor. The self-selection property comes out really sharply only in the $P_{\alpha \to \infty}$ case; and since only the neediest of claimants are covered by the works programme in this case, Basu (1981, 1990) points to the 'ethical' appropriateness of a 'low' wage in the sense just

[38] For details, see Gangopadhyay and Subramanian (1992). To keep the problem non-trivial, it is assumed that the wage bill is not large enough to eliminate poverty.

discussed (but see also, in this connection, the contributions of Dandekar and Sathe [1980] and Panda [1981]).

Notice that fixing the wage at some socially specified minimum
level such as the poverty line entails relatively limited coverage, while
fixing the wage relatively low, such as under the $P_{\alpha \to \infty}$ minimizing
strategy, will maximize coverage. These two sorts of wage-setting
schemes are referred to by Ravallion (1991, Chapter 11 in this volume)
as, respectively, LIMCOV (for 'Limited Coverage') and WIDCOV
(for 'Wide Coverage') schemes. Under LIMCOV, the demand for jobs
will exceed their available number, and some segment of the poor
population that is willing to work at the going wage will have to be
denied access; under WIDCOV, every person wishing to work at the
going wage is guaranteed employment. Ravallion looks at the sorts of
considerations under which one type of scheme rather than the other
will be preferred: these considerations, typically, revolve around the
measure of poverty employed, and on the magnitude of budgetary
outlays and administrative costs involved (the last of which we have
not allowed for at all in our earlier simplified review of budgetary
rules). Ravallion also provides an empirical application of his results,
using data from Bangladesh for the purpose.

The self-selection property inherent in wage-employment programmes has been an important reason for viewing this form of intervention
in a favourable light (see in this context, for example, Dreze and Sen
1989:[39] especially ch. 7). While it is possible that the self-selection
property is sharp in employment schemes, there may be other logistical
and administrative overheads that are non-negligible; in addition, the
wage rate must cover the claimant's forgone benefit, whereas in a direct
transfer programme (assuming perfect targeting), only the difference
between the guaranteed minimum and the claimant's income needs to
be transferred to the claimant. From his analysis of the indicators that
are available in India, Guhan (1994, Chapter 12 in this volume) turns
in a less-than-wholly-enthusiastic report on wage-employment schemes.

Social Security as an Ingredient in Anti-poverty Policy

Much of our discussion thus far has been at a certain level of abstrac-
tion, revolving around the elucidation of certain principles of anti-
poverty policy within the context of measurement issues. Guhan (1994;

---

[39] It should be clarified that Drèze and Sen are concerned with a specifically
famine-prevention setting.

Chapter 12) provides a succinct account of various preventive and protective measures of poverty alleviation, including the provision of social security, with specific reference to principles and problems as they have presented themselves in the experience of the developing world in general and India in particular. We have in this paper an assessment of both conceptual and practical problems encountered in the implementation of various poverty redressal schemes, encompassing land reform, asset creation, employment generation, minimum wage legislation, food subsidies and, finally, social assistance linked to specific contingencies of distress. On social security,[40] Guhan underlines the need to adapt social security models of the industrialized West to the requirements and specificities of the developing world; and he envisages for India the possibility of devising a feasible and affordable contingency-related package of measures covering, *inter alia*, old age pensions, survivor benefits, accident relief and maternity assistance, which should cost no more than 3 per cent of India's GDP.

NON-INCOME DIMENSIONS OF DEPRIVATION

For the most part we have hitherto considered deprivation only in relation to the space of incomes. But if there is a case for viewing the standard of living as being related to the actual capability of individuals to be or do this or that, then an exclusive concern with the domain of incomes can, at best, result in only a partial and, at worst, a misleading picture of deprivation (or its obverse, achievement). The 'basic needs' approach to assessing achievement (Hicks and Streeten 1979), the concern with measuring the 'quality of life' (Morriss 1979; Sen 1981), the centrality accorded to individuals' 'capability to function' (Sen 1985a; Sen et al. 1987), the significance attached to the evaluation of 'human development' (UNDP 1993) — all these are expressions (with admitted differences in content and emphasis) of a certain shared reservation against exclusive reliance on the level and growth of income as an adequate and meaningful indicator of well-being.

Morriss' (1979) work on the 'Physical Quality of Life Index' is an important forerunner to the construction of the UNDP's Human Development Index (HDI) (see UNDP 1993: especially 'Technical Notes', pp. 100–14). The components of the HDI are longevity, knowledge and income. Longevity (L) is measured by the expectation of life

[40] Some important recent contributions to the study of social security in developing countries include the collections of essays in Drèze and Sen (1990) and Ahmed et al. (1991).

at birth; education (E) is measured by two indicators: the adult literacy rate (l) and the mean years of schooling (s) of the population of age 25 or more; and the income component is measured by Atkinson's (1970) utility transform of income, which we can represent by W. For each indicator I, let $\bar{I}$ and I_o be the maximum and minimum values respectively attained by any country among those compared. Let D_I be a normalized measure of the extent of deprivation for the indicator I, where D_I is expressed as a ratio of the shortfall of I from its maximum value to the difference between its maximum and minimum values. Then, $D_L = (\bar{L} - L)/(\bar{L} - L_o)$; $D_E = 0.67\,(\bar{l} - l)/(\bar{l} - l_o) + 0.33\,(\bar{s} - s)/(\bar{s} - s_o)$ (educational deprivation is expressed as a weighted average, with weights of 0.67 and 0.33 respectively, of deprivation in literacy and in mean years of schooling); and $D_W = (\bar{W} - W)/(\bar{W} - W_o)$. The overall index of deprivation, D, is expressed as a simple average of the component-wise indices of deprivation:

$$D = (1/3)\,(D_L + D_E + D_W);$$ and the HDI, which is an index of *achievement*, is given by $HDI = 1 - D$.

Clearly, a number of criticisms, refinements and extensions of the HDI are possible; and these issues are very ably reviewed in UNDP (1993, pp. 100–14). Are the components of the HDI too few in number,[41] or too many, or just not the right ones? Should the maximum and minimum values for each indicator be fixed in relation to actual country performance or in relation to independent 'absolute' limits, so that over-time comparisons are not affected by changes in the performance of 'best' and 'worst' countries? In assessing improvement over time, should the deprivation indices be modified so as to be sharper — for a given improvement in the relevant indicator — the higher is the base level value of the indicator (on this, see Kakwani 1993)? Should the weighting system in the construction of the HDI be modified to reflect rationalizable values that may not accord with assigning an equal weight to all the components that constitute the HDI? Is there a case for adjusting the HDI to reflect any discriminatory differences that may show up between gender-specific HDIs, and HDIs for different well-defined socio-economic groups classified according to, say, region, caste, ethnicity, etc.?

Many of these issues are taken up for discussion in the essay by Dutta, Panda and Wadhwa (1995, Chapter 13 in this volume) who, in

---

[41] Dasgupta (1994), for example, would want an index of civil and political rights also to be included in the construction of the overall index.

addition, present a detailed picture of human development in India, by employing suitably adapted versions of the HDI for their purpose. The essay presents a comprehensive assessment of interstate differences in the achievement of human development in the last two decades. Apart from facilitating an identification of the laggards and the frontrunners, the paper also considers the crucial question of how closely human development is correlated with per capita income and social sector spending. The findings here carry the strong suggestion that the passive policy of waiting for growth to happen and its benefits to trickle down should sensibly yield place to measures of public action and active state intervention.

INEQUALITY, POVERTY AND WELFARE: GATHERING THE THREADS

We have thus far tended to treat the topics of inequality and poverty after a somewhat compartmentalized fashion, with welfare darting in and out of the picture. In this section I shall try to spell out some aspects of the nature and extent of the interrelationship between inequality, poverty and welfare, touching on areas of both congruence and conflict.

First, while the notions of inequality and poverty are clearly related, it is important to recognize that they also constitute *distinct* categories of enquiry. In particular — and as Sen (1983: Chapter 6 in this volume) has pointed out — recognizing an 'absolute' core to poverty makes it difficult to view poverty as anything more than just an aspect of relative inequality.

Second, there is a sort of 'deterministic' sense in which many indices of poverty respond positively to changes in inequality. In a general way, the restrictions in terms of 'dominance conditions' that have been discussed in the context of obtaining unambiguous poverty rankings, provide a clue to this aspect of the relationship between poverty and inequality. To put it in a simplified way, suppose, for specificity, that poverty is measured by the headcount ratio. (Let us also assume that the mean income μ is at least as large as the poverty line z.) Now it is easy to verify that at any given income level x, the slope of the Lorenz curve is given by $s(x) = x/\mu$, a relationship which makes it easy to read off the headcount ratio from the Lorenz curve, as illustrated in Figure 0.2. Figure 0.2 makes it clear that for any two distributions x and y sharing the same mean μ, if xLy, then the headcount ratio for x will be lower than for y, for the given poverty line z. It should, at the same time, be obvious that for two distributions x and y which share

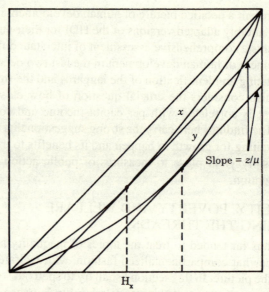

x and y have the same mean μ; x L y;
and $H_x < H_y$, where H is the headcount ratio.

Figure 0.2

the same Lorenz curve, if the mean μ_x of x exceeds the mean μ_y of y, then the headcount ratio for x will be lower than for y, for the given poverty line z. These considerations suggest that it should be possible to decompose a change in the value of a poverty index into a 'growth' component (obtained by estimating the change attendant on keeping the Lorenz curve fixed and permitting only the mean to vary) and an 'inequality' component (obtained by estimating the change attendant on keeping the mean fixed and permitting only the Lorenz curve to vary), together with a residual component attributable to the interaction of the 'growth' and 'inequality' components. In fact, Kakwani and Subbarao (1990) have undertaken this decomposition exercise in a study of the relative contributions of growth and inequality changes to changes in poverty in India; and for applications to both India and Brazil, the reader should consult Datt and Ravallion (1992).

Third, the extent of inequality in a society — assessed rather specifically in terms of the hiatus between the income shares of the poor and the non-poor — provides a clue to the ease with which poverty in the society can be eliminated through redistributive effort.

This is most clearly seen from a consideration of Anand's (1977) poverty index. One way of writing Anand's index is in the form $P^A = D/(X^P + X^N)$, when D is the shortfall of the aggregate income of the poor from the income that would be required to eliminate poverty, and X^P (respectively, X^N) is the aggregate income of the poor (respectively, the non-poor). For given D and X^P, it is clear that P^A declines with X^N: the 'relative burden of poverty' becomes smaller as, *ceteris paribus*, the income of the non-poor increases, i.e. as the gap in between-group incomes widens.

Fourth, Sen's approach to the measurement of poverty reveals how inequality in the distribution of incomes *among* the poor could enter naturally into an assessment of the extent of poverty that obtains: for the entire class of 'distributionally sensitive' poverty indices which satisfy the weak transfer axiom, an increase in inequality in the distribution of poor incomes (which leaves the numbers of individuals on either side of the poverty line unchanged) will cause measured poverty to rise.

What can we say of how welfare is mediated by the presence of inequality and poverty? On this not vastly over-researched subject, some important contributions are the essays by Brent (1986), Hagenaars (1987), Vaughan (1987), Lewis and Ulph (1988), and Beath, Lewis and Ulph (1994). It is useful to note first that it has been conventional to view welfare as being contributed to by two factors: the level of mean income μ, and the extent of inequality in the distribution of income. (Sen's 1976b index of 'real national income', given by the quantity $\mu[1-G]$ where G is the Gini coefficient of inequality in the distribution of income, is a good example of a summary welfare indicator which is increasing in average income and declining in the extent of inequality.) A view of welfare of this type is subsumed in a social welfare function (SWF) which Brent (1986) calls the 'two-objective' social welfare function.

The question arises: is there a basis to the view, which often seems to be held implicitly, that entering poverty as an argument in the welfare function is a matter of ' . . . a three objective SWF [being] merely the two objective version in disguise' (Brent 1986, p. 93)? In answering this question, Brent considers the class of SWFs each of which can be written as a weighted average of incomes: a typical SWF in this class can be written as $W = 1/n \sum_{i=1}^{n} v_i x_i$, where the weight v_i declines as x_i increases: such an SWF responds positively to mean income and negatively to inequality (via the 'egalitarian' weighting structure employed). A special case of such an SWF is one in which all poor incomes receive a weight v_1 and all non-poor incomes a weight v_2, with the egalitarian tilt secured by requiring that v_1 be larger than $v_2 (\geq 0)$. Suppose now, specifically, that $v_1 = (2\mu^N/\mu^P)v_2$, where μ^N (respectively, μ^P) is the average income of the non-poor (respectively, the poor). Then it can be shown that if H is the headcount ratio, $\partial W/\partial H = v_2 \mu^N \geq 0$: an increase in poverty (as measured by the headcount ratio) can actually lead to an increase in welfare. This implies that a 'three objective' SWF is not necessarily just a 'two objective' SWF in fancy dress.

That a conflict between the objectives of reducing inequality and reducing poverty can arise is already suggested by the fact that any ('proper') inequality measure must satisfy the transfer axiom, while a number of poverty measures (including distributionally sensitive indices like Sen's) can violate this axiom (recall that Sen's index only satisfies the 'weak' transfer axiom). Pyatt (1987) refers to such poverty indices as being 'badly behaved'. Of course, it is possible to construct an SWF which never betrays any tension between the objectives of reducing inequality and reducing poverty. Pyatt presents an ingenious way of doing this, and shows that — under suitably defined restrictions — the only 'acceptable' poverty index in this context is Thon's (1979) index. But getting ill-mannered poverty indices to yield place to well-behaved ones in order to achieve a satisfying congruence amongst the objectives of increasing welfare, reducing inequality and reducing poverty may have costs that deserve closer scrutiny.

Specifically, two questions of some moment are the specific interpretation conferred on the poverty line and the magnitude of mean income μ in relation to z. Virtually all of our analysis so far has been conducted on the strength of the implicit assumption that $\mu \geq z$. But we cannot discount the possibility that $\mu < z$. In such situations where μ is less than z, poverty minimization under the headcount ratio may turn out to be an unpleasant but pragmatic necessity:[42] an equal

---

[42] In the context of interventionary measures aimed at providing nutritional relief, Seckler (1985, p. 135) observes: 'Gross overestimations of the incidence of malnutrition in the world have simply provided aid and comfort to the advocates of Triage, Food as a Weapon, and other forms of barbarism.' By pitching the norm of nutritional adequacy 'low', it can be ensured that a headcount-minimizing strategy of budgetary allocation will direct resources to the most deprived of the deprived: it is some such calculation as this which appears to supply the motivation for some nutritionists' prescription of setting the 'cut-off' point of nutritional adequacy at a low level. While one can be sympathetic to the concern motivating such a view, it appears that nutritionists of this persuasion should fight their battle on the front of the appropriate choice of poverty

distribution of income may leave everybody in severely impaired circumstances. This is an instance of a situation wherein the 'man-overboard' solution to the lifeboat dilemma may achieve some harsh plausibility in relation to the 'equal rations' solution. (On these and related questions, see Sharma 1983 — cited in Hagenaars 1987; Lewis and Ulph 1988; Subramanian 1989; and Beath, Lewis and Ulph 1994).

Further, if the poverty line is a sharp dividing line such that there is a discontinuous increase in well-being from transiting the line, then many of our 'standard' notions of welfare, inequality and poverty may have to undergo some revision. Specifically, if the poverty line is to be invested with some special significance such that the ability to cross it is a particularly valued achievement, then poverty minimization in the light of this view must be pursued as an independent objective, irrespective of its implications for welfare and inequality. On the other hand, if no such special significance is seen as attaching to the poverty line, there can be no compelling justification for a poverty index to be 'badly behaved' in Pyatt's sense of that term. Pyatt's (1987) essay has the merit of confronting the poverty analyst with the need to effect a choice. One imagines that the second alternative, entailing a painless assimilation of poverty analysis into 'standard' welfare analysis, would knock the basis out of the distinctive concern for poverty, as such, that motivates its study. What remains then is to recognize the potential for conflict, the possibility of having to do without an overarching framework of welfare in which any move toward reducing deprivation is always and entirely in harmony with the pursuit of equality.

A SUMMING UP

In summing up, I should like, all in one place, to quickly touch on the essays in this volume. Since the chapters have all already been introduced at the appropriate places in the course of the preceding overview, I shall here restrict myself to locating the various essays in this book within its broad thematic concerns.

Mayhew's piece (Chapter 1) stands by itself, as a classic descriptive account of aspects of both poverty and inequality as these tragedies affect the lives of people who are real people and not just counters in the calculus of measurement.[43] This essay on the one hand, and the

---

index (the aggregation issue) rather than on the front of appropriate choice of a poverty line (the identification issue). This question is discussed in Dasgupta and Ray (1990).

[43] James Agee's *Let Us Now Praise Famous Men* and several of P. Sainath's reports on poverty in contemporary India (written for the *Times of India*) are examples of work

rest on the other, reflect the possibility of adopting vastly disparate approaches to the study of a given phenomenon. The effect, I hope, will be to dispose the reader to the belief that Mayhew is as little an unscientific sentimentalist as an analyst of Schur-concavity is a heartless monster.

The remaining essays in the book fall more squarely within the ambit of its principal concern: measurement. Chapters 2 and 3 deal with various aspects of the technical issues that must be addressed in inequality measurement. In Chapter 2, Lorenz makes, as it were, an original appearance as the persona behind the Lorenz curve. The piece is a vintage classic. Anand's contribution (Chapter 3) is a remarkably clear survey of measurement issues — covering both 'positive' and 'ethical' approaches — in inequality.

Chapters 4 and 5 are concerned more with 'applications' than with 'pure' conceptualization. Haddad and Kanbur (Chapter 4) investigate the possibility of underestimating overall inequality by failing to take account of intra-family distributional features, with specific reference to food intake and in the specific context of data for the Philippines; in the process, the authors shed some interesting sidelights on the issue of decomposability in inequality and poverty measurement. Anand and Kanbur (Chapter 5) review the soundness of claims regarding the empirical validation of Kuznets' hypothesis on the relationship between inequality and per capita GDP as it manifests itself in the course of economic development.

In so far as the measurement of poverty is concerned, it appears to be sensible to deal with the following categories of problems: (a) the identification problem; (b) the aggregation problem; (c) evaluation of specific country experience; and (d) policy for the alleviation of poverty. Sen's paper (Chapter 6) deals lucidly with the 'absolutist' vs 'relativist' debate on approaches to the identification problem; it presents a quick review of alternative ways of defining a poverty line; and it also usefully highlights both the relationship and the contrast between inequality and poverty. Just one of the many approaches to identification — the 'biological or 'nutrition-based' approach — has itself been a source of considerable acrimony between Sukhatme/Seckler/Associates and the Rest of the World; an essay which deals with the controversy and also has a bearing on the Indian experience is Gopalan's piece on the measurement of undernutrition (Chapter 7).

---

which similarly involves the reader's conscience in her or his response to the text.

Introduction   43

Sen (Chapter 8) makes a reappearance, as he must in any consideration of the aggregation issue in poverty measurement: his paper is a
classic which has triggered off an immense subsequent literature on
the subject. A significant component of that literature is constituted by
the slim piece by Foster, Greer and Thorbecke (Chapter 9): subgroup
consistency and decomposability (both missing in Sen's index) are
importantly useful properties in a poverty index, and apart from this,
the P_α family of indices has found wide application in policy analysis.
Anand's work on poverty in Malaysia is one of the most careful and
illuminating reviews of country experience which the literature offers;
and Chapter 10 is an excerpt from that work.

Chapters 11 and 12 deal with anti-poverty policy. Ravallion (Chapter
11) looks at optimal budgetary policy in relation to how poverty is
measured, in the context of wage employment schemes. Guhan (Chapter
12) presents a comprehensive review of various protective and preventive forms of anti-poverty intervention; and in the process, he elaborates
on certain issues of pragmatic import for developing countries in general
and India in particular — in a way which has a greater sense of 'realistic'
immediacy that is conveyed by the use of 'stylized facts' in more formal
models. Finally, Dutta et al. (Chapter 13) provide both a substantive
and measurement-oriented picture of some non-economic dimensions
of deprivation in India, by looking at state-wise trends and magnitudes
of 'human development' in the country.

This collection, then, taken as a whole, is not 'pure theory', nor
'pure application', nor exclusively an appraisal of experiences with a
developing country slant — but some mix of all of these with a central
focus on measurement. I have little doubt that the ground covered by
the book has been small, and even less doubt that this Introduction has
gone nowhere near making good the gaps. But I believe there is enough
material here to convey a flavour of the sorts of issues and problems
with which the measurement of inequality and poverty is concerned.
Also on evidence is the fact that this book deals with a complex of
issues that are the very opposite of a set of settled questions. In the
chapters in this collection, as also in this general introduction, the reader
will encounter again and again instances of controversy, disagreement,
paradox, ambiguity, fuzziness and ethical inconclusiveness. These
difficulties are inherent in the measurement of poverty and inequality,
and it is far better to acknowledge this than to seek comfort in a few
contrived and shabby certainties.

The measurement issues reviewed in this book do however serve to identify the sources of many of our confusions, and to impart a degree of clarity to the way in which we pose our questions even if we cannot always be sure of receiving completely satisfactory answers to these questions. It may be neither fair nor realistic to expect much more than this from the enterprise of measurement.

Acknowledgements: This is an abridged version of an earlier draft. The larger paper is available with the author. Many people have helped most generously with one or more of the following activities: the selection of essays in this volume; drawing the author's attention and giving him access to various aspects of the literature of which he was ignorant; discussing and clarifying many issues in the course of writing this Introduction; and reading and commenting on earlier versions of the Introduction. My greatest debt is to Kaushik Basu, A. Vaidyanathan, M.H. Suryanarayana, S. Guhan, Barbara Harriss-White and Paul Appasamy for help and advice. Thanks are also due to D. Jayaraj, Manabi Majumdar, K. Nagaraj and C. Annadurai. R. Dhaumaperumal and C. Kalai Selvi word-processed the entire draft against heavy odds, for which my deepest gratitude.

REFERENCES

Ahluwalia, M.S. (1974). 'Income Inequality: Some Dimensions of the Problem', in H.B. Chenery, M.S. Ahluwalia, C.L.G. Bell, J.H. Deloy and R. Jolly (eds), *Redistribution with Growth*. London: Oxford University Press.

—— (1976a). 'Income Distribution and Development: Some Stylized Facts', *American Economic Review (Papers and Proceedings)*, 66.

—— (1976b). 'Inequality, Poverty and Development', *Journal of Development Economics*, 3.

—— (1978). 'Rural Poverty and Agricultural Performance in India', *Journal of Development Studies*, 14.

—— (1986). 'Rural Poverty, Agricultural Production and Prices: A Re-examination', in Mellor and Desai (1986).

Ahluwalia, M.S., N.G. Carter and H.B. Chenery (1979). 'Growth and Poverty in Developing Countries', *Journal of Development Economics*, 6.

Ahmed, E., J. Drèze, J. Hills and A. Sen (eds) (1991). *Social Security in Developing Countries*. Oxford: Clarendon.

Aigner, D.J. and A.J. Heins (1967). 'A Social Welfare View of the Measurement of Income Inequality', *Review of Income and Wealth*, 13.

Anand, S. (1977). 'Aspects of Poverty in Malaysia', *Review of Income and Wealth*, 23.

—— (1983). *Inequality and Poverty in Malaysia: Measurement and Decomposition*. New York: Oxford University Press.

Anand, S. and S.M.R. Kanbur (1993a). 'The Kuznets Process and the Inequality–Development Relationship', *Journal of Development Economics*, 40.

—— (1993b). 'Inequality and Development: A Critique', *Journal of Development Economics*, 41.

Arrow, K.J. (1963). *Social Choice and Individual Values*. New York: Wiley.

—— (1977). 'Extended Sympathy and the Possibility of Social Choice', *American Economic Review*, 67.

Atkinson, A.B. (1970). 'On the Measurement of Inequality', *Journal of Economic Theory*, 2.

—— (1987). 'On the Measurement of Poverty', *Econometrica*, 5.

Bagchi, A. (ed.) (1988). *Economy, Society and Polity: Essays in Honour of Professor Bhabatosh Dutta*. Calcutta: Oxford University Press.

Bandyopadhyay, N. (1988). 'The Story of Land Reforms in Indian Planning', in Bagchi (1988).

Bardhan, P.K. (1973). 'On the Incidence of Rural Poverty in Rural India in the Sixties', *Economic and Political Weekly*, Annual Number, February.

Basu, K. (1981). 'Food for Work Programmes: Beyond Roads That Get Washed Away', *Economic and Political Weekly*, 16.

—— (1985). 'Poverty Measurement: A Decomposition of the Normalization Axiom', *Econometrica*, 53.

—— (1987). 'Axioms for a Fuzzy Measure of Inequality', *Mathematical Social Sciences*, 14.

—— (1990). 'The Elimination of Persistent Hunger in South Asia: Policy Options', in Drèze and Sen (1990).

—— (1995). 'On Interpersonal Comparisons and the Concept of Equality', in W. Eichorn (ed.), *Models of Measurement of Welfare and Inequality*. Springer Verlag.

Besley, T. (1990). 'Means Testing versus Universal Provisioning in Poverty Alleviation Programmes', *Economica*, 57.

Besley, T. and R. Kanbur (1988). 'Food Subsidies and Poverty Alleviation', *Economic Journal*, 98.

—— (1993). 'The Principles of Targeting', in M. Lipton and J. van der Gaag (eds), *Including the Poor*. Washington, D.C.: The World Bank.

Bhatty, I.Z. (1974). 'Inequality and Poverty in Rural India', in Srinivasan and Bardhan (1974).

Blackorby, C. and D. Davidson (1980). 'Ethical Indices for the Measurement of Poverty', *Econometrica*, 48.

Bossert, W., P.K. Pattanaik and Y. Xu (1994). 'Ranking Opportunity Sets: An Axiomatic Approach', *Journal of Economic Theory*, 63.

Bourguignon, F. and G.S. Fields (1990). 'Poverty Measures and Anti-Poverty Policy', *Recherches Economiques de Louvain*, 56.

Brent, R.J. (1986). 'An Axiomatic Basis for the Three Objective Social Welfare Function within a Poverty Context', *Economics Letters*, 20.

Chakravarty, S.R. (1983a). 'A New Index of Poverty', *Mathematical Social Sciences*, 6.

—— (1983b). 'Ethically Flexible Measures of Poverty', *Canadian Journal of Economics*, 16.

Clark, S., R. Hemming and D. Ulph (1981). 'On Indices for the Measurement of Poverty', *Economic Journal*, 91.

Cowell, F. (1986). 'Welfare Benefits and the Economics of Take-up', ESRC Programme on Taxation, Incentives and the Distribution of Income, Discussion Paper No. 89.

Dalton, H. (1920). 'The Measurement of Inequality of Incomes', *Economic Journal*, 30.

Dandekar, K. and M. Sathe (1980). 'Employment Guarantee Scheme and Food for Work Programme', *Economic and Political Weekly*.

Dandekar, V.M. (1981). 'On Measurement of Poverty', *Economic and Political Weekly*, 25.

Dandekar, V.M. and N. Rath (1971). *Poverty in India*. Pune: Indian School of Political Economy.

Dasgupta, P.S. (1993). *An Inquiry into Well-Being and Destitution*. Oxford: Clarendon Press.

Dasgupta, P.S., A.K. Sen and D. Starrett (1973). 'Notes on the Measurement of Inequality', *Journal of Economic Theory*, 6.

Dasgupta, P.S. and D. Ray (1990). 'Adapting to Undernutrition: The Clinical Evidence and Its Implications', in Drèze and Sen (1991), vol. 1.

Datt, G. and M. Ravallion (1992). 'Growth and Redistribution of Changes in Poverty Measures: A Decomposition with Applications to Brazil and India in the 1980s', *Journal of Development Economics*, 38.

Donaldson, D. and J.A. Weymark (1986). 'Properties of Fixed-Population Poverty Indices', *International Economic Review*, 27.

Drèze, J. and A. Sen (1989). *Hunger and Public Action*. Oxford: Clarendon Press.

Drèze, J. and A. Sen (1990). *The Political Economy of Hunger*, 3 vols. Oxford: Clarendon Press.

—— (1995). *India: Economic Development and Social Opportunity.* Delhi: Oxford University Press.

Dutta, B. (1980). 'Intersectoral Disparities and Income Distribution in India: 1960–61 to 1973–74', *Indian Economic Review*, 15.

—— (1994). 'Poverty in India: Trends, Determinants and Policy Issues'. Delhi: Indian Statistical Institute, Discussion Paper No. 94–16.

Dutta, B., M. Panda and W. Wadhwa (1995). 'Human Development in India', Discussion Papers in Economics. Delhi: Indian Statistical Institute, Discussion Paper No. 95–01.

Dworkin, R. (1977). *Taking Rights Seriously*. Harvard University Press.

Economic and Political Weekly Research Foundation (1993). 'Poverty Levels in India: Norms, Estimates and Trends', *Economic and Political Weekly*, August.

FAO (1973). *Energy and Protein Requirements*, FAO Nutrition Meetings Report Series No. 52, Rome.

Foster, J. (1984). 'On Economic Poverty: A Survey of Aggregate Measures', *Advances in Econometrics*, 3.

—— (1985). 'Inequality Measurement', in H.P. Young (ed.), *Fair Allocation*. Providence, RI: American Mathematical Society.

Foster, J., J. Greer and E. Thorbecke (1984). 'A Class of Decomposable Poverty Measures', *Econometrica*, 42.

Foster, J. and A.F. Shorrocks (1988a). 'Poverty Orderings', *Econometrica*, 56.

—— (1988b). 'Poverty Orderings and Welfare Dominance', *Social Choice and Welfare*, 5.

—— (1988c). 'Inequality and Poverty Orderings', *European Economic Review*, 32.

—— (1991). 'Subgroup Consistent Poverty Indices', *Econometrica*, 59.

Gangopadhyay, S. and S. Subramanian (1992). 'Optimal Budgetary Intervention in Poverty Alleviation Schemes', in Subramanian (1992).

Glewwe, P. (1992). 'Targeting Assistance to the Poor: Efficient Allocation of Transfers When Household Income Is Not Observed', *Journal of Development Economics*.

Gopalan, C. (1992). 'Undernutrition: Measurement and Implications', in Osmani (1992).

Grilli, E. (1994). 'Long-term Economic Growth, Income Distribution and Poverty in Developing Countries: The Evidence', Centro Studi Luca D'Agliano — Queen Elizabeth House Development Studies Working

Paper No. 69. (Paper prepared for E. Grilli and D. Salvatore (eds), *Handbook of Economic Development*. Greenwood Publishing Group).

Guhan, S. (1994). 'Social Security Options for Developing Countries', *International Labour Review*, 133.

Hagenaars, A. (1987). 'A Class of Poverty Indices', *International Economic Review*, 28.

Hadar, J. and W.R. Russell (1969). 'Rules for Ordering Uncertain Prospects', *American Economic Review*, 59.

Haddad, L. and R. Kanbur (1990). 'How Serious is the Neglect of Intra-Household Inequality?', *Economic Journal*, 100.

Hammond, P.J. (1976). 'Equity, Arrow's Conditions, and Rawls' Difference Principle', *Econometrica*, 44.

Harriss, B. (1990). 'The Intra-family Distribution of Hunger in South Asia', in Drèze and Sen (1990), vol. 1.

Hicks, N. and P. Streeten (1979). 'Indicators of Development: The Search for a Basic Needs Yardstick', *World Development*, 7.

Jain, L.R., K. Sundaram and S. Tendulkar (1989). 'Levels of Living and Incidence of Poverty in Rural India: A Cross Section Analysis', *Journal of Quantitative Economics*, 5.

Janakarajan, S. (1992). 'Interlinked Transactions and the Market for Water in the Agrarian Economy of a Tamil Nadu Village', in Subramanian (1992).

Jayaraj, D. and S. Subramanian (1995a). 'Poverty-eradication through Redistribution Taxation: Some Elementary Considerations', mimeo.

—— (1995b). 'Poverty and Discrimination: Measurement, and Evidence from Rural India', mimeo.

Kakwani, N.C. (1980a). *Income Inequality and Poverty: Methods of Estimation and Policy Applications*. New York: Oxford University Press.

—— (1980b). 'On a Class of Poverty Measures', *Econometrica*, 48.

—— (1984). 'Issues in Measuring Poverty', *Advances in Econometrics*, 3.

—— (1993). 'Performance in Living Standards: An International Comparison', *Journal of Development Economics*, 41.

Kakwani, N.C. and K. Subbarao (1990). 'Rural Poverty and Its Alleviation in India', *Economic and Political Weekly*, 25.

Kanbur, R. (1985). 'Inequality, Poverty, and Development: With An Application to Fiji' (paper based on a talk given to the Fiji Economic Association, September 1984), mimeo.

—— (1987). 'Measurement and Alleviation of Poverty: With an Application to the Effects of Macroeconomic Adjustment', *IMF Staff Papers*.

Keen, M. (1992). 'Needs and Targeting', *Economic Journal*, 102.

Kolm, S.Ch. (1969). 'The Optimum Production of Social Justice', in J. Margolis and H. Guitton (eds), *Public Economics*. London: Macmillan.

—— (1976a). 'Unequal Inequalities, I', *Journal of Economic Theory*, 12.

—— (1976b). 'Unequal Inequalities, II', *Journal of Economic Theory*, 13.

Krishnaji, N. (1981). 'On Measuring the Incidence of Undernutrition: A Note on Sukhatme's Procedure', *Economic and Political Weekly*, 16.

Krishnaswamy, K.S. (ed.) (1990). *Poverty and Income Distribution*. Bombay: Oxford University Press.

Kumar, B.G. and F. Stewart (1992). 'Tackling Malnutrition: What Can Targeted Nutritional Intervention Achieve?', in B. Harriss, S. Guhan and R. Cassen (eds), *Poverty in India: Research and Policy*. Bombay: Oxford University Press.

Kundu, A. and T.E. Smith (1983). 'An Impossibility Theorem on Poverty Indices', *International Economic Review*, 24.

Kuznets, S. (1955). 'Economic Growth and Income Inequality', *American Economic Review*, 45.

Kynch, J. and A.K. Sen (1983). 'Indian Women: Well-Being and Survival', *Cambridge Journal of Economics*, 7.

Lewis, G.W. and D.T. Ulph (1988). 'Poverty, Inequality and Welfare', *Economic Journal*, 98.

Lorenz, M.O. (1905). 'Methods for Measuring Concentration of Wealth', *Journal of the American Statistical Association*, 9.

Mayhew, H. (1985). *London Labour and the London Poor. Selections Made and Introduced by Victor Neuburg*. London: Penguin Books.

Mellor, J.W. and G.M. Desai (eds) (1986). *Agricultural Change and Rural Poverty: Variations on a Theme by Dharm Narain*. Delhi: Oxford University Press.

Minhas, B.S. (1971). 'Rural Poverty, Numbers Games and Polemics', *Indian Economic Review*, 6.

Minhas, B.S., L.R. Jain, S.M. Kansal and M.R. Saluja (1987). 'On the Choice of Appropriate Consumer Price Indices and Data Sets for Estimating the Incidence of Poverty in India', *Indian Economic Review*, 22.

Morris, M.D. (1979). *Measuring the Condition of the World's Poor: The Physical Quality of Life Index*. Oxford: Pergamon Press.

National Institute of Public Finance and Policy (1986). *Aspects of Black Economy in India*. Report submitted to the Ministry of Finance, Government of India.

Nozik, R. (1973). 'Distributive Justice', *Philosophy and Public Affairs*, 3.

Ojha, P.D. (1970). 'A Configuration of Indian Poverty, Inequality and Levels of Living', *Reserve Bank of India Bulletin*, January.

Ok, E.A. (1995). 'Fuzzy Measurement of Income Inequality: A Class of Fuzzy Inequality Measures', *Social Choice and Welfare*, 12, 2.

Osmani, S.R. (1992a). 'On Some Controversies in the Measurement of Undernutrition', in Osmani.

—— (ed.) (1992b). *Nutrition and Poverty*. Oxford: Clarendon Press.

Panda, M.K. (1981). 'Productivity Aspects of Wages in Food for Work Programmes', *Economic and Political Weekly*, 16.

Pattanaik, P.K. and Y. Xu (1990). 'On Ranking Opportunity Sets in Terms of Freedom of Choice', *Recherches Economique de Louvain*, 56.

Planning Commission, Government of India (1962). 'Perspective of Development: 1961–1976 — Implications of Planning for a Minimum Level of Living'. Reprinted in Srinivasan and Bardhan (1974).

—— (1969). *Report of the Committee on Distribution of Income and Levels of Living (Part II: Changes in Levels of Living)*. New Delhi.

—— (1981). *A Technical Note on the Sixth Plan of India (1980–85)*. New Delhi.

—— (1993). *Report of the Expert Group on Estimation of Proportion and Number of Poor*. New Delhi.

Pyatt, G. (1987). 'Measuring Welfare, Poverty and Inequality', *Economic Journal*, 97.

Rae, D. (1975). 'Maximin Justice and an Alternative Principle of General Advantage', *American Political Science Review*, 69.

Raj, K.N. (1973). 'Direct Taxation of Agriculture', Centre for Development Studies, Working Paper No. 11.

Ravallion, M. (1991). 'On the Coverage of Public Employment Schemes for Poverty Alleviation', *Journal of Development Economics*, 34.

Ravallion, M. and K. Chao (1989). 'Targeted Policies for Poverty Alleviation under Imperfect Information: Algorithms and Applications', *Journal of Policy Modelling*, 11.

Rawls, J. (1971). *A Theory of Justice*. Cambridge, Mass.: Harvard University Press.

Rothschild, M. and J. Stiglitz (1973). 'Some Further Results on the Measurement of Inequality', *Journal of Economic Theory*, 6.

Rudra, A. (1974). 'Minimum Level of Living — A Statistical Examination', in Srinivasan and Bardhan (1974).

Seckler, D. (1982). ' "Small But Healthy": A Basic Hypothesis in the Theory, Measurement and Policy of Malnutrition', in P.V. Sukhatme (ed.), *Newer Concepts in Nutrition and Their Implications for Policy*. Pune.

Sen, A.K. (1970). 'The Impossibility of a Paretian Liberal', *Journal of Political Economy*, 78. (Reprinted in Sen [1982].)

—— (1973). *On Economic Inequality*. Oxford: Clarendon Press.

—— (1976a). 'Poverty: An Ordinal Approach to Measurement', *Econometrics*, 44. (Reprinted in Sen [1982].)

—— (1976b). 'Real National Income', *Review of Economic Studies*, 43. (Reprinted in Sen [1982]).

—— (1977). 'Social Choice Theory: A Reexamination', *Econometrica*, 45. (Reprinted in Sen [1982].)

Sen, A.K. (1978). 'Ethical Measurement of Inequality: Some Difficulties', in W. Krelle and A.F. Shorrocks (eds), *Personal Income Distribution*. Amsterdam: North Holland. (Reprinted in Sen [1982].)

—— (1979). 'Personal Utilities and Public Judgments: Or What's Wrong with Welfare Economics?', *Economic Journal*, 89. (Reprinted in Sen [1982].)

—— (1980). 'Equality of What?', in S.M. McMurrin (ed.), *Tanner Lectures on Human Values, 1*. Salt Lake City: University of Utah Press and Cambridge: Cambridge University Press. (Reprinted in Sen [1982].)

—— (1981a). *Poverty and Famines: An Essay on Entitlement and Deprivation*. Oxford: Clarendon Press.

—— (1981b). 'Public Action and the Quality of Life in Developing Countries', *Oxford Bulletin of Economics and Statistics*, 43.

—— (1982). *Choice, Welfare and Measurement*. Oxford: Blackwell, Cambridge, Mass.: MIT Press and Delhi: Oxford University Press.

—— (1983). 'Poor, Relatively Speaking', *Oxford Economic Papers*, 35.

—— (1984a). *Resources, Values and Development*. Oxford: Blackwell, Cambridge, Mass.: Harvard University Press and Delhi: OUP.

—— (1984b). 'Rights and Capabilities', in Sen (1984a). (Also in T. Honderich (ed.), *Morality and Objectivity: A Tribute to J.L. Mackie*. London: Routledge.)

—— (1985a). *Commodities and Capabilities*. Amsterdam: North-Holland.

—— (1985b). 'A Reply to Professor Townsend', *Oxford Economic Papers*, 37.

—— (1986). 'Dharm Narain on Poverty: Concepts and Broader Issues', in Mellor and Desai (1986).

—— (1992). *Inequality Reexamined*. New York: Russell Sage Foundation and Oxford: Clarendon Press.

Sen, A.K., J. Muellbauer, R. Kanbur, K. Hart and B. Williams (1987). *The Standard of Living*. Cambridge: Cambridge University Press.

Sharma, B.D. (1987). 'Measuring Poverty and Equalitarian Trends', *North Eastern Hill University Journal of Social Sciences and Humanities*, 1.

Shorrocks, A.F. (1988). 'Aggregation Issues in Inequality Measurement', in W. Eichhorn (ed.), *Measurement in Economics: Theory and Applications in Economic Indices*. Heidelberg: Physica Verlag.

Shorrocks, A.F. and J. Foster (1987). 'Transfer Sensitive Inequality Measures', *Review of Economic Studies*, 54.

Srinivasan, T.N. and P.K. Bardhan (eds) (1974). *Poverty and Income Distribution in India*. Calcutta: Statistical Publishing Society.

Srinivasan, T.N. and P.K. Bardhan (eds) (1988). *Rural Poverty in South Asia*. New York: Columbia University Press.

Subramanian, S. (1989). 'Poverty-Minimization in the Light of "Life-Boat Ethics" ', *Journal of Quantitative Economics*, 5.

—— (1990). 'Unemployment, Poverty and Inequality' (Section II of Chapter 12), in Malcolm S. Adiseshiah (ed.), *Eighth Plan Perspectives*. New Delhi: Lancer International.

—— (ed.) (1992). *Themes in Development Economics: Essays in Honour of Malcolm Adiseshiah*. New Delhi: Oxford University Press.

Sukhatme, P.V. (1978). 'Assessment of Adequacy of Diets at Different Income Levels', *Economic and Political Weekly*, 13.

—— (1981). 'On Measurement of Poverty', *Economic and Political Weekly*, 16.

—— (1982). 'Measurement of Undernutrition', *Economic and Political Weekly*, 17.

Sukhatme, P.V. and S. Margen (1980). 'Relationship between Undernutrition and Poverty', *Indian Economic Review*, 16.

Sundrum, R.M. (1987). *Growth and Income Distribution in India: Policy and Performance since Independence*. Sage Publications: New Delhi.

Suryanarayana, M.H. (1991). 'A Note on Lorenz Ratios Based on NSS Consumption Distributions', *Journal of Quantitative Economics*, 7.

—— (1995). 'Growth, Poverty and Levels of Living: Hypotheses, Methods and Policies', *Journal of the Indian School of Political Economy*, 7.

Suryanarayana, M.H. and S. Geetha (1994). 'P* Poverty Measure: An Estimable Approach'. Indira Gandhi Institute of Development Research, Bombay, *mimeo*.

Takayama, N. (1979). 'Poverty, Income Inequality and their Measures: Professor Sen's Axiomatic Approach Reconsidered', *Econometrica*, 47.

Tendulkar, S.D. and L.R. Jain (1995). 'Economic Reforms and Poverty', *Economic and Political Weekly*, 30.

Tendulkar, S.D., K. Sundaram and L.R. Jain (1993). 'Poverty in India: 1970–71 to 1988–89'. ILO-ARTEP: New Delhi.

Thon, D. (1979). 'On Measuring Poverty', *Review pf Income and Wealth*, 25.

Townsend, P. (1985). 'A Sociological Approach to the Measurement of Poverty: A Rejoinder to Prof. Amartya Sen', *Oxford Economic Papers*, 37.

UNDP (1993). *Human Development Report (1993)*. New York: Oxford University Press.

Vaidyanathan, A. (1974). 'Some Aspects of Inequalities in Living Standards in Rural India', in Srinivasan and Bardhan (1974).

—— (1990). 'Asset Holdings and Consumption of Rural Households in India: A Study of Spatial and Temporal Variations', in Indian Society of Agricultural Economics, *Agricultural Development Policy: Adjustments and Reorientation*. New Delhi: Oxford and IBH.

Varian, H. (1975). 'Distributive Justice, Welfare Economics and the Theory of Fairness', *Philosophy and Public Affairs*, 4.

Vaughan, R.N. (1987). 'Welfare Approaches to the Measurement of Poverty', *Economic Journal*, 97.

Watts, H. (1968). 'An Economic Definition of Poverty', in D.P. Moynihan (ed.), *On Understanding Poverty*. New York: Basic Books.

Weale, A. (1980). 'The Impossibility of Liberal Egalitarianism', *Analysis*, 40.

Zubrigg, S. (1983). 'Ideology and the Poverty Line Debate', *Economic and Political Weekly*, 18.

Of the Dustmen of London

HENRY MAYHEW

Dust and rubbish accumulate in houses from a variety of causes, but principally from the residuum of fires, the white ash and cinders, or small fragments of unconsumed coke, giving rise to by far the greater quantity. Some notion of the vast amount of this refuse annually produced in London may be formed from the fact that the consumption of coal in the metropolis is, according to the official returns, 3,500,000 tons per annum, which is at the rate of a little more than 11 tons per house; the poorer families, it is true, do not burn more than 2 tons in the course of the year, but then many such families reside in the same house, and hence the average will appear in no way excessive. Now the ashes and cinders arising from this enormous consumption of coal would, it is evident, if allowed to lie scattered about in such a place as London, render, ere long, not only the back streets, but even the important thoroughfares, filthy and impassable. Upon the officers of the various parishes, therefore, has devolved the duty of seeing that the refuse of the fuel consumed throughout London is removed almost as fast as produced; this they do by entering into an agreement for the clearance of the 'dust-bins' of the parishioners as often as required, with some person who possesses all necessary appliances for the purpose — such as horses, carts, baskets, and shovels, together with a plot of waste ground whereon to deposit the refuse. The persons with whom this agreement is made are called 'dust-contractors', and are generally men of considerable wealth.

The collection of 'dust', is now, more properly speaking, the removal of it. The collection of an article implies the voluntary seeking after it, and this the dustmen can hardly be said to do; for though they parade the streets shouting for the dust as they go, they do so rather to fulfil a certain duty they have undertaken to perform than in any expectation of profit to be derived from the sale of the article.

Formerly the custom was otherwise; but then, as will be seen hereafter, the residuum of the London fuel was far more valuable. Not many years ago it was the practice for the various master dustmen to send in their tenders to the vestry, on a certain day appointed for the purpose, offering to pay a considerable sum yearly to the parish authorities for liberty to collect the dust from the several houses. The sum formerly paid to the parish of Shadwell, for instance, though not a very extensive one, amounted to between 400*l*. or 500*l*. per annum; but then there was an immense demand for the article, and the contractors were unable to furnish a sufficient supply from London; ships were frequently freighted with it from other parts, especially from Newcastle and the northern ports, and at that time it formed an article of considerable international commerce — the price being from 15*s*. to 1*l*. per chaldron. Of late years, however, the demand has fallen off greatly, while the supply has been progressively increasing, owing to the extension of the metropolis, so that the contractors have not only declined paying anything for liberty to collect it, but now stipulate to receive a certain sum for the removal of it. It need hardly be stated that the parishes always employ the man who requires the least money for the performance of what has now become a matter of duty rather than an object of desire. Some idea may be formed of the change which has taken place in this business, from the fact that the aforesaid parish of Shadwell, which formerly received the sum of 450*l*. per annum for liberty to collect the dust, now pays the contractor the sum of 240*l*. per annum for its removal.

The Court of Sewers of the City of London, in 1846, through the advice of Mr Cochrane, the president of the National Philanthropic Association, were able to obtain from the contractors the sum of 5000*l*. for liberty to clear away the dirt from the streets and the dust from the bins and houses in that district. The year following, however, the contractors entered into a combination, and came to a resolution not to bid so high for the privilege; the result was that they obtained their contracts at an expense of 2200*l*. By acting on the same principle in the year after, they not only offered no premium whatever for the contract, but the City Commissioners of Sewers were obliged to pay them the sum of 300*l*. for removing the refuse, and at present the amount paid by the City is as much as 4900*l*.! This is divided among four great contractors, and would, if equally apportioned, give them 1250*l*. each.

All the metropolitan parishes now pay the contractors various amounts for the removal of the dust, and I am credibly informed that there is a system of underletting and jobbing in the dust contracts extensively carried on. The contractor for a certain parish is often a different person from the master doing the work, who is unknown in the contract. Occasionally the work would appear to be subdivided and underlet a second time.

The parish of St Pancras is split into no less than 21 districts, each district having a separate and independent 'Board', who are generally at war with each other, and make separate contracts for their several divisions. This is also the case in other large parishes, and these and other considerations confirm me in the conclusion that of large and small dust-contractors, job-masters, and middle-men of one kind or the other, throughout the metropolis there cannot be less than the number I have stated — 90. With the exception of Bermondsey, there are no parishes who remove their own dust.

It is difficult to arrive at any absolute statement as to the gross amount paid by the different parishes for the removal of the entire dust of the metropolis. From Shadwell the contractor, as we have seen, receives 250*l.*; from the city the four contractors receive as much as 5000*l.*; but there are many small parishes in London which do not pay above a tithe of the last-mentioned sum. Let us, therefore, assume that one with another, the several metropolitan parishes pay 200*l.* a year each to the dust-contractor. According to the returns before given, there are 176 parishes in London. Hence, the gross amount paid for the removal of the entire dust of the metropolis will be between 30,000*l.* and 40,000*l.* per annum.

The removal of the dust throughout the metropolis is, therefore, carried on by a number of persons called contractors who undertake, as has been stated, for a certain sum, to cart away the refuse from the houses as frequently as the inhabitants desire it. To ascertain the precise numbers of these contractors is a task of much greater difficulty than might at first be conceived.

The London Post Office Directory gives the following number of tradesmen connected with the removal of refuse from the houses and streets of the metropolis.

Dustmen	9
Scavengers	10
Nightmen	14
Sweeps	32

But these numbers are obviously incomplete, for even a cursory passenger through London must have noticed a greater number of names upon the various dust carts to be met with in the streets than are here set down.

A dust-contractor who has been in the business upwards of 20 years, stated that from his knowledge of the trade, he should suppose that at present there might be about 80 or 90 contractors in the metropolis. Now, according to the returns before given, there are within the limits of the Metropolitan Police District 176 parishes, and comparing this with my informant's statement, that many persons contract for more than one parish (of which, indeed, he himself is an instance), there remains but little reason to doubt the correctness of his supposition — that there are, in all, between 80 or 90 dust-contractors, large and small, connected with the metropolis. Assuming the aggregate number to be 88, there would be one contractor to every two parishes.

These dust-contractors are likewise the contractors for the cleansing of the streets, except where that duty is performed by the street-orderlies; they are also the persons who undertake the emptying of the cesspools in their neighbourhood; the latter operation, however, is effected by an arrangement between themselves and the landlords of the premises, and forms no part of their parochial contracts. At the office of the street orderlies in Leicester Square, they have knowledge of only 30 contractors connected with the metropolis; but this is evidently defective, and refers to the 'large masters' alone; leaving out of all consideration, as it does, the host of small contractors scattered up and down the metropolis, who are able to employ only two or three carts and six or seven men each; many of such small contractors being merely master sweeps who have managed to 'get on a little in the world', and who are now able to contract, 'in a small way', for the removal of dust, street-sweepings, and nightsoil. Moreover, many of even the 'great contractors' being unwilling to venture upon an outlay of capital for carts, horses, &c., when their contract is only for a year, and may pass at the end of that time into the hands of any one who may underbid them — many such, I repeat, are in the habit of underletting a portion of their contract to others possessing the necessary appliances, or of entering into partnership with them. The latter is the case in the parish of Shadwell where a person having carts and horses shares the profits with the original contractor. The agreement made on such occasions is, of course, a secret, though the practice is by no means uncommon; indeed, there is so much secrecy maintained concerning all matters connected with this business, that the inquiry is beset with every possible difficulty. The gentleman who communicated to me the amount paid by the parish of Shadwell and who informed me, moreover, that parishes in his neighbourhood paid twice and three times more than Shadwell did, hinted to me the difficulties I should experience at the commencement of my inquiry, and I have certainly found his opinion correct to the letter. I have ascertained that in one yard intimidation was resorted to and the men were threatened with instant dismissal if they gave me any information but such as was calculated to mislead.

I soon discovered, indeed, that it was impossible to place any reliance on what some of the contractors said; and here I may repeat that the indisputable result of my inquiries has been to meet with far more deception and equivocation from employers generally than from the employed; working men have little or no motive for mis-stating their wages; they know well that the ordinary rates of remuneration for their labour are easily ascertainable from other members of the trade, and seldom or never object to produce accounts of their earnings, whenever they have been in the habit of keeping such things. With employers, however, the case is far different; to seek to ascertain from them the profits of their trade is to meet with evasion and prevarication at every turn; they seem to feel that their gains are dishonestly large, and hence resort to every means to prevent them being made public. That I have met with many honourable exceptions to this rule, I most cheerfully acknowledge; but that the *majority* of tradesmen are neither so frank, communicative, nor truthful, as the men in their employ, the whole of my investigations go to prove. I have already, in the *Morning Chronicle*, recorded the character of my interviews with an eminent Jew slop-tailor, an army clothier, and an enterprising free-trade stay-maker (a gentleman who subscribed his 100 guineas to the League), and I must in candour confess that now, after two years' experience, I have found the industrious poor a thousand-fold more veracious than the trading rich.

With respect to the amount of business done by these contractors, or gross quantity of dust collected by them in the course of the year, it would appear that each employs, on an average, about 20 men, which makes the number of men employed as dustmen through the streets of London amount to 1800. This, as has been previously stated, is grossly at variance with the number given in the Census of 1841, which computes the dustmen in the metropolis at only 254. But, as I said before, I have long ceased to place confidence in the government returns on such subjects. According to the above estimate of 254, and deducting from this number the 88 master dustmen, there would be only 166 labouring men to empty the 300,000 dust-bins of London, and as these men always work in couples, it follows that every two dustmen would have to remove the refuse from about 3600 houses; so that assuming each bin to require emptying once every six weeks they would have to cart away the dust from 2400 houses every month, or 600 every week, which is at the rate of 100 a day, and as each dust-bin contains about half a load, it would follow that at this rate each cart would have to collect 50 loads of dust daily, whereas 5 loads is the average day's work.

Computing the London dust-contractors at 90, and the inhabited houses at 300,000, it follows that each contractor would have 3333 houses to remove the refuse from. Now it has been calculated that the ashes and cinders alone with each house average about three loads per annum, so that each contractor would have, in round numbers, 10,000 loads of dust to remove in the course of the year. I find, from inquiries, that every two dustmen carry to the yard about five loads a day, or about 1500 loads in the course of the year, so that at this rate, there must be between six and seven carts, and twelve and fourteen collectors employed by each master. But this is exclusive of the men employed in the yards. In one yard that I visited there were fourteen people busily employed. Six of these were women who were occupied in sifting, and they were attended by three men who shovelled the dust into their sieves, and the foreman, who was hard at work loosening and dragging down the dust from the heap, ready for the 'fillers-in'. Besides these there were two carts and four men engaged in conveying the sifted dust to the barges alongside the wharf. At a larger dust-yard, that formerly stood on the banks of the Regent's-canal, I am informed that there were sometimes as many as 127 people at work. It is but a small yard, which has not 30 to 40 labourers connected with it; and the lesser dust-yards have generally from four to eight sifters, and six or seven carts. There are, therefore, employed in a medium-sized yard twelve collectors or cartmen, six sifters, and three fillers-in, besides the foreman or forewoman, making altogether 22 persons; so that, computing the contractors at 90, and allowing 20 men to be employed by each, there would be 1800 men thus occupied in the metropolis, which appears to be very near the truth.

One who has been all his life connected with the business estimated that there must be about ten dustmen to each metropolitan parish, large and small. In Marylebone he believed there were eighteen dust-carts, with two men to each, out every day; in some small parishes, however, two men are sufficient. There would be more men employed, he said, but some masters contracted for two or three parishes, and so 'kept the same men going', working them hard, and enlarging their regular rounds. Calculating then that ten men are employed to each of the 176 metropolitan parishes, we have 1760 dustmen in London. The suburban parishes, my informant told me, were as well 'dustmaned' as any he knew; for the residents in such parts were more particular about their dust than in busier places.

It is curious to observe how closely the number of men engaged in the collection of the 'dust' from the coals burnt in London agrees, according to the above estimate, with the number of men engaged in delivering the coals to be burnt. The coal-whippers, who 'discharge the colliers', are about 1800, and the coal-porters, who carry the coals from the barges to the merchants' wagons, are about the same in number. The amount of residuum from coal after burning cannot, of course, be equal either in bulk or weight to the original substance; but considering that the collection of the dust is a much slower operation than the delivery of the coals, the difference is easily accounted for.

We now come to speak of the labourers engaged in collecting, sifting, or shipping off the dust of the metropolis.

The dustmen, scavengers, and nightmen are, to a certain extent, the same people. The contractors generally agree with the various parishes to remove both the dust from the houses and the mud from the streets; the men in their employ are discriminately engaged in these two diverse occupations, collecting the dust to day, and often cleansing the streets on the morrow, and are designated either dustmen or scavengers, according to their particular avocation at the moment. The case is somewhat different, however, with respect to the nightmen. There is no such thing as a contract with the parish for removing the nightsoil. This is done by private agreement with the landlord of the premises whence the soil has to be removed. When a cesspool requires emptying, the occupying tenant communicates with the landlord, who makes an arrangement with a dust-contractor or sweep-nightman for this purpose. This operation is totally distinct from the regular or daily labour of the dust-contractor's men, who receive extra pay for it; sometimes one set go out at night and sometimes another, according either to the selection of the master or the inclination of the men. There are, however, some dustmen who have never been at work as nightmen, and could not be induced to do so, from an invincible antipathy to the employment; still, such instances are few, for the men generally go whenever they can, and occasionally engage in nightwork for employers unconnected with their masters. It is calculated that there are some hundreds of men employed nightly in the removal of the nightsoil of the metropolis during the summer and autumn, and as these men have often to work at dust-collecting or cleansing the streets on the following day, it is evident that the same persons cannot be thus employed every night; accordingly the ordinary practice is for the dustmen to 'take it in turns', thus allowing each set to be employed every third night, and to have two nights' rest in the interim.

The men, therefore, who collect the dust on one day may be cleaning the streets on the next, especially during wet weather, and engaged at night, perhaps, twice during the week, in removing nightsoil; so that it is difficult to arrive at any precise notion as to the number of persons engaged in any one of these branches *per se*.

But these labourers not only work indiscriminately at the collection of dust, the cleansing of the streets, or the removal of nightsoil, but they are employed almost as indiscriminately at the various branches of the dust business; with this qualification, however, that few men apply themselves continuously to any one branch of the business. The labourers employed in a dust-yard may be divided into two classes: those paid by the contractor; and those paid by the foreman or forewoman of the dust-heap, commonly called hill-man or hill-woman. They are as follows:

I. Labourers paid by the Contractors or,
   1. *Yard foreman*, or superintendent. This duty is often performed by the master, especially in small contracts.
   2. *Gangers or dust-collectors*. These are called 'fillers' and 'carriers', from the practice of one of the men who go out with the cart filling the basket, and the other carrying it on his shoulder to the vehicle.
   3. *Loaders* of carts in the dust-yard for shipment.
   4. *Carriers* of cinders to the cinder-heap, or bricks to the brick-heap.
   5. *Foreman* or *forewoman* of the heap.

II. Labourers paid by the Hill-man or Hill-woman
   1. *Sifters*, who are generally women, and mostly the wives or

concubines of the dustmen, but sometimes the wives of badly paid labourers.

2. *Fillers-in*, or shovellers of dust into the sieves of the sifters (one man being allowed to every two or three women).

3. *Carriers off* of bones, rags, metal, and other perquisites to the various heaps; these are mostly children of the dustmen.

A medium-sized dust-yard will employ about twelve collectors, three fillers-in, six sifters, and one foreman or forewoman; while a large yard will afford work to about 150 people.

There are four different modes of payment prevalent among the several labourers employed at the metropolitan dust-yards: (1) by the day; (2) by the piece or load; (3) by the lump; (4) by perquisites.

1st. *The foreman of the yard*, where the master does not perform this duty himself, is generally one of the regular dustmen picked out by the master, for this purpose. He is paid the sum of 2s. 6d. per day, or 15s. per week. In large yards there are sometimes two and even three yard-foremen at the same rate of wages. Their duty is merely to superintend the work. They do not labour themselves, and their exemption in this respect is considered, and indeed looked on by themselves, as a sort of premium for good services.

2nd. *The gangers or collectors* are generally paid 8d. per load for every load they bring into the yard. This is, of course, piece work, for the more hours the men work the more loads will they be enabled to bring, and the more pay will they receive. There are some yards where the carters get only 6d. per load, as, for instance, at Paddington. The Paddington men, however, are not considered inferior workmen to the rest of their fellows, but merely to be worse paid. In 1826, or 25 years ago, the carters had 1s. 6d. per load; but at that time the contractors were able to get 1l. per chaldron for the soil and 'brieze' or cinders; then it began to fall in value, and according to the decrease in the price of these commodities, so have the wages of the dust-collectors been reduced. It will be at once seen that the reduction in the wages of the dustmen bears no proportion to the reduction in the price of soil and cinders, but it must be borne in mind that whereas the contractors formerly paid large sums for liberty to collect the dust, they now are paid large sums to remove it. This in some measure helps to account for the apparent disproportion, and tends, perhaps, to equalize the matter. The gangers, therefore, have 4d. each, per load when best paid. They consider from four to six loads a good day's work, for where the contract is large, extending over several parishes, they often have to travel a long way for a load. It thus happens that while the men employed by the Whitechapel contractor can, when doing their utmost, manage to bring only four loads a day to the yard, which is situated in a place called the 'ruins' in Lower Shadwell, the men employed by the Shadwell contractor can easily get eight or nine loads in a day. Five loads are about an average day's work, and this gives them 1*s*. 8½*d*. per day each, or 10*s*. per week. In addition to this, the men have their perquisites 'in aid of wages'. The collectors are in the habit of getting beer or money in lieu thereof, at nearly all the houses from which they remove the dust, the public being thus in a manner compelled to make up the rate of wages, which should be paid by the employer, so that what is given to benefit the men really goes to the master, who invariably reduces the wages to the precise amount of the perquisites obtained. This is the main evil of the 'perquisite system of payment' (a system of which the mode of paying waiters may be taken as the special type). As an instance of the injurious effects of this mode of payment in connection with the London dustmen, the collectors are forced, as it were, to extort from the public that portion of their fair earnings of which their master deprives them; hence, how can we wonder that they make it a rule when they receive neither beer nor money from a house to make as great a mess as possible the next time they come, scattering the dust and cinders about in such as manner, that, sooner than have any trouble with them, people mostly give them what they look for? One of the most intelligent men with whom I have spoken, gave me the following account of his perquisites for the last week, viz.: Monday, 5½*d*.; Tuesday, 6*d*.; Wednesday, 4½*d*.; Thursday, 7*d*.; Friday, 5½*d*.; and Saturday, 5*d*. This he received in money, and was independent of beer. He had on the same week drawn rather more than five loads each day, to the yard, which made his gross earnings for the week, wages and perquisites together, to be 14*s*. 0½*d*. which he considers to be a fair average of his weekly earnings as connected with dust.

3rd. *The loaders of the carts* for shipment are the same persons as those who collect the dust, but thus employed for the time being. The pay for this work is by the 'piece' also, 2*d*. per chaldron between four persons being the usual rate, or ½*d*. per man. The men so engaged have no perquisites. The barges into which they shoot the soil or 'brieze', as the case may be, hold from 50 to 70 chaldrons, and they consider the loading of one of these barges a good day's work. The average cargo is about 60 chaldrons, which gives them 2s. 6d. per day, or somewhat more than their average earnings when collecting.

4th. *The carriers of cinders* to the cinder heap. I have mentioned that, ranged round the sifters in the dust-yard, are a number of baskets, into which are put the various things found among the dust, some of these being the property of the master, and others the perquisites of the hill-man or -woman, as the case may be. The cinders and old bricks are the property of the master, and to remove them to their proper heaps boys are employed by him at 1s. per day. These boys are almost universally the children of dustmen and sifters at work in the yard, and thus not only help to increase the earnings of the family, but qualify themselves to become the dustmen of a future day.

5th. *The hill-man or hill-woman.* The hill-man enters into an agreement with the contractor to sift *all* the dust in the yard throughout the year at so much per load and perquisites. The usual sum per load is 6d., nor have I been able to ascertain that any of these people undertake to do it at a less price. Such is the amount paid by the contractor for Whitechapel. The perquisites of the hill-man or hill-woman, are rags, bones, pieces of old metal, old tin or iron vessels, old boots and shoes, and one-half of the money, jewellery, or other valuables that may be found by the sifters.

The hill-man or hill-woman employs the following persons, and pays them at the following rates:

1st. *The sifters* are paid 1s. per day when employed, but the employment is not constant. The work cannot be pursued in wet weather, and the services of the sifters are required only when a large heap has accumulated, as they can sift much faster than the dust can be collected. The employment is therefore precarious; the payment has not, for the last 30 years at least, been more than 1s. per day, but the perquisites were greater. They formerly were allowed one-half of whatever was found; of late years, however, the hill-man has gradually reduced the perquisites 'first one thing and then another', until the only one they have now remaining is half of whatever money or other valuable article may be found in the process of sifting. These valuables the sifters often pocket, if able to do so unperceived, but if discovered in the attempt, they are immediately discharged.

2nd. *The fillers-in*, or shovellers of dust into the sieves of sifters, are in general any poor fellows who may be straggling about in search of employment. They are sometimes, however, the grown-up boys of dustmen, not yet permanently engaged by the contractor. These are paid 2s. per day for their labour, but they are considered more as casualty men, though it often happens, if 'hands' are wanted, that they are regularly engaged by th. ntractors, and become regular dustmen for the remainder of their lives.

3rd. The little fellows, the children of the dustmen, who follow their mothers to the yard, and help them to pick rags, bones, &c., out of the sieve and put them into the baskets, as soon as they are able to carry a basket between two of them to the separate heaps, are paid 3d. or 4d. per day for this work by the hill-man.

The wages of the dustmen have been increased within the last seven years from 6d. per load to 8d. among the large contractors — the 'small masters', however, still continue to pay 6d. per load. This increase in the rate of remuneration was owing to the men complaining to the commissioners that they were not able to live upon what they earned at 6d.; an enquiry was made into the truth of the men's assertion, and the result was that the commissioners decided upon letting the contracts to such parties only as would undertake to pay a fair price to their workmen. The contractors, accordingly, increased the remuneration of the labourers; since then the principal masters have paid 8d. per load to the collectors. It is right I should add, that I could not hear — though I made special enquiries on the subject — that the wages had been in any one instance reduced since Free-trade has come into operation.

The usual hours of labour vary according to the mode of payment. The 'collectors', or men out with the cart, being paid by the load, work as long as the light lasts; the 'fillers-in' and sifters, on the other hand, being paid by the day, work the ordinary hours, viz., from six to six, with the regular intervals for meals.

The summer is the worst time for all hands, for then the dust decreases in quantity; the collectors, however, make up for the 'slackness' at this period by nightwork, and, being paid by the 'piece' of load at the dust business, are not discharged when their employment is less brisk.

It has been shown that the dustmen who perambulate the streets usually collect five loads in a day; this, at 8d. per load, leaves them about 1s. 8d. each, and so makes their weekly earnings amount to about 10s. per week. Moreover, there are the 'perquisites' from the houses whence they remove the dust; and further, the dust-collectors are frequently employed at the nightwork, which is always a distinct matter from the dust-collecting, &c., and paid for independent of their regular weekly wages, so that, from all I can gather, the average wages of the men appear to be rather more than 15s. Some admitted to me, that in busy times they often earned 25s. a week.

Then, again, dustwork, as with the weaving of silk, is a kind of family work. The husband, wife, and children (unfortunately) all work at it. The consequence is, that the earnings of the whole have to be added together in order to arrive at a notion of the aggregate gains.

The following may therefore be taken as a fair average of the earnings of a dustman and his family *when in full employment*. The elder boys when able to earn 1s. a day set up for themselves, and do not allow their wages to go into the common purse.

	£	s.	d.	£	s.	d.
Man, 5 loads per day, or 30 loads per week,						
at 4d. per load	0	10	0			
Perquisites, or beer money	0	2	9½			
Nightwork for 2 nights a week	0	5	0			
				0	17	9½
Woman, or sifter, per week, at 1s. per day	0	6	0			
Perquisites, say 3d. a day	0	1	6			
				0	7	6
Child, 3d. per day, carrying rags, bones, &c.				0	1	6
Total				1	6	9½

These are the earnings, it should be borne in mind, of a family in full employment. Perhaps it may be fairly said that the earnings of the single men are, on an average, 15s. a week, and 1l. for the family men all the year round.

Now, when we remember that the wages of many agricultural labourers are but 8s. a week, and the earnings of many needlewomen not 6d. a day, it must be confessed that the remuneration of the dustmen, and even of the dustwomen, is *comparatively* high. This certainly is not due to what Adam Smith, in his chapter on the Difference of Wages, terms the 'disagreeableness of the employment'. 'The wages of labour', he says, 'vary with the ease or hardship, the cleanliness or dirtiness, the honourableness or dishonourableness, of the employment'. It will be seen — when we come to treat of the nightmen — that the most offensive, and perhaps the least honourable, of all trades, is far from ranking among the best paid, as it should, if the above principle held good. That the disagreeableness of the occupation may in a measure tend to decrease the competition among the labourers, there cannot be the least doubt, but that it will consequently induce, as political economy would have us believe, a larger amount of wages to accrue to each of the labourers, is certainly another of the many assertions of that science which must be pronounced 'not proven'. For the dustmen are paid, if anything, less, and certainly not more, than the usual rate of payment to the London labourers; and if the earnings rank high, as times go, it is because all the members of the family, from the very earliest age, are able to work at the business, and so add to the general gains.

I visited a large dust-yard at the east end of London, for the purpose of getting a statement from one of the men. My informant was, at the time of my visit, shovelling the sifted soil from one of the lesser heaps, and, by a great effort of strength and activity, pitching each shovel-full to the top of a lofty mound, somewhat resembling a pyramid. Opposite to him stood a little woman, stoutly made, and with her arms bare above the elbow; she was his partner in the work, and was pitching shovel-full for shovel-full with him to the summit of the heap. She wore an old soiled cotton gown, open in front, and tucked up behind in the fashion of the last century. She had clouts of old rags tied round her ancles to prevent the dust from getting into her shoes, a sort of coarse towel fastened in front for an apron, and a red handkerchief bound tightly round her head. In this trim she worked away, and not only kept pace with the man, but often threw two shovels for his one, although he was a tall, powerful fellow. She smiled when she saw me noticing her, and seemed to continue her work with greater assiduity. I learned that she was deaf, and spoke so indistinctly that no stranger could understand her. She had also a defect in her sight, which latter circumstance had compelled her to abandon the sifting, as she could not well distinguish the various articles found in the dust-heap. The poor creature had therefore taken to the shovel, and now works with it every day, doing the labour of the strongest men.

From the man above referred to I obtained the following statement: — 'Father vos a dustie; — vos at it all his life, and grandfather afore him for I can't tell how long. Father vos allus a rum 'un; — sich a beggar for lush. Vhy I'm blowed if he vouldn't lush as much as half-a-dozen on 'em can lush now; somehow the dusties hasn't got the stuff in 'em as they used to have. A few year ago the fellers 'u'd think nothink o' lushin away for five or six days without niver going anigh their home. I niver vos at a school in all my life; I don't know what it's good for. It may be wery well for the likes o' you, but I doesn't know it 'u'd do a dustie any good. You see, ven I'm not out with the cart, I digs here all day; and p'raps I'm up all night, and digs avay agen the next day. Vot does I care for reading, or anythink of that there kind, ven I gets home arter my vork? I tell you vot I likes, though! vhy, I jist likes two or three pipes o' baccer, and a pot or two of good heavy and a song, and then I tumbles in with my Sall, and I'm as happy as here and there von. That there Sall of mine's a stunner — a riglar stunner. There ain't never a voman can sift a heap quickerer nor my Sall. Sometimes she yarns as much as I does; the only thing is, she's sitch a beggar for lush, that there Sall of mine, and then she kicks up sitch jolly rows, you niver see the like in your life. That there's the only fault, as I know on, in Sall; but, barring that, she's a hout-and-houter, and worth a half-a-dozen of t' other sifters — pick 'em out vare you likes. No, we ain't married 'zactly, though it's all one for all that. I sticks to Sall, and Sall sticks to I, and there's an end on 't: — vot is it to any von? I rec'lects a-picking the rags and things out of mother's sieve, when I were a young 'un, and a putting 'em all in the heap jist as it might be there. I vos allus in a dust-yard. I don't think I could do no how in no other place. You see I vouldn't be 'appy like; I only knows how to vork at the dust 'cause I'm used to it, and so vos father afore me, and I'll stick to it as long as I can. I yarns about half-a-bull [2s. 6d.] a day, take one day with another. Sall sometimes yarns as much, and ven I goes out at night I yarns a bob or two more, and so I gits along pretty tidy; sometimes yarnin more and sometimes yarnin less. I niver vos sick as I knows on; I've been queerish of a morning a good many times, but I doesn't call that sickness; it's only the lush and nothink more. The smells nothink at all, ven you gits used to it. Lor' bless you! You'd think nothink on it in a veek's time, — no, no more nor I do. There's tventy on us vorks here — riglar. I don't think there's von on 'em 'cept Scratchey Jack can read, but he can do it stunning; he's out vith the cart now, but he's the chap as can patter to you as long as he likes.'

Concerning the capital and income of the London dust business, the following estimate may be given as to the amount of property invested in and accruing to the trade.

It has been computed that there are 90 contractors, large and small; of these upwards of two–thirds, or about 35, may be said to be in a considerable way of business, possessing many carts and horses, as well as employing a large body of people; some yards have as many as 150 hands connected with them. The remaining 55 masters are composed of 'small men', some of whom are known as 'running dustmen', that is to say, persons who collect the dust without any sanction from the parish; but the number belonging to this class has considerably diminished since the great deterioration in the price of 'brieze'. Assuming, then, that the great and little master dustmen employ on an average between six and seven carts each, we have the following statement as to the capital of the London dust trade:

600 Carts, at 20*l.* each	£12,000
600 Horses, at 25*l.* each	15,000
600 Sets of harness, at 2*l.* per set	1200
600 Ladders, at 5*s.* each	150
1200 Baskets, at 2*s.* each	120
1200 Shovels, at 2*s.* each	120
Being a total capital of	£28,590

If, therefore, we assert that the capital of this trade is between 25,000*l.*, and 30,000*l.* in value, we shall not be far wrong either way.

Of the annual income of the same trade, it is almost impossible to arrive at any positive results; but, in the absence of all authentic information on the subject, we may make the subjoined conjecture:

Sum paid to contractors for the removal of dust from the 176 metropolitan parishes, at 200*l.* each parish	£35,200
Sum obtained for 900,000 loads of dust, at 2*s.* 6*d.* per load	112,500
	£147,700

Thus it would appear that the total income of the dust trade may be taken at between 145,000*l.* and 150,000*l.* per annum.

Against this we have to set the yearly out-goings of the business, which may be roughly estimated as follows:

Wages of 1800 labourers, at 10s. a week each (including sifters and carriers)	£46,800
Keep of 600 horses, at 10s. a week each	15,600
Wear and tear of stock in trade	4000
Rent for 90 yards, at 100l. a year each (large and small)	9000
	£75,400

The above estimates give us the following aggregate results:

Total yearly incomings of the London dust trade	£147,700
Total yearly out-goings	75,400
Total yearly profit	£72,300

Hence it would appear that the profits of the dust-contractors are very nearly at the rate of 100l. per cent, on their expenditure. I do not think I have over estimated the incomings, or under estimated the out-goings; at least I have striven to avoid doing so, in order that no injustice might be done to the members of the trade.

This aggregate profit, when divided among the 90 contractors, will make the clear gains of each master dustman amount to about 800l. per annum: of course some derive considerably more than this amount, and some considerably less.

Methods of Measuring
the Concentration of Wealth

M.O. LORENZ

There may be wide difference of opinion as to the significance of a very unequal distribution of wealth, but there can be no doubt as to the importance of knowing whether the present distribution is becoming more or less unequal. For this purpose we need some method of interpreting such statistics as we have that show the condition of a country at different epochs or of different countries at the same epoch; that is we wish to be able to say at what point a community is to be placed between the two extremes — equality, on the one hand, and the ownership of all wealth by one individual on the other. It is the purpose of the present chapter to discuss some of the methods that have been used, and to suggest an additional one, but not to enter upon a discussion of the reliability of the data used for illustration. Let us consider first the numerical measures, taking up later the graphic representations.

It has been a common practice to construct a table of class divisions of wealth or income with the per cent of the population falling within each class. An increase in the percentage of the middle class is supposed to show a diffusion of wealth. For example the following table of income tax returns in England is supposed to show a 'tendency of wealth among the income-tax paying classes to distribute itself in smaller amounts in a larger number of hands':[1]

It is impossible to tell from such a table whether there has been a concentration or diffusion of wealth because it might be true that the incomes over five thousand pounds, although a smaller proportion of the total number in the second epoch, nevertheless constitute a much

---

[1] Goscher (1887). *Journal of the Royal Statistical Society*, 1, p. 600.

larger proportion of the total income.[2] It should be added, however, that comparisons of fixed classifications are of use in noting the absolute increase or decrease in wealth on the part of the lower classes. It is important to know, for example, that 29 per cent in 1892 and 39 per cent in 1901 of the people of Prussia (according to the income tax returns) had more than nine thousand marks a year income.[3]

Table 2.1
Income Tax Assessments under Schedule D

	1877	1886	Per cent of increase or decrease
Between £150 and £500	285,754	347,021	21.4 (Increase)
Between 500 and 1000	32,085	32,033	nil
Between 1000 and 5000	19,726	19,250	2.4 (Decrease)
Over 5000	3122	3048	2.3 (Decrease)

Another method of interpreting a table like the one just quoted has been suggested by Dr Julius Wolf.[4] Instead of paying attention to the change in the percentage of members in a certain class, we should observe, he says, the movement of persons from one class to another. To illustrate his way of attacking the problem, he gives the following table of the number of tax-payers in the Canton Zürich (p. 234):

Table 2.2
Number of Tax Payers in the Canton Zürich

Class		1848	1888
I.	100–2000 Fr.	25,991	21,108
II.	2100–20,000	13,959	24,406
III.	20,100–25,000	2469	6584
IV.	25,000 and over	81	484

[2] For a further discussion of this point, see Ely, 'Evolution of Industrial Society', p. 259.

[3] *Zeitschrift des käniglich preussischen statistischen Bureaus*, 1902, p. 246.

[4] J. Wolf (1892). 'Sozialismus und kapitalistische Gesellschaftsordnung' (being vol. 1 of 'System der Sozialpolitik'), Stuttgart.

According to the method which he is criticizing, the statement would be made that there has been an increase in the second class of 75 per cent, in the third of 174, and in the fourth of 500. This would look unfavourable, as the increase in the lowest class has been least. But, according to this method, we find that there has been a movement between classes, as follows:

I to II	14,622 or 56 per cent of those originally in class I.
II to III	5578 or 33 per cent of those originally in class II.
III to IV	403 or 17 per cent of those originally in class III.

This makes it appear that the lowest classes have progressed most rapidly. He proceeds in a similar manner (p. 239) with regard to the wealth of the various classes. Instead of calculating the per cent of the total wealth falling in each class, he observes the per cent of the increase in the total income of a community that accrues to each class. Taking statistics of incomes for Prussia for 1876 and 1888, he finds that the lowest class got 22.1 per cent of the increase in the total Prussian income, and the other classes (proceeding upward) participated as follows: 30.5, 18.1, 16.7, 8.8 and 3.7. This, he thinks, indicates a diffusion of wealth.

Wolf's method of interpretation is fallacious. Without stopping to consider minor objections, it will be sufficient to show the erroneous results to which it leads by the following hypothetical case. Let the individuals of a certain group possess wealth as indicated in the following table:

Table 2.3

Class (Dollars)	Wealth of each individual in each class (Dollars)	Number of individuals
0 to 9	1, 3, 5, 7, 9	5
10 to 24	10, 12, 14, 16, 18	5
25 to 49	25, 28, 31, 34, 37	5
50 to 99	50, 60, 70, 80, 90	5
100 and over	100, 110, 120, 130, 140	5

Now imagine the wealth of each specific individual doubled. The relation between the wealth of individuals has not changed, and hence the degree of concentration must be the same.[5] The classification will now be as follows:

Table 2.4

Class (Dollars)	Wealth of each individual (Dollars)	Number
0 to 9	2, 6	2
10 to 24	10, 14, 18, 20, 24	5
25 to 49	28, 32, 36	3
50 to 99	50, 56, 62, 68, 74	5
100 and over	{ 100, 120, 140, 160, 180, 200, 220, 240, 260, 280 }	10

We find that the movement between classes has been as follows:

Table 2.5

	Number	Per cent of those originally in the class from which the movement took place
I to II	3	60
II to III	3	60
III to IV	5	100
IV to V	5	100

This indicates a concentration, which we know has not taken place. The root fallacy here is the ignoring of the change in the meaning of a fixed classification with a change in general wealth. Again, if we examine, as he does, the sharing of various classes in the increase in the community's wealth, we find the first class actually lost, the second

[5] It has been objected that doubling incomes does not leave individuals in the same relation to each other because (owing to the law of diminishing utility) doubling a rich man's income does not add proportionately as much to his well-being as in the case of a poor man. But this does not affect the argument above, because, according to this view, doubling incomes would tend to diffuse enjoyment, not concentrate it, as Wolf's method would indicate. In the present problem no error will result from confining our attention to nominal incomes.

got 0.1 per cent of the increase, the third and fourth lost, and the fifth secured 99.9 per cent. Yet there was no change in the concentration.

It is apparent that we need to take account simultaneously of changes in wealth and changes in population. Here also several erroneous methods have been used. Dr Soetbeer sought to show that there had been no concentration in Prussia between 1876 and 1888 because 'the average income of tax-payers in the higher classes had shown no tendency to increase'.[6] But that average income is no safe criterion is shown by the hypothetical case just presented, where the average income of the highest class shows a market increase, although there was no change in the degree of concentration.

Again, the 'triple measure' presented by Mr George K. Holmes[7] is not trustworthy. According to this we are to note, first, the average wealth in order to get the plane of distribution, or the relation of the whole population to its total mass of wealth; secondly, the per cent of people owning wealth shows the 'width of distribution'; and, finally, to find the state of the distribution among the possessing class, he takes the median of the number of owners and the median of the amount of wealth, and observes the distance between these medians (p. 116). That distance is the measure of the inequality of the distribution. To the first two parts of this triple measure no objection can be taken, but the last part would lead to error. Its method of application is shown by the following hypothetical case given in the article: A group of 64 persons is divided into 15 classes according to their wealth:

Class	$1	$2	$3	$4	$5	$6	$7	$8	$9	$10	$11	$12	$13	$14	$15
Number	1	2	3	4	5	6	7	8	7	6	5	4	3	2	1
Wealth of each class	1	4	9	16	25	36	49	64	63	60	55	48	39	28	15

Here the median of the number is in the centre of the eighth class, or $8.50, and the median of the amount of wealth is in the ninth class, or at the point represented by $9.82, and the difference between the two is $1.32, which is the measure of concentration. The error in this measure lies in the fact that the distance between the medians varies not only with the degree of concentration (for it does this), but also

---

[6] Soetbeer (1889). *Jahrbücher für Nationalökonomic und Statistik*, p. 420.

[7] George K. Holmes (1893). *Publications of the American Statistical Association*, p. 141.

with changes in the total wealth. Let us suppose each individual's wealth in the above case is doubled. The two medians would now be $17 and $19.65, and their difference $2.65, showing an increase in concentration, but by hypothesis the relative position of the members has not changed.

Another method of taking account of changes both in wealth and of population is simply to state in a table the per cent of total wealth and of total population in each class in each epoch. The following table, for example, does this with regard to Prussian incomes in the years 1892 and 1901:

Table 2.6[*]

Class	1892		1901	
	Per cent of number	Per cent of total income	Per cent of number	Per cent of total income
Under 900	70.1	41.2	60.5	31.7
900–3000	26.0	30.0	34.8	35.3
3000–6000	2.5	8.6	3.0	9.3
6000–9500	.7	4.2	.8	4.5
9500–30,500	.6	7.4	.7	8.1
30,500 and over	.1	8.6	.2	11.1
	100.0	100.0	100.0	100.0

Constructed from data in the *Zeitschrift* of the Prussian Statistical Bureau, 1902, the incomes below 900 marks being estimated on the assumption that their average was 700 in both epochs, and that the persons assessed are the same per cent of the total number of income-receivers as the taxable part of the population (*Einkommens Keuerpfuchliger Theil*) is of the total population.

What can such a table tell us? We can make such statements as the following: 70 per cent of the number in 1892 had 41 per cent of the income, and 60 per cent of the number in 1901 had 31 per cent of the income; but does this indicate concentration or diffusion? If we knew what per cent of the income was received in 1901 by 70, 26, 2.5, 0.7, 0.6 and 0.1 per cents, respectively, of the number, we could make a comparison. This, it is true, is not a theoretical difficulty, but a practical one due to the insufficiency of data, to be encountered by any method. But suppose we had complete data, could we then interpret the results by this method? The difficulty would be in attempting to comprehend the significance of changes in half a dozen classes, especially when some would indicate diffusion and some concentration. However, we can always arrive at definite though very general results by merely reducing the number of classes to two, the richer and the poorer halves of the community, and noting changes in their proportion of the total income or wealth.[8] If the poorer half has acquired a larger proportion of the total income, we should probably be warranted in saying that there had been on the whole a movement towards equality. It is apparent, however, that such a measure does not tell the whole story. It covers up some of the changes that may be going on within each half.

The objection that the foregoing method does not tell the whole story is obviated in *part* by Dr T.S. Adams[9] in applying to the present problem the measures of dispersion suggested by Mr A.L. Bowley.[10] For example, assuming the members of a community arranged in order according to their wealth, we find the first and second quartiles, and divide their difference by their sum. This quotient will vary from 0 to 1, and the nearer 1, the greater the concentration. This is the best numerical measure that has as yet been suggested, although it may also hide some of the changes that are going on.

Turning now to the graphic measures, a simple plotting of wealth along one axis and the numbers of the population along another is not satisfactory for the reason that changes in the shape of the curve will not show accurately changes in the relationships of individuals. To escape this objection, one naturally resorts to logarithmic curves. Professor Pareto, in his 'Cours d'Economie Politique',[11] does this, but in an erroneous way. He represents logarithms of class divisions in wealth along one axis, and the logarithms of the number of persons having more than each class division along the other. The error in this procedure lies in adhering to a fixed classification for two epochs. The number of persons having more than, say, $10 in each of the two periods of time is, as we have seen, of no significance in the question of degree of concentration when the per capita wealth of the community is growing. It will be found, for example, that plotting such curves for the hypothetical case given in Tables 2.3, 2.4 and 2.5 shows a steeper curve for the second epoch. The method is especially inapplicable to data in which the highest class is given as those having more than a

8 Suggested in Ely's 'Evolution of Industrial Society', p. 257.
9 Adams and Sumner, 'Labour Problems', pp. 534 and 538.
10 'Elements of Statistics', second edition, p. 136.
11 vol. ii, p. 304.

certain amount (as in Table 2.6); for, imagine a community in which the wealth is nearly equally distributed, and then assume that the richest individual becomes a multi-millionaire, with no change in the wealth of the remainder. Professor Pareto's curve would tell us nothing about this change.

If one wishes to use logarithmic curves, the following method would be better: measure along the horizontal axis cumulated per cents of the population from poorest to richest, and along the vertical axis logarithms of the *cumulated amounts* of wealth held by the successive per cents of the population from poorest to richest. In interpreting these curves, it is necessary to pay attention solely to their shape, and to ignore the actual distance from the base line. The steeper the curve, the greater the concentration. It should be noted that according to this method an equal distribution does not give a horizontal line.

However, logarithmic curves are more or less treacherous. Forgetting that they are logarithms, we are apt to think of them as absolute amounts, when plotted. For this reason it is believed that the following graphic method will be found more satisfactory. It takes account of changes in wealth and population, thus putting upon a comparable basis any two communities of the most diverse conditions. Where guessing is necessary, owing to insufficient data, it enables us to do this guessing in the most impersonal way. The method is as follows:

Plot along one axis cumulated per cents of the population from poorest to richest, and along the other the per cent of the total wealth held by these per cents of the population. To illustrate, take a population in which wealth is distributed equally. No matter what the average wealth or size of the population, we should always plot the following sets of figures:[12]

The poorest 1 per cent of the population have 1 per cent of the wealth.
The poorest 2 per cent of the population have 2 per cent of the wealth.
The poorest 3 per cent of the population have 3 per cent of the wealth.

        etc.   etc.

This will give a straight line. With an unequal distribution, the curves will always begin and end in the same points as with an equal

[12] In practice the method will not be found labourious, because it is not necessary to plot each per cent.

distribution, but they will be bent in the middle; and the rule of interpretation will be, as the bow is bent, concentration increases. If we plot in this way the figures for Prussian income given in Table 2.6, we get the following results:

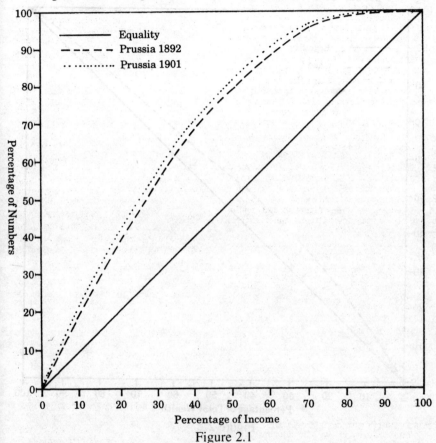

Figure 2.1

It is evident at a glance that the figures for 1901 show a greater concentration than those for 1892.

The curves may not always give so clear an answer as in the previous illustration, because opposing tendencies may exist at the same time, but the diagram will always tell what has happened. To take an extreme case, let the following figures represent the distribution of $100 among a group of ten persons at two epochs:

| Case I | 6 | 7 | 8 | 9 | 10 | 12 | 12 | 12 | 12 | 12 |
| Case II | 8 | 8 | 8 | 8 | 8 | 8 | 8 | 14 | 14 | 16 |

We get curves as follows:

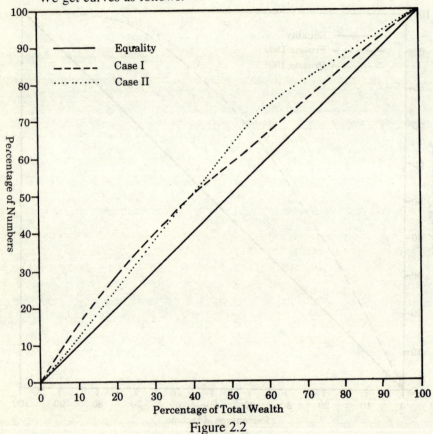

Figure 2.2

There has been a tendency towards an equal distribution in the lower half, but a contrary tendency in the upper half. Notice that we can tell from the diagram that in each case the poorest half of the community have 40 per cent, but the poorest two–thirds have a smaller per cent of the total wealth in the second case.

The Measurement of Income Inequality

S. ANAND

A: A Brief Review

Most of the important results in inequality measurement, and many inequality indices themselves, are based on the Lorenz curve for an income distribution. This brief review begins with a definition of the Lorenz curve for a continuous income distribution specified as an income density function $f(y)$;[1] the definition for a discrete distribution is provided later (see Section C). Let

$$F(x) = \int_0^x f(y)\, dy$$

be the cumulative population share corresponding to income level x, so that $F(x)$ is the proportion of the population that receives income less than or equal to x. Let

$$\Phi(x) = (1/\mu) \int_0^x yf(y)\, dy$$

be the cumulative income share corresponding to income level x, where $\mu = \int_0^\infty yf(y)\, dy$ is the mean of the distribution. This defines an implicit relation between F and Φ in terms of the parameter x. The graph $F(x)$, $\Phi(x)$ is said to be the Lorenz curve of the income distribution $f(y)$.

Alternatively, starting with the pth percentile in the income distribution, we can define x as the income level which cuts off the bottom p per cent, that is $p = F(x)$ or $x = F^{-1}(p)$. The income share of the bottom p per cent in the distribution is then $\Phi[F^{-1}(p)]$. This function gives the Lorenz curve of the distribution, $L(p)$, which shows the

---

[1] As $f(y)$ is a density function for income, $y \geq 0$, $f(y) \geq 0$, and $\int_0^\infty f(y)\, dy = 1$.

cumulative income share corresponding to percentile p ($0 \leq p \leq 1$). Thus $L(p) = \Phi[F^{-1}(p)]$ on the support of $F(x)$. It is easy to check the following propositions, which are illustrated in Figure 3.1.

1. $0 \leq F \leq 1$, $0 \leq \Phi \leq 1$; $F(0) = \Phi(0) = 0$, $F(\infty) = \Phi(\infty) = 1$.
2. The Lorenz curve $L(p)$ ($0 \leq p \leq 1$) is *convex*, and its derivative $L'(p)$ is given by

$$L'(p) = \frac{F^{-1}(p)}{\mu} = \frac{x}{\mu}$$

where $x = F^{-1}(p)$ is the income level which cuts off the bottom p per cent.
3. The slope of the Lorenz curve equals unity at the percentile $p^* = F(\mu)$, so that the fraction of the population receiving income less than or equal to the mean μ can be read off immediately.

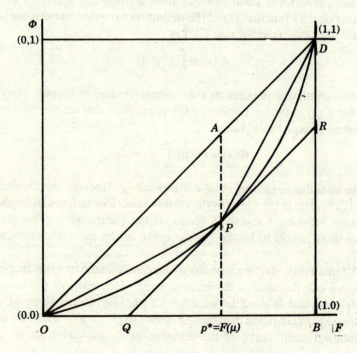

Figure 3.1:   The Lorenz Diagram

INDICES BASED DIRECTLY ON THE LORENZ DIAGRAM

The Lorenz curve corresponding to the distribution in which everyone receives the same income is the line OD in Figure 3.1;[2] this is referred to as the line (or diagonal) of perfect equality. There are several inequality indices which attempt to measure the divergence between the Lorenz curve for a given income distribution and the line of perfect equality. The best-known and most widely used among these is the Gini coefficient. It is described below together with some other indices based on the Lorenz diagram.

The Gini coefficient G is defined as the area between the Lorenz curve and the line of equality divided by the area of the triangle OBD below this line. The Gini coefficient varies between the limits of 0 (perfect equality) and 1 (perfect inequality), and the greater the departure of the Lorenz curve from the diagonal, the larger is the value of the Gini coefficient.

An alternative definition for the Gini coefficient can be specified in algebraic terms as

$$G = \tfrac{1}{2} \, (\Delta / \mu)$$

where $\Delta = \int_0^\infty \int_0^\infty |x - y| f(x) f(y) \, dx \, dy$ is the absolute mean difference (see Kendall and Stuart 1963). Thus G can also be defined as one-half the relative mean difference. In appendix B these two definitions are shown to be equivalent.

Another measure of inequality based on the Lorenz diagram is the value of the maximum discrepancy between the line of perfect equality and the Lorenz curve (see Schutz 1951). The distance between the diagonal and the Lorenz curve is evidently maximized at the point p^* in Figure 3.1 where the slope of the Lorenz curve is equal to unity; hence the value of the maximum discrepancy is AP or $[p^* - L(p^*)]$.

The value of the maximum discrepancy turns out to be equal to one-half the relative mean deviation M, which is another measure of inequality (see Sen 1973). It is not difficult to prove that

$$[p^* - L(p^*)] = M/2 = \tfrac{1}{2} \, (\delta / \mu)$$

where $\delta = \int_0^\infty |y - \mu| f(y) \, dy$ is the absolute mean deviation.

Yet another measure has been proposed which tries to capture the divergence between the Lorenz curve and the line of perfect equality. This is defined as the area of the largest triangle that can be inscribed

---

[2] This distribution has a point-mass income density function.

between the Lorenz curve and the line of equality, divided by the area of the triangle OBD below this line. As shown below, this measure reduces to the value of the maximum discrepancy, or $M/2$.

The triangle with the largest area that can be inscribed in the convex set defined by the Lorenz curve and the line of equality is OPD. This is seen by constructing the quadrilateral OQRD which contains the convex set; OQRD has OD as base and opposite side QR parallel to OD and tangential to the Lorenz curve. Now OPD is clearly a triangle of maximal area that can be inscribed in the larger set OQRD. A fortiori, it is a triangle of maximal area that can be inscribed in the required subset. The area of triangle OPD is $(1/2) (OD) (AP/\sqrt{2}) = [p^* - L(p^*)]/2$, while that of triangle OBD is $1/2$. Hence the value of the inequality measure is $[p^* - L(p^*)]$, or $M/2$.

OTHER INDICES

There are three basic properties that one would like an inequality index to satisfy: (1) mean or scale independence, that is the index remains invariant if everyone's income is changed by the same proportion; (2) population-size independence, that is the index remains invariant if the number of people at each income level is changed by the same proportion;[3] and (3) the Pigou–Dalton condition, that is any transfer from a richer to a poorer person that does not reverse their relative ranks reduces the value of the index (Sen 1973, p. 27).

The properties of mean independence and population-size independence together imply that the index can be computed directly from the Lorenz curve of the income distribution: knowledge of mean income and total population size are unnecessary (see Section C). Conversely, an index that can be computed directly from the Lorenz curve obviously satisfies the properties of mean independence and population-size independence.

The inequality indices in the previous section are defined in terms of the Lorenz diagram and thus satisfy the properties of mean independence and population-size independence. The Gini coefficient satisfies the Pigou–Dalton condition also,[4] but the other indices, which

---

[3] With this property, the index depends only on the relative population frequencies at each income level, not the absolute population frequencies. In the continuous case this is equivalent to the index being computable from the income density function alone.

[4] This is plain from the geometrical definition of the Gini coefficient. A transfer of income from a richer to a poorer person raises the entire Lorenz curve between the corresponding percentiles; hence it reduces the Gini coefficient.

are equivalent to the relative mean deviation up to a scalar multiple, do not. From the definition of the relative mean deviation, it is clear that it is insensitive to income transfers between people on the same side of the mean.[5]

There are two common statistical measures of dispersion for a distribution: the range and the variance. The range can be defined as the absolute difference between the highest and lowest income levels divided by the mean income. Since it ignores the distribution *inside* the extremes, the range obviously violates the Pigou–Dalton condition. The variance, however, does satisfy this property — but it violates mean independence. A way around this deficiency is to deflate the variance by the square of the mean. This gives the squared coefficient of variation, which satisfies all three properties. In addition, the squared coefficient of variation satisfies a (weak) decomposability property.

The other inequality indices considered are defined in terms of a discrete income distribution. Let the vector $y = (y_1, y_2, \ldots, y_n)$ denote an income distribution among n persons, where $y_i \geq 0$ is the income of person i $(i = 1, 2, \ldots, n)$. Let the arithmetic mean income of the distribution be μ, so that

$$\mu = \frac{1}{n} \sum_{i=1}^{n} y_i$$

The variance of income var(y) can then be written as

$$\text{var}(y) = \frac{1}{n} \sum_{i=1}^{n} (y_i - \mu)^2$$

If all incomes are multiplied by the factor λ, the variance of income changes by the factor λ^2. It is easily checked that for a positive scalar λ

$$\text{var}(\lambda y) = \lambda^2 \, \text{var}(y).$$

Unlike the variance of income, the variance of the *logarithm* of income var(log y) is a mean-independent measure of inequality. Let $\tilde{\mu}$ be the geometric mean income of the distribution, so that by definition

$$\log \tilde{\mu} = \frac{1}{n} \sum_{i=1}^{n} \log y_i.$$

[5] Again this is evident from the geometrical representation of the relative mean deviation. In Figure 3.1, the length of AP is unaltered by income transfers on one side only of $p^* = F(\mu)$ (see also Atkinson 1970).

Then the variance of log-income or var(log y) can be written as

$$\text{var}(\log y) = \frac{1}{n} \sum_{i=1}^{n} (\log y_i - \log \tilde{\mu})^2$$

Now if all incomes are multiplied by the positive factor λ, the variance of log-income does not change at all. It is easily checked that for a scalar $\lambda > 0$,

$$\text{var}(\log \lambda y) = \text{var}(\log y).$$

The variance of log-income also obviously satisfies the property of population-size independence. However, it does not satisfy the Pigou–Dalton condition for the entire range of incomes.[6]

The deviation of the logarithms of income is sometimes taken from the logarithm of the arithmetic mean log μ rather than the logarithm of the geometric mean log $\tilde{\mu}$ (see Sen 1973). This yields a slightly different measure which is also mean-independent

$$v = \frac{1}{n} \sum_{i=1}^{n} (\log y_i - \log \mu)^2.$$

It can easily be verified that

$$v = \text{var}(\log y) + (\log \mu - \log \tilde{\mu})^2.$$

But (log μ – log $\tilde{\mu}$) is itself a measure of inequality, namely Theil's second measure L (see below). Thus v is really the sum of two distinct inequality measures, var(log y) and the square of the Theil L measure.

Both var(log y) and v suffer from a rather serious practical defect. The measures are *not* defined if there is a person in the distribution with zero income. Unfortunately, this happens to be the case with some of the Malaysian distributions considered. To overcome this problem, some have suggested that the zero-income recipients be assigned a small positive income (such as 1). But the choice of the amount assigned makes all the difference to the value of the measure. The sensitivity of the measure to this arbitrary procedure, and the inability to defend the particular amount assigned, render the measure unusable in such situations. One attractive feature of the variance of log-income, however, is that it is decomposable around group geometric mean

---

[6] The Pigou–Dalton condition is not satisfied for incomes above $\tilde{\mu}e$, where e is the base of the natural logarithms.

incomes. Another derives from its relation to the lognormal distribution (see Aitchison and Brown 1957) and to the estimating form of the human capital model.

Finally, two inequality measures of Theil (1967) are considered. The first is Theil's entropy index T based on the notion of entropy in information theory. It is defined as

$$T = \frac{1}{n} \sum_{i=1}^{n} \frac{y_i}{\mu} \log \frac{y_i}{\mu}$$

where $n\mu = \sum_{i=1}^{n} y_i = Y$ is the total income. Note that (y_i/μ) is simply the slope of the Lorenz curve at the percentile corresponding to income level y_i. Hence T, like the measures in the previous section, can be computed directly from the Lorenz curve of the income distribution. The motivation for T, however, derives from the 'entropy' $H(y)$ associated with the income shares $(y_1/Y), \ldots, (y_n/Y)$:

$$H(y) = \sum_{i=1}^{n} (y_i/Y) \log \frac{1}{(y_i/Y)}.$$

The closer are the income shares (y_i/Y) to the population shares $(1/n)$, the greater is $H(y)$; and when each (y_i/Y) equals $(1/n)$, $H(y)$ attains its maximum value of $\log n$. On the other hand, if one income share tends to unity and all the others tend to zero, $H(y)$ tends to its minimum value of zero. Thus the entropy $H(y)$ of an income distribution can be regarded as a measure of income *equality*. Theil obtains a measure of income *inequality* by subtracting $H(y)$ from its maximum value, $\log n$.[7] This inequality measure is T, which can be written as

$$T = \log n - H(y)$$
$$= \sum_{i=1}^{n} (y_i/Y) \log \frac{(y_i/Y)}{(1/n)}.$$

As $(1/n)$ is the population share and (y_i/Y) the income share of person i, Theil interprets T as 'the expected information of a message which transforms population shares into income shares' (1967, p. 95). When there is perfect equality, each person's income share (y_i/Y) and

---

[7] The difference between the maximum entropy value, $\log n$, and the actual entropy value, $H(y)$, is called redundancy in communication theory.

population share $(1/n)$ are equal, and T assumes the value zero.[8] When there is perfect inequality, however, a single person receives all the income and everyone else receives zero income: one of the y_i's is then equal to Y, and all other y_i's are equal to zero. In this case, T assumes its maximum value of $\log n$; all terms with a zero income share tend to zero, since $x \log x \to 0$ as $x \to 0$.

The Theil entropy index T fulfills most of the desirable properties specified for a measure of inequality. It is mean-independent and population-size-independent; it satisfies the Pigou–Dalton condition; it is defined for distributions with zero-income recipients; and, finally, it is additively decomposable in the weak sense, with income-share weights for the within-group component — which sum to unity.

Another inequality index of Theil (1967) I call Theil's second measure L. It is analogous to the entropy index T except that it reverses the roles of income share (y_i/Y) and population share $(1/n)$ in the formula for T. Thus Theil's second measure can be written as

$$L = \sum_{i=1}^{n} (1/n) \log \frac{(1/n)}{(y_i/Y)}.$$

Theil interprets L as 'the expected information content of the indirect message which transforms the income shares as prior probabilities into the population shares as posterior probabilities' (1967, p. 125). Like T, the index L attempts to measure the divergence between income shares and population shares, but it uses a somewhat different distance function. Since $Y = n\,\mu$, Theil's second measure L can also be written as

$$L = \frac{1}{n} \sum_{i=1}^{n} \log \frac{\mu}{y_i}.$$

As (y_i/μ) is the slope of the Lorenz curve at the percentile corresponding to income level y_i, the measure L can be computed directly from the Lorenz curve of the income distribution. Rewriting the expression for L,

$$L = \log \mu - \frac{1}{n} \sum_{i=1}^{n} \log y_i$$
$$= \log \mu - \log \tilde{\mu}$$
$$= \log \frac{\mu}{\tilde{\mu}}$$

---

[8] T may be thought of as a general distance function which measures the divergence between income shares and population shares.

where $\tilde{\mu}$ is the geometric mean income of the distribution. In other words, L is the logarithm of the ratio of the arithmetic mean income of the distribution to the geometric mean income.[9]

Theil's second measure L obviously satisfies the properties of mean independence and population-size independence; it also satisfies the Pigou–Dalton condition. Moreover, L is additively decomposable in the strict sense, with population-share weights for the within-group component — which sum to unity. One disadvantage, however, is that it is not defined for distributions with zero incomes, since $\log x \rightarrow -\infty$ as $x \rightarrow 0$.

B: The Gini Coefficient

The most common definition of the Gini coefficient is in terms of the Lorenz diagram — as the ratio of the area between the Lorenz curve and the line of equality, to the area of the triangle below this line (see Section A). Various other definitions have also been discussed in the literature and are useful for different purposes. Here several definitions of the Gini coefficient are reviewed, and their equivalence is demonstrated.

Suppose there are n individuals (or households) who are labeled in non-descending order of income as: $y_1 \leq y_2 \leq \ldots \leq y_n$. Denote this (ordered) income distribution by the vector $y = (y_1, y_2, \ldots, y_n)$, and let μ be its mean. Let F_i be the cumulative population share and Φ_i the cumulative income share corresponding to individual i ($i = 1, 2, \ldots n$). Define $F_0 = \Phi_0 = 0$. Thus

$$F_i = \frac{i}{n} \text{ and } \Phi_i = \frac{1}{n\mu} \sum_{k=1}^{i} y_k \text{ for } i = 0, 1, \ldots, n.$$

The first definition is the one used in this study to estimate Gini coefficients for Malaysia.

Definition 1 (Geometric)

$$G_1 = 1 - \sum_{i=0}^{n-1} (F_{i+1} - F_i)(\Phi_{i+1} + \Phi_i).$$

[9] L is also a simple monotonic increasing transform of Atkinson's (1970) index I when the inequality aversion parameter ε is equal to unity. In this case, the Atkinson equally distributed equivalent income is just the geometric mean income $\tilde{\mu}$ of the distribution, and $I = 1 - (\tilde{\mu}/\mu)$. Hence $L = -\log(1 - I)$.

It is shown that G_1 is equivalent to the geometric definition of the Gini coefficient given above. Figure 3.2 illustrates the Lorenz curve for the discrete income distribution $y = (y_1, y_2, \ldots, y_n)$ where $y_1 \leq y_2 \leq \ldots \leq y_n$. The shaded part shows a typical segment of the area below the Lorenz curve. The total area below the Lorenz curve

$$= \frac{1}{2} \sum_{i=0}^{n-1} (F_{i+1} - F_i)(\Phi_{i+1} + \Phi_i).$$

Therefore the Gini coefficient

$$= \frac{1}{1/2} \left[\frac{1}{2} - \frac{1}{2} \sum_{i=0}^{n-1} (F_{i+1} - F_i)(\Phi_{i+1} + \Phi_i) \right]$$

$$= 1 - \sum_{i=0}^{n=1} (F_{i+1} - F_i)(\Phi_{i+1} + \Phi_i)$$

$$= G_1 . \; ||$$

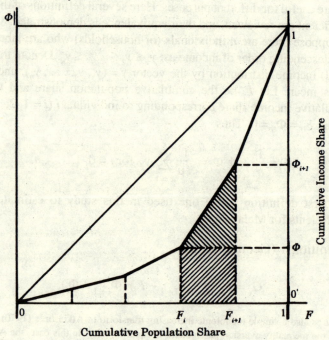

Figure 3.2:   The Lorenz Curve for a Discrete Income Distribution

Definition 2 (Rao 1969)

$$G_2 = \sum_{i=1}^{n-1} (F_i \Phi_{i+1} - F_{i+1} \Phi_i).$$

It is shown that $G_1 = G_2$.

$$G_1 = 1 - \sum_{i=0}^{n-1} (F_{i+1} - F_i)(\Phi_{i+1} + \Phi_i)$$

$$= 1 + \sum_{i=0}^{n-1} (F_i \Phi_{i+1} - F_{i+1} \Phi_i) - \sum_{i=0}^{n-1} (F_{i+1} \Phi_{i+1} - F_i \Phi_i)$$

But

$$\sum_{i=0}^{n-1} (F_{i+1} \Phi_{i+1} - F_i \Phi_i) = F_n \Phi_n - F_0 \Phi_0 = 1,$$

since $F_n = \Phi_n = 1$, and $F_0 = \Phi_0 = 0$. Therefore

$$G_1 = \sum_{i=1}^{n-1} (F_i \Phi_{i+1} - F_{i+1} \Phi_i)$$

$$= G_2 . ||$$

Definition 3 (Kendall and Stuart 1963)

Kendall and Stuart define the Gini coefficient as one-half the relative mean difference, that is one-half the average value of absolute differences between *all* pairs of incomes divided by the mean income. Thus

$$G_3 = \frac{1}{2n^2 \mu} \sum_{i=1}^{n} \sum_{j=1}^{n} |y_i - y_j|.$$

This definition implies that $2n^2 \mu G_3$ is the sum of every element of the symmetrical $n \times n$ matrix whose $(i, j)^{\text{th}}$ element is $|y_i - y_j|$. It is shown that $G_3 = G_2$. Since individuals are labelled in non-descending order of income

$$y_1 \le y_2 \le \ldots \le y_n,$$

G_3 can be written as:

$$G_3 = \frac{1}{2n^2 \mu} \left[2 \sum_{i=1}^{n} \sum_{j \le i} (y_i - y_j) \right]$$

$$= \frac{1}{n^2 \mu} \sum_{i=1}^{n} \left[iy_i - \sum_{j=1}^{i} y_j \right] = \frac{1}{n^2 \mu} \sum_{i=1}^{n} [i\, y_i - n\, \mu\, \Phi_i]$$

Substituting $\dfrac{y_i}{n\,\mu} = (\Phi_i - \Phi_{i-1})$ and $\dfrac{i}{n} = F_i$,

one has

$$G_3 = \sum_{i=1}^{n} \left[F_i (\Phi_i - \Phi_{i-1}) - \frac{1}{n} \Phi_i \right] = \sum_{i=1}^{n} \left[\left(F_i - \frac{1}{n} \right) \Phi_i - F_i \Phi_{i-1} \right]$$

$$= \sum_{i=1}^{n} (F_{i-1}\Phi_i - F_i \Phi_{i-1}) \qquad \text{since } F_i - F_{i-1} = \frac{1}{n}$$

$$= \sum_{i=1}^{n-1} (F_i \Phi_{i+1} - F_{i+1}\Phi_i)$$

$$= G_2 . \;\Vert$$

Definition 4 (Sen 1973)

With individuals labelled in non-descending order of income so that $y_1 \le y_2 \le \ldots \le y_n$, Sen defines the Gini coefficient as

$$G_4 = 1 + \frac{1}{n} - \frac{2}{n^2 \mu} [ny_1 + (n-1) y_2 + \ldots + 2y_{n-1} + y_n]$$

$$= \frac{n+1}{n} - \frac{2}{n^2 \mu} \sum_{i=1}^{n} (n+1-i)\, y_i .$$

This form makes clear the income-weighting scheme in the welfare function behind the Gini coefficient. Rank-order weights are applied to different people's income levels so that the poorest person receives a weight of n, the ith poorest person a weight of $(n+1-i)$, and the richest (or n^{th} poorest) person a weight of unity. It is shown that $G_3 = G_4$. As before, G_3 can be written as

$$G_3 = \frac{1}{n^2 \mu} \sum_{i=1}^{n} \sum_{j \le i} (y_i - y_j),$$

which is the sum of all the elements of the lower triangular matrix:

$$
\begin{bmatrix}
(y_1 - y_1) & 0 & \cdots & 0 \\
(y_2 - y_1) & (y_2 - y_2) & \cdots & 0 \\
\cdot & \cdot & & \cdot \\
\cdot & \cdot & & \cdot \\
\cdot & \cdot & & 0 \\
(y_n - y_1) & (y_n - y_2) & \cdots & (y_n - y_n)
\end{bmatrix}
$$

Summing the first element in each bracket horizontally by row gives $\sum_{i=1}^{n} iy_i$; summing the second element in each bracket vertically by column gives $-\sum_{j=1}^{n} (n + 1 - j) y_j$.

Hence

$$
G_3 = \frac{1}{n^2 \mu} \left[\sum_{i=1}^{n} iy_i - \sum_{i=1}^{n} (n + 1 - i) y_i \right]
$$

$$
= \frac{1}{n^2 \mu} \left[\sum_{i=1}^{n} (n + 1) y_i - 2 \sum_{i=1}^{n} (n + 1 - i) y_i \right]
$$

$$
= \frac{n + 1}{n} - \frac{2}{n^2 \mu} \sum_{i=1}^{n} (n + 1 - i) y_i
$$

$$
= G_4 . \; ||
$$

Definition 5 (Fei and Ranis 1974)

Fei and Ranis express the Gini coefficient as a linear transform of the rank index of the income distribution. The rank index R is defined as a weighted average of the *ranks* of persons in the income distribution, where the weights are their income shares. With individuals labelled in non-descending order of income as $y_1 \leq y_2 \leq \ldots \leq y_n$, the rank index R can be written:

$$
R = \sum_{i=1}^{n} iy_i \; \bigg/ \; \sum_{i=1}^{n} y_i.
$$

The Gini coefficient G_5 is then defined as

$$G_5 = \frac{2}{n} R - \frac{n+1}{n}$$

$$= \frac{2}{n^2 \mu} [1y_1 + 2y_2 + \ldots + ny_n] - \frac{n+1}{n}.$$

It is shown that $G_4 = G_5$.

$$G_4 = \frac{n+1}{n} - \frac{2}{n^2 \mu} \sum_{i=1}^{n} (n+1-i) y_i$$

$$= \frac{n+1}{n} - \frac{2}{n^2 \mu} \left[\sum_{i=1}^{n} (n+1) y_i - \sum_{i=1}^{n} iy_i \right]$$

$$= \frac{2}{n^2 \mu} \sum_{i=1}^{n} iy_i - \left(\frac{n+1}{n} \right)$$

$$= G_5 . \; ||$$

Up to a multiplicative constant, G_5 can also be expressed as the *covariance* of income and its rank:

$$G_5 = \frac{2}{n \mu} \; \text{cov}(i, y_i).$$

This is easily checked as follows. By definition of covariance,

$$\text{cov}(i, y_i) = \frac{1}{n} \sum_{i=1}^{n} (i - \bar{i}) (y_i - \bar{y})$$

$$= \frac{1}{n} \sum_{i=1}^{n} iy_i - \bar{i}\bar{y},$$

where a bar above a variable denotes its mean. But since

$$\bar{i} = \frac{1}{n} \sum_{i=1}^{n} i = \frac{(n+1)}{2}, \quad \text{and} \quad \bar{y} = \mu,$$

$$\text{cov}(i, y_i) = \frac{1}{n} \sum_{i=1}^{n} iy_i - \frac{(n+1)}{2} \mu.$$

Therefore $\dfrac{2}{n\mu}\,\text{cov}(i, y_i) = \dfrac{2}{n^2\mu}\sum_{i=1}^{n} iy_i - \dfrac{(n+1)}{n}$

$$= G_5 . \;\|$$

The equivalence of five alternative definitions of the Gini coefficient has thus been demonstrated.

THE EFFECT OF CHANGES IN CERTAIN INCOMES

It is often useful to predict the effect on inequality of changes in certain incomes in the distribution.

It is clear that if the income of every individual is raised by the same proportionate amount, the Gini coefficient, being mean-independent, will remain unchanged. But if the income of everyone is raised by the same *absolute* amount, say $\varepsilon > 0$, the Gini coefficient will decrease as a straightforward function of ε. This is easily seen. Starting with the distribution $y = (y_1, y_2, \ldots, y_n)$, let $x = (x_1, x_2, \ldots, x_n)$ be the distribution with $x_i = (y_i + \varepsilon)$, $i = 1, 2, \ldots, n$. Then if the mean of distribution y is μ, the mean of distribution x is $(\mu + \varepsilon)$. Using definition 3 of the Gini coefficient, one has

$$G(x) = \frac{1}{2n^2(\mu+\varepsilon)}\sum_{i,j}\left|x_i - x_j\right|$$

$$= \frac{1}{2n^2(\mu+\varepsilon)}\sum_{i,j}\left|y_i - y_j\right|$$

$$= \frac{\mu}{(\mu+\varepsilon)}\,G(y)$$

$$< G(y) .$$

Indeed the Lorenz curve for distribution x lies above that for distribution y. Distribution x evidently tends to perfect equality as the absolute amount ε by which everyone's income is raised becomes indefinitely large. From the expression for $G(x)$, it follows that $G(x) \to 0$ as $\varepsilon \to \infty$.

Now suppose the income of only certain individuals in the distribution is changed. For example suppose the income of the richest person is raised and the income of the poorest person is reduced. In this case, the ranks of these two persons in the distribution are unaltered and, from the rank index definition, the Gini coefficient can be seen to increase. Indeed the new distribution will show more inequality in the Lorenz sense. In the general case, let the income of the jth poorest person in the distribution be changed *without* altering this person's rank; the effect on the Gini coefficient can then be measured by using the rank index definition. By definition 5 of the Gini coefficient,

$$G = \frac{2}{n} R - \frac{n+1}{n}$$

where

$$R = \sum_{i=1}^{n} i y_i \bigg/ \sum_{i=1}^{n} y_i$$

is the rank index of the income distribution. Differentiating G partially with respect to y_j, one has

$$\frac{\partial G}{\partial y_j} = \frac{2}{n} \left(\frac{\partial R}{\partial y_j} \right)$$

$$= \frac{2}{n} (j - R) \bigg/ \sum_{i=1}^{n} y_i$$

which is $\lessgtr 0$ as $j \lessgtr R$. Hence if the jth poorest person's income is raised without altering the rank order of individuals, G falls if $j < R$ and G rises if $j > R$. If the jth poorest person's income is reduced without altering the rank order, then G rises if $j < R$ and G falls if $j > R$.

It can be shown that $(n+1)/2 \leq R \leq n$.[10] Hence if the income of anyone below the median income level[11] is raised (reduced) without altering the rank order of individuals, the Gini coefficient will fall (rise).

---

[10] Since it is always the case that $G \geq 0$ (see definition 3 of the Gini coefficient).

$$G = (2/n) R - (n+1)/n \geq 0, \text{ or } R \geq (n+1)/2.$$

And since $i \leq n$, it follows that

$$R = \sum_{i=1}^{n} i y_i \bigg/ \sum_{i=1}^{n} y_i \leq \sum_{i=1}^{n} n y_i \bigg/ \sum_{i=1}^{n} y_i = n.$$

Therefore, $(n+1)/2 \leq R \leq n$.

[11] The median income level may be defined as $y_{n/2}$ or $y_{(n+1)/2}$ depending on whether n is even or odd.

C: Lorenz Dominance and Inequality

In this section I first prove Atkinson's celebrated theorem about the ranking of income distributions in terms of welfare, Lorenz dominance, and the principle of transfers. Using Atkinson's theorem, I then go on to show that Lorenz dominance is a useful property to establish even when welfare comparisons are not possible between the underlying distributions — but the purpose is purely a positive or descriptive comparison of inequality.[12]

It is easier here to deal with discrete distributions, so let the vector $y = (y_1, y_2, \ldots, y_n)$ denote the ordered income distribution $y: 0 \le y_1 \le y_2 \le \ldots \le y_n$ among n individuals (or households). The Lorenz curve $L_y(.)$ of this distribution can be defined at the discrete points (i/n), for $i = 0, 1, \ldots, n$, as follows:

$$L_y(0) = 0$$

$$L_y(i/n) = \sum_{k=1}^{i} y_k \Big/ \sum_{k=1}^{n} y_k \qquad \text{for } i = 1, 2, \ldots, n.$$

For all other points p in the interval $[0, 1]$, $L_y(p)$ is defined by linear interpolation.

Now suppose x and y are two ordered distributions with the same number of individuals n and the same total income

$$\sum_{k=1}^{n} x_k = \sum_{k=1}^{n} y_k.$$

Consider three criteria for ranking these income distributions:

(i) $x \succeq_L y$, that is, x Lorenz-dominates y, which means that

$$L_x(i/n) \ge L_y(i/n) \qquad \text{for } i = 0, 1, \ldots, n.$$

(ii) $x \succeq_T y$, which means that distribution x can be obtained from distribution y by a finite sequence of income transfers from richer to poorer individuals, where each transfer preserves the relative ranks of the two individuals affected. This criterion is the ranking of distributions x and y according to the *principle of transfers*. Given an ordered distribution y, a *single* progressive transfer d from a richer individual j

[12] See Sen (1973) for a distinction between positive and normative comparisons and measures of inequality.

to a poorer individual i $(y_i < y_j)$ which preserves their relative ranks leads to a new distribution x defined as:

$$x_k = y_k \qquad k \neq i, j$$
$$x_i = y_i + d$$
$$x_j = y_j - d$$

where $x_i \leq x_j$, that is $d \leq (y_j - y_i)/2$.[13]

(iii) x $\gtrsim_U$ y, which means that $\Sigma_{k=1}^{n} U(x_k) \geq \Sigma_{k=1}^{n} U(y_k)$ for *all* non-decreasing concave functions $U(y)$. This criterion says that distribution x yields at least as much welfare as distribution y for any additively separable, symmetric, non-decreasing, concave social welfare function $\Sigma U(y)$.

It may not always be possible to rank two arbitrary distributions x and y by criterion (i), (ii), or (iii).[14] However, when it *is* possible to rank them by one criterion, it will also be possible to rank them by the other criteria, and in that case all three criteria will give the *same* ranking. This is Atkinson's theorem.

Theorem (Atkinson 1970): The ranking of income distributions x and y by criteria (i), (ii) and (iii) is *identical*. Formally, the following statements are equivalent:

(i)   x $\gtrsim_L$ y
(ii) x $\gtrsim_T$ y
(iii) x $\gtrsim_U$ y.

Proof: It is shown that (i) => (ii) => (iii) => (i). The proof given here is adapted from Rothschild and Stiglitz (1973).

$$\frac{\text{(i)} \Rightarrow \text{(ii)}}{\text{x} \gtrsim_L \text{y} \Rightarrow \text{x} \gtrsim_T \text{y}}$$

[13] Given symmetry, nothing would be altered if, instead of imposing the condition that the income transfer preserves the relative ranks of individuals i and j, that is $d \leq (y_j - y_i)/2$, the size of the transfer was limited to their income difference, that is $d \leq (y_j - y_i)$. This is the more usual way of defining x $\gtrsim_T$ y (see Atkinson 1970; Sen 1973; and Dasgupta, Sen and Starrett 1973).

[14] In other words, the criteria $\gtrsim_L$, $\gtrsim_U$, and $\gtrsim_T$ provide only a *partial* ordering among distributions with the same number of people and the same total income.

Since x and y have the same total income, $x \gtrsim_L y$ implies that

$$\sum_{k=1}^{i} x_k \geq \sum_{k=1}^{i} y_k \qquad \text{for } i = 1, 2, \ldots, n.$$

Let i be the *first* integer for which $x_i > y_i$, so that $x_k = y_k$ for $k \leq (i-1)$. Define a new distribution $x(i)$ from x as follows. Transfer an amount $(x_i - y_i)$ from individual i to individual $(i+1)$; this lowers i's income to y_i and raises $(i+1)$'s income to $x_{i+1} + (x_i - y_i)$. Then the new distribution $x(i)$ has the properties:

$$
\begin{aligned}
x_k(i) &= x_k \ y_k && \text{for } k \leq (i-1) \\
x_i(i) &= x_i - (x_i - y_i) = y_i \\
x_{i+1}(i) &= x_{i+1} + (x_i - y_i) \\
x_k(i) &= x_k && \text{for } k > (i+1).
\end{aligned}
$$

Thus $x(i)$ agrees with y in one more place than x — the first i places instead of the first $(i-1)$ places — and it is still true that $x(i) \gtrsim_L y$ since

$$\sum_{k=1}^{i+1} x_k(i) = \sum_{k=1}^{i+1} x_k.$$

The same procedure may be applied to $x(i)$ to find an income transfer from poor to rich which produces a new distribution which agrees with y in at least one more place than $x(i)$ and still Lorenz-dominates y. Continuing in this manner, the distribution y is eventually obtained from x by a sequence of at most $(n-1)$ transfers from poor individuals to rich. Hence $x \gtrsim_T y$.

(ii) => (iii)

$$x \gtrsim_T y \Rightarrow x \gtrsim_U y$$

Since $x \gtrsim_T y$ means that x can be obtained from y by a finite sequence of income transfers from rich individuals to poor, it will suffice to show that a single transfer from rich to poor does not lower welfare. Without loss of generality, suppose that x is obtained from y by a single transfer d from individual 2 to individual 1, where $d \leq (y_2 - y_1)/2$. Then,

$$x_1 = y_1 + d$$

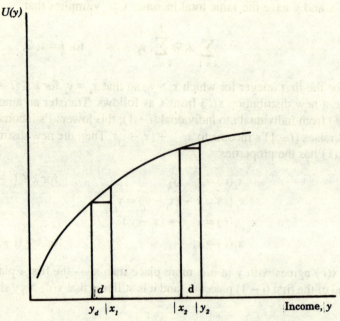

Figure 3.3:   The Concave Function $U(y)$

$$x_2 = y_2 - d$$
$$x_k = y_k \qquad \text{for } k \geq 3.$$

Let $U(y)$ be any non-decreasing concave function, as shown in Figure 3.3.

Given the relation between x_1, x_2 and y_1, y_2, it is obvious from the concavity of $U(y)$ that $[U(x_1) - U(y_1)] \geq [U(y_2) - U(x_2)]$. Thus

$$[U(x_1) + U(x_2)] \geq [U(y_1) + U(y_2)],$$

and therefore

$$\sum_{i=1}^{n} U(x_i) \geq \sum_{i=1}^{n} U(y_i).$$

Hence $x \gtrsim_U y$.

$$\underline{(iii) \Rightarrow (i)}$$
$$x \gtrsim_U y \Rightarrow x \gtrsim_L y$$

$x \gtrsim_U y$, implies that $\sum_{k=1}^{n} U(x_k) \geq \sum_{k=1}^{n} U(y_k)$ for any non-decreasing

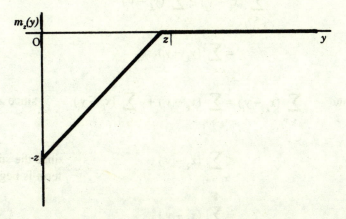

Figure 3.4: The Concave Function $m_z(y)$

concave function $U(y)$. Consider the function: $m_z(y) = \min(y - z, 0)$. For each z, $m_z(y)$ is a non-decreasing concave function of y, as shown in Figure 3.4. Hence

$$\sum_{k=1}^{n} m_z(x_k) \geq \sum_{k=1}^{n} m_z(y_k) \qquad \text{for each } z,$$

That is

$$\sum_{x_k \leq z} (x_k - z) \geq \sum_{y_k \leq z} (y_k - z). \qquad (C.1)$$

Now suppose that $x \geq_L y$ is *not* true. Then it is not the case that

$$\sum_{k=1}^{i} x_k \geq \sum_{k=1}^{i} y_k \qquad \text{for each } i = 1, 2, \ldots, n.$$

Let i be the *first* integer such that

$$\sum_{k=1}^{i} x_k < \sum_{k=1}^{i} y_k. \qquad (C.2)$$

Since

$$\sum_{k=1}^{i-1} x_k \geq \sum_{k=1}^{i-1} y_k,$$

it follows that $x_i < y_i$. Putting $z = y_i$ in (C.1) gives

$$\sum_{x_k \le y_i} (x_k - y_i) \ge \sum_{y_k \le y_i} (y_k - y_i)$$

$$= \sum_{k=1}^{i} (y_k - y_i). \tag{C.3}$$

Now $\qquad \displaystyle\sum_{x_k \le y_i} (x_k - y_i) = \sum_{x_k \le x_i} (x_k - y_i) + \sum_{x_i < x_k \le y_i} (x_k - y_i) \qquad$ since $x_i < y_i$

$$\le \sum_{x_k \le x_i} (x_k - y_i) \qquad \text{since the second term is negative}$$

$$= \sum_{k=1}^{i} (x_k - y_i). \tag{C.4}$$

Stringing together (C.4) with (C.3), it follows that

$$\sum_{k=1}^{i} (x_k - y_i) \ge \sum_{k=1}^{i} (y_k - y_i)$$

$$\text{or} \sum_{k=1}^{i} x_k \ge \sum_{k=1}^{i} y_k,$$

which contradicts (C.2). So it must be true that $x \ge_L y$, and the proof is complete. ||

In fact, a stronger theorem than this can be proved by adopting a weaker criterion for the welfare ranking (iii). The welfare function

$$\sum_{i=1}^{n} U(y_i)$$

can be replaced by a symmetric non-decreasing quasi-concave function of individual incomes $W(y_1, y_2, \ldots, y_n)$ (see Dasgupta, Sen and Starrett 1973). Defining the criterion $\ge_W$ as $x \ge_W y$ if $W(x) \ge W(y)$ for all symmetric non-decreasing quasi-concave functions W, the theorem can also be proved with $\ge_U$ replaced by $\ge_W$ in (iii).

The quasi-concavity restriction on the welfare function can be weakened still further. For the theorem to go through, it is clear that the *weakest* requirement on the function is that welfare does *not decrease* by a transfer of income from a richer to a poorer individual, where the size of transfer is less than or equal to their income difference. I call a function $E(y_1, y_2, \ldots, y_n)$ which satisfies this property 'egalitarian'; it is called 'locally equality preferring' by Rothschild and Stiglitz (1973). Defining the criterion $\geq_E$ as $x \geq_E y$ if $E(x) \geq E(y)$ for all symmetric non-decreasing egalitarian functions E, the theorem is also valid with $\geq_U$ replaced by $\geq_E$ in (iii).

Since the class of additively separable concave functions is contained in the class of quasi-concave functions, which in turn is contained in the class of egalitarian (or locally equality preferring) functions, it follows that $x \geq_E y \Rightarrow x \geq_W y \Rightarrow x \geq_U y$. But by the very definition of $\geq_E$, $x \geq_T y \Rightarrow x \geq_E y$, and from Atkinson's theorem, $x \geq_U y \Rightarrow x \geq_T y$; therefore, $x \geq_U y \Rightarrow x \geq_E y$. The chain of implications is complete and

$$x \geq_E y \Rightarrow x \geq_W y \Rightarrow x \geq_U y \Rightarrow x \geq_E y.$$

Thus the rankings of distributions by the three criteria $\geq_U, \geq_W$, and $\geq_E$ are equivalent, and each is equivalent to $\geq_L$ and $\geq_T$.

Given two distributions with the same number of individuals and the same mean income, Atkinson uses Lorenz dominance to establish an unambiguous welfare ranking between them in terms of *all* welfare functions from a wide class. But in any actual comparison of income distributions (for example between countries or over time), the population size and mean income are likely to be different. With different population sizes but the same mean income, a simple extension of Atkinson's theorem shows that Lorenz dominance still gives an unambiguous ranking between the distributions in terms of per capita welfare.[15] With different mean incomes, the unambiguous welfare ranking survives only when it is the Lorenz-dominant distribution that has the higher mean income. Thus Lorenz dominance cannot always be used for normative comparisons of inequality between two distributions.

I put the Lorenz ranking to a somewhat different use in this study. Even if normative comparisons are not possible, for example because the underlying distributions refer to different population units or income concepts, the Lorenz ordering can still reveal a good deal about

---

[15] If the criterion $\geq_W$ or $\geq_E$ is being used instead of Atkinson's $\geq_U$, then a 'symmetry axiom for population' is needed (see Sen 1973).

inequality in a positive or descriptive sense. The next result shows that Lorenz dominance provides an unambiguous ranking of distributions by *all* positive inequality indices from a wide class.

Proposition: Let L be the class of inequality indices that satisfy three basic properties: mean independence, population-size independence, and the Pigou–Dalton condition. If the Lorenz curve of a distribution $x(\mu_x, n_x)$ with mean μ_x and population size n_x dominates the Lorenz curve of another distribution $y(\mu_y, n_y)$ with mean μ_y and population size n_y, then *all* indices from the class L will show less inequality for $x(\mu_x, n_x)$ than for $y(\mu_y, n_y)$.

Proof: Let I be a typical inequality index from the class L of inequality indices. Replicate n_y times the number of people at each income level in $x(\mu_x, n_x)$, and replicate n_x times the number of people at each income level in $y(\mu_y, n_y)$. Then multiply each person's income in $x(\mu_x, n_x n_y)$ by μ_y, and each person's income in $y(\mu_y, n_x n_y)$ by μ_x. Then the new distributions $x(\mu_x \mu_y, n_x n_y)$ and $y(\mu_x \mu_y, n_x n_y)$ have the same population size $n = n_x n_y$ and the same mean $\mu = \mu_x \mu_y$; hence the hypotheses of Atkinson's theorem hold for them. Furthermore, $x(\mu, n)$ Lorenz-dominates $y(\mu, n)$ because the Lorenz curve of $x(\mu, n)$ is identical to the Lorenz curve of $x(\mu_x, n_x)$, and the Lorenz curve of $y(\mu, n)$ is identical to the Lorenz curve of $y(\mu_y, n_y)$. Therefore, by Atkinson's theorem, $x(\mu, n)$ can be obtained from $y(\mu, n)$ by a sequence of transfers from rich individuals to poor. Now as the index I satisfies the Pigou–Dalton condition, it will show less inequality for $x(\mu, n)$ than for $y(\mu, n)$. (A transfer from rich to poor decreases the value of such an index.) But since the index I is also mean-independent and population-size-independent, its values for $x(\mu_x, n_x)$ and $y(\mu_y, n_y)$ are identical to its values for $x(\mu, n)$ and $y(\mu, n)$, respectively. Hence the index I shows less inequality for $x(\mu_x, n_x)$ than for $y(\mu_y, n_y)$. ||

All the positive indices considered in this study belong to the class L, except for the variance of log-income (at high levels of income). Thus Lorenz dominance automatically implies less inequality according to such indices as the Gini coefficient, the two Theil measures, and the squared coefficient of variation. It also implies less inequality according to so-called normative indices belonging to this class, such as Atkinson's index, which may be used in a positive or descriptive sense. I call the class L the Lorenz class of inequality indices.

REFERENCES

Aitchison, J. and J.A.C. Brown (1957). *The Lognormal Distribution*. Cambridge: Cambridge University Press.

Atkinson, Anthony B. (1970). 'On the Measurement of Inequality', *Journal of Economic Theory*, 2(3), September.

Dasgupta, Partha S., Amartya K. Sen and David Starrett (1973). 'Notes on the Measurement of Inequality', *Journal of Economic Theory*, 6(2), April.

Fei, John C.H. and Gustav Ranis (1974). 'Income Inequality by Additive Factor Components', Economic Growth Center, Yale University.

Kendall, M.G. and A. Stuart (1963). *The Advanced Theory of Statistics*, vol. 1, *Distribution Theory*, 2nd ed., London: Griffin.

Rao, V.M. (1969). 'Two Decompositions of Concentration Ratio', *Journal of the Royal Statistical Society*, series A, 132, pt. 3.

Rothschild, Michael and Joseph E. Stiglitz (1973). 'Some Further Results on the Measurement of Inequality', *Journal of Economic Theory*, 6(2), April.

Schutz, R.R. (1951). 'On the Measurement of Income Inequality', *American Economic Review*, 41(1), March.

Sen, Amartya K. (1973). *On Economic Inequality*. Oxford: Clarendon Press.

Theil, Henri (1967). *Economics and Information Theory*. Amsterdam: North-Holland.

How Serious is the Neglect of Intra-Household Inequality?

Lawrence Haddad and Ravi Kanbur

In the measurement of inequality and poverty, the significance of intra-household inequality clearly depends on the objective of the exercise. In the growing literature on this subject, the reason for investigating intra-household inequality is that the ultimate object of concern for economic policy is the well-being of individuals. Yet most policy, and most policy analysis, has until recently equated the well-being of individuals with the average (adult-equivalent) well-being of the household to which they belong. The assumption is thus that within a household resources are divided according to need. If this were true, then policy could concentrate on increasing the resources of poor households without getting enmeshed in an intra-household policy that may be difficult to design and even more difficult to execute. However, a growing body of empirical literature has begun to question and examine whether resources within a household are indeed distributed according to need (see Sen 1984; Harriss 1986; Behrman 1989; Thomas 1989). The natural corollary is thus that conventional results on the extent and pattern of inequality and poverty as revealed by household-level resources have to be re-examined.

There is, however, little in the way of *quantification* of how much of a difference the existence of intra-household inequality would make to conventional measures of inequality and poverty. Is the understatement (if any) likely to be large? Even if the understatement of the *levels* of inequality and poverty is large, are the *patterns* of inequality and poverty grossly different when one takes account of intra-household inequality? An answer to the latter question is important since *policy design* (for example directing resources to particular regions, crop groups, etc.) often relies on the pattern of poverty and inequality (see, for example, the use by Anand [1983] of inequality and poverty decomposition to analyse the efficacy of various policies in Malaysia).

The object of this chapter is to present a framework in which these questions can be addressed and then to apply this framework to a data set from the Philippines on intra-household inequality in nutritional status. Our empirical conclusions are likely to be of interest to those who are considering undertaking the costly task of an intra-household focused survey in developing countries. These conclusions can be stated very crudely but simply as follows:

(i) The neglect of intra-household inequality is likely to lead to a considerable understatement of the levels of inequality and poverty.

(ii) However, while the patterns of inequality revealed by household-level data are somewhat different to those revealed by individual-level data, these differences can be argued to be not dramatic.

The first section in this chapter develops an analytical framework for assessing the impact of intra-household inequality on the levels of inequality and poverty. The second section applies this framework after introducing our data set. The third section concludes the paper.

A THEORETICAL ANALYSIS

We suppose that the object of interest is the well-being of individuals, which is measured by some agreed standard (consumption, nutrition, etc.) and denoted y. It is assumed that all relevant corrections and adjustments have been made and incorporated into y (price differences, needs differences, etc.) so that it really does represent the variable on which social welfare is defined. Now let x be the average of y *within* a household. Thus the mean of the distribution of individuals by x is the same as the mean of y. However, the distribution of individuals by x would ignore intra-household inequality and it is the difference between this distribution and the distribution of y that lies at the heart of the analysis in this chapter.

Denote the conditional density of y given x as $a(y \mid x)$. This captures inequality within a household whose average standard of living is x. If $p(x)$ is the marginal density of x in the population, then the density of y in the population, $f(y)$, is clearly

$$f(y) = \int a(y \mid x) p(x) \, dx, \qquad (1)$$

where the integration is over the permissible range of x.

Consider a convex function $h(\cdot)$. Note that

$$E[h(y)] = \int \left[\int h(y)\, a(y \mid x)\, dy \right] p(x)\, dx$$

$$\geq \int h(x)\, p(x)\, dx \text{ by Jensen's inequality}$$

$$= E[h(x)]. \tag{2}$$

What (2) tells us is that the expectation of all convex functions is greater under the distribution of y than under the distribution of x. It therefore follows (see Rothschild and Stiglitz 1970) that $f(y)$ is a mean preserving spread of $p(x)$, which is a fairly obvious result. It also follows, from Atkinson (1970), that the Lorenz curve of y will be unambiguously below the Lorenz curve of x on a Lorenz diagram. This is the sense in which inequality will always be understated by using only household-level information. The 'Lorenz class' of measures (see Anand 1983) will always be lower for x than for y — for example the Gini coefficient or the Theil index will always be understated.

To illustrate further the nature of the understatement, consider as a measure of inequality the coefficient of variation. Since the means of y and x are the same, in this case we might as well use the variance. Writing $V(y)$ as the variance of y, $V(x)$ as the variance of x and $V(y \mid x)$ as the variance of y conditional on x (that is the variance of well-being within a household whose average well-being is x), we know from the analysis of variance that

$$V(y) = \int V(y \mid x)\, p(x)\, dx + V(x). \tag{3}$$

In effect, the right-hand side of (3) decomposes the inequality of y into an intra-household component and an inter-household component. The size of the intra-household component — the discrepancy between $V(y)$ and $V(x)$ — is an empirical matter and in the following section we provide quantification of the discrepancy for a range of inequality measures, based on a particular data set.

So much for the measured *level* of inequality. What about the *pattern* of inequality? Suppose that our households could be split into two mutually exclusive and exhaustive groups U and R ('urban' and 'rural'). A typical investigation of the pattern of inequality involves two questions: (i) Which group has higher inequality? (ii) What fraction of inequality is accounted for by inequality within and inequality between these two groups? These questions are asked very commonly in inequality analysis (for example Theil 1967; Anand 1983; Tsakloglou 1988) and they are important for policy design. Would be answers differ greatly if we ignored intra-household inequality?

Taking the second question first, using subscripts U and R for the two groups we can write:

$$V(y) = \lambda_U V_U(y) + \lambda_R V_R(y) + \lambda_U \lambda_R [\mu_U(y) - \mu_R(y)]^2, \qquad (4)$$

where λ_U and λ_R are population proportions in the two groups ($\lambda_U + \lambda_R = 1$) and μ represents the mean. The between group component of overall inequality in (4) is that involving the group means. The between group *contribution* is defined as

$$C_B(y) = \frac{\lambda_U \lambda_R [\mu_U(y) - \mu_R(y)]^2}{V(y)}. \qquad (5)$$

The within group contribution is simply $1 - C_B(y)$. If we did not have individual-level data but relied on household means, then

$$V(x) = \lambda_U V_U(x) + \lambda_R V_R(x) + \lambda_U \lambda_R [\mu_U(x) - \mu_R(x)]^2, \qquad (6)$$

$$C_B(x) = \frac{\lambda_U \lambda_R [\mu_U(x) - \mu_R(x)]^2}{V(x)}. \qquad (7)$$

But it is easy to show that $\mu_U(y) = \mu_U(x)$ and $\mu_R(y) = \mu_R(x)$. Thus the *absolute* value of the between group component is the same whether y or x is used. Since from (3) we know that $V(y) > V(x)$, we have the result that

$$C_B(y) < C_B(x). \qquad (8)$$

Hence tne between group contribution to inequality is overstated and the within group contribution is correspondingly understated when intra-household inequality is ignored. While (for ease of exposition) we have derived the result for $V(\cdot)$, it holds true for any measure of inequality where the between group component depends only on group means (for this approach to defining 'decomposability', see Shorrocks 1980). For example it holds true for the well-known Theil index of inequality, which forms the basis of many empirical studies. The *extent* of overstatement or understatement is an empirical matter, and we shall investigate this in the next section in the context of our data set.

What of the *ranking* of groups by inequality? It can be shown (Haddad and Kanbur 1989) that

$$\{ [V_U(y) - V_R(y)] > 0 => [V_U(x) - V_R(x)] > 0 \}$$

$$<==>$$

$$\left\{ [V_U(y) - V_R(y)] > \left[\int V_U(y \mid x) p_U(x) \, dx - \int V_R(y \mid x) p_R(x) \, dx \right] \right\}. \quad (9)$$

Similar results can be derived for other indices such as the Theil index. The general point is that, if intra-household inequality in the two groups is sufficiently similar, the rankings will be preserved. However, if intra-household inequality is very much greater in the group with higher overall inequality, then suppression of this intra-household variation could lead to a ranking reversal. Whether this actually happens or not is an empirical matter, and we will investigate it further in the next section.

We turn now to an analysis of poverty. The standard approach in the literature (see Sen 1976) is to choose a poverty line and then define a poverty index based on the gap between the value of the variable measuring the standard of well-being, and its critical value as given by the poverty line.

If we define a 'gap function' as $h(y, z)$, where z is the poverty line, then a general definition of a class of poverty indices (see Atkinson 1987) is

$$P(y) = \int h(y, z) f(y) \, dy. \quad (10)$$

If we had information only on household averages then we would be forced to use

$$P(x) = \int h(x, z) p(x) \, dx. \quad (11)$$

But from (2) we know immediately that $P(y) \geq P(x)$ if $h(\cdot, z)$ is convex in its first argument.

To investigate this further, consider the class of poverty indices recently introduced by Foster, Greer and Thorbecke (FGT) in 1984. In terms of (10), their index assumes

$$h(y, z) = \begin{cases} \left(\dfrac{z - y}{z} \right)^x; & y \leq z, \\ \\ 0; & y > z. \end{cases} \quad (12)$$

Here, α is an index of poverty aversion. When $\alpha = 0$, P becomes simply the standard headcount ratio or incidence of poverty measure. When $\alpha = 1$, P emphasizes the average depth of poverty while with $\alpha > 1$, P is sensitive to intra-poor transfers. Notice that with $\alpha \geq 1$, $h(y, z)$ is convex in y and we can be sure that the FGT index on x will *understate* true poverty. However, for $\alpha < 1$ $h(y, z)$ is neither convex nor concave over its whole range so that Jensen's inequality can no longer be used. To investigate this further, consider $\alpha = 0$. A necessary and sufficient condition can be derived if we specialize to

$$
\left.
\begin{aligned}
y &= x + \varepsilon, \\
E(\varepsilon) &= 0, \\
Var(\varepsilon) &= \sigma_\varepsilon^2, \\
Cov(x, \varepsilon) &= 0.
\end{aligned}
\right\}
\tag{13}
$$

Then
$$
\begin{aligned}
E(y) &= E(x), \\
Var(y) &= Var(x) + \sigma_\varepsilon^2.
\end{aligned}
$$

If we further restrict ourselves to y and x being symmetric distributions (for example the normal distribution) then it follows easily that

$$
P_0(y) \lessgtr P_0(x) \text{ according as } z \lessgtr \mu.
\tag{14}
$$

This is in fact a special case of a more general result of Ravallion (1988) derived in a different context. Thus the x indicator *overstates* poverty if the poverty line exceeds the mean of y — we shall see an empirical verification of this result in our data set.

Let us now turn to the difference that can be made to an analysis of poverty patterns across mutually exclusive and exhaustive groups. As before, let these be indexed U and R, with population proportions λ_U and λ_R. We know from (10) and (11) that

$$
P(y) = \lambda_U P_U(y) + \lambda_R P_R(y); \quad P(x) = \lambda_U P_U(x) + \lambda_R P_R(x)
\tag{15}
$$

and the contribution of region U to poverty in the two cases is therefore

$$
C_U(y) = \frac{\lambda_U P_U(y)}{P(y)}; \quad C_U(x) = \frac{\lambda_U P_U(x)}{P(x)}.
\tag{16}
$$

Thus $\quad C_U(y) - C_U(x) = \dfrac{\lambda_U \lambda_R P_U(x) P_R(x)}{P(y) P(x)} \left[\dfrac{P_U(y)}{P_U(x)} - \dfrac{P_R(y)}{P_R(x)} \right]. \tag{17}$

We already know that if h is convex in y then $P_U(y) > P_U(x)$, and $P_R(y) > P_R(x)$, that is true poverty is understated in both groups when measured using x. However, for the measured *contributions* to poverty to be very different, the degree of understatement has to be greatly different in the two regions. In other words, intra-household inequality and its pattern have to be very different when comparing across the two groups. The same is of course also true when considering poverty-ranking reversals. If $P_U(y) > P_R(y)$ and the pattern of intra-household inequality is the same or very similar in the two groups then $P_U(x) > P_R(x)$ will also hold. Only if the patterns are significantly different will ranking reversals take place. Once again, whether this happens or not is an empirical matter and we turn now to an investigation of our theoretical framework as applied to a particular data set.

AN EMPIRICAL ANALYSIS

The Data Set and the Variables

Having developed a theoretical framework and some results on what difference the neglect of intra-household inequality can make to the measurement and decomposition of equality and poverty, it is now time to investigate a specific data set.

The data used in this study are described and evaluated fully in Bouis and Haddad (1989a). They come from a survey of the predominantly rural southern Philippine providence of Bukidnon. The survey was conducted in four rounds over a sixteen-month period in 1984–5, covering 448 households comprising 2880 individuals. The only good for which we can identify individual consumption is food. Therefore we focus on food, converting dietary intake into calories and standardizing by calorie requirements, to give calorie adequacy.

Calorie adequacy will be our measure of individual well-being. There is now a large and controversial literature on the appropriateness of this variable for welfare and policy analysis. However, recall that our object is to investigate the consequences of neglecting intra-household inequality for the measurement of inequality and poverty. Food consumption is one of the few variables on which intra-household data can be collected and, as such, is suited to our analysis.

Calorie intakes in our data set represent 24-hour recalls by the mother, of food eaten by individual family members. This information may be subject to a number of errors, both in overall quantity recall and allocative recall. However, as Burke and Pao's (1976) review of alternative food intake enumeration methods notes, 'no one method was consistently advantageous over all others'. Chavez and Huenemann (1984) arrive at a similar conclusion. In addition, we have minimized problems of representativeness by using only four-round *averages* of calorie intake for each individual in an attempt to make the dietary snapshots more typical. This technique has been used for a number of years by the USDA in its *National Food Consumption Surveys* (USDA 1986).

Concerning measurement errors, two sources of evidence attest to the accuracy of our enumerators' data-collection efforts. First, calorie consumption figures calculated from two different methodologies (24-hour recall and food expenditure data) exhibited a high degree of correspondence at the means of the data (Bouis and Haddad 1989b). Furthermore, the 24-hour recall intakes corresponded reasonably well to a small, overlapping subsample of food weighings conducted simultaneously (Corpus, et al. 1987).

The denominator of the calorie adequacy ratio is calorie requirement. We use orthodox recommended daily allowance (RDA) calorie figures for a healthy Philippino population with requirements disaggregated into thirty-two age–gender–pregnancy status categories (details in Bouis and Haddad 1989a). We recognize of course, the limitations of RDAs in the context in which we plan to use them (see, for example, Davidson, et al. 1979). These problems are not trivial, but until individual requirements for full functional capacity are available, the best we can do is to use the RDAs and note that they represent 'an order of magnitude' (Achaya 1983).

Our object is to assess the seriousness of neglecting intra-household inequality. In our data set, since we have individual-level data we can 'pretend' that we do not have this information by taking household averages. However, in the empirical context we now have a choice of whether to take the mean of individual adequacy ratios, or to take the ratio of the within-household mean of individual calorie intakes and individual requirements. There are thus three variables of interest: individual calorie adequacy, ϕ, mean individual calorie adequacy within the household, ϕ_1, and household calorie adequacy, ϕ_2. More precisely, let

$C_i =$ calorie intake of individual i,

$R_i =$ calorie requirement of individual i,

ϕ_i = calorie adequacy of individual i,

n_h = number of individuals in household h,

$$\phi_{1i} = \frac{1}{n_h} \sum_{i=1}^{n_h} \phi_i = \text{mean of individual calorie adequacy within the household, which is assigned to each household member,}$$

$$\phi_{2i} = \left(\sum_{i=1}^{n_h} C_i \right) \bigg/ \left(\sum_{i=1}^{n_h} R_i \right) = \text{household calorie adequacy, which is assigned to each household member.}$$

Referring to our theoretical discussion, ϕ corresponds to y and ϕ_1 to x. But in the empirical context we typically have to deal not with ϕ_1 but with ϕ_2 since information is only collected at the household level on calorie intake. While ϕ_1 and ϕ_2 will differ, we shall see that the difference, and its empirical effect, is not very great.

These three variables are calculated for all 2880 individuals in our sample. We should note that all individuals within a household will have identical values for ϕ_1. The same is true for ϕ_2. The mean of ϕ over the 2880 individuals in the sample is 0.87765, indicating that on average our sample is undernourished. The mean of ϕ_1 is by definition the same as the mean of ϕ. However, the mean of ϕ_2 is 0.88835, an excess of 1.2 per cent, indicating slight negative correlation between calorie intake and calorie requirement. Our real object, however, is to examine and compare measures of inequality and poverty defined over ϕ, ϕ_1 and ϕ_2. We start with inequality.

Measurement and Decomposition of Inequality

Figure 4.1 compares the Lorenz curve of ϕ with those of ϕ_1 and ϕ_2. We showed in the first section that the Lorenz curve of ϕ_1 would be unambiguously closer to the line of perfect equality than the Lorenz curve of ϕ and this is shown to be the case in Figure 4.1a. The same comparison holds for ϕ_2 and ϕ, and in fact the Lorenz curves of ϕ_1 and ϕ_2 are almost identical.

Table 4.1 quantifies inequality differences with respect to five commonly used measures of inequality: the coefficient of variation, the log-variance, the Gini coefficient, the Theil index T, Theil's second measure L and the Atkinson equally distributed equivalent measure of inequality with inequality aversion parameter equal to 2. The exact

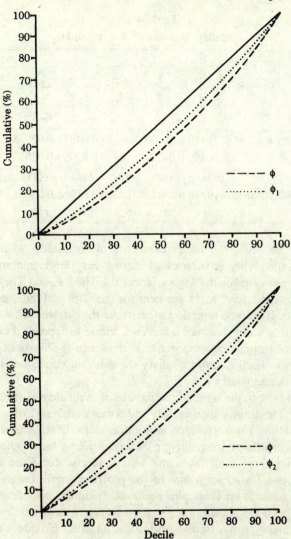

Figure 4.1: Lorenz Curves for ϕ, ϕ_1 and ϕ_2.

definitions of these measures are to be found in Kanbur (1984). The first point to note is how close the measures based on ϕ_1 and ϕ_2 are to each other. With this in mind, we concentrate on the differences between ϕ and ϕ_1.

Table 4.1
Inequality Measures for ϕ, ϕ_1 and ϕ_2

Variable	n	Mean	Coefficient of variation	Log variance	Gini coefficient	Theil T (base e)	Theil L (base e)	Atkinson measure ($\varepsilon = 2$)
ϕ	2880	0.87765	0.31419	0.10897	0.1754	0.04873	0.05078	0.10229
ϕ_1	2880	0.87765	0.20386	0.04257	0.1148	0.02059	0.02083	0.04127
(% of ϕ)			(65)	(39)	(65)	(42)	(41)	(40)
ϕ_2	2880	0.88835	0.19998	0.04118	0.1090	0.01986	0.02012	0.03996
(% of ϕ)			(64)	(38)	(62)	(41)	(40)	(40)

As can be seen, the understatements of inequality when intra-household inequality is suppressed can be very large, ranging from around 60 per cent for the log-variance, the Theil T, and Theil L and the Atkinson measure, to 35 per cent for the Gini and the coefficient of variation. It may be tempting to attribute the difference to 'within' household inequality, but such a *precise* attribution depends on whether or not the measure is 'decomposable' in the sense of Shorrocks (1980). Only the two Theil measures satisfy the relevant conditions of strict sub-group decomposability.

We turn now to the issue of the *pattern* of inequality as revealed by the data. It is traditional in inequality and poverty analysis to decompose inequality along key socio-economic dimensions. Thus Anand (1983) provides a profile of inequality in Malaysia along racial lines while Tsakloglou (1988) undertakes the same exercise for Greece along regional lines. The exact nature of the profile depends on the policy question at hand. In the Philippine region of Bukidnon, one of the central issues has been the impact of a move from corn to sugar production on inequality and poverty. Bouis and Haddad (1989a) provide a detailed analysis of the nutrition and income effects of the introduction of sugar-cane cultivation in the study area. Our object here is more limited — to investigate the sensitivity of the pattern of inequality, across the sub-groups identified by Bouis and Haddad (1989a) as being important, to the use of individual- or household-level data.

The first panel of Table 4.2 shows a decomposition of the Theil T index across three mutually exclusive and exhaustive types of house-holds — corn producers, sugar producers and others. As can be seen,

Table 4.2

Theil T Inequality Measures for Selected Subgroups Using ϕ, ϕ_1 and ϕ_2

Group	N	$\mu(\phi)$	$\mu(\phi_1)$	$\mu(\phi_2)$	$T(\phi)$	$T(\phi_1)$	$T(\phi_2)$
Corn	1565	0.88379	0.88379	0.89338	0.04736	0.02019	0.01953
Sugar	1082	0.87938	0.87938	0.89144	0.04999	0.02065	0.01980
No crop	233	0.82843	0.82843	0.84025	0.05048	0.02141	0.02083
Within	–	–	–	–	0.04859	0.02046	0.01973
Between	–	–	–	–	0.00014	0.00014	0.00013
% Between	–	–	–	–	0.29	0.68	0.66
Owner	695	0.89826	0.89826	0.90311	0.05076	0.02113	0.01993
Mix	516	0.89603	0.89603	0.90497	0.04401	0.01815	0.01785
Tenant	758	0.88679	0.88679	0.90000	0.04728	0.02017	0.01964
Labourer	580	0.84614	0.84614	0.86168	0.04838	0.02018	0.01987
Other ten*	331	0.84004	0.84004	0.85154	0.05292	0.02203	0.02107
Within	–	–	–	–	0.04837	0.02024	0.01959
Between	–	–	–	–	0.00036	0.00036	0.00028
% Between	–	–	–	–	0.74	1.8	1.4
Corn own**	341	0.89133	0.89133	0.89588	0.05232	0.02227	0.02126
Corn mix	310	0.87277	0.87277	0.88165	0.04223	0.01715	0.01693
Corn share	549	0.89237	0.89237	0.90350	0.04491	0.02022	0.01996

Table 4.2 (cont.)

117

Table 4.2 (cont.)

Group	N	$\mu(\phi)$	$\mu(\phi_1)$	$\mu(\phi_2)$	$T(\phi)$	$T(\phi_1)$	$T(\phi_2)$
Corn lab	267	0.87524	0.87524	0.88847	0.04788	0.01968	0.01859
Sug own	354	0.90494	0.90494	0.91006	0.04922	0.01999	0.01861
Sug mix	206	0.93104	0.93104	0.94007	0.04529	0.01835	0.01795
Sug rent	209	0.87215	0.87215	0.89079	0.05347	0.01983	0.01871
Sug lab	313	0.82131	0.82131	0.83882	0.04787	0.01967	0.02023
Other occ	233	0.82843	0.82843	0.84025	0.05048	0.02141	0.02083
Corn othrnt	98	0.86765	0.86765	0.87838	0.05771	0.02269	0.02093
Within	–	–	–	–	0.04814	0.02001	0.01938
Between	–	–	–	–	0.00059	0.00059	0.00049
% Between	–	–	–	–	1.21	2.9	2.5

* 'Other ten' = Other tenure status.

** Abbreviations in this panel correspond to full labels given in Table 4.3.

the 2880 individuals in the sample are divided as follows: 1565 in corn-producing households, 1082 in sugar-producing households and 233 in other households. It is immediately seen that if we compare inequality as measured by the Theil T index defined on ϕ (individual-level data), inequality among individuals in sugar households is greater than that among individuals in corn households, while inequality among households that grow neither crop is greatest. A shift in favour of sugar, particularly if this creates landless labourers in the process, is therefore worrying from the point of view of inequality. Would this conclusion have been greatly affected if we had had information on calorie adequacy only at the household level? The answer is no. The inequality ranking of the three groups remains unchanged whether ϕ, ϕ_1 or ϕ_2 is used as the basis of inequality calculations. As was pointed out in the first section, for ranking reversals to take place it has to be the case that patterns of intra-household inequality are vastly different from group to group; this is clearly not the case for our data set.

An alternative dimension to be considered is tenure status, again identified by Bouis and Haddad (1989a) as important in Bukidnon. The second panel in Table 4.2 provides intra-group inequalities based on ϕ, ϕ_1 and ϕ_2 for five tenure status groups. Once again, we see that the rankings remain unaffected.

Table 4.3

Theil T Inequality Rankings for Crop-tenancy Groups by Household- and Individual-level Data

Group*	Ranking by		
	ϕ	ϕ_1	ϕ_2
Corn mixed tenancy	1	1	1
Corn share tenant	2	7	6
Sugar mixed tenancy	3	2	2
Sugar labourer	4	3	7
Corn labourer	5	4	3
Sugar owner	6	6	4
Other occupation	7	8	8
Corn owner	8	9	10
Sugar renter	9	5	5
Corn other rental arrangement	10	10	9

* Inequality increases from least to most down the Table.

The final level of disaggregation we tried was that given in the third panel of Table 4.2, where ten mutually exclusive and exhaustive groups of households are identified according to crop and tenure status. We would expect, of course, that as the disaggregation becomes finer and finer, and groups become more homogeneous, eventually ranking changes would begin to appear. Table 4.3 shows the ranks in question. In order to get a quantitative feel for the extent of rank reversal we calculated Spearman's rank correlation coefficients. The rank correlation coefficient between ϕ_1 and ϕ_2 is 0.85, indicating very close association between the two ranks. That between ϕ and ϕ_1 is 0.72. The lowest value for the coefficient is between ϕ and ϕ_2 and is 0.66. Thus we can conclude that while there are some rank changes when we switch from individual- to household-level data, the extent of the changes is not dramatic.

Finally, from Table 4.2 we note the empirical confirmation of our theoretical result that the between group component of inequality will be unchanged whether ϕ or ϕ_1 is used, since this depends only on group means and the conditional mean of ϕ is the same as the conditional mean of ϕ_1 for any conditioning variable. Since the within group component of inequality is inevitably greater with ϕ than with ϕ_1, it follows that the *contribution* of this component to total inequality when ϕ is used is greater than when ϕ_1 is used. Correspondingly, with ϕ the contribution of the between group component is lower than with ϕ_1. In our data set, these conclusions are unchanged when ϕ_1 is replaced by ϕ_2.

Measurement and Decomposition of 'Poverty' (Defined as Undernutrition)

In the first section we derived a number of theoretical results on the likely impact of intra-household inequality on measured poverty. The object of this subsection is to consider an empirical analysis based on our data set. Any measurement of poverty requires us to specify a poverty line. In the context of the variable of interest in this study — the calorie adequacy ratio — an appropriate poverty line is simply 1. All those with calorie adequacy ratio less than 1 can reasonably be argued to be undernourished or 'poor' in the terminology of income poverty. We will concentrate attention on the class of poverty indices put forward by Foster, et al. (1984). Adapting the notation of the first section, these can be written as

$$P_\infty = \int_0^1 (1 - \phi)^\infty f(\phi)\, d\phi,$$

TABLE 4.4

P_∞ Poverty Measures for Selected Subgroups Using ϕ, ϕ_1 and ϕ_2

Group	N	$P_0(\phi)$	$P_1(\phi)$	$P_2(\phi)$	$P_0(\phi_1)$	$P_1(\phi_1)$	$P_2(\phi_1)$	$P_0(\phi_2)$	$P_1(\phi_2)$	$P_2(\phi_2)$
All	2880	0.70243	0.18640	0.06759	0.76875	0.15201	0.04093	0.75764	0.14355	0.03756
Corn	1565	0.69521	0.18144	0.06483	0.75463	0.14661	0.03925	0.73738	0.13897	0.03632
Sugar	1028	0.70055	0.18592	0.06811	0.77634	0.15042	0.04029	0.77172	0.14125	0.03647
No crop	233	0.75966	0.22203	0.08369	0.82833	0.19571	0.05516	0.82833	0.18494	0.05097
Owner	695	0.68345	0.17584	0.06342	0.74964	0.14021	0.03716	0.74964	0.13459	0.03495
Mix	516	0.67636	0.17171	0.05930	0.70543	0.13731	0.03354	0.72093	0.13092	0.03137
Tenant	758	0.68865	0.17792	0.06445	0.76253	0.14202	0.03822	0.74802	0.13265	0.03441
Labourer	580	0.74310	0.20589	0.07605	0.83276	0.17269	0.04884	0.78276	0.16133	0.04424
Other ten	331	0.74320	0.21676	0.08159	0.80967	0.18633	0.05270	0.80967	0.17582	0.04822
Corn own	341	0.68622	0.18359	0.06663	0.73607	0.14803	0.03970	0.73607	0.14226	0.03797
Corn mix	310	0.71613	0.18241	0.06382	0.70968	0.15507	0.03895	0.70968	0.14857	0.03646
Corn share	549	0.68852	0.17219	0.06080	0.76138	0.13601	0.03740	0.74499	0.12825	0.03452
Corn lab	267	0.69288	0.18820	0.06766	0.81273	0.15036	0.04007	0.74532	0.14009	0.03578
Sug own	354	0.68079	0.16837	0.06034	0.76271	0.13269	0.03472	0.76271	0.12720	0.03204
Sug mix	206	0.61650	0.15562	0.05250	0.69903	0.11059	0.02541	0.73786	0.10435	0.02370
Sug rent	209	0.68900	0.19298	0.07404	0.76555	0.15781	0.04037	0.75598	0.14421	0.03412
Sug lab	313	0.78594	0.22099	0.08320	0.84984	0.19174	0.05632	0.81470	0.17946	0.05146
Other occ	233	0.75966	0.22203	0.08369	0.82833	0.19571	0.05516	0.82833	0.18494	0.05097
Corn othrnt	98	0.70408	0.20423	0.07661	0.76531	0.16404	0.04685	0.76531	0.15414	0.04168
Male	1484	0.72372	0.19017	0.06863	0.77089	0.15058	0.04016	0.76146	0.14262	0.03691
Female	1396	0.67980	0.18240	0.06648	0.76648	0.15353	0.04175	0.75358	0.14453	0.03826
Adult	1191	0.48615	0.10074	0.03259	0.75231	0.14757	0.03957	0.74139	0.13920	0.03633
Non-adult*	1689	0.85494	0.24681	0.09226	0.78034	0.15515	0.04189	0.76909	0.14661	0.03843

* Non-adults are defined as individuals less than or equal to nineteen years of age in accordance with definitions employed by the National Nutrition Council of the Philippines for calorie requirements (NNC 1976).

where ϕ is calorie adequacy, $f(\cdot)$ its frequency density, and α is the poverty aversion parameter. We focus on $\alpha = 0, 1, 2$ in our discussion.

The first panel of Table 4.4 presents values of P_0, P_1, and P_2 based on ϕ, ϕ_1 and ϕ_2. We have already proved that for $\alpha \geq 1$, P_∞ for ϕ will exceed P_∞ for ϕ_1. This is seen in the table. Ignoring intra-household inequality leads to an understatement of P_1 of 18.4 per cent if ϕ_1 is used and 23.0 per cent if ϕ_2 is used. Similarly, if P_2 is the accepted index of poverty then there is an understatement of 39.4 per cent with ϕ_1 and 44.4 per cent with ϕ_2. Clearly, then, there is a dramatic understatement of poverty if intra-household inequality is ignored, for $\alpha \geq 1$.

However, notice that with $\alpha = 0$ the situation is the other way round; there is now a substantial *overstatement* of poverty if intra-household inequality is ignored. Using ϕ there are 70.2 per cent of individuals below the calorie adequacy ratio of 1, while using ϕ_1 76.9 per cent of individuals fall below this critical value — an overstatement of 9.4 per cent. The explanation for this reversal is to be found in the discussion leading up to equation (14) of the first section. Under certain conditions we showed that the incidence of poverty (or undernutrition) will be overstated by household-level data if the poverty line exceeds the population mean. This is exactly what happens in our data: the mean of ϕ (and ϕ_1) is 0.88 while the chosen poverty line is 1.00.

Let us turn now to the pattern of poverty across socio-economic groups. The next three panels of Table 4.4 use the same mutually exclusive and exhaustive groups as in Table 4.2. The policy relevance of these household-level groupings has already been discussed in the subsection on Measurement and Decomposition of Inequality.

The theoretical significance of P_∞ rankings of sectors and groups has been discussed by Kanbur (1987) in the context of targeting and poverty alleviation. We note here that there are *no* ranking changes in the first or the second panel. As argued earlier, we would expect some rank changes to occur as the classification gets finer. However, even with ten groups the changes are very small. As can be seen from the relevant panel of Table 4.4, the three poorest and three least poor groups in the ranking are unchanged as between ϕ, ϕ_1 and ϕ_2. The rank correlation coefficient between ϕ and ϕ_1 is 0.96 and that between ϕ and ϕ_2 is 0.9. Clearly, then, the neglect of intra-household inequality is *not* leading to dramatic changes in poverty ranking.

The groupings used so far, and those discussed in the theoretical section, are those defined at the household level. For some policy purposes, however, individual-level groupings *are* required. The last two panels in Table 4.4 consider two such groupings which are of obvious interest — male/female and adult/non-adult. The adult/non-adult division reveals no P_∞ ranking differences as between ϕ, ϕ_1 and ϕ_2. However, we find that male/female P_1 and P_2 rankings are reversed when comparing ϕ with ϕ_1 and ϕ with ϕ_2. This could be potentially serious if targeting policy towards males and females (for example in supplemental feeding programmes) is to be based on the degree of observed undernutrition in these groups. However, this is the only case, in all of the decomposition in Table 4.4, where rank reversal is potentially serious.

Finally, we consider group contributions to poverty based on ϕ, ϕ_1 and ϕ_2. Table 4.5 presents this analysis. The first four panels in Table 4.5 show the similar contributions each group makes to overall poverty whether we use ϕ, ϕ_1 or ϕ_2. As we argued earlier, intra-household inequality would have to be very different when comparing across groups for the contributions to poverty to differ by much.

Although the only individual-level grouping that experiences a ranking reversal in Table 4.4 is the male/female classification, the difference between adult/non-adult poverty levels widens substantially as we move from poverty measures based on ϕ_1 and ϕ_2 to those based on ϕ. This is emphasized in the bottom panel of Table 4.5, which shows the non-adult contribution to poverty measures based on ϕ to be in the 70–80 per cent range, but falling to 60 per cent when ϕ_1 and ϕ_2 are used.

CONCLUSION

The object of this chapter has been, first, to develop a framework in which the consequences of ignoring intra-household inequality for the measurement and decomposition of inequality and poverty can be assessed and, second, to apply this framework to a particular data set. Our theoretical analysis suggested that potentially serious errors could be made so far as the *levels* of inequality and poverty are concerned. Empirically, we showed that this is indeed the case — the errors are of the order of 30 per cent or more. In the case of poverty measurement we showed theoretically and empirically that for certain measures of poverty the errors could be of either sign: a careful analysis is therefore required before any claims are made as to whether poverty is understated or overstated.

So far as the *patterns* of inequality and poverty are concerned, our

Table 4.5

Percentage Group Contributions to P_α Poverty Measures Using ϕ, ϕ_1 and ϕ_2

Group	N	$P_0(\phi)$	$P_1(\phi)$	$P_2(\phi)$	$P_0(\phi_1)$	$P_1(\phi_1)$	$P_2(\phi_1)$	$P_0(\phi_2)$	$P_1(\phi_2)$	$P_2(\phi_2)$
All	2800	100.0	100.0	100.0	100.0	100.0	100.0	100.0	100.0	100.0
Corn	1565	53.8	52.9	52.1	53.3	52.4	52.1	52.9	52.6	52.5
Sugar	1082	37.5	37.5	37.9	37.9	37.2	37.0	38.3	37.0	36.5
No crop	233	8.7	9.6	10.0	8.7	10.4	10.9	8.8	10.4	11.0
Owner	695	23.5	22.8	22.6	23.5	22.3	21.9	23.9	22.6	22.5
Mix	516	17.3	16.5	15.7	16.4	16.2	14.7	17.0	16.3	15.0
Tenant	758	25.8	25.1	25.1	26.1	24.6	24.6	26.0	24.3	24.1
Labourer	580	21.3	22.2	22.7	21.8	22.9	24.0	20.8	22.6	23.7
Other ten	331	12.2	13.4	13.9	12.1	14.1	14.8	12.3	14.1	14.8
Corn own	341	11.6	11.7	11.7	11.3	11.5	11.5	11.5	11.7	12.0
Corn mix	310	11.0	10.5	10.2	9.9	11.0	10.2	10.1	11.1	10.4
Corn share	549	18.7	17.6	17.1	18.9	17.1	17.4	18.7	17.0	17.5
Corn lab	267	9.1	9.4	9.3	9.8	9.2	9.1	9.1	9.0	8.8
Sug own	354	11.9	11.1	11.0	12.2	10.7	10.4	12.4	10.9	10.5
Sug mix	206	6.3	6.0	5.6	6.5	5.2	4.4	7.0	5.2	4.5
Sug rent	209	7.1	7.5	7.9	7.2	7.5	7.2	7.2	7.3	6.6
Sug lab	313	12.2	12.9	13.4	12.0	13.7	15.0	11.7	13.6	14.9
Other occ	233	8.7	9.6	10.0	8.7	10.4	10.9	8.8	10.4	11.0
Corn othrnt	98	3.4	3.7	3.9	3.4	3.7	3.9	3.4	3.7	3.8
Male	1484	53.1	52.6	52.3	51.7	51.0	50.6	51.8	51.2	50.6
Female	1396	46.9	47.4	47.7	48.3	49.0	49.4	48.2	48.8	49.4
Adult	1191	28.6	22.3	19.9	40.5	40.1	40.0	40.5	40.1	40.0
Non-adult*	1689	71.4	77.7	80.1	59.5	59.9	60.0	59.5	59.9	60.0

* Non-adults are defined as individuals less than or equal to nineteen years of age in accordance with definitions employed by the National Nutrition Council of the Philippines for calorie requirements (NNC 1976).

theoretical analysis was more equivocal — significant differences in the cross group patterns of intra-household inequality are required to reverse the true rankings of policy-relevant socio-economic groups by inequality and poverty, when intra-household inequality is ignored. Our empirical analysis lends support to this equivocation — the changes in patterns of inequality when intra-household inequality is ignored are by no means dramatic; sometimes, they hardly change at all.

There is clearly a need to confirm our results further for other data sets in other countries. We hope to have provided both a framework in which such analysis can proceed and a preliminary indication that the results are important to policy-makers who are considering whether or not to launch a costly intra-household-oriented survey. The conclusions based on our data set are that the collection of such data is important if the object is to get an estimate of the *levels* of inequality and poverty; but if the object is to discover the *patterns* of inequality and poverty across key socio-economic groups, the policy-maker would do well to assess carefully the costs and benefits of such an exercise.

Acknowledgements: We would like to thank the International Food Policy Research Institute, Washington D.C. for access to the Philippine data set.

REFERENCES

Achaya, K.T. (1983). 'RDAs: Their Limitations and Application', *Economic and Political Weekly*, 18(15), p. 587.

Anand, S. (1983). *Inequality and Poverty in Malaysia: Measurement and Decomposition*. Oxford: Oxford University Press.

Atkinson, A.B. (1970). 'On the Measurement of Inequality', *Journal of Economic Theory*, 2, pp. 244–63.

—— (1987). 'On the Measurement of Poverty', *Econometrica*, 55, pp. 749–64.

Behrman, J. (1989). 'Intrahousehold Allocation of Nutrients and Gender Effects: A Survey of Structural and Reduced-form Estimates', in Siddig R. Osmani (ed.), *Nutrition and Poverty*. Oxford: Oxford University Press.

Bouis, H.E. and L.J. Haddad (1989a). *A Case Study of the Commercialisation of Agriculture in the Southern Philippines: The Income, Consumption and Nutrition Effects of a Switch from Corn to Sugar Production in Bukidnon*, Research Report, IFPRI, Washington, D.C.

Bouis, H.E. and L.J. Haddad (1989b). 'Estimating the Relationship between Calories and Income: Does Choice of Survey Variable Matter?', IFPRI, mimeo., Washington, D.C.

Burke, M. and E. Pao (1976). 'Methodology for Large-scale Surveys of Household and Individual Diets', USDA, Home Economics Research Report No. 40, Washington, D.C.

Chavez, M. and R. Huenemann (1984). 'Measuring Impact by Assessing Dietary Intake and Food Consumption', in D. Sahn, R. Lockwood and N. Scrimshaw (eds), *Methods for the Evaluation of the Impact of Food and Nutrition Programmes*, UNU.

Corpus, V.A., A. Ledesma, A. Limbo and H. Bouis (1987). 'The Commercialisation of Agriculture in the Southern Philippines, Phase I Report', IFPRI, mimeo., Washington, D.C.

Davidson, S., R. Passmore, J.F. Brock and A.S. Truswell (1979). *Human Nutrition and Dietics*, 7th edn, Churchill Livingstone.

Foster, J., J. Greer and E. Thorbecke (1984). 'On a Class of Decomposable Poverty Measures', *Econometrica*, 52, pp. 761–5.

Haddad, L. and R. Kanbur (1989). 'How Serious is the Neglect of Intra-household Inequality? (What Difference Does it Make to the Measurement and Decomposition of Inequality and Poverty?)', Discussion Paper 95, Development Economics Research Centre, University of Warwick, May.

Harriss, B. (1986). 'The Intra-family Distribution of Hunger in South Asia', in J. Drèze and A.K. Sen (eds), *Hunger and Public Policy*. Oxford: Oxford University Press.

Kanbur, R. (1984). 'The Measurement and Decomposition of Inequality and Poverty', in F. van der Ploeg (ed.), *Mathematical Methods in Economics*. Bognor Regis: Wiley.

——— (1987). 'Measurement and Alleviation of Poverty', *I.M.F. Staff Papers*, 30, pp. 60–85.

NNC (1976). 'Philippine Recommended Dietary Allowances', Part I, National Nutrition Council of the Philippines.

Ravallion, M. (1988). 'Expected Poverty under Risk-induced Welfare Variability', *Economic Journal*, 98, pp. 1171–82.

Rothschild, M. and J.E. Stiglitz (1970). 'Increasing Risk I: A Definition', *Journal of Economic Theory*, 2, pp. 225–43.

Sen, A.K. (1976). 'Poverty: An Ordinal Approach to Measurement' *Econometrica*, 44, pp. 219–31.

——— (1984). 'Family and Food: Sex Bias in Poverty', in A.K. Sen (ed.), *Resources, Values and Development*. Oxford: Blackwell.

Shorrocks, A.F. (1980). 'The Class of Additively Decomposable Inequality Measures', *Econometrica*, 48, pp. 613–25.

Theil, H. (1967). *Economics and Information Theory*. Amsterdam: North–Holland.

Thomas, D. (1989). 'Intra-household Resource Allocation: An Inferential Approach', Yale University, mimeo., May.

Tsakloglou, P. (1988). 'Aspects of Inequality and Poverty of Greece', Unpublished Ph.D. dissertation, University of Warwick.

USDA (1986). *Nationwide Food Consumption Survey Continuing Survey of Food Intakes by Individuals*, Human Nutrition Information Service, NFCS, CSFII, No. 86–93.

Inequality and Development: A Critique

SUDHIR ANAND AND S.M.R. KANBUR

INTRODUCTION

The last decade or so has seen considerable revival of interest in the relationship between inequality and development, a relationship that was first discussed by Kuznets (1955) more than three decades ago. In that discussion Kuznets introduced the now famous U-hypothesis, that the relation between inequality and development follows an 'inverse-U' shape — with inequality first increasing and then decreasing with development.

Kuznets based his discussion on time-series data for England, Germany and the United States, but the recent literature is dominated by a cross-section view. Using data on a cross-section of currently developed and developing countries, a number of papers claim to have discovered support for the U-hypothesis. The work of Adelman and Morris (1973), Paukert (1973), Ahluwalia (1974, 1976a, b), Chenery and Syrquin (1975), Lydall (1977), Loehr (1981) and others has been of this nature. Fields (1980) surveys this literature and concludes:

Research studies suggest that the relationship between relative inequality and per capita GNP tends to have an inverted-U shape: among groups of countries in the cross section, inequality rises in the early stages of economic development and falls in the middle and later stages. [p. 122.]

Robinson (1976, p. 437) observes moreover that the inverse-U relationship has 'acquired the force of economic law'. This relationship has also been adopted by the World Bank to make projections of inequality and world poverty in the year 2000 (see *World Development Reports* 1978, 1979 and 1980).

The literature on inequality and development is thus of undoubted importance from the viewpoint of both economic analysis and policy. However, the centrepiece of this literature consists of the articles by

Ahluwalia (1976b) and Ahluwalia, Carter and Chenery (1979), published in the *Journal of Development Economics* (see also Ahluwalia 1974, 1976a). In an influential literature, these have become influential papers. They are widely cited and the Ahluwalia papers (1974, 1976b) have been excerpted or reprinted in collections of readings in development economics (Meier 1976, Livingstone 1981). The importance of Ahluwalia's (1976b) paper for the inequality–development literature is two-fold. First, it has served to 'confirm' the U-hypothesis originally put forward by Kuznets (1955). On the basis of his estimation, Ahluwalia (1976b, p. 338) claims that 'there is strong support for the proposition that relative inequality increases substantially in the early stages of development, with a reversal of this tendency in the later stages'.

Second, Ahluwalia's particular estimates have been used for projections of inequality and poverty by Ahluwalia, Carter and Chenery (1979) and by the World Bank in its *World Development Reports* (1978, 1979, 1980).

In commenting on Ahluwalia's estimation of the inequality–development relationship, Srinivasan (1977, p. 25) too concludes that 'the cross-country data seem to support the hypothesis of Kuznets that as development proceeds, income inequality worsens first before it improves', and reckons that it is ' . . . possible to make some limited and stylized policy simulations based on the curve' (p. 15). Given that Ahluwalia's estimation of the inequality–development relationship has been used for these two important purposes, we would like to investigate its empirical and econometric basis more closely, and it is the object of this essay to do just that.[1]

The plan of this chapter is as follows. After a brief outline in the next section of Ahluwalia's estimation, the third section investigates the sensitivity of the estimates to alternative functional forms. We find that Ahluwalia's estimates are not robust to such variations: different functional forms, between which the data cannot choose, give widely differing shapes to the inequality–development relationship. These differences are particularly important for the projection exercises of Ahluwalia, Carter and Chenery (1979) which are discussed in the fourth section. There are various problems with Ahluwalia's (1976b) data set, and the fifth section investigates the robustness of his estimates to

---

[1] Saith (1983) has also commented on certain aspects of the Ahluwalia (1976b) study, but we have reservations about his critique, some of which are expressed in nn. 2, 12 and 19 below.

variations in the data set. Using a data set whose quality is as good if not better, we get a reversal of the claimed inverse-U shape for the relationship. The sixth section concludes the chapter.

AHLUWALIA'S ESTIMATION OF THE INEQUALITY–DEVELOPMENT RELATIONSHIP

The inequality–development relationship in Ahluwalia (1976b) is estimated by means of the regression equation

$$I = a_0 + a_1 [\log_{10} Y] + a_2 [\log_{10} Y]^2 + a_3 D + \varepsilon.$$

The dependent variable, I, is an index of *equality*, the income share of the lowest 40 per cent of the population, while the independent variables are: (i) the logarithm of per capita GNP [$\log_{10} Y$]; (ii) the square of the logarithm of per capita GNP [$\log_{10} Y$]^2; and (iii) a dummy for socialist countries, D. The stochastic error term ε is assumed to be normally distributed with classical properties; this assumption is discussed further in the third section. The equation was estimated for a sample of sixty developing and developed countries, and also for a subsample of forty developing countries only (Ahluwalia's [1976b] data set is presented in his Table 8, pp. 340–1). From an examination of the data it becomes clear that the six socialist countries in the sample have a uniformly higher income share for the lowest 40 per cent. Thus a dummy variable is introduced which takes on a value of 1 for socialist countries and 0 for others.[2]

[2] Saith (1983, p. 376) criticizes Ahluwalia's use of the 'socialist dummy', arguing that

the correct procedure is to drop the 6 [socialist] countries from the sample altogether; when this is done, the $\bar{R}^2$ drops (from its original value of 0.57) . . . drastically to 0.18. Although the estimated coefficients still remain significant, one cannot any more place much reliance in the model as less than a fifth of the total variation is explained; it is quite possible that if other relevant variables were included in the equation, the GNP variables would lose significance.

This argument of Saith's is problematic on several counts. From a substantive point of view, the issue is whether socialist and non-socialist countries follow different relationships and how we should test for this difference. If the differences are nested, and they can be captured solely by an intercept dummy, then Ahluwalia's procedure is valid. (N.B. Ahluwalia's procedure could be extended to include slope dummies.) From an econometric point of view, Saith's critique is invalid. First, the 'drop' in $\bar{R}^2$ is of little significance since the data being explained in the two cases (sample sizes of sixty and fifty-four) are *different*. We have computed SEE in the two cases (N.B. Saith does not present this statistic), and this turns out to be virtually the same: hence $\bar{R}^2$ is much higher for the full sample of sixty countries precisely because — as Ahluwalia (1976b;

Equation (1.1A) in Table 5.1 reports the coefficient estimates of the above regression for the sample of sixty developing and developed countries (equation [1.1A] is the same as equation [A.4] in Ahluwalia [1976b, p. 311]). The coefficient estimates of $[\log_{10} Y]$ and $[\log_{10} Y]^2$ are significant and of the right signs to generate a U-shape:[3] for *non-socialist* countries the income share of the lowest 40 per cent falls from an average value of 17 per cent at a per capita GNP level of $100 to 11 per cent at the turning point of $468, and then rises to about 15 per cent at $2000.

Equation (1.1B) in Table 5.1 reports the coefficient estimates for the restricted sample of forty developing countries.[4] The coefficient estimates are significant and again of the right signs to generate a U-shape. However, the positions of the curves (1.1A) and (1.1B) are quite different: note the difference of almost $100 in the per capita GNP levels at which the respective turning points occur. This will be seen to be important in projection exercises. First, however, we investigate the sensitivity of the relationship to the functional form estimated.

ALTERNATIVE FUNCTIONAL FORMS AND THE INEQUALITY–DEVELOPMENT RELATIONSHIP

Alternative Functional Forms

The functional form appropriate for econometric estimation should ideally be derived from an economic theory of the underlying processes. We have in another article (Anand and Kanbur 1993) analysed a model of intersectoral population shifts during the course of development, formalizing the ideas of Kuznets (1955). Ahluwalia (1976b)

---

p. 313) states — 'the inclusion of socialist countries in this sample adds substantially to the intercountry variance in income shares' (without affecting *SEE* significantly). Second, Saith implies that because the $\bar{R}^2$ is low ('less than a fifth of the total variation is explained'), inclusion of other variables might render the GNP variables insignificant. While the latter is always a possibility, this has nothing to do with a particular low value of $\bar{R}^2$.

[3] Confirmation of the U-shape actually requires testing the significance of *combinations* of coefficients rather than the signs of individual coefficients.

[4] We have discovered that Ahluwalia's (1976b) estimates in his Table 1(B) for developing countries *exclude* Spain which is, however, classified as a developing country in his Table 8. We have not been able to ascertain the reason for this, but it does not affect the estimates greatly. In order to facilitate comparison with Ahluwalia's estimates, we too exclude Spain from our 'developing countries only' sample.

Further, since the six socialist countries are classed as 'developed' in Ahluwalia's data set, the socialist dummy does not make an appearance in this equation.

Table 5.1

Estimates of the Inequality–Development Relationship for Alternative Functional Forms

Equation number[a]	Independent variables[b]								Statistics				Turning point (1970 US dollars)	Sample size[c]
	Constant	log₁₀ Y	[log₁₀ Y]²	Y	Y²	1/Y	[1/Y]²	D	$\bar{R}^2$	F	SEE	DW		
(1.1A)	70.56 (5.38)	−44.38 (−4.61)	8.31 (4.82)					11.95 (8.44)	0.594	29.78	3.17	2.05	468.0	60
(1.1B)	106.80 (3.83)	−74.68 (−3.25)	14.53 (3.10)						0.242	7.24	3.18	2.18	371.1	40
(1.2A)	12.24 (16.07)			0.98×10^{-3} (0.82)	0.10×10^{-6} (0.34)			10.87 (7.04)	0.496	20.34	3.53	1.63	−5,444.4	60
(1.2B)	16.43 (11.37)			-20.42×10^{-3} (−3.10)	17.34×10^{-6} (2.98)				0.163	4.79	3.35	2.04	589.1	40
(1.3A)	−16.52 (−3.05)	9.41 (5.51)				1,307.17 (5.09)		11.49 (8.38)	0.607	31.39	3.12	2.10	319.9	60
(1.3B)	−17.33 (−1.27)	9.66 (2.03)				1,341.11 (2.93)			0.225	6.67	3.22	2.13	319.7	40
(1.4A)	23.28 (5.00)	−4.79 (−2.42)		3.16×10^{-7} (3.79)				11.84 (7.83)	0.543	24.34	3.36	1.82	658.3	60
(1.4B)	45.35 (5.15)	−15.72 (−3.68)		15.60×10^{-3} (3.09)					0.241	7.19	3.19	2.19	437.6	40

Equation number[a]	Independent variables[b]								Statistics				Turning point (1970 US dollars)	Sample size[c]
	Constant	$\log_{10} Y$	$[\log_{10} Y]^2$	Y	Y^2	$1/Y$	$[1/Y]^2$	D	$\bar{R}^2$	F	SEE	DW		
(1.5A)	15.66 (17.40)					−1,745.26 (−3.73)	162.83×10^3 (4.07)	10.52 (7.04)	0.532	23.38	3.40	1.76	182.2	60
(1.5B)	12.20 (7.69)					−437.72 (−0.65)	71.92×10^3 (1.38)		0.181	5.31	3.31	2.01	318.2	40
(1.6A)	9.27 (9.32)			2.29×10^{-3} (5.04)		557.76 (3.45)		11.97 (8.40)	0.583	28.51	3.21	1.99	493.5	60
(1.6B)	6.20 (3.00)			6.41×10^{-3} (2.22)		862.92 (3.68)			0.240	7.16	3.19	2.17	366.9	40

a   The dependent variable in the equation is I, the percentage income share of the lowest 40 per cent.

b   t-ratios are shown in parentheses below the coefficient estimates.

c   A sample size of sixty refers to the full sample of developing and developed countries, while a sample size of forty refers to the restricted sample of developing countries only.

appeals to this model in specifying his inequality–development relationship. But we show in Anand and Kanbur (1993) that the Kuznets process does *not* in general lead to a quadratic relationship between the share of the lowest 40 per cent (or indeed any of the common inequality indices) and the logarithm of per capita GNP. In the absence of a strong theoretical justification for the log-quadratic form,[5] it would seem prudent to estimate alternative functional forms which could generate a U-shape (see Anand and Kanbur 1984, pp. 157–60).

Table 5.1 presents estimates for five other functional forms capable of generating a U-shape.[6] The 'A' equations are estimated using Ahluwalia's (1976b) full sample of sixty developing and developed countries, while the 'B' equations are estimated for the restricted sample of forty developing countries. The socialist dummy turns out to be highly significant in each of the 'A' equations; but the similarity between the estimates of alternative functional forms ends there. Equation (1.2A), which represents a quadratic relationship between the share of the lowest 40 per cent and per capita GNP, shows equality continually increasing, or inequality continually *decreasing*, with development (see Figure 5.1 which is a plot of equation [1.2A] with D set at 0). This functional form, therefore, does not confirm the hypothesized U-relationship.

Equations (1.3A), (1.4A), (1.5A) and (1.6A) confirm the hypothesized U-relationship, and the income coefficients are all significant at the 95 per cent level of confidence. However, they imply markedly different turning points — from US $182.2 (equation [1.5A]) to US $658.3 (equation [1.4A]). Thus, depending on the functional form that is estimated, the prediction of the time path of inequality could be distinctly different. For example consider the case of India. In 1964, India had a per capita GNP of US $110.3 at 1970 prices (Ahluwalia 1976b, Table 8). Assuming a growth rate of 2 per cent per annum in per capita GNP, the point of maximum inequality on the basis of

[5] Ahluwalia (1976b, p. 309, n. 5) does attempt to justify the use of the logarithmic transform applied to per capita GNP: 'The logarithmic transformation gives equal weight to equal proportional differences in GNP in measuring "levels of development". This has an intuitive appeal since growth occurs at a compound rate over time.' But we are unclear how this statement helps to justify the logarithmic form for the relationship in question.

[6] The genesis of these functional forms is discussed in Anand and Kanbur (1993), where they are derived as the specifications that are appropriate for alternative indices of inequality under the Kuznets process. Their role in this paper is simply to provide empirical alternatives to Ahluwalia's log-quadratic form.

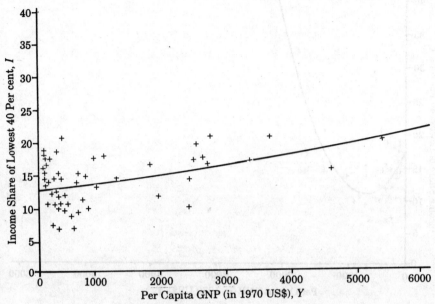

Figure 5.1:   Plot of Equation (1.2A) with D set at 0
(country observations corresponding to $D = 1$ suppressed).

Note: + denotes country observation.

equation (1.5A) would be reached in 1990, whereas on the basis of equation (1.4A) it would be reached in 2054! The more general point is that the estimated 'A' equations could generate strikingly different projections of inequality — a point which will be taken up in the fourth section.

The 'B' equations all confirm the U-shape. Notice once again, however, the great differences in shape and position of the estimated relationships, both among themselves and when compared to their corresponding 'A' equations (see Figures 5.1 and 5.2 which are, respectively, plots of equation [1.2A] with D set at 0, and equation [1.2B]). An immediate feature of Figure 5.2 is that the curve goes outside the permissible range of [0, 40] for the dependent variable in the per capita GNP range shown (this is also true of equation [1.4B] for which a plot has not been included here). The econometric implications of this limited dependent variable problem are taken up in a later subsection.

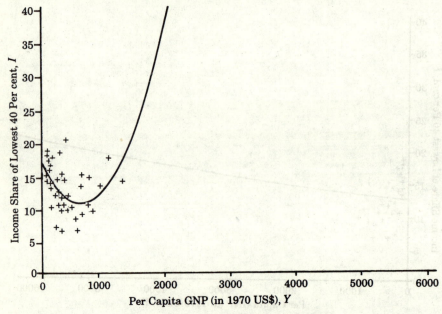

Figure 5.2: Plot of Equation (1.2B)

Note: + denotes country observation.

Testing Between Alternative Functional Forms

A major conclusion of our earlier discussion is the *sensitivity* of the relationship to the functional form estimated. Some forms support the U-shape while others do not (viz. equation [1.2A]). Even when two different functional forms both confirm the U-shape, the estimated relationships differ considerably — for example in their turning points. How, then, are we to select between these competing functional forms? In the absence of a strong prior theoretical model, we are forced to rely on an empirical criterion.

We discuss the 'A' equation estimates only. Taking the conventional goodness-of-fit criteria such as $\bar{R}^2$ or F, there is little to choose between the six forms; all of the $\bar{R}^2$s are around 0.5 and the F values are around 25. The Durbin–Watson statistic values do not pick up any misspecification in the equations.[7] According to the $\bar{R}^2$ and F criteria

---

[7] The Durbin–Watson statistic can be used in this context because the observations have been entered in the regressions in ascending order of per capita GNP.

(1.3A) dominates the Ahluwalia form (1.1A). The central equation of the inequality–development literature is thus beaten by an alternative functional form which, for example, generates a very different turning point.

Recent years have seen growing criticism of the use of such goodness-of-fit criteria for comparing alternative models. In particular, Pesaran (1974) and Pesaran and Deaton (1978) have argued that conventional criteria such as $\bar{R}^2$ have little statistical basis, especially when — as in our case — the models being compared are *non-nested*. To quote Pesaran and Deaton (1978, p. 678):

We are faced with a body of data and a set of alternative hypotheses. Since the latter are non-nested by assumption, we cannot rank them by level of generality as can be done when the models are nested. There is thus no maintained hypothesis; each model is on an equal footing with every other model. To follow Cox's procedure we take the alternatives one at a time, assuming each one in turn to be true and inferring from the behaviour of the alternatives against the data whether or not our temporarily maintained or working hypothesis can or cannot explain what we then observe. We thus make pairwise tests of each pair of hypotheses and we ask the question, is the performance of H_j against the data consistent with the truth of H_i?

Pesaran (1974) applies the general results of Cox (1961, 1962) to the problem of choosing between non-nested linear models, and derives a test statistic N_0 which is a standard normal variate under the maintained hypothesis H_0.[8] A test of H_0 against H_1 can then be conducted at the desired level of significance. The whole procedure

---

[8] For the purposes of this chapter a brief account of the test procedure will suffice. Suppose the log-likelihood functions of the two non-nested hypotheses H_0 and H_1 are $L_0 (\alpha_0)$ and $L_1 (\alpha_1)$, respectively, where α_0 and α_1 are the parameter vectors. Let the logarithm of the maximum-likelihood ratio be $\hat{L}_{10} = L_0 (\hat{\alpha}_0) - L_1 (\hat{\alpha}_1)$, where $\hat{\alpha}_0$ and $\hat{\alpha}_1$ are the maximum-likelihood estimators of α_0 and α_1 for the models H_0 and H_1, respectively. Then Cox's statistic T_0 for testing H_0 against the alternative H_1 is

$$T_0 = \hat{L}_{10} - n \left[\Plim_{n \to \infty} (\hat{L}_{10}/n) \right]_{\alpha_0 = \hat{\alpha}_0}$$

where the probability limit is taken assuming H_0 is true. Cox shows that under general conditions, when H_0 is true, T_0 will be asymptotically normally distributed with mean zero and variance $V_0 (T_0)$ — for which an explicit expression is provided. Then the standardized statistic $N_0 = T_0/[V_0 (T_0)]^{1/2}$ can be used to test H_0 against H_1 at the chosen level of significance. The test statistic N_0 can be calculated from a series of linear regressions involving the two models (see Pesaran 1974 and Dastoor 1978).

is repeated, with H_1 in turn becoming the maintained hypothesis. Hence, there is the possibility that both alternatives are rejected, or that neither is rejected. It is only when a hypothesis is *both* not rejected when it is the maintained hypothesis *and* succeeds in rejecting the other hypothesis when that is the maintained hypothesis, that it can be said to *dominate*. Such domination is only relative to the *pair* of hypotheses under consideration: no implication can be drawn relative to other alternatives.[9]

Table 5.2 provides a full account of these tests for our six functional forms. Comparing Ahluwalia's form (1.1A) with (1.2A), we see that (1.1A) cannot be rejected by (1.2A), the value of the test statistic N_0 being below the critical value of 1.96 at the 5 per cent level of significance. However, when (1.2A) is the maintained hypothesis, it is rejected by (1.1A). Thus Ahluwalia's form (1.1A) can be said to dominate (1.2A). However, what of the other functional forms? As can be seen from the next four comparisons in Table 5.2, the Ahluwalia form is not rejected by (1.3A)–(1.6A). But while the Ahluwalia form rejects (1.4A) and (1.5A), it cannot reject (1.3A) and (1.6A). In other words, the data *cannot* discriminate between the Ahluwalia form and at least two other forms, a fact which should caution against sole reliance on equation (1.1A) for projections.[10]

---

[9] The Pesaran and Deaton (1978) approach to hypothesis testing stems from their general view of empirical methodology that

hypotheses are responsible for organizing data in order to yield meaningful information and that, without such organization, observations are meaningless. . . . We thus consider that not only are procedures such as the Cox test necessary to make comparisons between hypotheses, but that the ability to make meaningful inferences about the truth of any single hypothesis demands the presence of at least one non-nested alternative. In econometrics, we never have a maintained hypothesis which we believe with certainty; we must always use the models we possess to organize the evidence in different ways and to ask whether the patterns which result are consistent with the views we currently hold. . . .

An hypothesis, which one would not wish to consider seriously in its own right, can be a perfectly effective tool for disproving an alternative, even if that alternative may in some respects seem much more promising. It is thus important that tests between non-nested hypotheses or models should encompass the possibility of rejecting both, as does the Cox procedure. This is notably not the case for tests which compare relative fits, for example comparisons of R^2 statistics or likelihoods [Pesaran and Deaton 1978, pp. 678–9.]

[10] The results for the 'B' equations are not shown here, but the conclusions are similar. The Ahluwalia (1976b) functional form does not emerge a clear winner when compared with many of these forms. The data would seem to leave us indifferent between his functional form and several others.

Table 5.2
Tests of Alternative Non-nested Functional Forms

Maintained hypothesis	*Alternative hypothesis*	N_0-*statistic value*
(1.1A)	(1.2A)	0.932
(1.2A)	(1.1A)	−14.629
(1.1A)	(1.3A)	−1.510
(1.3A)	(1.1A)	−0.161
(1.1A)	(1.4A)	1.248
(1.4A)	(1.1A)	−3.569
(1.1A)	(1.5A)	−1.203
(1.5A)	(1.1A)	−4.676
(1.1A)	(1.6A)	0.898
(1.6A)	(1.1A)	−1.633
(1.2A)	(1.3A)	−15.265
(1.3A)	(1.2A)	−0.038
(1.2A)	(1.4A)	−16.950
(1.4A)	(1.2A)	1.374
(1.2A)	(1.5A)	−4.584
(1.5A)	(1.2A)	−5.237
(1.2A)	(1.6A)	−36.786
(1.6A)	(1.2A)	1.008
(1.3A)	(1.4A)	−0.055
(1.4A)	(1.3A)	−4.193
(1.3A)	(1.5A)	0.479
(1.5A)	(1.3A)	−4.357
(1.3A)	(1.6A)	−0.054
(1.6A)	(1.3A)	−2.094
(1.4A)	(1.5A)	−3.850
(1.5A)	(1.4A)	−4.588
(1.4A)	(1.6A)	−3.771
(1.6A)	(1.4A)	1.614
(1.5A)	(1.6A)	−4.417
(1.6A)	(1.5A)	−1.548

An Econometric Problem

It is apparent from Figure 5.2 that the predicted value of *I* can lie outside the range of 0 to 40 per cent. There is also an inconsistency between the error term in the regression equation being a normally distributed

Table 5.3
Logistic Estimates of the Inequality–Development Relationship

Equation number[a]	Constant	Independent variables[b]							Statistics				Turning point (1970 US dollars)	Sample size[c]
		$\log_{10} Y$	$[\log_{10} Y]^2$	Y	Y^2	$1/Y$	$[1/Y]^2$	D	$\bar{R}^2$	F	SEE	DW		
(2.1A)	2.59 (3.80)	−2.25 (−4.49)	0.42 (4.69)					0.56 (7.62)	0.551	25.11	0.16	2.02	477.1	60
(2.1B)	4.67 (3.13)	−3.99 (−3.25)	0.78 (3.11)						0.235	7.00	0.17	2.17	361.2	40
(2.2A)	−0.37 (−9.42)			0.53×10^{-4} (0.85)	0.38×10^{-8} (0.26)			0.50 (6.30)	0.445	16.76	0.18	1.62	−6973.7	60
(2.2B)	−0.15 (−2.00)			-10.70×10^{-4} (−3.03)	91.73×10^{-8} (2.95)				0.156	4.61	0.18	2.03	583.2	40
(2.3A)	−1.83 (−6.53)	0.48 (5.41)				66.81 (5.02)		0.54 (7.57)	0.568	26.86	0.16	2.09	320.5	60
(2.3B)	−1.98 (−2.70)	0.53 (2.06)				71.64 (2.93)			0.217	6.39	0.17	2.12	311.2	40
(2.4A)	0.18 (0.75)	−0.24 (−2.33)		1.58×10^{-4} (3.63)				0.55 (7.04)	0.493	20.15	0.18	1.79	659.7	60
(2.4B)	1.38 (2.93)	−0.83 (−3.65)		8.37×10^{-4} (3.10)					0.234	6.97	0.17	2.18	430.7	40

Equation number[a]	Constant	Independent variables[b]							Statistics				Turning point (1970 US dollars)	Sample size[c]
		$\log_{10} Y$	$[\log_{10} Y]^2$	Y	Y^2	$1/Y$	$[1/Y]^2$	D	$\bar{R}^2$	F	SEE	DW		
(2.5A)	−0.20 (−4.28)					−88.97 (−3.69)	8336.35 (4.04)	0.49 (6.35)	0.491	19.99	0.18	1.77	186.5	60
(2.5B)	−0.37 (−4.36)					−24.26 (−0.67)	3842.06 (1.37)		0.169	4.97	0.18	2.00	316.7	40
(2.6A)	−0.52 (−10.10)			1.15×10^{-4} (4.88)		28.48 (3.38)		0.56 (7.58)	0.539	23.95	0.17	1.97	497.7	60
(2.6B)	−0.70 (−6.29)			3.50×10^{-4} (2.26)		45.66 (3.63)			0.232	6.90	0.17	2.17	361.2	40

a The dependent variable is I^*, the logistic transform of I, given by $I^* = \log_{10}[I/(40 - I)]$ where I is the percentage income share of the lowest 40 per cent.

b t-ratios are shown in parentheses below the coefficient estimates.

c A sample size of sixty refers to the full sample of developing and developed countries, while a sample size of forty refers to the subsample of developing countries only.

variate taking values in the range $-\infty$ to $+\infty$, and the dependent variable I being restricted to the range 0 to 40 (per cent). This is, of course, a common econometric problem which occurs when the dependent variable is limited.

The standard way around these problems is to transform the dependent variable of the regression in such a way that the original variable I can take values between 0 and 40 only. There are many such transforms available, but one which is commonly used is the *logistic* function. In this case the appropriate estimating form for Ahluwalia's basic equation becomes:

$$I^* = \log_{10} [I/(40-I)] = a_0 + a_1 [\log_{10} Y] + a_2 [\log_{10} Y]^2 + a_3 D + \varepsilon.$$

Here, for a given value of $[\log_{10} Y]$, as $\varepsilon \to -\infty$ $I \to 0$, and as $\varepsilon \to +\infty$ $I \to 40$. Moreover, since I^* is a monotonic increasing function of I, the turning point of I as a function of Y is the same as the turning point of I^* as a function of Y. Estimates of the logistic form corresponding to equations (1.1)–(1.6) are presented in Table 5.3 as equations (2.1)–(2.6). The logistic and non-logistic curves corresponding to both equation (1.2B) and equation (1.4B) turn out to be very different beyond a per capita GNP level of $1500 (figures not shown here).

PROJECTIONS OF INEQUALITY IN THE YEAR 2000: A SENSITIVITY ANALYSIS

In its *World Development Reports* 1978, 1979 and 1980, the World Bank used the inequality–development relationship to project inequality and poverty to the year 2000. These projections were based on the methodology developed by Ahluwalia, Carter and Chenery (1979) (henceforth ACC), which relied directly on Ahluwalia's (1976b) estimation of the relationship. We have elsewhere commented in detail on the ACC projections methodology (see Anand and Kanbur 1991). Our object here is to investigate the sensitivity of the projections to alternative estimates of the inequality–development relationship.

ACC present projections of the income share of the lowest 40 per cent in the year 2000 for their 'Base Case' scenario of growth assumptions (ACC, Table 2, pp. 312–13). Our Table 5.4 presents projections for a selection of alternative functional form estimates. This selection is meant to be illustrative rather than comprehensive.

Consider first of all projections based on Ahluwalia's functional

Table 5.4

Projections of the Income Share of the
Lowest 40 Per Cent in the Year 2000 for Selected Equations

		(1.1A)	(1.3A)	(1.1B)	(1.2B)	(2.2A)	(2.2B)
1	Bangladesh	17.2	14.8	16.0	18.8	19.7	18.7
2	Ethiopia	14.4	14.2	14.5	14.3	12.1	14.1
3	Burma	15.2	15.7	15.8	14.6	12.1	14.5
4	Indonesia	13.2	11.0	11.5	15.1	17.5	14.8
5	Uganda	14.0	13.6	14.0	14.1	12.1	14.0
6	Zaire	12.8	12.1	12.4	13.4	12.1	13.2
7	Sudan	12.0	11.3	11.4	12.5	12.2	12.3
8.	Tanzania	12.3	11.5	11.7	12.8	12.2	12.6
9	Pakistan	14.2	12.8	12.9	15.6	17.7	15.3
10	India	14.1	12.4	12.8	15.6	17.3	15.3
11	Kenya	7.4	7.5	6.8	7.4	9.6	7.8
12	Nigeria	11.6	11.2	11.0	11.8	12.3	11.6
13	Philippines	10.3	11.4	10.7	8.8	12.4	9.1
14	Sri Lanka	18.1	18.5	17.9	17.7	19.5	17.5
15	Senegal	8.9	9.3	9.0	8.5	9.5	8.7
16	Egypt	13.1	14.4	14.0	11.6	14.7	11.5
17	Thailand	11.0	12.0	11.4	9.7	13.8	9.9
18	Ghana	12.3	11.6	11.7	12.9	12.2	12.7
19	Morocco	11.4	11.8	11.5	10.4	12.6	10.3
20	Ivory Coast	10.3	11.3	11.1	8.9	11.0	9.1
21	Korea	20.3	21.7	22.8	32.1	20.5	32.9
22	Chile	14.2	15.2	16.5	17.6	13.9	18.4
23	Zambia	12.9	13.4	13.3	11.9	13.2	11.9
24	Colombia	11.6	12.9	14.6	18.6	11.2	19.8
25	Turkey	10.0	11.3	12.1	11.3	10.1	11.3
26	Tunisia	13.7	14.7	7.2	28.9	12.9	31.0
27	Malaysia	13.3	14.3	16.7	25.7	12.5	28.0
28	Taiwan	24.3	25.2	27.5	35.3	23.7	34.5
29	Guatemala	12.5	13.3	14.1	14.9	13.2	15.0
30	Brazil	12.0	12.8	16.0	33.8	10.6	34.4
31	Peru	8.8	9.6	11.3	14.5	8.0	14.1
32	Iran	13.0	13.7	16.9	35.2	11.7	35.3
33	Mexico	13.1	13.3	16.6	38.9	11.6	36.8
34	Yugoslavia	23.8	23.3	30.0	123.9	22.1	40.0
35	Argentina	18.5	18.1	23.2	81.9	17.0	40.0
36	Venezuela	14.8	13.7	19.5	128.3	12.9	40.0

form (1.1A) and the alternative functional form (1.3A).[11] The important feature of these two equations, as shown in the section on testing alternative functional forms, is that neither dominates the other in the sense of the hypothesis-testing procedure of Cox (1961, 1962) and Pesaran (1974). In other words, Ahluwalia's (1976b) data *cannot discriminate* between his log-quadratic form and an alternative form which has as independent variables $[\log_{10} Y]$ and $[1/Y]$. It is seen at a glance from Table 5.4 that the projections corresponding to these forms are widely different. For example in the case of Bangladesh the difference between the (1.1A) and (1.3A) projections is 15 per cent of their average value. For Indonesia, the relative discrepancy is even higher at 18.2 per cent. Even these comparisons may understate the discrepancy; for instance the range of the discrepancies relative to the average range (across countries) of the two sets of projections is 24.2 per cent. Thus, although for some countries the discrepancy between the (1.1A) and (1.3A) projections is small, the general impression is one of non-robustness of the ACC projections based on Ahluwalia's (1976b) estimates.

Up to now, like ACC, we have used the full sample estimates for projection. However, estimates using the subsample of forty developing countries are also available; yet ACC did not use them for projections of income share for their thirty-six developing countries. In any case, we would wish to investigate the sensitivity of the ACC projections to a change in the data set which leaves out the developed countries.[12] Comparing the (1.1A) and (1.1B) projections of income share for the year 2000 (see Table 5.4), the discrepancy is seen to be particularly

[11] It will be noticed that our projections (1.1A) in Table 5.4 are not exact replications of the ACC projections in their Table 2. The reason for these differences possibly arises from our inability to implement the ACC procedure exactly; their documentation (especially for projecting per capita GNP) is incomplete or ambiguous in places (see Anand and Kanbur 1991, Appendix B). Our implementation of the ACC procedure for projecting inequality (and poverty) in the year 2000 is described in Anand and Kanbur (1991).

[12] Saith (1983, p. 376) objects to the use of the pooled sample of developing and developed countries on the grounds that 'the context in which the LDCs have to struggle towards development is fundamentally different from that in which the DCs developed in the past . . . it cannot be assumed that the LDC group could, or will, tread the same path as the DCs'. Short of an explicit theory of these differences, and of their implications for cross-sectional estimation, it is not clear that the appropriate statistical procedure is simply to drop the DCs (developed countries) from the sample. Saith then proceeds to compare the $\bar{R}^2$s, invalidly, for the full sample and LDC sample estimates (see n. 2 above).

large for fast-growing countries such as Brazil and Venezuela.[13] Overall, the range of the discrepancies is 7.9 (from 1.7 for Indonesia to –6.2 for Yugoslavia). This compares with a range of 15.5 for the (1.1A) projections (from 24.3 for Taiwan to 8.8 for Peru) and a range of 23.2 for the (1.1B) projections (from 30.0 for Yugoslavia to 6.8 for Kenya). Thus the range of the discrepancies in projection is no less than 40.7 per cent of the average range of the two sets of projections.

Before leaving the 'B' equations notice that the projections of income share for the lowest 40 per cent in Yugoslavia, Argentina and Venezuela using equation (1.2B) are larger than 40 per cent. In other cases the projections are implausibly high: equation (1.2B) projects a share for the lowest 40 per cent in Brazil of 33.8 per cent, and in Mexico of 38.9 per cent. This is a consequence of the fact that although the dependent variable must lie between 0 and 40, the functional forms estimated allow projections of the dependent variable to go outside this range. This was noted in the section on an econometric problem, where the equations were re-estimated using a logistic transform for the dependent variable (Table 5.3). The projections based on two such equations are shown in Table 5.4. The use of the logistic transform is seen to make a considerable difference to the projections. For example the range of discrepancies for the (1.2B) and (2.2B) projections is 118.4 per cent of the average range of projections.

To conclude, the ACC projections of inequality in the year 2000 are found to be highly sensitive to variations in the functional form and sample size used to estimate the inequality–development relationship.[14]

THE DATA BASE OF THE INEQUALITY–DEVELOPMENT RELATIONSHIP: A SENSITIVITY ANALYSIS

The Ahluwalia (1976b) Data Set and Alternatives
Up to now we have used the Ahluwalia (1976b) data set in our estimation exercises. However, an empirical literature is only as good as its data

---

[13] This is seen from the plots of the two relationships, which are not included here. For low and middle income levels the (1.1A) relationship is above the (1.1B) relationship; hence for slow-growing countries like India and Pakistan equation (1.1A) predicts a higher share of the lowest 40 per cent than does equation (1.1B). However, for higher income levels the position of the two relationships is reversed, so that for fast-growing countries the projection of the share of the lowest 40 per cent for the year 2000 is much higher with the (1.1B) equation than with the (1.1A) equation.

[14] A detailed analysis and critique of the ACC poverty projections for the year 2000 may be found in Anand and Kanbur (1991).

base, and the literature on the estimation of the inequality–development relationship is no exception. Income distribution data, particularly in developing countries, are often unreliable and yet we find little analysis of the *sensitivity* of the estimates to use of alternative data. Moreover, a cross-section data set presents severe problems of comparability. A thorough review of the data problems is beyond the scope of this chapter (for more on international and intertemporal data comparability see, respectively, Anand and Kanbur 1991 and Anand 1983). Our object, rather, is to sound a note of caution by demonstrating the sensitivity of Ahluwalia's (1976b) estimates to changes in his data set.

Ahluwalia's (1976b) data set is presented and discussed in the appendix to his paper (Table 8, and pp. 338–42). Per capita GNP figures in US dollars at 1970 prices are shown in his Table 8 for the sixty countries considered, but ˙he source for these figures is not cited. Income distribution data are presented as quintile shares for each of the sixty countries. The data are taken from sources cited in the income distribution compilation by Jain (1975).[15] Ahluwalia (1976b, p. 339) notes that 'the source for each observation is given by the number of parentheses which corresponds to the source number reported in Jain (1975)'. However, for ten of the sixty countries, Ahluwalia's references in his Table 8 do not uniquely identify the source in Jain (1975).[16]

The quintile shares shown in Ahluwalia's Table 8 differ from those given in Jain (1975) for the same country sources (where these can, in fact, be uniquely identified). Jain's estimates of income share were obtained by fitting a Lorenz curve to the survey data in cumulative form and then reading off the decile shares from the estimated Lorenz curve. The functional form fitted was one due to Kakwani and Podder (1976) and is described in Jain (1975, p. xiii). Ahluwalia's estimates of quintile share, however, were read off from a Lorenz curve drawn *free-hand* through the observed points of the survey data. His defence of this method is as follows:

The main reason for preferring this method is that the [Kakwani–Podder] fitted curve does not necessarily pass through the observed points and since these

[15] See Ahluwalia (1976b, p. 338–9): 'The sample of 60 countries was selected from a recent compilation of available cross-country data undertaken in the World Bank's Development Research Center and reported in Jain (1975).'

[16] These countries are: India, Honduras, Malaysia, Brazil, Peru, Costa Rica, Uruguay, Spain, Argentina and Yugoslavia. Note also that for one country, Taiwan, although there are sources available in Jain (1975), Ahluwalia uses Kuo (1975) without any specific justification.

points correspond to deciles or quintiles in many cases, it is arguably more appropriate to use the exact figures [Ahluwalia 1976b, p. 339].

Our review of the data sources shows that the 'observed points' do not in general correspond to deciles or quintiles. (The survey authorities could not, of course, have chosen the 'observed points' on this basis as that would have required knowledge of the income distribution in advance of the survey.) Moreover, Kakwani and Podder's methodology is based on the hypothesis that there is a sampling error between the 'true' population frequencies in an income interval and the recorded frequencies. If one accepts their approach, there would seem to be no justification for forcing the Lorenz curve to pass through the observed points.

The main problem, however, with Ahluwalia's free-hand method of fitting the Lorenz curve is that his estimates of quintile share are *not replicable* by independent researchers. For this reason we prefer to use the Jain (1975) data on income shares as our 'base data' for regression analysis — even though we have some reservations about the Kakwani and Podder approach which is used to estimate the Jain decile shares.

From a potential total of eighty-one countries for which income distribution data are reported in Jain (1975), Ahluwalia chooses a sample of sixty countries. This choice was ' . . . dictated by particular judgements about the reliability of data in some cases' (Ahluwalia 1976b, p. 339). Unfortunately, the nature of these judgments is not made explicit. In cases where there are multiple observations available for countries, his data set is restricted to one distribution per country, again without justification for the particular choice of observation.[17]

A major problem for this cross-country analysis is that the income distribution data for these sixty countries are *not comparable* with respect to income concept, population unit and survey coverage. For some countries the income shares in Ahluwalia's Table 8 refer to the distribution of *individuals* (economically active population, income recipients, male employees, etc.), and for other countries they refer to the distribution of *households* by household income/consumption or by

[17] Ahluwalia (1976b, p. 339) justifies the use of just one observation per country 'on the grounds that adding more than one observation for some countries would give too much weight to particular country experience'. But if the cross-section estimation is supposed to capture the time-series relationship (as evidenced by its use for projections to the year 2000), then excluding multiple observations over time for a country is *inefficient* because information is lost.

per capita household income/consumption.[18] For some countries the incomes are gross-of-tax and for others net-of-tax; for some they refer to cash incomes and for others certain items of income-in-kind are included. For some countries the survey coverage is national, for others it is restricted to particular geographical regions of the country (for example urban areas only). The variation in the income share of the lowest 40 per cent in a country can be considerable depending on the distribution chosen. For example in the case of Malaysia, the income share of the lowest 40 per cent varies from 9.6 per cent to 17.7 per cent for different distributions from the *same* 1970 Post Enumeration Survey (Jain 1975; see also Anand 1983). Some standardization of distributions across countries is clearly required. Thus for each country, we might choose the *national* distribution of *households* by *household income*.

Given that Ahluwalia's (1976b) data set is an idiosyncratic selection of non-comparable distributions, we feel that at the very least there is a case for testing the robustness of his estimates with respect to alternative data sets of comparable or superior quality. From the Ahluwalia list of countries, we have constructed a data set 'C' which is comparable in terms of survey coverage (national), population unit (household) and income concept (household income).[19] Of the sixty countries in Ahluwalia (1976b), *no* Household–National (HH–NL) source is presented in Jain (1975) for twenty-six countries; these countries have therefore been dropped. For the remaining thirty-four countries, the income share figures for HH–NL distributions from Jain (1975) are presented in Table 5.5.[20] The table also presents per capita

---

[18] Ahluwalia (1976b, p. 339) claims that 'wherever available, household distributions have been used, but in many cases we have had to use the distribution of individuals'. However, in cases such as India and New Zealand, for which household distributions are available in Jain (1975), Ahluwalia chooses the distribution of individuals.

[19] Saith (1983, p. 379) re-estimates Ahluwalia's regression by using 'alternative data for half a dozen countries' including 'income-shares and GNP per capita data for Pakistan for the year 1970–1971 relating to the population rather than for 1963–1964 for households as in Ahluwalia's equation'. He concludes from his equation (V)(b) in Table 3 that 'the $\bar{R}^2$ is reduced to 0.10 and the significance of the estimated coefficients is also cut' (Saith 1983, p. 379). Quite apart from the questionable use of $\bar{R}^2$ as the criterion for choice (see n. 2 above), we are not told in what way the alternative data set is superior to that of Ahluwalia: Saith's alternative data set is also composed of non-comparable distributions!

[20] Our review of the data (Anand and Kanbur 1991) has revealed that Jain's classification of sources may not be true to the original. Thus, for example, the source for Korea (68) HH–NL in Jain (1975, p. 65) is shown as 'Korea Statistical Yearbook,

GNP figures, in US dollars at 1970 prices, for the years to which these income distribution data refer.[21]

Table 5.5
A Minimally Consistent Data Set

Country	Year of survey	Per capita GNP in year of survey, US $ at 1970 prices	Percentage income share of the lowest 40 per cent
Malawi	1969	80.0	15.0
Pakistan –a	1963–4	93.7	17.5
–b	1966–7	104.7	19.2
–c	1968–9	112.6	20.3
–d	1969–70	116.8	20.2
–e	1970–1	118.6	20.6
Tanzania–a	1967	103.8	13.5
–b	1969	110.3	7.8
Sri Lanka–a	1953	83.5	14.6
–b	1963	91.2	13.7
–c	1969–70	108.6	17.9
–d	1969–70	108.6	17.8
–e	1973	111.3	19.3

Table 5.5 (cont.)

1970'. An examination of this source book reveals that the coverage of the survey is restricted to cities in Korea — it is *not* a national survey. This source is accordingly not used for Korea in our Table 5.6 regressions.

[21] Ahluwalia presents per capita GNP figures in US dollars at 1970 prices (Table 8, pp. 340–1) without specifying his sources. We assume these per capita GNP figures correspond to the years of the income distribution surveys, but there is no way to verify. Using these per capita GNP figures as the base, we have estimated per capita GNP for the years to which our own income distribution sources refer by using country-specific growth rates for the relevant periods. Estimates for growth rates during 1960–75 were obtained from the World Bank (1972) Atlas (for Japan, France, UK, New Zealand, West Germany, Canada, USA, Yugoslavia, East Germany and Costa Rica) or from ACC (for the remaining countries). In the latter case we have used separate GDP growth rates for the subperiods 1960–5, 1965–70 and 1970–5 as shown in ACC (Table A.2, p. 335), and average population growth rates for the entire period 1960–75 shown in ACC (Table 2, pp. 312–13). In some cases, we require growth rates for per capita GNP before 1960. For these countries we have used the following sources: Sri Lanka — Fields (1980); India — Streeten and Lipton (1968); Philippines — Philippines (1978); Taiwan — Fei, Ranis and Kuo (1979); Malaysia — Rao (1976); France — Denison (1967).

Table 5.5 (cont.)

Country		Year of survey	Per capita GNP in year of survey, US $ at 1970 prices	Percentage income share of the lowest 40 per cent
India	–a	1953–7	94.2	20.2
	–b	1960	102.9	13.6
	–c	1964–5	111.3	17.2
	–d	1967–8	120.1	13.1
Thailand		1962	142.8	13.2
Philippines	–a	1956	191.8	12.9
	–b	1961	207.2	12.7
	–c	1961	207.2	11.9
	–d	1961	207.2	12.0
	–e	1965	224.4	11.6
	–f	1965	224.4	11.7
	–g	1965	224.4	11.5
	–h	1971	261.8	11.9
Egypt		1964–5	232.8	14.1
Korea	–a	1966	190.5	23.2
	–b	1966	190.5	18.4
	–c	1968	226.5	21.4
	–d	1969	246.5	21.4
	–e	1970	269.2	17.7
	–f	1970	269.2	17.5
	–g	1971	289.9	18.7
	–h	1971	289.9	23.7
Honduras	–a	1967–8	301.0	7.3
	–b	1967–8	301.0	6.4
Zambia		1959	308.2	13.0
Turkey		1968	322.2	9.4
Taiwan	–a	1953	178.6	8.6
	–b	1959–60	216.4	14.9
	–c	1961	234.2	13.5
	–d	1964	283.9	20.3
	–e	1972	457.7	22.3
Malaysia	–a	1957–8	274.1	17.7
	–b	1957–8	274.1	15.7
	–c	1960	286.3	9.6
	–d	1967–8	372.3	10.4
	–e	1970	401.4	11.8
	–f	1970	401.4	11.2

Country		Year of survey	Per capita GNP in year of survey, US $ at 1970 prices	Percentage income share of the lowest 40 per cent
Brazil	–a	1970	456.5	9.2
	–b	1970	456.5	7.7
Jamaica		1958	515.6	8.2
Lebanon		1955–60	588.3	12.3
Costa Rica	–a	1961	450.4	13.0
	–b	1971	617.1	14.6
Mexico	–a	1963	564.7	10.4
	–b	1963	564.7	10.9
	–c	1963	564.7	9.9
	–d	1967–8	662.6	11.2
	–e	1968	673.8	9.8
	–f	1969	696.9	10.2
Uruguay		1967	720.8	14.2
Spain		1964–5	852.1	16.5
Chile		1968	903.5	13.0
Argentina		1961	1004.6	16.6
Puerto Rico		1963	1217.4	13.7
Japan	–a	1962	988.2	15.3
	–b	1962	988.2	16.9
	–c	1963	1083.1	20.4
	–d	1965	1301.0	16.8
	–e	1968	1712.8	16.0
	–f	1971	2255.0	14.8
	–g	1971	2255.0	22.3
France	–a	1956	1886.5	11.8
	–b	1962	2303.1	10.0
United Kingdom	–a	1960	2028.5	18.1
	–b	1968	2414.3	18.5
New Zealand		1966	2278.2	20.9
Australia		1967–8	2632.4	20.0
West Germany	–a	1968	2995.3	16.8
	–b	1969	3100.1	18.9
	–c	1970	3208.6	16.4
Canada	–a	1961	3046.6	19.7
	–b	1965	3509.6	19.0
United States	–a	1960	3827.1	15.9
	–b	1966	4623.3	15.4

Table 5.5 (cont.)

Table 5.5 (cont.)

Country		Year of survey	Per capita GNP in year of survey, US $ at 1970 prices	Percentage income share of the lowest 40 per cent
United States	–c	1970	5244.1	15.3
	–d	1971	5411.9	15.5
	–e	1972	5585.1	14.1
Yugoslavia	–a	1963	488.0	19.0
	–b	1968	602.3	18.4
East Germany	–a	1967	1808.7	26.8
	–b	1970	2046.3	26.3

Source: Jain (1975) for percentage income shares of the lowest 40 per cent.

Note: The method of estimation of per capita GNP in the year of survey, in US $ at 1970 prices, is described in n. 21 in the text.

Sensitivity Analysis

As Table 5.5 demonstrates, for the same country there can be considerable variation in the estimated share of the lowest 40 per cent for different years. If we follow Ahluwalia in choosing one observation per country, then given such a *minimally consistent* alternative data set, what is the sensitivity of the estimated inequality–development relationship to variations in functional form? Equations (1.1C) and (1.2C) in Table 5.6 provide the answer to this question for one particular data set.[22] The sample size of thirty-four in Table 5.6 refers to the full sample of developing and developed countries, including two socialist countries for which a dummy was introduced. Turning to the estimates, notice that the coefficients of (1.1C), with the exception of that on the dummy variable, are not significantly different from zero. Although the coefficient signs of (1.1C) imply a U-shaped

---

[22] This data set is as follows. For those countries in Table 5.5 for which a single observation is available, that observation is used. For those countries for which there is a choice, the following selections have been made: Pakistan — a; Tanzania — b; Sri Lanka — b; India — d; Philippines — a; Korea — h; Honduras — a; Taiwan — e; Malaysia — a; Brazil — a; Costa Rica — b; Mexico — d; Japan — c; France — b; UK — a; West Germany — c; Canada — b; United States — e; Yugoslavia — a; East Germany — b. Each observation on the share of the lowest 40 per cent was paired with the per capita GNP estimate for that year, and the observations were introduced into the regressions in ascending order or per capita GNP.

Table 5.6
Estimates of the Inequality–Development Relationship for a Minimally Consistent Data Set

Equation number[a]	Constant	Independent variables[b]				D	Statistics				Turning point (1970 US dollars)	Sample size
		$\log_{10} Y$	$[\log_{10} Y]^2$	Y	Y^2		$\bar{R}^2$	F	SEE	DW		
(1.1C)	21.23 (1.01)	-7.50 (-0.48)	1.80 (0.65)			7.53 (2.45)	0.181	3.43	4.17	2.36	122.7	34
(1.2C)	12.65 (10.92)			3.27×10^{-3} (2.02)	-0.53×10^{-6} (-1.55)	7.03 (2.33)	0.218	4.07	4.08	2.41	3108.0	34

a The dependent variable in the equation is I, the percentage income share of the lowest 40 per cent.

b t-ratios are shown in parentheses below the coefficient estimates.

relationship, its turning point is considerably different from that of Ahluwalia's equation (1.1A).

Consider now equation (1.2C), the estimate of the ordinary (non-log) quadratic form using our minimally consistent alternative data set 'C'. The coefficients indicate a *reversal* of the U-shape: see Figures 5.3 and 5.4, which are plots of equations (1.1C) and (1.2C), respectively with D set at 0. Moreover, the fit of equation (1.2C) is *better* than that of the log-quadratic form (1.1C). Table 5.7 sets out the non-nested hypotheses test between (1.1C) and (1.2C). As shown, the log-quadratic form is *rejected* at the 0.1 per cent level of significance when it is the maintained hypothesis, but does *not* reject the ordinary quadratic form when that is the maintained hypothesis.

Table 5.7
Test of the Non-nested Hypotheses (1.1C) and (1.2C)

Maintained hypothesis	Alternative hypothesis	N_0-statistic value
(1.1C)	(1.2C)	−6.869
(1.2C)	(1.1C)	0.376

We have already argued in an earlier section that different functional forms fitted to the same data set (Ahluwalia's) can lead to estimates of the inequality–development relationship which differ widely in shape and position. However, the results in this section call into question even the 'confirmation' of the famous U-shape. They provide an instance where the functional form *which is supported by the data* is precisely the one which indicates a *reversal* of the customary U-shape. This is particularly important since our alternative data set has the merit of being *minimally consistent*, in direct contrast to Ahluwalia's (1976b) data set. It is obvious that these results will have significant implications for any projection exercises of the ACC or World Bank type.

CONCLUSION

The object of this chapter has been to undertake a critical appraisal of the empirical literature on inequality and development, and particularly the influential examples of it due to Ahluwalia (1976b) and Ahluwalia, Carter and Chenery (1979). Their results are central to this literature, since they have served to confirm the Kuznets U-hypothesis and have

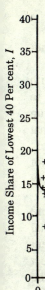
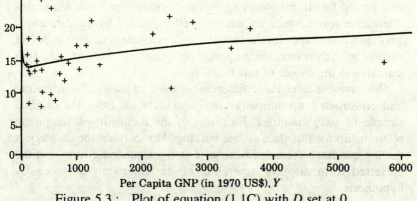

Figure 5.3.: Plot of equation (1.1C) with *D* set at 0
(country observations corresponding to *D* = 1 suppressed).

Note: + denotes country observation.

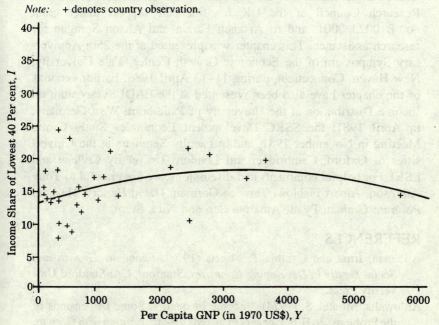

Figure 5.4: Plot of equation (1.2C) with *D* set at 0
(country observations corresponding to *D* = 1 suppressed).

Note: + denotes country observation.

been used as the basis of projections of inequality and poverty (including by the World Bank).

We have tested for the robustness of Ahluwalia's estimates with respect to variations in functional form and data set, and find them to be lacking. A rigorous statistical methodology is used for testing non-nested functional forms against one another, and it is found that alternative forms which are equally well supported by the data imply very different shapes for the inequality–development relationship. Not surprisingly, therefore, the inequality projections of ACC are also very sensitive to the choice of functional form.

We have indicated the deficiencies of the data used in this literature and constructed a minimally consistent data set from the original sample of sixty countries. Estimates of the inequality–development relationship for this data set are striking. Not only do the data reject the log-quadratic form in favour of a straight quadratic form, but the preferred form displays a *reversal* of the commonly accepted U-hypothesis.

Acknowledgements: We are grateful to the Economic and Social Research Council of the UK for financial support under grant no. B 0023 0001, and to Afsaneh Farzin and Alison Sprague for research assistance. This chapter was presented at the 25th Anniversary Symposium of the Economic Growth Center, Yale University, New Haven. Connecticut, during 11–13 April 1986. Earlier versions of the chapter have also been presented at the EADI Symposium on Income Distribution at the University of Paderborn, West Germany, in April 1981, the SSRC Development Economics Study Group Meeting in November 1981, and at Faculty Seminars at the Universities of Oxford, Cambridge, and London (University College and LSE). For helpful comments and discussions, we are grateful to Tony Atkinson, Albert Fishlow, Terence Gorman, David Hendry, Hashem Pesaran, Graham Pyatt, Amartya Sen and Nick Stern.

REFERENCES

Adelman, Irma and Cynthia T. Morris (1973). *Economic Growth and Social Equity in Developing Countries.* Stanford, CA: Stanford University Press.

Ahluwalia, Montek S. (1974). 'Income Inequality: Some Dimensions of the Problem', in H.B. Chenery et al. (eds), *Redistribution with Growth.* London: Oxford University Press.

Ahluwalia, Montek S. (1976a). 'Income Distribution and Development: Some Stylized Facts', *American Economic Review*, Papers and Proceedings, 66(2), pp. 128–35.

—— (1976b). 'Inequality, Poverty and Development', *Journal of Development Economics*, 3, pp. 307–42.

Ahluwalia, Montek S., Nicholas G. Carter and Hollis B. Chenery (1979). 'Growth and Poverty in Developing Countries', *Journal of Development Economics*, 6, pp. 299–341.

Anand, Sudhir (1983). *Inequality and Poverty in Malaysia: Measurement and Decomposition.* New York: Oxford University Press.

Anand, Sudhir and S.M.R. Kanbur (1984). 'Inequality and Development: A Reconsideration', in H.-P. Nissen (ed.), *Towards Income Distribution Policies.* EADI Book Series 3, Tilburg, Netherlands, pp. 131–67.

—— (1991). 'International Poverty Projections', Ld'A/QEH Working Paper No. 32, Oxford: Queen Elizabeth House, Feb.; and PRE Working Paper WPS 617 (Washington, DC: World Bank) March; forthcoming in M.O.L. Bacharach, M.A.H. Dempster and J.L. Enos (eds), *Mathematical Models in Economics.* Oxford: Clarendon Press.

—— (1993). 'The Kuznets Process and the Inequality–Development Relationship', *Journal of Development Economics*, 40(1), Feb., pp. 25–52.

Chenery, Hollis B. and Moises Syrquin (1975). *Patterns of Development, 1950–1970.* New York: Oxford University Press.

Chenery, Hollis B., et al. (1974). *Redistribution with Growth.* London: Oxford University Press.

Cox, D.R. (1961). 'Tests of Separate Families of Hypotheses', in *Proceedings of the Fourth Berkeley Symposium, Vol. I.* Berkeley, CA: University of California Press, pp. 105–23.

—— (1962). 'Further Results on Tests of Separate Families of Hypotheses', *Journal of the Royal Statistical Society*, Series B, 24(2), pp. 406–24.

Dastoor, N.K. (1978). 'Non-nested Hypothesis Testing', Discussion Paper No. 117, Department of Economics, University of Essex, Colchester, Aug.

Denison, Edward F. (1967). *Why Growth Rates Differ.* Washington, DC: The Brookings Institution.

Fei, John H., Gustav Ranis and Shirley W.Y. Kuo (1979). *Growth with Equity: The Taiwan Case.* New York: Oxford University Press.

Fields, Gary S. (1980). *Poverty, Inequality, and Development.* Cambridge: Cambridge University Press.

Jain, Shail (1975). *Size Distribution of Income: A Compilation of Data*. Baltimore, MD: Johns Hopkins University Press (for the World Bank).

Kakwani, N.C. and N. Podder (1976). Efficient Estimation of the Lorenz Curve and Associated Inequality Measures from Grouped Observations, *Econometrica*, 44(1), pp. 137–48.

Kuznets, Simon (1955). 'Economic Growth and Income Inequality', *American Economic Review*, 45(1), March, pp. 1–28.

Livingstone, Ian (ed.) (1981). *Development Economics and Policy: Readings*. London: George Allen & Unwin.

Loehr, William (1981). 'Economic Growth, Distribution and Incomes of the Poor', *Journal of Economic Studies*, 7(3), pp. 127–39.

Lydall, Harold F. (1977). 'Income Distribution during the Process of Development', World Employment Programme Research Working Paper No. WEP 2–23/WP 52, Geneva: International Labour Office, Feb.

Meier, Gerald M. (1976). *Leading Issues in Economic Development*, Third edition. New York: Oxford University Press.

Paukert, Felix (1973). 'Income Distribution at Different Levels of Development: A Survey of Evidence', *International Labour Review*, 108(2–3), Aug.–Sept., pp. 97–125.

Pesaran, M.H. (1974). 'On the General Problem of Model Selection', *Review of Economic Studies*, 41, pp. 153–71.

Pesaran, M.H. and Angus S. Deaton (1978). 'Testing Non-nested Non-linear Regression Models', *Econometrica*, 46(3), May, pp. 677–94.

Philippines (1978). *1978 Philippine Statistical Yearbook*. Manila: National Economic and Development Authority.

Rao, V.V. Bhanoji (1976). *National Accounts of West Malaysia, 1947–1971*. Singapore: Heinemann Educational Books (Asia) Ltd.

Robinson, Sherman (1976). 'A Note on the U-hypothesis Relating Income Inequality and Economic Development', *American Economic Review*, 66(3), June, pp. 437–40.

Saith, Ashwani (1983). 'Development and Distribution: A Critique of the Cross-country U-hypothesis', *Journal of Development Economics*, 13, pp. 367–82.

Srinivasan, T.N. (1977). 'Development, Poverty, and Basic Human Needs: Some Issues', *Food Research Institute Studies*, 16(2), pp. 11–28.

Streeten, Paul and Michael Lipton (1968). *The Crisis of Indian Planning*, London: Oxford University Press.

World Bank (1972). *World Bank Atlas 1972*. Washington, DC: World Bank.

World Bank (1978, 1979, 1980). *World Development Report*. New York: Oxford University Press (for the World Bank).

Poor, Relatively Speaking[*]

A.K. SEN

INTRODUCTION

When on 6 January 1941, amidst the roar of the guns of the Second World War, President Roosevelt announced that 'in the future days . . . we look forward to a world founded upon four essential freedoms', including 'freedom from want', he was voicing what was soon to become one of the major themes of the post-War era. While the elimination of poverty all over the world has become a much-discussed international issue, it is in the richer countries that an immediate eradication seemed possible. That battle was joined soon enough after the War in those affluent countries, and the ending of poverty has been a major issue in their policy discussions.

There are, however, great uncertainties about the appropriate way of conceptualizing poverty in the richer countries, and some questions have been repeatedly posed. Should the focus be on 'absolute' poverty or 'relative' poverty? Should poverty be estimated with a cut-off line that reflects a level below which people are — in some sense — 'absolutely impoverished', or a level that reflects standards of living 'common to that country' in particular? These questions — it will be presently argued — do not bring out the real issues clearly enough. However, a consensus seems to have emerged in favour of taking a 'relative' view of poverty in the rich countries. Wilfred Beckerman and Stephen Clark put it this way in their important recent study (1982) of poverty and social security in Britain since 1961: 'We have measured poverty in terms of a "relative" poverty line, which is generally accepted as being the relevant concept for advanced countries.'

There is indeed much merit in this 'relative' view. Especially against

---

* Revised version of a Geary Lecture given on 6 September 1982, at the Economic and Social Research Institute, Dublin, Ireland.

the simplistic absolute conceptualization of poverty, the relative view has represented an entirely welcome change. However, I shall argue that ultimately poverty must be seen to be primarily an absolute notion, even though the specification of the absolute levels has to be done quite differently from the way it used to be done in the older tradition. More importantly, the contrast between the absolute and the relative features has often been confused, and I shall argue that a more general question about ascertaining the absolute standard of living lies at the root of the difficulty. In particular, it will be claimed that *absolute* deprivation in terms of a person's *capabilities* relates to *relative* deprivation in terms of commodities, incomes and resources.

That is going to be my main theme, but before I get to that general issue, I ought to make clear the sense in which I believe that even the narrow focus on relative poverty has been valuable in the recent discussions on poverty. In the post-War years there was premature optimism about the elimination of poverty in rich countries based on calculations using poverty lines derived from nutritional and other requirements of the kind used by Seebohm Rowntree in his famous poverty studies of York in 1899 and 1936, or by Charles Booth in his nineteenth-century study of poverty in London. The post-War estimates using these given standards yielded a very comforting picture of the way things had improved over the years, and indeed in terms of old standards the picture certainly looked greatly more favourable than in the darker pre-War days. For example the third York survey of 1951 (Rowntree and Lavers 1951, p. 40), following Rowntree's earlier ones, indicated that using the same standard, the proportion of working class population in poverty appeared to have fallen from 31 per cent at the time of the last survey in 1936 to less than 3 per cent in the new survey of 1951. This was partly the result of general economic growth and a high level of employment, but also the consequence of various welfare legislations following the Beveridge Report of 1942, covering family allowances, national insurance, national assistance and national health service. Deducting public transfers would have made the poverty ratio higher than 22 per cent rather than less than 3 per cent. The changed situation — despite some statistical problems — was indeed genuine, but it was much too slender a basis on which to declare victory in the war against poverty. While the Labour government did go to the electorate in 1950 with the emphatic claim in its manifesto that 'destitution has been banished' and that the government has 'ensured full employment and fair shares of the necessities of life',[1] there was little real reason to be smug about eradication of poverty in Britain. There were lots of people who were in misery and clearly deprived of what they saw (as I shall presently argue, *rightly*) as necessities of life, and the battle against poverty was far from over.

It is in this context that the change of emphasis in the academic literature from an absolutist to a relativist notion of poverty took place, and it has had the immediate effect of debunking the smug claims based on inadequate absolute standards. But instead of the attack taking the form of disputing the claim that the old absolute standards were relative still, it took the investigation entirely in the relativist direction, and there it has remained through these years. The relativist response to the smugness was effective and important. Using what he regarded as the orthodox or conventional poverty line fixed at a level 40 per cent higher than the basic National Assistance scale, plus rent, Peter Townsend (1962) showed that as many as one in seven Britons were in poverty in 1960. Other important questions were also raised, for example by Dorothy Wedderburn (1962), and more detailed and comprehensive estimates soon followed, and the poverty battle was seen as wide open.[2] While I shall question the conceptualization underlying this change, I certainly would not dispute the value of the relativist contribution in opening up the question of how poverty lines should be determined, as well as in preventing a premature declaration of victory by the old absolutist school.

A THOROUGH-GOING RELATIVITY?

Peter Townsend, who — along with other authors such as Gary Runciman — has made pioneering and far-reaching contributions to the relativist view of poverty puts the case thus:

Any rigorous conceptualization of the social determination of need dissolves the idea of 'absolute' need. And a thorough-going relativity applies to time as well as place. The necessities of life are not fixed. They are continuously being adapted and augmented as changes take place in a society and in its products. Increasing stratification and a developing division of labour, as well as the growth of powerful new organisations, create, as well as reconstitute, 'need'. Certainly no standard of sufficiency could be revised only to take account of changes in prices, for that would ignore changes in the goods and services consumed as well as new obligations and expectations placed on

---

1 Quoted by David Bull (1971, p. 13).
2 See especially Abel–Smith and Townsend (1965) and Atkinson (1970b).

members of the community. Lacking an alternate criterion, the best assumption would be to relate sufficiency to the average rise (or fall) in real incomes [Townsend 1979b, pp. 17–18.][3]

The last remark — that the best assumption would be to relate sufficiency to 'the average rise (or fall) in real incomes' — is obviously *ad hoc*. But the more general argument is undoubtedly quite persuasive. However, I think this line of reasoning suffers from two quite general defects. First, *absoluteness* of needs is not the same thing as their *fixity over time*. The relativist approach sees deprivation in terms of a person or a household being able to achieve *less than what others* in that society do, and this relativity is not to be confused with *variation over time*. So the fact that 'the necessities of life are not fixed' is neither here nor there as far as the competing claims of the absolutist and relativist views are concerned. Even under an absolutist approach, the poverty line will be a function of *some* variables, and there is no *a priori* reason why these variables might not change over time.

The second problem is perhaps a more difficult one to sort out. There is a difference between achieving *relatively less than others*, and achieving *absolutely less because of falling behind others*. This general distinction, which I think is quite crucial to this debate, can be illustrated with a different type of interdependence altogether — that discussed by Fred Hirsch (1976) in analysing 'positional goods'. Your ability to enjoy an uncrowded beach may depend on your knowing about that beach when others do not, so that the *absolute* advantage you will enjoy — being on an uncrowded beach — will depend on your *relative* position — knowing something that others do not. You want to have that information, but this is not because you particularly want to do *relatively better than or as well as others*, but you want to do *absolutely well*, and that in this case requires that you must have some differential advantage in information. So your absolute achievement — not merely your relative success — may depend on your relative position in some other space. In examining the absolutist versus the relativist approach it is important to be clear about the space we are talking about. Lumping together needs, commodities, etc. does not help to discriminate between the different approaches, and one of the items in our agenda has to be a closer examination of the relationship between these different spaces.

Before I come to that, let me consider a different approach to the relativist view — this one occurring in the important study of 'poverty

---

[3] See also his major study of poverty in the UK, Townsend (1979a).

and progress in Britain' between 1953 and 1973 by Fiegehen, Lansley and Smith (1977). They put the question thus:

In part the renewed concern with 'want' reflected generally increased prosperity and the feeling that the standard of living which society guaranteed should be raised accordingly. This led to 'relative' concepts of poverty, by which the extent of poverty is judged not by some absolute historically defined standard of living, but in relation to contemporary standards. By such a moving criterion poverty is obviously more likely to persist, since there will always be certain sections of society that are badly off in the sense that they receive below-average incomes. Thus renewed interest in poverty stemmed to a considerable extent from a recognition that it is incumbent on society to assist the *relatively* deprived [pp. 2–3.]

One consequence of taking this type of rigidly relativist view is that poverty cannot — simply cannot — be eliminated, and an anti-poverty programme can never really be quite successful. As Fiegehen, Lansley and Smith note, there will always be certain sections of society that are badly off in relative terms. That particular feature can be changed if the relative approach is differently characterized, for example checking the number below 60 per cent of median income (the answer *can* be zero). But it remains difficult to judge, in any purely relative view, how successful an anti-poverty programme is, and to rank the relative merits of different strategies, since gains shared by all tend to get discounted. It also has the implication that a general decline in prosperity with lots of additional people in misery — say due to a severe recession or depression — need not show up as a sharp increase in poverty since the relative picture need not change. It is clear that somewhere in the process of refining the concept of poverty from what is viewed as the crudities of Charles Booth's or Seebohm Rowntree's old-fashioned criteria, we have been made to abandon here an essential characteristic of poverty, replacing it with some imperfect representation of *inequality* as such.

That poverty should in fact be viewed straightforwardly as an issue of inequality has, in fact, been argued by several authors. The American sociologists Miller and Roby (1971) have put their position thus:

Casting the issue of poverty in terms of stratification leads to regarding poverty as an issue of inequality. In this approach, we move away from efforts to measure poverty lines with pseudo-scientific accuracy. Instead, we look at the nature and size of the differences between the bottom 20 or 10 per cent and the rest of the society.[4]

4 See also Miller, et al. (1967). Contrast Townsend's (1979a) rejection of the

I have tried to argue elsewhere (Sen 1981, ch. 2) that this view is based on a confusion. A sharp fall in general prosperity causing widespread starvation and hardship must be seen by any acceptable criterion of poverty as an intensification of poverty. But the stated view of poverty 'as an issue of inequality' can easily miss this if the *relative* distribution is unchanged and there is no change in 'the differences between the bottom 20 or 10 per cent and the rest of the society'. For example recognizing starvation as poverty is scarcely a matter of 'pseudo-scientific accuracy'!

It can, however, be argued that such sharp declines are most unlikely in rich countries, and we can forget those possibilities. But that empirical point does nothing to preserve the basic adequacy of a conceptualization of poverty which should be able to deal with a wide variety of counter-factual circumstances. Furthermore, it is not clear that such declines cannot really take place in rich countries. A measure of poverty should have been able to reflect the Dutch 'hunger winter'[5] of 1944–5, when widespread starvation was acute. And it must not fail to notice the collapse that would surely visit Britain if Mrs Thatcher's quest for a 'leaner and fitter' British economy goes on much longer. The tendency of many of these measures to look plausible in situations of growth, ignoring the possibility of contraction, betrays the timing of the birth of these measures in the balmy 1960s, when the only possible direction seemed forward.

THE POLICY DEFINITION

While one could easily reject a *fully* relativized view of poverty, making poverty just 'an issue of inequality', it is possible to adopt a *primarily* relativized view without running into quite the same problems. The poverty line that has been most commonly used in recent studies of British poverty is the one given by the Official Supplementary Benefit scale,[6] and this scale has been consistently revised with attention being paid to the average level of British income. In fact, the scale has been revised upwards faster than the average income growth, and the poverty line in real terms did in fact double between July 1948 and November

identification of poverty with inequality (p. 57).

[5] This famine was indeed spread very widely across the Dutch population, thereby making the relative extents of deprivation quite muddled; see Aykroyd (1974) and Stein, et al. (1975).

[6] See, for example, Atkinson (1970b), Bull (1971), Fiegehen, Lansley and Smith (1977), Berthoud and Brown with Cooper (1981) and Beckerman and Clark (1982).

1975 (Beckerman and Clark 1982, p. 4). Using this poverty line, adjusted for cost-of-living changes on a month to month basis, Beckerman and Clark have estimated that the number of persons in poverty in Britain went *up* by about 59 per cent between 1961–3 and 1974–6 (p. 3). This rise is not entirely due to the upward revision of the poverty line, and another important factor is the demographic change associated with an increase in the number of pensioners in the British population, but the upward trend of the poverty line is certainly a major influence in this direction (Beckerman and Clark 1982, pp. 3–4).[7]

This practice of using the Supplementary Benefit scale as the poverty line is open to some obvious problems of its own. Not the least of these is the perversity whereby an increase in the attempt by the state to deal with poverty and low incomes by raising the Supplementary Benefit scale will tend to increase rather than diminish the measured level of poverty, by raising the poverty line. In this view, *helping* more is read as more help being *needed*. The most effective strategy for the government to adopt to reduce the number of the 'poor', under this approach, is to *cut*, rather than *raise*, the level of assistance through Supplementary Benefits. This can scarcely be right.

Identifying the poverty line with the Supplementary Benefit scale belongs to a more general tradition, which the United States President's Commission on Income Maintenance in 1969 called the 'policy definition' of poverty (p. 8). It is a level of income that is seen as something 'the society feels some responsibility for providing to all persons'. This approach too is, I believe, fundamentally flawed (see Sen 1981, pp. 17–21). The problem is that the level of benefits is determined by a variety of considerations going well beyond reflecting the cut-off point of identified poverty. For one thing, it reflects what is feasible. But the fact that the elimination of some specific deprivation — even of starvation — might be seen, given particular circumstances, as unfeasible does not change the fact of that deprivation. Inescapable poverty is still poverty. Furthermore, the decisions regarding state assistance will reflect — apart from feasibility considerations — other pressures, for example pulls and pushes of politically important groups,

---

[7] A big factor in this increase in the Beckerman–Clark calculation is their procedure of adjusting the poverty line for cost-of-living increase every month in between the official adjustments of the Supplementary Benefit scale, so that those whose incomes were raised exactly to the Supplementary Benefit level through that scheme would shortly appear as being *below* the Beckerman–Clark poverty line as a result of the monthly adjustments.

policy objectives *other than* poverty removal (such as reduction of inequality). Attempts to read the poverty line from the assistance level are riddled with pitfalls. If Mrs Thatcher decides today that the country 'cannot afford' the present level of Supplementary Benefits and the scale must be cut, that decision in itself will not reduce poverty in Britain (through lowering the poverty line below which people count as poor).

THE ABSOLUTIST CORE

Neither the various relativist views, nor seeing poverty as 'an issue in inequality', nor using the so-called 'policy definition', can therefore serve as an adequate theoretical basis for conceptualizing poverty. There is, I would argue, an irreducible absolutist core in the idea of poverty. One element of that absolutist core is obvious enough, though the modern literature on the subject often does its best to ignore it. If there is starvation and hunger, then — no matter what the *relative* picture looks like — there clearly is poverty. In this sense the relative picture — if relevant — has to take a back seat behind the possibly dominating absolutist consideration. While it might be thought that this type of poverty — involving malnutrition or hunger — is simply irrelevant to the richer countries, that is empirically far from clear, even though the frequency of this type of deprivation is certainly much less in these countries.

Even when we shift our attention from hunger and look at other aspects of living standard, the absolutist aspect of poverty does not disappear. The fact that some people have a lower standard of living than others is certainly proof of inequality, but by itself it cannot be a proof of poverty unless we know something more about the standard of living that these people do in fact enjoy. It would be absurd to call someone poor just because he had the means to buy only one Cadillac a day when others in that community could buy two of these cars each day. Absolute considerations cannot be inconsequential for conceptualizing poverty.

The temptation to think of poverty as being altogether relative arises partly from the fact that the *absolute* satisfaction of some of the needs might depend on a person's *relative* position *vis-à-vis* others in much the same way as — in the case discussed earlier — the absolute advantage of a person to enjoy a lonely beach may depend upon his relative advantage in the space of knowledge regarding the existence of and access to such beaches. The point was very well caught by Adam

Smith when he was discussing the concept of necessities in *The Wealth of Nations*:

By necessaries I understand not only the commodities which are indispensably necessary for the support of life, but what ever the custom of the country renders it indecent for creditable people, even the lowest order, to be without. . . . Custom . . . has rendered leather shoes a necessary of life in England. The poorest creditable person of either sex would be ashamed to appear in public without them (Smith 1776, pp. 351–2).

In this view to be able to avoid shame, an eighteenth-century Englishman has to have leather shoes. It may be true that this situation has come to pass precisely because the typical members of that community happen to possess leather shoes, but the person in question needs leather shoes not so much to be *less ashamed* than others — that relative question is not even posed by Adam Smith — but simply not to be ashamed, which as an achievement is an absolute one.

CAPABILITIES CONTRASTED WITH COMMODITIES, CHARACTERISTICS AND UTILITIES

At this stage of this discussion I would like to take up a somewhat more general question, viz. that of the right focus for assessing standard of living. In my Tanner Lecture (given at Stanford University in 1979) and my Hennipman Lectures (given at the University of Amsterdam in 1982), I have tried to argue that the right focus is neither commodities, nor characteristics (in the sense of Gorman and Lancaster), nor utility, but something that may be called a person's capability (Sen 1980; 1982b; also Sen 1982a, Introduction, pp. 30–1). The contrasts may be brought out by an illustration. Take a bicycle. It is, of course, a commodity. It has several characteristics. Let us concentrate on one particular characteristic, namely transportation. Having a bike gives a person the ability to move about in a certain way that he may not be able to do without the bike. So the transportation *characteristic* of the bike gives the person the *capability* of moving in a certain way. That capability may give the person utility or happiness if he seeks such movement or finds it pleasurable. So there is, as it were, a *sequence* from a commodity (in this case a bike), to characteristics (in this case, transportation), to capability to function (in this case, the ability to move), to utility (in this case, pleasure from moving).

It can be argued that it is the third category — that of capability to function — that comes closest to the notion of standard of living. The commodity ownership or availability itself is not the right focus since it does not tell us what the person can, in fact, do. I may not be able to use the bike if, say, I happen to be handicapped. Having the bike — or something else with that characteristic — may provide the basis for a contribution to the standard of living, but it is not in itself a constituent part of that standard. On the other hand, while utility reflects the use of the bike, it does not concentrate on the use itself but on the mental reaction to that use. If I am of a cheerful disposition and enjoy life even without being able to move around because I succeed in having my heart leap up every time I behold a rainbow in the sky, I am no doubt a happy person, but it does not follow that I have a high standard of living. A grumbling rich man may well be less happy than a contented peasant, but he does have a higher standard of living than that peasant; the comparison of standard of living is not a comparison of utilities. So the constituent part of the standard of living is not the good, nor its characteristics, but the ability to do various things by using that good or those characteristics, and it is that ability rather than the mental reaction to that ability in the form of happiness that, in this view, reflects the standard of living.

ABSOLUTE CAPABILITIES AND RELATIVE COMMODITY REQUIREMENTS

If this thesis of the capability focus of standard of living is accepted (and I believe the case for it is quite strong), then several other things follow. One of them happens to be some sorting out of the absolute–relative disputation in the conceptualization of poverty. At the risk of oversimplification, I would like to say that poverty is an absolute notion in the space of capabilities but very often it will take a relative form in the space of commodities or characteristics.

Let us return to Adam Smith. The capability to which he was referring was the one of avoiding shame from the inability to meet the demands of convention.[8] The commodity needed for it, in a particular

---

[8] This particular capability, emphasized by Adam Smith, clearly has a strong psychological component in a way that other capabilities that have been thought to be basic may not have, e.g. the ability to be well nourished or to move about freely or to be adequately sheltered (see Sen 1980). The contrast between capability and utility may, in some ways, be less sharp in the case of capabilities involving psychology, even though it would be impossible to catch the various psychological dimensions within the undifferentiated metric of utility (no matter whether defined in terms of pleasure and pain, or choice, or desire fulfilment). In fact, the capability of being happy can be seen

illustration that Smith considered, happened to be a pair of leather shoes. As we consider richer and richer commodities, the commodity requirement of the same capability — avoiding this type of shame — increases. As Adam Smith (1776) noted, 'the Greeks and Romans lived . . . very comfortably though they had no linen', but 'in the present time, through the greater part of Europe, a creditable day-labourer would be ashamed to appear in public without a linen shirt' (pp. 351–2). In the commodity space, therefore, escape from poverty in the form of avoiding shame requires a varying collection of commodities — and it is this collection and the resources needed for it that happen to be relative *vis-à-vis* the situations of others. But on the space of the capabilities themselves — the direct constituent of the standard of living — escape from poverty has an absolute requirement, to wit, avoidance of this type of shame. Not so much having equal shame as others, but just not being ashamed, absolutely.

If we view the problem of conceptualizing poverty in this light, then there is no conflict between the irreducible absolutist element in the notion of poverty (related to capabilities and the standard of living) and the 'thoroughgoing relativity' to which Peter Townsend refers, if the latter is interpreted as applying to commodities and resources. If Townsend puts his finger wrong, this happens when he points towards the untenability of the idea of absolute needs. Of course, needs too can vary between one society and another, but the cases that are typically discussed in this context involve a different bundle of commodities and a higher real value of resources fulfilling the *same* general needs. When Townsend estimates the resources required for being able to 'participate in the activities of the community', he is in fact estimating the varying resource requirements of fulfilling the same absolute need.

In a poor community the resources or commodities needed to participate in the standard activities of the community might be very little indeed. In such a community the perception of poverty is primarily concerned with the commodity requirements of fulfilling nutritional needs and perhaps some needs of being clothed, sheltered and free from disease. This is the world of Charles Booth or Seebohm Rowntree in nineteenth-century or early twentieth-century London or York, and that of poverty estimation today, say, in India. The more

---

as just one particular capability, and utility — shorn of its claim to unique relevance — can be given some room *within* the general approach of capabilities. These issues have been further discussed in Sen (1982b).

physical needs tend to dominate over the needs of communal participation, on which Townsend focuses, at this less affluent stage both because nutritional and other physical needs would tend to have a more prominent place in the standard-of-living estimation and also because the requirements of participation are rather easily fulfilled. For a richer community, however, nutritional and other physical requirements (such as clothing as protection from climatic conditions) are typically already met, and the needs of communal participation — while absolutely no different in the space of capabilities — will have a much higher demand in the space of commodities and that of resources. Relative deprivation, in this case, is nothing other than a relative failure in the commodity space — or resource space — having the effect of an absolute deprivation in the capability space.

The varying commodity requirements of meeting the same absolute need applies not merely to avoiding shame from failing to meet conventional requirements, and to being able to participate in the activities of the community, but also to a number of other needs. It has been pointed out by Theo Cooper in a regrettably unpublished paper (Cooper 1972) that in West Europe or North America a child might not be able to follow his school programme unless he happens to have access to a television. If this is in fact the case, then the child without a television in Britain or in Ireland would be clearly worse off — have a lower standard of living — in this respect than a child, say, in Tanzania without a television. It is not so much that the British or the Irish child has a brand new need, but that to meet the same need as the Tanzanian child — the need to be educated — the British or the Irish child must have more commodities. Of course, the British child might fulfil the need better than the Tanzanian with the help of the television — I am not expressing a view on this — but the fact remains that the television is a necessity for the British child for school education in a way it is not for the Tanzanian child.

Similarly, in a society in which most families own cars, public transport services might be poor, so that a carless family in such a society might be *absolutely poor* in a way it might not have been in a poorer society. To take another example, widespread ownership of refrigerators and freezers in a community might affect the structure of food retailing, thereby making it more difficult in such a society to make do without having these facilities oneself.

It is, of course, not my point that there is no difference in the standards of living of rich and poor countries. There are enormous differences in the fulfilment of some of the most basic capabilities, for example to meet nutritional requirements, to escape avoidable disease, to be sheltered, to be clothed, to be able to travel and to be educated. But whereas the commodity requirements of these capability fulfilments are not tremendously variable between one community and another, such variability is enormous in the case of other capabilities. The capability to live without shame emphasized by Adam Smith, that of being able to participate in the activities of the community discussed by Peter Townsend, that of having self-respect discussed by John Rawls (1971, pp. 440–6), are examples of capabilities with extremely variable resource requirements.[9] And, as it happens, the resource requirements typically go up in these cases with the average prosperity of the nation, so that the relativist view acquires plausibility despite the absolutist basis of the concept of poverty in terms of capabilities and deprivation.

It is perhaps worth remarking that this type of *derived* relativism does not run into the difficulties noted earlier with thoroughgoing relativity of the kind associated with seeing poverty as 'an issue of inequality'. When the Dutch in the hunger winter of 1944–5 found themselves suddenly in much reduced circumstances, their commodity requirements of capability fulfilment did not go down immediately to reduce the bite of poverty, as under the rigidly relativist account. While commodity requirements are sensitive to the opulence and the affluence of the community in general, this relationship is neither one of instant adjustment, nor is it a straightforward one to be captured simply by looking at the average income, or even the current Lorenz curve of income distribution. Response to communal standards is a more complex process than that.

PRIMARY GOODS AND VARYING REQUIREMENTS BETWEEN AND WITHIN COMMUNITIES

I should also remark on a point of some general philosophical interest related to this way of viewing personal advantage and social poverty. The philosophical underpinning of the recent poverty literature has been helped enormously by John Rawls' far-reaching analysis of social justice. One respect in which Rawls differs sharply from utility-based theories such as utilitarianism is his focus on what he calls 'primary goods' rather than on utility in judging a person's advantage. Our focus

---

[9] Education is perhaps an intermediate case, where the resource variability is important but perhaps not as extreme as with some of these other capabilities related to social psychology.

on capability differs *both* from the utilitarian concern with just mental reactions and from the Rawlsian concern with primary goods as such, though the approach of capabilities is much influenced by Rawls' moral analysis. Making comparisons in the capability space is quite different from doing that either in the utility space (as done by utilitarians), or in the space of commodities or primary goods (even when this is done very broadly, as Rawls does). In this view the variables to focus on consist of such factors as *meeting* nutritional requirements rather than either the pleasure from meeting those requirements (as under utilitarianism), or the *income* or *food* needed to meet those requirements (as in the Rawlsian approach). Similarly, the capability approach focuses on meeting the need of self-respect rather than *either* the pleasure from having self-respect, *or* what Rawls calls 'the social basis of self-respect' (Rawls 1971, pp. 60–5).[10] The capability approach differs from the traditional utility-based analysis as strongly as the Rawlsian approach does, but it continues to concentrate on human beings — their capabilities in this case — rather than moving with Rawls to incomes, goods and characteristics.[11] Rawls himself motivated his focus on primary goods, using arguments that rely on the importance of capabilities. What the capability approach does is to make that basis explicit and then it goes on to acknowledge the enormous variability that exists in the commodity requirements of capability fulfilment. In this sense, the capability approach can be seen as one possible *extension* of the Rawlsian perspective.

The extension makes a substantial practical difference not merely because the commodity requirements of capability fulfilment vary between one community and another, or one country and another, but also because there are differences *within* a given country or community in the mapping from commodities to capabilities. In a country with various racial groups, even the food requirements of nutritional fulfilment may vary a great deal from one group to another.[12] For example in India the people in the state of Kerala have both the lowest level of average calorie intake in the country and the highest level of longevity

[10] Note, however, that Rawls vacillates between taking 'the *bases* of self-respect' as a primary good (this is consistent with taking income as a primary good), and referring to 'self-respect' itself as a primary good, which is closer to our concern with capabilities.

[11] I have discussed this contrast more extensively in Sen (1980, 1982a, pp. 30–1, 1982b). See also Rawls (1982, pp. 168–9).

[12] This is in addition to inter-individual and intertemporal variations emphasized by Sukhatme (1977), Srinivasan (1979) and others. See also Scrimshaw (1977).

and high nutritional fulfilment. While part of the difference is certainly due to distributional considerations and the availability of back-up medical services, the physiological differences in the calorie requirements of the Malayali in Kerala compared with, say, the larger Punjabi, is also a factor.

This type of *intra*-country or *intra*-community difference can be very important even in rich countries and even those with a basically homogeneous population. This is because of other variations, for example that of age. Of particular relevance in this context is the fact that a high proportion of those who are recognized as poor in the richer countries are also old or disabled in some way (see Wedderburn 1961 and Atkinson 1970b). Inability to earn an adequate income often reflects a physical disadvantage of some kind and this disadvantage is not irrelevant to the conversion of goods into capabilities. While nutritional requirements may not increase with age or disability — may even decrease somewhat — the resource requirements of, say, movement, or of participation in the activities of the community, may be considerably larger for older or disabled people. The focus on absolute capabilities brings out the importance of these *intra*-community variations in the commodity space, going well beyond the *inter*-community variations emphasized in the typical relativist literature.

While it might not be easy to take full note of such intra-community variations in practical studies of poverty, it is important to have conceptual clarity on this question and to seek more sensitive practical measures in the long run. I should think the direction in which to go would be that of some kind of an efficiency-adjusted level of income with 'income' units reflecting command over capabilities rather than over commodities. This will be, I do not doubt, quite a rewarding field of research.

AGGREGATE POVERTY MEASURES AND RELATIVITIES

Even when incomes are not thus adjusted within a given country or community, conceptualization of poverty does, of course, involve more than just fixing a poverty line. I have so far said nothing at all on that question, and I should now briefly turn to it. The predicaments of people below the poverty line are not by any means homogeneous even when their respective abilities to convert commodities into capabilities are identical, since they differ from each other in the size of their respective shortfalls of income from the poverty line. Traditionally, poverty measurement has tried to make do with operating on two aggregate magnitudes, namely the headcount ratio (that is the proportion of population below the poverty line) and the income-gap ratio (that is the average income shortfall of all the poor taken together as a proportion of the poverty line itself, or alternatively as a proportion of the mean income of the community). But it is easy to show that these two magnitudes taken together cannot capture poverty adequately since any sensible measure of poverty must be sensitive also to the distribution of that income shortfall among the poor. Bearing this in mind, several of us in recent years have tried to propose various distribution-sensitive measures of poverty.

The one I proposed in *Econometrica* of 1976 is based on an axiomatic structure that gets numerical weights from ordinal information regarding relative incomes much in the same way as Borda — in his theory of voting — obtained his rank-order method by converting ranks into weights. With such an axiomatization, and a chosen procedure of normalization, it can be shown that one gets a measure of poverty P that depends on three parameters, namely the headcount ratio H, the income-gap ratio I as a proportion of the poverty line and the Gini coefficient G of the distribution of income among the poor:[13]

$$P = H(I + [1 - I] G)$$

Equivalently, this measure P can be expressed as a function of the headcount ratio H, the poverty line π, and the equally distributed equivalent income e^g of the poor (as defined by Kolm 1969 and Atkinson 1970a) using the Gini social evaluation function,[14]

$$P = H(\pi - e^g)/\pi$$

A generalization of this measure, proposed by Blackorby and Donaldson (1980) replaces the equally distributed equivalent income e^g based on the specific Gini social evaluation function by any member e of equally distributed equivalent incomes for a whole class of such social evaluation functions:

$$P = H(\pi - e)/\pi$$

Other variations have also been proposed by such authors as Kakwani;

[13] Sen (1976a, Theorem 1). An earlier version, with slight axiomatic variations, was presented in Sen (1973).

[14] On the Gini social evaluation function, see Sen (1974, 1976b) and Hammond (1978). On related issues see Graaft (1977), Kakwani (1980) and Roberts (1980).

Takayama; Hamada and Takayama; Anand; Osmani; Thon; Szal; Fields; Pyatt; Clark, Hemming and Ulph; Foster; Foster, Greer and Thorbecke; Chakravarty; Foster and Shorrocks; and others.[15] I do not propose to discuss here the various properties of these different variants. But there is one slightly contrary property that is worth a comment because it links up with the absolute–relative question with which this chapter has been concerned. In presenting my measure in *Econometrica* 1976, I expressed some support for the view that the poverty measure must satisfy an adapted version of the so-called Pigou–Dalton condition of transfer, to wit, any transfer of income to a poor person from a person who is richer must reduce the recorded poverty level. This axiom was not used in deriving my measure P, and indeed as I noted the following year in *Econometrica* (Sen 1977, p. 77), it is possible for the measure P to violate this Pigou–Dalton condition, albeit in rather rare circumstances. It turns out that all the variants of this measure mentioned above — with a few exceptions involving other unattractive characteristics — can also violate the Pigou–Dalton condition (Sen 1981, App. C). For the violation result to hold it is necessary, though not sufficient, that the transfer from the rich person should make him fall from above to below the poverty line as a consequence of the transfer. Is this violation of the Pigou–Dalton transfer condition a disturbing characteristic?

The Pigou–Dalton condition is certainly an appealing one as a requirement of a measure of *inequality*, and this is indeed how it has been used by Kolm (1969) and Atkinson (1970a), and how it has been related to the property of S-concavity in a paper on economic inequality by Dasgupta, Starrett and myself (Dasgupta, Sen and Starrett 1973; see also Rothschild and Stiglitz 1973). But does this make sense for a measure of poverty as opposed to inequality? If one takes the thorough-going relativist view that poverty is nothing other than 'an issue in equality', as Miller and Roby put it, then clearly the Pigou–Dalton axiom must be unexceptionable as a restriction on permissible poverty measures.[16] But if the absolutist view is taken, then the poverty line is not just a reflection of some relative characteristic of the distributional statistics, but represents a line with some absolute justification of its

---

15 Many of these variations are discussed in Sen (1981, ch. 3 and App. C), and in Sen (1982a, Intro., pp. 31–6).

16 This will, of course, not be the case when there are efficiency differences in converting resources into capability, as discussed above.

own. For example in the capability view, the poverty line may be defined to represent the level at which a person can not only meet nutritional requirements, etc. but also achieve adequate participation in communal activities (as characterized by Townsend) and be free from public shame from failure to satisfy conventions (as discussed by Adam Smith). In this case if a transfer drags a person from above to below that threshold while reducing the income gap of a poorer person, it is not obvious that the overall poverty measure must invariably be expected to decline. The poverty line has some absolute significance and to cross it is a change of some importance. Thus the absolutist approach to conceptualizing poverty — even though it involves a relativist reflection in the commodity space — will tend to reject the invariable insistence on the Pigou–Dalton condition of transfer when such a transfer changes the number of people below the poverty line.

There is a weaker version of the transfer axiom, which I called the Weak Transfer Axiom (see Sen 1977, p. 77; and also Sen 1981, p. 186), which insists on the Pigou–Dalton condition being invariably satisfied whenever the transfer to the poor person from the richer person does not change the number below the poverty line, and this of course is fully consistent with the absolutist approach, and is indeed satisfied by the measure P and most of its variants.

CONCLUDING REMARKS

I end with a few concluding statements. First, I have argued that despite the emerging unanimity in favour of taking a relative as opposed to an absolute view of poverty, there is a good case for an absolutist approach. The dispute on absolute versus relative conceptualization of poverty can be better resolved by being more explicit on the particular space (for example commodities, incomes or capabilities) in which the concept is to be based.

Second, I have outlined the case for using an absolute approach to poverty related to the notion of *capability*. Capabilities differ both from commodities and characteristics, on the one hand, and utilities, on the other. The capability approach shares with John Rawls the rejection of the utilitarian obsession with one type of mental reaction, but differs from Rawls' concentration on primary goods by focusing on capabilities of human beings rather than characteristics of goods they possess.

Third, an absolute approach in the space of capabilities translates into a relative approach in the space of commodities, resources and incomes in dealing with some important capabilities, such as avoiding shame from failure to meet social conventions, participating in social activities and retaining self-respect.

Fourth, since poverty removal is not the only object of social policy and inequality removal has a status of its own, taking an absolutist view of poverty must not be confused with being indifferent to inequality as such. While poverty may be seen as a failure to reach some absolute level of capability, the issue of inequality of capabilities is an important one — in its own right — for public policy (see Sen 1980; 1982b).

Fifth, while inter-country and inter-community differences have been much discussed in the context of conceptualizing poverty, the differences *within* a country and *within* a community need much more attention because of interpersonal variations in converting commodities into capabilities. This is particularly important since poverty is often associated with handicaps due to disability or age. This problem could perhaps be handled by using efficiency-income units reflecting command over capabilities rather than command over goods and services.

Finally, I have argued that the reasonableness of various axioms that aggregative measures of poverty may or may not be asked to satisfy depend (sometimes in an unobvious — certainly unexplored — way) on whether fundamentally a relative or an absolute approach is being adopted. This has practical implications on the choice of statistical measures to be used. It is important to know whether the poor, relatively speaking, are in some deeper sense absolutely deprived. It makes a difference.

Acknowledgements: For helpful comments I am most grateful to Wilfred Beckerman, Graciela Chichilnisky, Theo Cooper, Jan Graaff, Kieran A. Kennedy, Paul Seabright, Peter Townsend and Dorothy Wedderburn.

REFERENCES

Abel–Smith, B. and P. Townsend (1965). *The Poor and the Poorest.* London: Bell.

Atkinson, A.B. (1970a). 'On the Measurement of Inequality', *Journal of Economic Theory*, 2.

—— (1970b). *Poverty in Britain and the Reform of Social Security.* Cambridge: Cambridge University Press.

Aykroyd, W.R. (1974). *The Conquest of Famine.* London: Chatto and Windus.

Beckerman, W. and S. Clark (1982). *Poverty and Social Security in Britain Since 1961*. Oxford: Oxford University Press.

Berthoud, R. and J.C. Brown with S. Cooper (1981). *Poverty and the Development of Anti-poverty Policy in the UK*. London: Heinemann.

Blackorby, C. and D. Donaldson (1980). 'Ethical Indices for the Measurement of Poverty', *Econometrica*, 48.

Bull, D. (ed.) (1971). *Family Poverty* (London: Duckworth).

Cooper, T.C. (1971). 'Poverty', unpublished note, St Hugh's College, Oxford.

Dasgupta, P., A. Sen and D. Starrett (1973). 'Notes on the Measurement of Inequality', *Journal of Economic Theory*, 6.

Fiegehen, G.C., P.S. Lansley and A.D. Smith (1977). *Poverty and Progress in Britain 1953–73*. Cambridge: Cambridge University Press.

Graaff, J. de V. (1977). 'Equity and Efficiency as Components of General Welfare', *South African Journal of Economics*, 45.

Hammond, P.J. (1978). 'Economic Welfare with Rank Order Price Weighting', *Review of Economic Studies*, 45.

Hirsch, F. (1976). *Social Limits to Growth*. Cambridge, Mass.: Harvard University Press.

Kakwani, N. (1980). *Income, Inequality and Poverty*. New York: Oxford University Press.

Kolm, Ch. S. (1969). 'The Optimal Production of Social Justice', in J. Margolis and H. Guitton (eds), *Public Economics*. London: Macmillan.

Miller, S.M., M. Rein, P. Roby and B. Cross (1967). 'Poverty, Inequality and Conflict', *Annals of the American Academy of Political Science*.

Miller, S.M. and P. Roby (1971). 'Poverty: Changing Social Stratification', in P. Townsend (ed.), *The Concept of Poverty*. London: Heinemann.

Rawls, J. (1971). *A Theory of Justice*. Cambridge, Mass.: Harvard University Press and Oxford: Clarendon Press.

—— (1982): 'Social Unity and Primary Goods', in A. Sen and B. Williams (eds), *Utilitarianism and Beyond*. Cambridge: Cambridge University Press.

Roberts, K. (1990). 'Price Independent Welfare Prescriptions', *Journal of Public Economics*, 13.

Rothschild, M. and J.E. Stiglitz (1973). 'Some Further Results in the Measurement of Inequality', *Journal of Economic Theory*, 6.

Rowntree, Seebohm B. and G.R. Lavers (1951). *Poverty and the Welfare State*. London: Longmans.

Scrimshaw, N.S. (1977). 'Effect of Infection on Nutrition Requirements', *American Journal of Clinical Nutrition*, 30.

Sen, A.K. (1973). 'Poverty, Inequality and Unemployment: Some Conceptual Issues in Measurement', *Economic and Political Weekly*, 8.

—— (1974). 'Informational Bases of Alternative Welfare Approaches: Aggregation and Income Distribution', *Journal of Public Economics*, 4.

—— (1976a). 'Poverty: An Ordinal Approach to Measurement', *Econometrica*, 44; reprinted in Sen (1982a).

—— (1976b). 'Real National Income', *Review of Economic Studies*, 43; reprinted in Sen (1982a).

—— (1977). 'Social Choice Theory: A Re-examination', *Econometrica*, 45; reprinted in Sen (1982a).

—— (1980). 'Equality of What?', in S. McMurrin (ed.), *The Tanner Lectures on Human Values*. Cambridge: Cambridge University Press; reprinted in Sen (1982a).

—— (1981). *Poverty and Famines: An Essay on Entitlement and Deprivation.* Oxford: Clarendon Press.

—— (1982a). *Choice, Welfare and Measurement.* Oxford: Blackwell and Cambridge, Mass.: MIT Press.

—— (1982b). *Commodities and Capabilities*, Hennipman Lecture given on 22 April 1982; to be published by North-Holland, Amsterdam.

Smith, Adam (1776). *An Inquiry into the Nature and Causes of the Wealth of Nations.* Everyman Edition: London: Home University Library.

Srinivasan, T.N. (1979). 'Malnutrition: Some Measurement and Policy Issues', mimeograph, World Bank, Washington, D.C.

Stein, Z., M. Susser, G. Saenger and F. Marolla (1975). *Famine and Human Development: The Dutch Hunger Winter of 1944–1945.* London: Oxford University Press.

Sukhatme, P.V. (1977). *Nutrition and Poverty.* New Delhi: Indian Agricultural Research Institute.

Townsend, P. (1962). 'The Meaning of Poverty', *British Journal of Sociology*, 8.

—— (1979a). *Poverty in the United Kingdom.* London: Allen Lane and Penguin Books.

—— (1979b). 'The Development of Research on Poverty', in Department of Health and Social Security, *Social Security Research: The Definition and Measurement of Poverty*. London: HMSO.

US President's Commission on Income Maintenance (1969). *Poverty amid Plenty.* Washington, D.C.: US Government Printing Office.

Wedderburn, Dorothy (1961). *The Aged in the Welfare State.* London: Bell.

—— (1962). 'Poverty in Britain Today — The Evidence', *Sociological Review*, 10.

Undernutrition:
Measurement and Implications

C. GOPALAN

INTRODUCTION

In this chapter it is the measurement of undernutrition in population groups rather than individuals that is under consideration. It is important to make this distinction at the very outset because yardsticks and procedures that may be adequate for evaluation of the nutritional status of whole communities may not be suitable for the assessment of the nutritional status of a given individual. Individual genetic variations with respect to requirements of nutrients and response to their deprivations could get largely neutralized when large population groups in nearly similar socio-economic and environmental status are considered.

Economists and planners, understandably, look for tidy methods of quantifying undernutrition in population groups. Biologists, however, would readily recognize the inherent limitations and pitfalls of exercises that seek to 'measure' undernutrition with mathematical precision. These limitations stem from the very nature of the undernutrition process — the multiplicity of interacting, often mutually reinforcing, factors involved in its causation; its evolution, often so insidious that it is hard to decide where normalcy has ended and subnormality (or abnormality) has set in; and its multiple clinical dimensions. It is not the purpose of this paper to discuss these limitations in detail, but a broad appreciation of them is essential for any meaningful discussion of the problem of measuring undernutrition.

The chapter is organized as follows. The following section describes the biological processes involved in the genesis and development of undernutrition. The third section reviews the conceptual issues involved in the two major approaches to the measurement of undernutrition.

These issues have been the subject of intense controversy in recent times, leading to sharply contrasting views on how undernutrition should be measured. These controversies are reviewed briefly, and my own views on the subject are presented. The fourth section is concerned with some of the practical problems of measuring undernutrition, bearing in mind the limitations of data on the one hand and the multifaceted nature of undernutrition on the other. Here I argue that the measurement of undernutrition in large populations should be based on dietary surveys supplemented by weight-for-age measurements of children under the age of 5.

My emphasis on the weight-for-age criterion is in sharp opposition to a recent trend which favours the alternative weight-for-height criterion. As I explain, the choice between these alternative criteria has a lot to do with the views one holds on the conceptual issues discussed in the third section. It is, however, important to point out that my choice of the weight-for-age criterion for the under-fives in no way implies a negative judgement on the usefulness of height-for-age measurements: it is just that there are certain special problems in the height-for-age measurement of very young children. However, as is argued in the fifth section, monitoring the height of older children is an exceedingly useful exercise; indeed, it is perhaps the best possible way of assessing the long-term changes in the nutritional status of a community. Finally, my major conclusions are summarized in the last section.

THE BIOLOGY OF UNDERNUTRITION

The Aetiology

Undernutrition, widely prevalent among socially and economically deprived population groups around the world, is associated with a cluster of related, often coexistent, factors which together constitute what may be termed the 'poverty syndrome', the major attributes of which are (1) income levels that are inadequate to meet basic needs of food, clothing, and shelter; (2) diets that are quantitatively and often qualitatively deficient; (3) poor environment, poor access to safe water, and poor sanitation; (4) poor access to health care; and (5) large family size and high levels of illiteracy — especially female illiteracy. Among most undernourished population groups, these factors often tend to coexist, though their relative severity and extent may vary in different locations. In the evaluation of undernutrition, and indeed in its progression and perpetuation, these factors often act synergistically.

The effects of all these factors, both socio-economic and environmental, are, however, ultimately mediated through a final common pathway. The ultimate determinant of nutritional status is the availability at the cellular level — in adequate amounts, in proper combinations, and at appropriate times — of all the essential nutrients required for normal growth, development, maintenance, repair, and functioning of the organism. This, in turn, is determined by two broad sets of factors: (1) the diet, which must provide adequate amounts of the essential nutrients, and (2) factors that condition the requirement, absorption, assimilation, and utilization of the nutrients of the diet. These latter include the activity level and environmental factors, particularly infections and stress situations.

Correlation Between Dietary Intake and Nutritional Status

The correlation between the levels of dietary inadequacy prevailing in households and communities on the one hand and the degree of severity of undernutrition (as assessed by anthropometric criteria and clinical signs) obtaining among them on the other is not always strict. Three major reasons for this may be mentioned.

1. The severity of effects of primary dietary inadequacy in a population can be aggravated by superadded conditioning factors such as infections and parasitic diseases, the extent of such aggravation being determined by the nature of such infections, their duration, frequency, and severity, and the promptness and efficiency with which they are prevented and treated in the community. Infections can increase requirements of nutrients and inhibit their absorption and assimilation. For example in communities subject to the same order of dietary deficiency right through the year, clinical manifestation of undernutrition could be more pronounced in seasons characterized by a high prevalence of infections than at other times. Thus in Coonoor in India, in poor communities subject to the same monotonous dietary deficiency throughout the year, the peak incidence of 'kwashiorkor' (a disease caused by severe protein–calorie deficiency) in children in successive years was noticed in May–June, following the peak incidence of diarrhoeal diseases in the 'fly season' of April–May (Gopalan 1955). In parts of Kerala in India, nearly three decades ago, when health services were less adequate than at present, the peak prevalence of 'kwashiorkor' was noticed in the weeks following the monsoon when, again, diarrhoeal diseases attained their peak.

While the level of dietary inadequacy is undoubtedly the dominant determinant of undernutrition, the level of primary health care in the community can significantly modify the severity of its clinical manifestations.

2. Where diets of entire households rather than of individuals within the family are being used as yardsticks in the assessment of community nutritional status, differences in the nature of intra-familial distribution of food, and in particular in infant feeding and child-rearing practices, between the families and between communities can result in important differences with respect to nutritional status (especially of children) between households, and between communities with nearly similar overall levels of dietary inadequacy.

Differences with respect to nutritional status of infants and young children between households with nearly similar dietary and socio-economic status can arise from differences with respect to duration and intensity of breast-feeding, the time of introduction of supplements, and the nature and amount of such supplements. Relatively small proportions of the overall family diet can make a significant difference to the level of adequacy or inadequacy of the diet of the preschool child. The level of female literacy in the household is often a major determinant of child-rearing practices and, therefore, of the level of child nutrition in poor households.

3. Furthermore, except in acute famine situations, the current nutritional status of a community is often a reflection of its erstwhile rather than (necessarily) its present dietary status. There is a variable time-lag between dietary deprivation and the onset of clinical undernutrition. This consideration, however, may not matter in the case of communities wherein no significant or striking changes in dietaries have taken place, and where seasonal fluctuations in dietaries are not marked. Current dietaries may then well reflect the situation responsible for the prevailing nutritional state.

The time-lag between the onset of nutrient deprivation and the appearance of clinical (or functional) manifestation can vary, depending on the nutrient and the clinical sign. Thus, for example, it could take much longer for eye lesions to appear following a vitamin A deprivation than for growth retardation to occur following calorie–protein undernutrition. In the case of growth retardation consequent on calorie–protein undernutrition itself, retardation in linear growth (stunting) is generally the outcome of a more long-standing dietary deprivation than retardation in body-weight increment (wasting).

These considerations will underscore the limitations with respect to the measurement of nutritional status of communities on the basis of the level of dietary inadequacy alone, and will highlight the need for additional yardsticks. This is not to minimize the importance of diet surveys in the assessment of nutritional status of population groups, but only to explain some of the seeming incongruities such as the lack of strict parallelism between dietary intakes and nutritional status. It will also explain the reasons why nutrition scientists rely not only on diet survey data but also on nutrition surveys (actual examination of human subjects — both adults and children) for the assessment of nutritional status of population groups.

Growth Retardation

In children of poor communities, habitually subsisting on inadequate diets, there is a continuous and insidious transition from the stage of normalcy usually obtaining up to about the fourth or sixth month (many infants being small-for-date may never start from normalcy) to that of full-fledged, clinically manifest undernutrition which generally super-venes before the third year. The speed of this downward slide from normalcy to full-fledged disease will depend on the extent of the dietary inadequacy, its duration, and the presence or absence of superadded aggravating factors such as infection. In poor communities we may expect to see children in different stages of this transition. Not all will go through the entire transition: the downward slide may be arrested at different stages, or it may be so slow that the child may manage to cross the critical age period of 4 to 5 years before the 'end point' is reached. It is necessary to emphasize that, unlike many infectious diseases, in the case of undernutrition there is no point of striking or dramatic onset and no easily (visually) discernible dividing line between normalcy and the commencement of 'disease'. In children whose growth is carefully monitored, a faltering in the growth rate and the point at which the growth curve begins to flatten and deviate from the normal standard could provide the earliest indication of undernutrition; however, few children in poor communities of the developing world enjoy the benefit of such close and careful growth monitoring. Bio-chemical tests could reveal subclinical undernutrition, but these are hardly feasible in large-scale community surveys.

Retardation of growth and downward deviation from normalcy become progressively more pronounced with the passage of time, and children pass insidiously from the so-called 'mild' to the 'severe' grades of growth retardation. A considerable proportion of children presently in the 'mild' grades of growth retardation are potential candidates for the 'moderate' and 'severe' grades; those presently in the 'severe' grades were probably in the 'mild' and 'moderate' categories a few weeks or months earlier. A fortunate small proportion may even reverse their direction.

In order to arrive at a given level of growth retardation, not all children need follow the same route in the growth chart. The shape of the growth curve could vary. The speed and intensity of growth retardation and the consequent duration over which a given order of growth retardation results will differ depending on the nature and extent of dietary inadequacy and of superadded infections. Under these circumstances, as important as the child's current position in the growth chart will be the route which that child took in order to arrive at the point — whether the child is the victim of an acute fairly severe deficiency over a short duration, or of a chronic less severe deficiency spread out over a longer period. For the same low weight-for-age, the child in the latter category could be more 'stunted' (less height for age) than the one in the first, and might require a much longer duration of more intensive nutritional rehabilitation for recovery. Quantification of undernutrition purely on the basis of degree of deficit of weight-for-age thus has its complexities and limitations. These have been discussed in detail in an earlier study (Gopalan 1984).

Multiple Nutrient Deficiencies

Children in poor communities suffer not merely from calorie deficiency but from other nutrient deficiencies as well. Thus Indian children in poor rural communities often suffer from moderate and severe iron deficiency, anaemia (63 per cent of children below 3 years belonging to poor rural communities were found to suffer from such anaemia, according to one study of the National Institute of Nutrition), vitamin A deficiency, and less frequently from deficiencies of vitamins of the B group. Iodine deficiency resulting in endemic goitre is a massive problem of a special kind and may be treated as a separate category; it lends itself to a simple technological solution capable of successful implementation even within the prevailing context of poverty.

The severity of deficiency of the different nutrients does not necessarily run parallel, possibly because of differences in the composition of diets and in the efficiency of absorption of different nutrients. The severity of iron deficiency or vitamin A deficiency may show a much lower positive correlation with the degree of weight deficit than the severity of calorie deficiency. Under the circumstances, different combinations of multiple nutrient deficiencies of varying orders of severity are seen in poor children. To quantify undernutrition under these circumstances, we need to be able to give a 'value' to different specific nutritional deficiencies in the total composite of undernutrition.

A recognition of these complexities inherent in the biology of the process of undernutrition will help us understand the problems and difficulties involved in the measurement of undernutrition in a community.

Practical Approaches to Measurement

Despite these difficulties and limitations, a fairly reliable estimate of the quantum of undernutrition in a community may be made through two approaches which are practicable under the real-life conditions obtaining in the field, and which will largely serve the needs of the public health scientist and developmental economist:

1. a survey of the diets of representative households (supported by a survey of diets of individual members of the family in a sub-sample of households) in a community, in order to derive information on nutrient intake — especially calorie intake;

2. anthropometric and clinical examination of children — especially the under-fives (who constitute the 'most sensitive' segment of the population from the point of view of nutritional vulnerability).

In the conventional procedure employed by nutrition scientists for the assessment of nutritional status of communities, these two approaches are combined with a broad survey of the socio-economic and environmental status of the community, which could not only facilitate the interpretation of data but could also provide valuable practical leads for combating undernutrition in the community.

The approaches described above have been widely used and, subject to their inherent limitations, they are valid. The major controversies with respect to measurement of undernutrition pertain not so much to the choice of the above two approaches, as to the interpretation and evaluation of the data derived from them.

SOME BASIC ISSUES

In any discussion about the measurement of undernutrition, there are some basic issues which need to be considered and some crucial questions which need to be answered.

If we are going to use the two practical approaches described above, the following questions arise: What are the normal standards against which the prevailing level of calorie intake and the observed growth performance should be compared in order to determine adequacy or otherwise? Are the widely used standards that are recommended by international agencies and adopted with slight variations by most countries valid for both the rich and the poor? More specifically, with respect to calorie intake, is it necessary to use the recommended mean requirement level (M), or will it be more appropriate, especially in the case of poor populations, to use a level equivalent to the mean minus two standard deviations ($M - 2\,SD$) as the standard yardstick? With respect to growth, how appropriate are the 'international standards' for developing countries? Even if we accept the position that the genetic potential for growth between populations is nearly similar, can we not accept some levels of growth retardation (as revealed by comparisons with international or the 'best indigenous' standard) as acceptable for poor children consistent with their 'economy and ecology'? Should small body size cause any concern, and is it of any functional significance? Does 'stunting', so widely seen in developing countries, really matter?

We may consider some recent hypotheses which touch on these questions.

Sukhatme's Hypothesis

With respect to calorie intake, a sharp debate as to whether, for the purpose of assessing the adequacy of a given level of calorie intake, the recommended mean energy requirement level (M) need be used as the standard for comparison, or whether a level corresponding to the mean minus two standard deviations ($M - 2\,SD$) would suffice has been ongoing for some time. This debate was touched off largely by the postulate of Sukhatme (1978, 1981) that a human subject can permanently 'adapt' himself to a low calorie intake level representing the lowest limit of his 'intra-individual variation' and that, therefore, $M - 2\,SD$ rather than M would be the appropriate yardstick for comparison. Sukhatme's postulate has been dealt with in earlier publications (Gopalan 1983a), and it is therefore proposed to touch on it only briefly here.

Sukhatme's contention that the energy requirement of normal individuals is not static and that there is intra-individual variation in calorie intake may not be disputed. In fact, it is to be expected that calorie intake of individuals not subject to socio-economic constraint will show daily variation depending on the level of activity and the presence or absence of stress.

What is unacceptable, however, is the second postulate of Sukhatme, that subjects permanently obliged to subsist on calorie intakes representing the lowest levels of what he terms 'intra-individual variation' (equivalent to recommended mean level minus the standard deviations) can permanently adapt their requirement to this low intake without any functional impairment. In short, Sukhatme suggests that the pendulum of daily calorie intake in an individual, which normally oscillates between two points on either side of the mean, can be safely and permanently arrested at the lowest end of its oscillation. If intra-individual variation in energy intake is a physiological mechanism providing for daily variation in energy requirements, Sukhatme's postulate would imply that the human organism could do without this physiological adjustment and that that requirement will somehow get adjusted to a lower level in keeping with the lowered intake. A healthy subject responds to alterations in energy intake by burning body fat when dietary energy is deficient or by storing body fat when dietary energy is in excess, resulting in a continuous process of breakdown and synthesis of body energy reserves. Individuals subsisting permanently on low-energy intakes have no scope for this and lose the advantage of an important regulatory mechanism. We have no evidence that fluctuations in efficiency of energy utilization in the absence of variations in levels of activity or stress contribute significantly to prevailing intra-individual variation even over a short period. We have no evidence to believe that populations engaged in their expected levels of occupational activity and obliged permanently to subsist at nearly 70 per cent of the recommended mean energy intake can 'adapt' themselves to such a low level of calorie intake without suffering loss of body weight and consequent impairment of function.

Seckler's and Payne's Hypotheses

Seckler (1982) had gone so far as to suggest that 'smallness' is an appropriate and welcome attribute of poor people, consistent with their good health. He advised Indian nutrition scientists not only not to use 'international standards' of growth (as these would yield an 'over-estimation' of undernutrition) but also not to use even the 'best indigenous standard' of the Indian high socio-economic groups, because even these will be 'abnormally large' for the majority of Indians who are poor. This subject has been dealt with in an earlier publication (Gopalan 1983b).

More recently, Payne has argued that, even if children of developing countries have the same genetic potential for growth as those of the more fortunate countries of Europe and the USA, they will settle for a lower level of growth in keeping with their 'economy and ecology' (Pacey and Payne 1985). It is not surprising that this plea for acquiescence in growth retardation has been sharply rejected as an exercise in 'perpetuation of undernutrition' (Jaya Rao 1986).

The three hypotheses referred to above have one thing in common: they have all relied on the body's ability to permanently 'adapt' itself to environmental and dietary stress without any detriment whatsoever to functional competence. Unfortunately, 'adaptation' has apparently been loosely interpreted in the debate to signify an acceptable state of normalcy instead of being viewed as no more than a 'strategic retreat from normalcy' on the part of the organism ('a contraction of its metabolic frontiers') in order to face the stress and escape with minimal permanent damage to its vital tissues. 'Adaptation' thus represents a state of siege. A population that is permanently reduced to this state cannot be normal. I shall discuss this central issue at some length in the next section and shall try to highlight the 'cost' and functional implications involved in the so-called 'adaptation' process.

'Adaptation': Meaning and Implications

When an organism is subject to the stress of dietary inadequacy, it responds to the stress in a number of ways in order to minimize permanent tissue damage. A reduction of physical activity to conserve energy and a retardation of growth to minimize nutrient requirement are well-known responses. However, these responses are not without their inevitable functional consequences and costs. Individuals responding to stress in this way should not be considered normal and indeed are not normal, as several functional studies have shown. They generally function at a substandard level.

Thus an adult can (within limits) successfully 'adapt' himself to low calorie intake through a corresponding reduction in work output to reduce energy expenditure. Such adaptation will, however, result in limiting his productivity and earning capacity and thus could only serve to perpetuate his poverty. Payne would perhaps argue that the individual is 'adapted' to function as well as he needs to in his 'economy and ecology', meaning his poverty situation, in which he is often either unemployed or underemployed. This would imply that we accept a situation in which the economic status of a poor country decides the level of development of its human resources, and that efforts at improvement of the quality of human resources of a country could wait until economic improvement has been registered. This would be contrary to the present strategies, whereby vigorous efforts at promoting the quality of human resources go hand in hand with efforts at economic improvement.

To take another example, children can adapt to energy deficiency by reducing play and other physical activities, but such restriction could impair their mental and physical development. The fascinating work of Torun, et al. (1975) has in fact shown the importance of physical activity in children in promoting linear growth and ensuring an efficient pattern of energy utilization. A restriction of physical activity in children can, by reducing opportunities for stimulation and learning experiences, retard mental development as well. Adjustment to low energy inputs through restriction of necessary physical activity cannot, therefore, be considered an acceptable form of adaptation.

Rutishauser and Whitehead (1972) observed that the level of physical activity of Ugandan children was less than that of European counterparts of comparable age and that their caloric intake was also correspondingly low (80 kcal per kilogram of body weight as against 100 kcal for European children). We should avoid drawing the conclusion that the low physical activity of African children is perhaps a 'cultural attribute' and that the low energy intake is the result rather than the cause of the decreased activity. We may safely predict that, if European children were to subsist on the habitual diets of Ugandan children, their activity pattern would be no different. Several 'natural' and controlled studies have clearly demonstrated that the response of human beings to calorie undernutrition is identical, irrespective of their race and nationality. The picture of semi-starvation was the same in Belsen and Bengal, in Madras and Minnesota. There is no scientific evidence to show that people of different cultures will show different physiological responses when faced with the same order of restriction in calorie intake.

Implications with Respect to Protein Nutrition

An important point that seems to have been totally lost sight of in discussions of Sukhatme's hypothesis of 'adaptation' to low calorie intake is its serious implications with respect to protein nutrition.

Policy-makers, planners, and some economists apparently labour under the mistaken impression that, with the acceptance of that hypothesis, the current estimates of undernutrition among populations in developing countries will be reduced to 'manageable proportions'. Far from this being the case, the acceptance of this hypothesis would actually imply that the nutrition situation in many developing countries is far worse than what the present estimates indicate — indeed, that the solution of the problem will be possible only through a drastic qualitative upgrading of the current dietaries, which would be clearly well beyond the economic resources of these countries. Let me explain why this is so.

At the height of the great protein debate, which finally led to the 'protein fiasco' and the winding up of the PAG (Protein Advisory Group of the UN), we in India had argued that the problem of protein–calorie malnutrition was essentially a problem of calorie defi- ciency, and that such protein deficiency as existed was an incidental secondary by-product of primary calorie deficiency. Sukhatme himself was very much in the forefront in this endeavour. We had shown that, if the habitual cereal–legume dietaries of poor Asian population groups were consumed at levels adequate to meet the full caloric needs (and here we were talking of caloric needs as conforming to present international recommended mean levels of intake, and not of $M - 2\,SD$ levels), then protein needs would be automatically met. A study carried out at the National Institute of Nutrition (Gopalan, et al. 1973), which had then attracted international attention, actually helped to demonstrate how, in an undernourished community of children, an additional provision of 310 calories (even when such calories were derived from food sources practically devoid of proteins — 'empty calories') could bring about a significant improvement in their nutritional status and a reduction in protein–calorie malnutrition. We therefore took the position that, under the circumstances, the right and feasible strategy was to bridge the calorie gap with existing habitual dietaries and not to go in for expensive protein concentrates or for drastic dietary changes which in any case were well beyond the economic resources of these countries. Our policy was based on the principle that children needed to be fed the cereal–legume diets, which alone they could afford, at levels that would at least provide their full calorie needs as per internationally accepted recommendations — levels at which they would not need to restrict play and physical activity in order to conserve energy. We sought to overcome the problem of low calorie density ('bulk factor') of cooked cereal diets through invoking traditional practices like malting, so that children could be fed such predominantly cereal-based diets in quantities that would provide them their full caloric needs as per current recommendations (and therefore also, incidentally, their protein needs).

If, in consonance with Sukhatme's hypothesis, we now take the position that what children (and adults) need is no more than 70 per cent of the recommended mean levels of calorie intake, then on such restricted levels, clearly, they cannot meet their protein requirements with their present habitual cereal–legume diets. As the intake of energy is restricted, protein requirement increases — by as much as 20–30 per cent. Individuals will need to include in their dietaries other, relatively expensive, items of protein-rich foods. Several studies carried out at the National Institute of Nutrition in Hyderabad provide experimental support for this in both children and adults, as shown in Tables 7.1 and 7.2. Not only is the protein concentration in the habitual poor Asian dietaries too low to provide the protein requirement at the $M - 2\,SD$ levels of calorie intake, but the utilization of protein at this lower level is also relatively poor.

Thus a child of 3 years subsisting on a 1200 calorie diet could obtain 22 gm protein daily with a diet that provides no more than just 7.2 per cent of its overall calorific value through protein. (Low-cost cereal–legume diets provide more than 8 per cent of protein calories.) Against this, if calorie intake using the same diet is reduced to 70 per cent of mean recommended levels ($M - 2\,SD$ level), the protein–calorie percentage in the diet that will be needed to provide the same 22 gm of protein daily would be 10.3 per cent (clearly, more than is possible with existing poor Indian dietaries). Moreover, we have also to take into account the fact that with low levels of calorie intake the utilization of protein is poor. Thus in a study of under-fives it was found that, while with a calorie intake of 100 kcal/kg per day the children need 1.35 gm protein per kg to achieve a retention of 40 mg of nitrogen per day, they would need 1.64 gm per kg from the same protein source to achieve the same level of nitrogen retention when calorie intake is reduced to 80 kcal/kg per day. Thus a decrease in calorie intake to 70 per cent will call for an increase of protein intake by an additional 20 per cent. In a study of adults it was found that, with a calorie intake of 2066 kcal daily, as much as 60 gm protein

Table 7.1
Recommended Dietary Intakes of Protein
and Energy for Indians, 1981

	Net calories (kcal)	Proteins (gm)	Protein–calorie %	Net calories at 70% level	Protein–calorie % at low level of energy re- quirement
Men					
Sedentary work	2400	55	9.2	1680	13.1
Moderate work	2800	55	7.9	1960	11.2
Heavy work	3900	55	5.6	2730	8.1
Women					
Sedentary work	1900	45	9.5	1330	13.5
Moderate work	2200	45	8.2	1540	11.7
Heavy work	3000	45	6.0	2100	8.6
During pregnancy	2500	59	9.4	1750	13.5
Lactation	2750	70	10.2	1925	14.5
Children					
1–3 years	1220	22.0	7.2	854	10.3
4–6 years	1720	29.4	6.8	1204	9.8
7–9 years	2050	35.6	6.9	1435	9.9
Boys 10–12 years	2420	42.5	7.0	1694	10.0
Girls 10–12 years	2260	42.1	7.5	1582	10.6
Boys 13–15 years	2660	51.7	7.8	1862	11.1
Girls 13–15 years	2360	43.3	7.3	1652	10.5
Boys 16–18 years	2820	53.1	7.5	1974	10.8
Girls 16–18 years	2200	44.00	8.0	1540	11.4

Source: Recommended Dietary Intakes for Indians 1981 (Indian Council of Medical Research)

Note: This table presents the RDA of calories and proteins for adults (at different physiological levels) and children. Also, it provides the protein–calorie percentage at requirement level and at the low level of energy intake. This shows that at low level of energy ($M - 2\,SD$) intake the protein–calorie percentage of the dietaries should be at higher levels to meet the recommended allowance of protein. The protein–calories percentage of the habitual rice-legume-based Indian dietaries is around 8–9 per cent. Also, since the protein requirement is known to increase when calories are restricted because of poorer utilization, the actual protein–calorie percentage required at the low energy will be higher by another 20–50 per cent.

Table 7.2

Effect of Energy Restriction on Protein Requirements in India

Preschool children

Energy intake (kcal/kg/day)	Protein requirement[a] (gm/kg)
100	1.33
80	1.64

Adults 1

Protein intake (gm/day)	Energy required for nitrogen(N) balance (cal)
60	2066
40	2249

Adults 2: Heavy casual labourers

Energy intake (kcal/kg/day)	Protein intake (gm/kg/day)	Mean N balance (gm/day)
55.5	1.0	+ 1.0
44.4	1.0	− 0.3

Source: Provided at the author's request by Dr B.S. Narasinga Rao, Director, National Institute of Nutrition, Hyderabad, India.

[a]   A retention of 40 mg of nitrogen per kilogram was taken on meeting the requirement of preschool children.

was necessary to achieve nitrogen balance, while with a calorie intake of 2250 calories, the protein intake needed for achieving nitrogen balance was just 40 gm daily.

   In effect, then, it would appear that in recommending lower levels of calorie intake for poor populations in the expectation that they will 'adapt' to such low levels, we are also implying that they substitute 'cake' for their usual 'bread'.

Growth Retardation: The Minimal Role of Genetic Factor

It has now been conclusively shown, on the basis of data from countries throughout the world, that differences currently observed with respect to growth patterns of children in the rich countries of Europe and North America on the one hand and in the poor countries of Asia, Africa, and Latin America on the other (and between the rich and poor within the developing countries themselves) are mostly attributable to differences in their socio-economic status, and not to genetic differences (Habicht, et al. 1974; Stephenson, et al. 1983). The remarkable secular trend in heights of children and adults witnessed in post-War Japan underscores this fact. While a great majority of Indian children show varying degrees of growth retardation, Indian children who are not subject to dietary constraints have been shown to have growth levels that correspond closely to the international (Harvard) standards (Gopalan 1989). The genetic potential for growth and development is nearly similar among most peoples of the world.

The Lancet (1984), discussing the use in developing countries of international growth standards (particularly the WHO/NCHS standards), on the basis of data from different parts of the world, concluded in its editorial that 'recent evidence suggests that the growth of privileged groups of children in developing countries does *not* differ importantly from these standards' and that 'the poorer growth so commonly observed in the underprivileged is due to social factors — among which malnutrition–infection complex is of primary importance — rather than to ethnic or geographic differences'.

Also there are no known ethnic differences in human physiology with respect to metabolism of nutrients. Africans and Asians do not burn their dietary calories or use their dietary protein any differently from Europeans and Americans. It follows, then, that dietary requirements for normal growth, development, and function cannot vary widely between different races, unless we accept different standards between them with respect to normal growth and function.

It is not so much the retardation of physical growth *per se* and the relatively small body size of the poor that need bother us: it is the fact that there is now mounting evidence, thanks to sophisticated functional tests which measure physical stamina and work capacity on the one hand and mental development and learning ability on the other, that impairment in physical growth (as assessed by the failure to achieve the full genetic potential for the attainment of physical stature) is accompanied by varying degrees of functional incompetence. The fascinating work of Spurr, et al. (1982, 1983, 1984) in Colombia, Chavez and Martinez (1982) in Mexico, Viteri (1971) in Guatemala, and Satyanarayana, et al. (1977) in India has provided ample evidence of the functional implications of growth retardation. Indeed, there is often a linear relationship between the degree of growth retardation and the degree of physical and mental functional impairment. Measurement of the degree of growth retardation thus could serve as a proxy for the assessment of functional competence.

It will be difficult for any biologist to agree with Payne's strange suggestion that the term 'undernutrition' should be reserved only for children whose state of nutrition has deteriorated to the point where they are close to death, and that other children with less severe degrees of nutritional deprivation, who do not actually face the risk of imminent death, even if they happen to show clear evidence of functional impairment of various kinds, should not be included in the 'undernourished' category. This is almost like saying that a person should be considered 'unhealthy' only when he has reached the point of death.

Weight-for-height

A view that is now being widely propagated is that, irrespective of deficits in height-for-age or weight-for-age, children with weights 'appropriate' to their heights ('normal' weight–height ratio) could be considered to have successfully adapted themselves to their dietary deprivation, and to be practically 'normal' and free from undernutrition! According to this postulate, it is not so much height-for-age or weight-for-age that matters but the weight–height ratio that is the crucial indicator of normalcy. This convenient hypothesis could lend legitimacy to the 'small but healthy' hypothesis. However, there is not an iota of hard scientific evidence to justify this sweeping postulate. Indeed, such evidence as is available points to a near-linear relationship between deficits in height-for-age or weight-for-age and functional impairment, irrespective of weight-for-height.

The above postulate is an unwarranted distortion of Waterlow's morphological classification of growth retardation into stunting, wasting, and stunting + wasting. Waterlow clearly did not invest this classification with functional significance. All that he implied was that, in the case of such stunted children with a normal weight–height ratio, it could be argued that their *current* level of calorie intake is probably adequate to sustain them in the context of their stunted stature. He did not claim that stunted children with appropriate weights for their heights were functionally normal or that stunting, even if associated with appropriate body weight-for-height, was an acceptable state.

Satyanarayana has shown a direct correlation between productivity and body weight in industrial workers drawn from the poor socioeconomic groups, even with respect to operations in which body weight may not be expected to make a difference. In a longitudinal study on undernourished boys in India, Satyanarayana, Naidu and Rao (1979) showed that the wages earned by adolescent boys employed by farmers in rural areas were significantly related to body weight and height. Men and women with better nutritional anthropometry earned 30–50 per cent additional incentive money (over and above the uniform basic pay) in factories where an individual incentive system based on work output was in operation.

Agarwal, et al. (1987) have provided convincing evidence, on the basis of an intensive study of over 1300 children in rural areas of Uttar Pradesh in India, that stunted children with a 'normal' weight–height ratio show the same order of functional (physical and mental) impairment as equally stunted children with poorer weight–height ratios. The view that a stunted child may be considered 'adapted' if it happens to have a weight appropriate to its stunted height is apparently untenable.

A considerable proportion of girls in developing countries who are stunted and of low body size because of undernutrition during the crucial years of their growth and development end up with heights of below 145 cm when they enter motherhood. It is now known that there is a direct relationship between stunting of mothers and the occurrence of low birth weights in their offspring. According to the recommendations of international agencies, maternal heights below 145 cm may be considered indicative of risk of obstetric complications and low birth weight. It will be seen from the data presented in Table 7.3 that a distinctly higher proportion of offspring of mothers with heights of less than 145 cm were of low birth weight. In India, as in many other developing countries, more than one-third of all infants born alive have birth weights below 2500 gm. It is now known that, with respect to both height and weight, infants who start with the initial handicap of a low birth weight apparently never fully recover from it. Thus low birth weights in full-term infants make a lasting contribution to stunting.

Stunting is the outstanding feature of so-called 'adaptation'. It is the feature that ensures that not only this generation, but also the next, does not escape from the poverty trap. Stunted children with impaired learning abilities and schooling end up as stunted adults with low levels of productivity, educational attainment, and resourcefulness, earning low incomes and thus continuing to be enmeshed in the poverty trap, and so proving unable to feed their children adequately. Stunted women beget offspring with low birth weights who start their lives with an initial handicap from which they never fully recover. Thus stunting and the poverty with which it is invariably associated continue from one generation to another. To view this scenario as 'acceptable adaptation' is cruel irony!

Table 7.3
Maternal Height and Incidence of
Low Birth Weight (LBW) in Offspring, India

Maternal height (cm)	Income group (Rs/head/month)	Incidence of LBW (%)
< 145	< 50	35.5
> 145	< 50	24.2
> 145	> 200	15.0

Source: Ghosh, et al. (unpublished research).

A country or community in which large segments of the population suffer from growth retardation is one in which the quality and calibre of human resources is eroded and of substandard quality. A level of dietary intake and nutrition which can permit only substandard growth must inevitably lead to an erosion of the quality of human resources in developing countries or a perpetuation of such erosion where it already exists.

A sensible developmental policy of any country must obviously aim at providing for a level of calorie intake that will permit the full productivity and work output from its labour force, and a level of growth and development for its children that represents the fullest expression of their genetic potential. It is possible that many poor countries may be in no position to achieve these targets in the near future, and may have to settle for a policy that will enable them to reach these goals in a phased manner. It will, however, be an act of self-deception and political expediency to tailor standards of growth, physical and mental function, and dietary requirements in order to minimize the problem of undernutrition and win the war against poverty *on paper*. Standards are meant to determine the magnitude of a problem: it will be perverse to let this magnitude frighten us or tempt us to tailor the standard so that the 'problem' is reduced to 'manageable proportions'.

There is no scientific justification for double standards between rich and poor countries in the matter of dietary requirements of their populations or growth levels of their children. We may, of course, argue as to whether current levels of body weight (not height) observed in European and American infants and preschool children are not some-what high and are representative of *over*nutrition and obesity. This is a different matter; it could call for a revision of standards for American and European children as well. Establishment by each country of a standard yardstick of its own in conformity with the pattern observed among affluent children of that country, who are not subject to dietary and environmental constraints, will be in order. On the basis of all available evidence, we may expect that the standards thus established by different countries (including developing countries) will not be widely different. What we should guard against, however, is an acceptance of the concept that levels of growth and of dietary intake known and accepted to be subnormal and substandard for the affluent are appropriate and good enough for the poor and consistent with their poverty status. In the measurement of undernutrition, we should be guided by these considerations.

SOME PROBLEMS IN MEASUREMENT

I shall now briefly consider the two practical approaches referred to earlier. There are inherent practical limitations involved in the use of these approaches as measures of undernutrition. For our present pur-pose, we will not consider the limitations that pertain to the actual collection of data and the possibilities of measurement errors, but merely the broader issues.

The Calorie Intake Yardstick

Estimations of levels of dietary intake of calories have been widely used in the evaluation of nutritional status of population groups. The limitations of the calorie intake yardstick have been discussed in an earlier study (Gopalan 1983a); these need only be recapitulated briefly here.

First, as pointed out earlier, poor diets are deficient not in calories alone but in several nutrients as well, though in dietaries based mostly on a single major staple there is close correlation between calorie intake and intake of essential nutrients. Where the major dietary item is lacking in an important nutrient (as is the case with cassava and tapioca with respect to protein), the diet could be quite adequate with respect to calories while being highly deficient with respect to protein. This is not unusual in Africa. Under the circumstances, calorie intake levels may provide a flattering picture of the nutritional status. Therefore calorie intake measurements generally provide a quantitative and not necessarily a qualitative measure of the adequacy of diets.

Second, measurements of calorie intake, especially under field conditions, lack precision; daily and seasonal fluctuations in dietary intake could add to this problem, which even seven-day weighment methods cannot entirely solve. Repeated diet surveys in different seasons may be necessary to obtain a reliable picture.

Third, where diets of entire households (and not of individual members therein) are estimated, as is generally the case, the actual calorie intake of the most vulnerable segment of the population, namely the children, is often indirectly derived through the application of certain arbitrary coefficients based on the assumption that the intrafamilial distribution of food conforms to relative physiological needs — an assumption not often valid. Actual estimations of individual dietary intakes within families in a representative sub-sample of households surveyed, and the application of necessary correction based on these data to the figures for individual intakes, may obviate the error to some extent.

For the purpose of assessment of dietary/nutritional status, the actual observed calorie intake for a given age/sex/occupational group is compared with the mean energy requirement level for that group as recommended by international (and national) expert bodies on the basis of well-conducted, fairly reliable intensive studies in several laboratories of the world. The Indian Council of Medical Research, for example, has recommended energy intake levels appropriate for different categories (age, sex, and occupation) based on Indian studies as well as on published observations from elsewhere and the recommendation of international agencies. Through such comparison, it will be possible to determine proportions of population groups — manual labourers (male and female), sedentary workers (male and female), children between 5 and 12 years of age, and children below 5 years of age — in the community surveyed, obtaining, say, 90, 80–90, 70–80, 60–70, and less than 60 per cent of the respective recommended intake energy level.

Growth Retardation as a Measure of Undernutrition

Children under 5 years of age represent the most vulnerable segment of the population from the nutritional standpoint. For all practical purposes, the growth performance of children of this age group is a convenient measure of the nutritional status of the community. This procedure is now being widely employed in many developing countries. The pitfalls and limitations of this approach have been discussed in an earlier publication (Gopalan 1984).

Among the different anthropometric measurements — namely weight-for-age, height-for-age, weight-for-height, and arm circumference — taking practical considerations into account, the balance of advantage rests heavily with weight-for-age measurements as far as infants and under-fives are concerned. Heights (or lengths) for age in children are more difficult to measure accurately, and height measurements are also less sensitive to dietary deprivation. The significance of weight-for-height measurements, and of the classification of growth retardation into 'wasting' and 'stunting', are debatable. Arm circumference measurements are simple to carry out but there are doubts on the one hand about their being age-independent (a merit often claimed in their favour), and on the other hand about their reliability in comparison to weight measurements. For all practical purposes, therefore, as far as under-fives are concerned, it may be best to rely on weight-for-age surveys.

The procedure that is now being widely adopted is to compare the weight-for-age of the child with the weight-for-age in the international (Harvard or NCHS) standard. According to the Gomez scale, which is generally used (Gomez, et al. 1956), children with weights within 90 per cent of the standard are considered 'normal', those between 90 and 75 per cent of the standard as being in 'mild' malnutrition, those between 75 and 60 per cent of the standard as being 'moderately' malnourished, and those below 60 per cent of the standard as being 'severely' malnourished.

The cut-off points of 90, 75, and 60 per cent, are admittedly arbitrary and have no real scientific basis. The use of the international standard rather than the 'best indigenous' standard as the yardstick for comparison has also been questioned. Even so, Gomez's classification has proved useful in enabling health/nutrition scientists to quantify undernutrition in the children of a community and to assess the impact of nutrition intervention programmes. However, in order that weight-for-age measurements in under-fives could be thus used for comparisons of nutritional status between population groups and between two time-points in the same population group, some precautions are absolutely necessary. These precautions are not being currently observed, with the result that the data from different locations and at different time-points are not truly comparable.

In all comparisons that use cut-off points that are percentages of the standard median, it is extremely important to ensure that the age and sex composition of the under-five groups are very similar. A given order of weight deficit in a child under 2 years of age carries a far greater significance than the same order of weight deficit in a child of 5 years. Also, where there are wide seasonal fluctuations with regard to food availability, comparisons of measurements between two populations in two such different seasons may prove fallacious. Mistakes in age assessment, especially in children under 3 years, can modify results significantly.

According to available data, generally less than 10 per cent of under-fives in South East Asian countries suffer from 'severe malnutrition' (weight-for-age less than 60 per cent of the standard), less than 15 per cent are normal (weight-for-age more than 90 per cent of standard), while the remaining belong to the 'mild' and 'moderate' grades of undernutrition.

If used with due precautions, weight-for-age surveys among under-fives and the quantification of the order of weight deficit observed among them provides the health/nutrition scientist with a convenient and practicable tool for the quantification of weight deficits in children and therefore, indirectly, for the quantification of undernutrition. This procedure will be specially useful in comparisons of different population groups within a country in order to identify the most depressed groups requiring special attention, and also to monitor changes in the profile of undernutrition (the quantum and pattern) following from nutrition intervention programmes.

The Gomez scale and other similar methods attempt to classify undernutrition in terms of various cut-off points defined as a stipulated percentage of the median of the reference population. The limitation of this approach is that it does not take into account the variability of the relative width of the distribution of weight-for-age across different age periods. For example 60 per cent of median weight-for-age indicates a much more severe state of malnutrition for infants and young children than for older children. In order to overcome this problem, a new method has been developed which measures the deviation of the anthropometric measurement from the reference median in terms of standard deviation units or 'Z' scores (Waterlow, et al. 1977). This is coming into increasing use.

Unfortunately, weight-for-age measurements are now being put to the improper use of subserving a nutrition policy of brinkmanship in some developing countries, not for the promotion of child health/nutrition and prevention of undernutrition, but mainly to identify cases of so-called 'severe' malnutrition (that is children with weight-for-age of less than 60 per cent of the standard) who could be chosen as beneficiaries for supplementary feeding programmes. In a longitudinal study among children of Bangladesh, Chen, Chowdhury and Huffman (1980) observed that the risk of increased mortality was observed only in under-fives who suffered from 'severe' malnutrition. This has unfortunately been misinterpreted to imply that children suffering from 'mild' and 'moderate' malnutrition can somehow muddle through and that only the 'severely' malnourished need attention in nutrition intervention programmes. Though Chen tried to rebut this inference in a later publication (Chen, et al. 1982), the impression conveyed by his original paper has continued to misguide health workers in developing countries.

Such exclusive attention to the severely malnourished to the point of neglect of the 'moderately' and 'mildly' malnourished (nutrition policy of brinkmanship) can only result in reducing the size of the tip of the iceberg and in further increasing the pool of moderate and mild malnutrition cases in the community. But children who are currently in the so-called 'moderate' stage could move into the 'severe' stage within a few weeks or months. To withhold action until they are actually at that end-stage would be poor strategy. The inputs needed to prevent children who are in the mild and moderate stages of malnutrition from passing into the severe stage are far less than those that would be needed to rehabilitate the severely undernourished ones. It may even be possible for mothers of poor households to provide the inputs of the former category in their own homes with their own resources, if they are properly assisted and educated by health workers in the course of domiciliary visits. The inputs needed for rehabilitation of the severely undernourished, on the other hand, will be clearly beyond the means of poor households and will need expensive institutional support. Apart from this practical consideration, there is now evidence that even the so-called moderately undernourished children show functional (physical and mental) impairment.

HEIGHT AS AN INDICATOR OF NUTRITIONAL STATUS

It was earlier pointed out that, as far as infants and very young children are concerned, height measurements may not be feasible in large-scale field studies; moreover, height (length) is less sensitive to dietary fluctuations in the short run. For these reasons, it was recommended that weight-for-age measurements would suffice for all practical purposes as far as under-fives are concerned.

However, the merit of height measurements as an indication of socio-economic status of a community deserves special emphasis. Serial height measurements of children of 6–7 years of age have an important place in national nutrition surveys. Cross-sectional measurement of heights in adult populations of different classes can provide valuable indicators of disparities with respect to nutritional status arising from socio-economic inequalities. Tanner (1982), in his remarkable paper on 'The Potential of Auxological Data for Measuring Economic and Social Well-being', has provided a fascinating historical account which highlights the great value of height measurements as an instrument for monitoring progress with respect to the state of health, nutrition, and well-being of communities. Steckel (1983) found a close correlation between height and per capita income in a study based on the result of fifty-six height studies and per capita income estimates for twenty countries. When it is recognized that 'socio-economic' factors and per capita income could affect height only by mediating changes in nutritional inputs, the importance of height as a measure of nutritional status of a community becomes obvious.

The most convenient age group that could be captured for large-scale height surveys would be schoolchildren of the 6–7-year age group — that is those belonging to the first or second standard (the stage at which drop-outs are few). In fact, such surveys must constitute an important item of any national nutrition survey.

Height measurements and quantification of height deficit (in comparison with an international or national standard) will help to identify differences in nutritional status between different regions, population groups, and social classes in a country and to monitor changes over a period of time. Indeed, height deficits in a population group could be considered to provide an even more reliable indication of nutritional status than weight deficits. It may be argued that the standards against which weight measurements are being compared have been derived from relatively obese affluent American subjects and may not necessarily reflect optimal nutrition. Also, temporary diminution in weights occurring in communities of children or even adults can be caused by short-lived epidemics. These criticisms will not apply to height measurements. Overnutrition and resultant obesity can result in more than optimal weights, but not in more than optimal heights.

Height-for-age deficits can be quantified in the same way as weight-for-age deficits using international standards and applying the procedures of 'Z' scores. Where facilities exist, each country could develop its own weight-for-age and height-for-age standards based on measurements carried out on truly affluent sections of its own population which are free from dietary and environmental constraints. Many developing countries do not at present have such standards of their own. Under the circumstances, in view of the mounting evidence that genetic differences with respect to growth potential between population groups are relatively minor, it will be quite in order for international standards (WHO/NCHS/Harvard) to be used for all practical purposes for the assessment of weight and height deficits. It is possible that even standards developed by each developing country based on observations on its affluent sections could fall short of the widely used international standards to some extent. This is because of the strong likelihood that the secular trend with respect to growth has not as yet reached its maximum limit in many developing countries. It may probably need two or three generations of affluence for populations in many such countries to attain their fullest growth potential, which can be expected to be almost similar to the prevailing pattern in Europe and America, as has been revealed by experience in Japan during the last two to three decades.

Biological Significance of Height Measurement

Tanner (1982) quotes Villerme, who wrote as long ago as 1928 that

human height becomes greater and growth takes place more rapidly, other things being equal, in proportion as the country is richer, comfort more general, houses, clothes and nourishment better, and labour, fatigue and privations during infancy and youth less; in other words, circumstances which accompany poverty delay the age at which complete stature is reached and stunt adult height.

In Japan, between 1957 and 1977 average mature height increased by 4.3 cm in males and 2.7 cm in females; age at maximum increment dropped by 0.97 years in males and 0.53 years in females. Practically all the height increase was due to increase in leg length, not in sitting height, with the result that within twenty years of economic advancement the entire body proportions of the Japanese had changed. This is perhaps the most striking and spectacular evidence of the importance of height measurements as an index of the nutritional status of a population which parallels economic advancement, and it reveals that height measurement is clearly an indicator of as much importance to the developmental economist and planner as it is to the health/nutrition scientist.

There is a large body of evidence pointing to a relationship between height and mental function. Indeed, as early as 1893, William Porter (quoted by Tanner 1982) had shown in the schools of St Louis that pupils who were academically advanced for their age were also taller. There have been quite a few similar observations in recent years pointing to a correlation between height and IQ.

Tanner also quotes findings from a massive study in Norway, in which height measurements were recorded in 1.8 million subjects over 15 years of age: there it was found that mortality in those 185–9 cm tall was half the rate of that in those 150–5 cm tall. A similar lower mortality among taller children less than 5 years old in Ghana has also been reported by Billewicz and McGregor (1982).

Reviewing all the available evidence on height measurements and attempting an answer to the question, 'Is being taller better?', Tanner (1982) concludes:

It does look, therefore, as though height indeed can be a proxy for health and for the attainment of biological potential. This is true, of course, only when comparing groups, not in comparing isolated individuals, the variation between whom is due overwhelmingly to genetic causes. But between social classes, urban and rural dwellers, educated and uneducated, height is a useful proxy for 'aisance de vie'.

Height measurements will not only be helpful in monitoring *secular* trends in nutrition and economic status: they will also be useful in making interregional and interclass comparisons of nutritional status. Height measurements could help to bring out glaring socio-economic inequalities and the consequent disparities in nutritional status among classes within countries. Tanner refers to a report on Trinidad slaves in 1815 which showed that Trinidad foremen were on average an inch taller than the fieldhands. Bielicki, et al. (1981) showed that the sons of Polish peasants raised in villages in families containing four children had an average height of about 172 cm, while sons of professional men with small families working in large cities averaged 176 cm. Goldstein

(1971) reported a similar phenomenon in the UK on the basis of a national sample survey of heights of 7-year-olds in 1971.

The difference between the average heights of non-manual classes (class III) and labouring classes (classes IV and V) was also reported as being roughly 1 in. by Clements and Picket in 1957 (quoted by Tanner 1982); strangely enough, the data of the office of Population Censuses and Surveys of 1980 show that this difference still persists.

It is only with respect to Scandinavian countries — Sweden and Norway — that there is, today, convincing evidence of an absence of significant differences with respect to height between occupational classes. The attainment of such a situation of equity and distributive justice wherein there are no striking differences with respect to nutritional status between different occupational and income groups must be considered the hallmark of truly successful socio-economic development; in such a situation, even the groups with the lowest income levels are apparently able to achieve an optimal level of nutrition. Unfortunately, most developing countries still appear to be far away from this goal. Not only is the general level of health and nutrition in their populations low, but there is also apparently far greater evidence of disparities among populations. Evidence of differences in height between different occupation groups in India is unfortunately quite striking, as the observations that follow will show.

Indian Studies

Three Indian studies covering fairly large numbers of subjects indicate the value of height as a measure of nutritional status. In these studies, height measurements (along with weight measurements) have been carried out in subjects of different socio-economic groups. It was presumed that 'the dietary intake would largely parallel the socio-economic status; and in any case, as was pointed out earlier, there is no way in which socio-economic or occupational status can exert a direct metabolic effect on the body in order to influence height except through its effect on nutritional inputs. So it will be justifiable to view the observed relationship in these studies between height and economic status as in fact a relationship between height and nutritional status.

1. Shanti Ghosh and her colleagues have carried out an extensive longitudinal study on growth and development of children of different socio-economic groups, from birth to nearly 15 years of age. Nearly 8200 children were covered in the study. The communities investigated

ranged from the poorest (less than Rs 50 per head per month — 1969 level) to the fairly well-to-do upper middle class (more than Rs 200 per head per month — 1969 level). The longitudinal data from children belonging to these two income groups (Figure 7.1) show a clear relationship between socio-economic status and heights and weights of children.

2. Satyanarayana and colleagues (1980) have assembled data from longitudinal observations on the heights and weights of children of different socio-economic groups in rural Hyderabad observed over a fifteen-year period from 5 to 20 years of age. The children belonging to their Group I, with heights between M and $M - 2\,SD$ of Boston standard, mostly came from families of affluent landlords owning more than 5 acres of fertile land; those of their Group III were from the poorest rural households owning no land of their own, with adults being illiterate and eking out their living from seasonal agricultural wage-

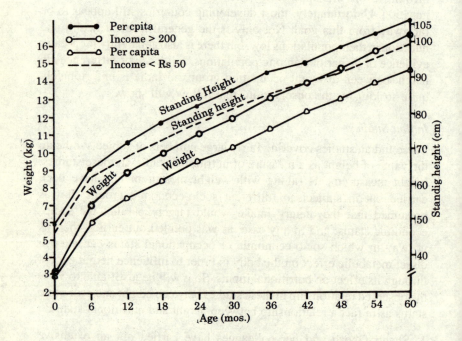

Figure 7.1:   Weight and standing heights of Indian girls,
by per capita income and age

Source: Ghosh, et al., unpublished research.

labour. In Table 7.4 some of their observations have been set out. The table also shows data on heights and weights of children of the most affluent Indian communities as observed and reported by Hanumantha Rao and Sastry (1977) on the basis of their cross-sectional studies. The striking differences between the various socio-economic groups will again be obvious.

Table 7.4
Longitudinal Studies of Growth of Indian
Children of Different Socio-economic Groups

Group	Initial (aged 5)		Final (aged 20)	
	Ht (cm)	Wt (kg)	Ht (cm)	Wt (kg)
Mostly from families of well-to-do landlords[a] (owning about 5 acres of fertile land)	104.7	15.3	167.8	51.5
Mostly from families of agricultural labourers on seasonal/daily wages[a]	89.2	11.5	157.8	44.0
Highly affluent[b]	108.0	18.3	171.8	59.6

[a] Based on Satyanarayana (1986).
[b] Based on Hanumantha Rao and Sastry (1977).

3. The National Nutrition Monitoring Bureau (1980) has recently completed a study of the dietary, nutritional, and anthropometric status of 32,332 subjects (12,925 adults and the rest children) drawn from fifteen major cities of India. The sample households were classified into five major socio-economic categories. The high-income group (HIG) and slum labour (SL) represented the two extreme ends of the economic spectrum, with the other three groups lying in between. SL was the group subject to the greatest socio-economic deprivation — poor, largely illiterate or semi-literate, living in highly overcrowded and unhygienic conditions, and having to depend mostly on unskilled manual labour to eke out a precarious livelihood. Their diets were decidedly lower in energy content, and their children showed a higher prevalence of signs of vitamin deficiencies. The heights and weights of children and adults faithfully reflected the socio-economic gradient, with HIG at one end, SL at the other, and the remaining groups falling in between. For the sake of convenience, only part of the data from the

two groups at the extreme ends (HIG and SL) have been set out in Tables 7.5 and 7.6.

Table 7.5
Heights and Weights of Children in Urban India, 1975–1979

	Height (cm)		Weight (kg)	
	HIG[a]	SL[b]	HIG[a]	SL[b]
At 5 years				
Boys	110.4	99.8	18.2	13.9
Girls	107.6	98.7	16.2	13.6
At 12 years				
Boys	144.2	132.6	30.8	25.1
Girls	140.4	133.7	29.9	26.8
At 16 years				
Boys	164.5	154.7	46.2	38.6
Girls	156.2	148.6	43.1	39.1

Source: National Nutrition Monitoring Bureau (1980).
  [a]   High-income group.   [b] Slum labour.

Table 7.6
Heights and Weights of Adults in India, 1975–1979

	Height (cm)		Weight (kg)	
	HIG[a]	SL[b]	HIG[a]	SL[b]
	(1)	(2)[c]	(3)	(4)[c]
At 20–5 years				
Males	166.4	161.4	50.4	46.6
		(161.0–164)		(47.2–49.8)
Females	154.6	150.1	46.8	41.7
		(149.4–151.9)		(41.0–44.2)
At 40–5 years				
Males	166.8	161.2	66.3	48.1
Females	153.1	149.6	56.0	41.6

Source: National Nutrition Monitoring Bureau (1980).
  [a]   High-income group.   [b] Slum labour.
  [c]   Figures in parentheses in columns (2) and (4) are measurements of corresponding rural groups.

The Poverty Trap

The outstanding finding in all the three Indian studies cited above is the striking relationship between income and occupational status on the one hand and physical stature on the other. It would appear that the more 'lowly' (using the expression for the sake of convenience) the job that a community is engaged in, the greater the degree of stunting in its children and adults. The cart-pullers, scavengers, manual labourers (including those engaged in strenuous work), stone-cutters, porters having to carry heavy loads, and agricultural labourers are apparently the ones who are most stunted and have the lowest body weights; unfortunately, these are precisely the occupation groups (rather than the business executives and academicians) who are in greatest need of a strong and sturdy body for optimal productivity and output and for earning a reasonable wage from their occupation.

As was pointed out earlier, my concern is not over small body size *per se*. Earlier in this chapter I pointed out the functional implications of stunting. Stunting in a community is but a proxy for current substandard function and for past malnutrition which must have involved a considerable cost to society.

A community in which a considerable part of the population is stunted is usually a community with high infant and child mortality, high levels of morbidity in children, and a high rate of drop-outs from schools. This is also a community in which children have lost valuable time for learning skills, mothers have lost considerable part of their daily wages, and health services are so overburdened with curative work that preventive and promotive health programmes are relegated to the background.

SUMMARY AND CONCLUSIONS

The major propositions of this chapter can be briefly recapitulated.

1. There are two practical approaches to the measurement of undernutrition: (*a*) through a survey of diets of representative households (supported by surveys of diets of individual members of the family in a sub-sample of households), in order to derive information about the nutrient intake, especially calorie intake; and (*b*) through an anthropometric and clinical examination of children, especially the under-fives. These two procedures, combined with a broad survey of socio-economic and environmental status of the community, will yield

data which, when properly interpreted and evaluated, could provide valuable practical leads for combating undernutrition in the community.

2. The basic issue that arises in the interpretations of the data gathered through these above approaches is, what are the normal standards against which prevailing levels of calorie intake or observed growth performance should be compared in order to determine adequacy or otherwise? The three hypotheses — of Sukhatme, Seckler, and Payne — that have been advanced in this connection have been critically examined. Sukhatme has argued that human subjects can permanently adapt themselves to a low calorie intake level representing the lowest limit of their intra-individual variations and that, therefore, $M - 2\ SD$ (recommended mean energy requirement level M minus two standard deviations) rather than M would be the appropriate yardstick for an assessment of calorie intake. Sukhatme's hypothesis is unacceptable because there is no convincing evidence that populations engaged in their expected levels of occupational activity and obliged to subsist on only about 70 per cent of their recommended mean energy intake can permanently adapt themselves to such a low calorie intake through metabolic adjustment and increased efficiency of energy utilization without suffering a loss of body weight or consequent impairment of function. With a calorie intake that is around 70 per cent of the currently recommended levels, it will be difficult for children to meet their protein requirements with cereal-based diets: a drastic qualitative upgrading of current cereal-based diets would be necessary. This implies a reversal to the discredited view that the answer to the problem of protein–calorie malnutrition in developing countries lies in increasing use of expensive protein concentrates, a view that has been convincingly rejected on the basis of extensive studies.

3. Seckler's hypothesis that moderate degrees of growth retardation are a welcome attribute of poor people consistent with their good health and an acceptable form of adaptation is untenable because of the evidence that even moderate degrees of growth retardation have been shown to be associated with an impairment of physical and mental function.

4. Payne's hypothesis that even if children of developing countries have been shown to have the same genetic potential for growth as those of the more fortunate countries of Europe and the USA, their lower levels of growth should not be viewed as evidence of under-

nutrition but as an adjustment to their 'economy and ecology' is also untenable. Payne does not deny that such growth-retarded children suffer from impaired function; but he considers that, despite such impairment, the subjects can function as well as they need to in their economy and ecology, and therefore, he would not consider them undernourished. The acceptance of this postulate can lead to the perpetuation of the present substandard state of growth and development in populations of the poor countries and is therefore wholly unacceptable.

5. In all the above three hypotheses the word 'adaptation' has been loosely employed to signify an acceptable state of normalcy instead of being viewed as a strategic retreat from normalcy which involves compromise with respect to both physical and mental function.

6. The view propounded by Payne that only those children whose state of nutrition has deteriorated to the point where they face the risk of imminent death should be considered undernourished obviously cannot be accepted. This is almost like saying that a person is 'unhealthy' only when he is on the point of death. The so-called moderately malnourished children of today could gravitate into severe malnutrition in a few weeks or months. It is far easier and far less expensive to prevent them from sliding to such a severe stage of undernutrition than to rehabilitate them after they have reached that stage. Moreover, the so-called moderate degree of growth retardation is also associated with impaired function. Populations subjected to such retardation represent a substandard human resource.

7. The view sometimes propagated that, irrespective of deficit in height-for-age or weight-for-age, children with weights appropriate to their heights (normal weight-for-height ratio) could be considered adapted is also untenable. Stunting, irrespective of body weight, has been shown to be associated with impaired function. Stunted children with normal weight-for-height ratio also show evidence of impaired physical and mental function.

8. A level of dietary intake and nutrition which can permit only substandard growth must inevitably lead to an erosion of the quality of human resources of developing countries or a perpetuation of such erosion where it already exists. It must, therefore, be the policy of developing countries to achieve for their children a level of growth and development which represents the fullest expression of their genetic potential.

REFERENCES

Agarwal, D.K., S.K. Upadhyay, A.M. Tripathi and K.N. Agarwal (1987). *Nutritional Status, Physical Work Capacity and Mental Function in School Children*, Scientific Report no. 6. New Delhi: Nutrition Foundation of India.

Bielick, T.W., et al. (1981). 'The Influence of Three Socioeconomic Factors on Body Height in Polish Military Conscripts', *Human Biology*, 53.

Billewicz, W.Z. and I.A. McGregor (1982). 'A Birth-to-Maturity Longitudinal Study of Heights and Weights in Two West African [Gambian] Villages, 1951–1975', *Annals of Human Biology*, 9.

Chavez, A. and C. Martinez (1982). 'Growing up in a Developing Community'. Institute of National Nutrition, Mexico, mimeo.

Chen, L.C., A.K.M. Chowdhury and S.L. Huffman (1980). 'Anthropometric Assessment of Energy — Protein Malnutrition and Subsequent Risk of Mortality among Pre-school-aged Children', *American Journal of Clinical Nutrition*, 33.

Chen, L.C., et al. (1982). 'Malnutrition and Mortality', *Nutrition Foundation of India Bulletin*, 3.

Goldstein, W. (1971). 'Factors Influencing the Height of Six-Year-Old Children: Results from the National Child Development Study', *Human Biology*, 43.

Gomez, F., et al. (1956). 'Mortality in Second and Third Degree Malnutrition', *Journal of Tropical Paediatrics*, 2.

Gopalan, C. (1955). 'Clinical Aspects and Treatment', in J.C. Waterlow (ed.), *Protein Malnutrition*. Rome: FAO.

Gopalan, C., M.C. Swaminathan, K.K. Kumar, D. Hanumantha Rao, and K. Vijayaraghavan (1973). 'Effect of Calorie Supplementation on Growth of Undernourished Children', *American Journal of Clinical Nutrition*, 26.

—— (1983a). 'Measurement of Undernutrition: Biological Considerations', *Nutrition Foundation of India Bulletin*, 4.

—— (1983b). ' "Small is Healthy?" for the Poor, Not for the Rich', *Nutrition Foundation of India Bulletin*, 4; reprinted in *Future*, Autumn 1983 (page references relate to the reprint).

—— (1984). 'Classification of Undernutrition: Their Limitations and Fallacies', *Nutrition Foundation of India Bulletin*, 5.

—— (1989). 'Growth Standard for Indian Children', *Nutrition Foundation of India Bulletin*, 10.

Habicht, J.P., R. Martorell, C. Yarbrough, R.M. Malina and R.E. Klein (1974). 'Height and Weight Standards for Pre-school Children: How

Relevant are Ethnic Differences in Growth Potential?', *Lancet*, 7 April.

Hanumantha Rao, D. and G. Sastry (1977). 'Growth Pattern of Well-to-do Indian Adolescents and Young Adults', *Indian Journal of Medical Research*, 66.

Jaya Rao, K.S. (1986). 'Perpetuating Undernutrition', *Economic and Political Weekly*, 14 June.

Lancet (1984). 'A Measure of Agreement on Growth Standard' (editorial), *Lancet*, 21 January.

National Nutrition Monitoring Bureau (1980). *Report on Urban Population, 1975–1979*. Hyderabad: National Institute of Nutrition.

Pacey, A. and P. Payne (eds) (1985). *Agricultural Development and Nutrition*. London: Hutchinson Press.

Rutishauser, I.H.E. and R.G. Whitehead (1972). 'Energy Intake and Expenditure in 1–3-Year-Old Ugandan Children Living in a Rural Environment', *British Journal of Nutrition*, 28.

Satyanarayana, K., A.N. Naidu, B. Chatterjee and B.S.N. Rao (1977). 'Body Size and Work Output', *American Journal of Clinical Nutrition*, 30.

Satyanarayana, K. and B.S.N. Rao (1979). 'Nutritional Deprivation in Childhood and the Body Size, Activity and Physical Work Capacity of Young Boys', *American Journal of Clinical Nutrition*, 32.

Satyanarayana, K., A.N. Naidu and B. Chatterjee (1980). 'Adolescent Growth Spurt among Rural Indian Boys in Relation to Their Nutritional Status in Early Childhood', *Annals of Human Biology*, 7.

Seckler, D. (1982). 'Small But Healthy: A Basic Hypothesis in the Theory, Measurement and Policy of Malnutrition', in Sukhatme (1982).

Spurr, G.B., et al. (1982). 'Maximum Oxygen Consumption of Nutritionally Normal White, Mestizo and Black Colombian Boys 6–16 Years of Age', *Human Biology*, 54.

Spurr, G.B., J.C. Reina, H.W. Dahners and M. Barac-Nieto (1983). 'Marginal Malnutrition in School-Aged Colombian Boys: Functional Consequences in Maximum Exercise 1–3', *American Journal of Clinical Nutrition*, 37.

Spurr, G.C., J.C. Reina and R. Ramiret (1984). 'Marginal Malnutrition in School-Aged Colombian Boys: Efficiency of Treadmill Walking in Submaximal Exercise 1–3', *American Journal of Clinical Nutrition*, 39.

Steckel, R.H. (1983). 'Height and Per Capita Income', *Historical Methods*, 16.

Stephenson, L.S., et al. (1983). 'A Comparison of Growth Standards:

Similarities between NCHS, Harvard, Denver and Privileged African Children and Differences with Kenyan Rural Children', International Nutrition Monograph Series no. 12.

Sukhatme, P.V. (1978). 'Assessment of Adequacy of Diets and Different Income Levels', *Economic and Political Weekly*, Special Number, August.

——(1981). 'On Measurement of Poverty', *Economic and Political Weekly*, 8 August.

—— (ed.) (1982). *Newer Concepts in Nutrition and Their Implications for Policy*. Pune: Maharashtra Association for the Cultivation of Science.

Tanner, J.M. (1982). 'The Potential of Auxological Data for Measuring Economic and Social Well-Being', *Social Science History*, 6.

Torun, B., Y. Schutz, R. Bradfield and F.E. Viteri (1975). 'Effect of Physical Activity upon Growth of Children Recovering from Protein Calorie Malnutrition (PCM)', *Proceedings of Tenth International Congress of Nutrition*, Kyoto.

Viteri, F. (1971). 'Considerations on the Effect of Nutrition on the Body Composition and Physical Capacity of Young Guatemalan Adults', in N. Scrimshaw and A.M. Altshull (eds), *Amino-acid Fortification of Protein Foods*. Cambridge, Mass.: MIT Press, pp. 350–75.

Waterlow, et al. (1977). 'The Presentation and Use of Height and Weight Data for Comparing the Nutritional Status of Groups of Children under the Age of 10 years', *World Health Organization Bulletin*, 55.

Poverty:
An Ordinal Approach to Measurement

A.K. SEN

MOTIVATION

In the measurement of poverty two distinct problems must be faced: (i) identifying the poor among the total population; and (ii) constructing an index of poverty using the available information on the poor. The former problem involves the choice of a criterion of poverty (for example the selection of a 'poverty line' in terms of real income per head), and then ascertaining those who satisfy that criterion (for example fall below the 'poverty line') and those who do not. In the literature on poverty significant contributions have been made in tackling this problem (see, for example, Rowntree 1901, Weisbrod 1965, Townsend 1954 and Atkinson 1970a), but relatively little work has been done on problem (ii) with which this chapter will be concerned.

The most common procedure for handling problem (ii) seems to be simply to count the number of the poor and check the percentage of the total population belonging to this category. This ratio, which we shall call the headcount ratio H, is obviously a very crude index. An unchanged number of people below the 'poverty line' may go with a sharp rise in the extent of the shortfall of income from the poverty line.[1]

The measure is also completely insensitive to the distribution of income among the poor. A pure transfer of income from the poorest poor to those who are better off will either keep H unchanged, or make it go down — surely a perverse response. Measure H thus violates both of the following axioms.

[1] Cf. 'Its [the new Poor Law's] only effect was that whereas previously three to four million half paupers had existed, a million of total paupers now appeared, and the rest, still half paupers, merely went without relief. The poverty in the agricultural districts has increased every year' (Engels 1969, p. 288).

Monotonicity Axiom.   *Given other things, a reduction in income of a person below the poverty line must increase the poverty measure.*

Transfer Axiom.   *Given other things, a pure transfer of income from a person below the poverty line to anyone who is richer must increase the poverty measure.*[2]

Despite these limitations, the headcount ratio is very widely used.[3]

Another common measure is the so-called 'poverty gap' (used by the United States Social Security Administration((see Batchelder 1971, p. 30) which is the aggregate shortfall of the income of all the poor taken together from the poverty line. This satisfies the monotonicity axiom but violates the transfer axiom.[4]

Though it will not be necessary to formally use the monotonicity axiom and the transfer axiom in deriving the new poverty measure (they will be satisfied anyway, implied by a more demanding axiomatic structure[†]), the motivation of our search for a new measure can be understood by noticing the violation of these elementary conditions by the poverty measures currently in wide use.

INCOME SHORTFALL AND POVERTY

Consider a community S of n people. The set of q people with income no higher than x is called $S(x)$. If z is 'the poverty line', that is the level of income at which poverty begins, $S(z)$ is the set of 'the poor'. $S(\infty)$

---

[2] Cf. Dalton's 'principle of transfers' in measuring inequality; see Atkinson (1970b, pp. 247–9). See also Dasgupta, Sen and Starrett (1973) and Rothschild and Stiglitz (1973).

[3] The vigorous and illuminating debate on whether or not rural poverty is on the increase in India, which took place recently, was based almost exclusively on using the headcount ratio. See particularly Ojha (1970), Dandekar and Rath (1971), Minhas (1970 and 1971), Bardhan (1970 and 1971), Srinivasan and Vaidyanathan (1971), Vaidyanathan (1971) and Mukherjee, Bhattacharya and Chatterjee (1972). A remarkable amount of sophistication in correcting consumption data, calculating class-specific deflators, etc. was coupled with the use of this rather crude criterion of measuring poverty.

[4] It is also completely insensitive to the *number* of people (or the *percentage* of people) who are poor, sharing a given poverty gap.

[†] This is not correct. The poverty measure P, which is axiomatically derived here, does not, in fact, invariably satisfy the 'strong' version of the transfer axiom used here; this was noted in 'Social Choice Theory: A Re-examination', *Econometrica*, 45 (January 1977), p. 185. The strong version of the transfer axiom takes no note whatsoever of poverty line, which is quite legitimate for a measure of inequality but not perhaps for a measure of poverty. The measure P does satisfy a weaker version of the transfer axiom proposed in 'Social Choice Theory'.

is, of course, the set of all, that is S. The income gap g_i of any individual i is the difference between the poverty line z and his income y_i.

$$g_i = z - y_i. \tag{1}$$

Obviously, g_i is non-negative for the poor and negative for others.

For any income configuration represented by an n-vector y, 'the aggregate gap' $Q(x)$ of the set $S(x)$ of people with income no higher than x is a normalized weighted sum of the income gaps g_i of everyone in $S(x)$, using non-negative weights $v_i(z, y)$:

$$Q(x) = A(z, q, n) \sum_{i \in S(x)} g_i v_i(z, y). \tag{2}$$

The specification of A and v_i will depend on a set of axioms to be proposed presently. It should, however, be noted at this stage that the form of (2) is very general indeed, and that v_i has been defined as a function of the vector y, and not of y_i alone (along with z). In particular no requirement of additive separability has been imposed.

The index of poverty P of a given income configuration y is defined to be the maximal value of the aggregate gap $Q(x)$ for all x:

$$P = \max_x Q(x). \tag{3}$$

Since the weights v_i are all non-negative, it is obvious from (1) and (2) that

$$P = Q(z). \tag{4}$$

That is the index of poverty P of a community is given by the value of the weighted aggregate gap of the poor in that community.

RELATIVE DEPRIVATION AND INTERPERSONAL COMPARABILITY

In line with the motivation of the transfer axiom, it may be reasonable to require that if person i is accepted to be worse off than person j in a given income configuration y, then the weight v_i on the income shortfall g_i of the worse-off person i should be greater than the weight v_j on the income shortfall g_j. Let $W_i(y)$ and $W_j(y)$ be the welfare levels of i and j under configuration y.

Axiom E (Relative Equity). *For any pair i, j: if $W_i(y) < W_j(y)$, then $v_i(z, y) > v_j(z, y)$.*

If the individual welfare functions were cardinal, interpersonally fully comparable and identical for all persons, and furthermore if the Benthamite additive utilitarian form of social welfare were accepted, then it would be natural to relate v_i in Axiom E to the marginal utility of income of person i. But in this chapter the utilitarian approach is not taken; nor are the assumptions of cardinality and full interpersonal comparability made.[5] Individual welfare is taken to be ordinally measurable and level comparable. There is agreement on who is worse off than whom, for example 'poor i is worse off than wealthy j', but no agreement on the values of the welfare differences is required.

While Axiom E can be justified on the grounds of a strictly concave interpersonally comparable cardinal welfare function, that is not the only possible justification. The idea that a greater value should be attached to an increase in income (or reduction of shortfall) of a poorer person than that of a relatively richer person can also spring from considerations of interpersonal equity.[6] The appeal of Axiom E is, I believe, much wider than that which can be obtained from an exclusive reliance on utilitarianism and diminishing marginal utility.

Axiom E gives expression to a very mild requirement of equity. Another axiom is now proposed, which incorporates Axiom E, but is substantially more demanding.

Axiom R (Ordinal Rank Weights)   *The weight $v_i(z, y)$ on the income gap of person i equals the rank order of i in the interpersonal welfare ordering of the poor.*

The method of constructing weights on the basis of rank orders is not new, and since the classic discussion of the procedure by Borda in 1781 (extracts trans. in Black 1958), it has been extensively analysed and axiomatized in voting theory (see, especially Fine and Fine 1974; Fishburn 1973, ch. 13, Gärdenfors 1973 and Hansson 1973). Axiom R is taken as an axiom here, though it can be easily made a theorem derived from more primitive axioms (see Sen 1973b and 1974).

There are essentially two ways of doing this. The first is to follow Borda in equidistanced cardinalization of an ordering. If A, B, and C are ranked in that order in terms of their weights, and if there is no

[5] Alternative frameworks for interpersonal comparability were explored in Sen (1970a and 1972) in which the possibility of *partial* comparability of cardinal individual welfare functions was also explored.
[6] On various aspects of equity considerations in welfare economics, see Graaff (1967), Runciman (1966), Kolm (1969), Sen (1970b) and Pattanaik (1971).

intermediate alternative between A and B, and none between B and C, 'I say that the degree of superiority that this elector has given to A over B should be considered the same as the degree of superiority that he has accorded to B over C' (Borda 1781, p. 659, trans. Black 1958, p. 157). We know from Axiom E that if i is worse off than j, then the weight on i's income gap should be greater than on j's income gap. Using Borda's procedure combined with appropriate normalization of the origin and the unit, we arrive at Axiom R.

The second is to take a 'relativist' view of poverty, viewing deprivation as an essentially relative concept (see Runciman 1966). The lower a person is in the welfare scale, the greater his sense of poverty, and his welfare rank among others may be taken to indicate the weight to be placed on his income gap.[7] Axiom R can be derived from this approach as well.

We turn now to the relation between income and welfare, since Axioms E and R are in terms of welfare rankings, whereas the observed data are on income rankings. There are, of course, good reasons to think that sometimes a richer person may have lower welfare than a poorer person, for example if he is a cripple, and this may raise interesting issues of equity (see Sen 1973a, ch. 1). When dealing with a general measure of poverty for the community as a whole, however, it is not easy to bring such detailed considerations into the exercise. Axiom M proceeds on the cruder assumptions that a richer person is also better off. Furthermore, the individual welfare relation is taken to be a strict complete ordering to avoid some problems that arise with rank-order methods in the case of indifference. This last assumption is less arbitrary than it may at first seem.[8]

Axiom M (Monotonic Welfare). *The relation > (greater than) defined on the set of individual welfare numbers* $[W_i(y)]$ *for any income configuration y is a strict complete ordering, and the relation > defined on the corresponding set of individual incomes* $[y_i]$ *is a sub-relation of the former, i.e. for any i, j: if $y_i > y_j$, then $W_i(y) > W_j(y)$.*

---

[7] This can be axiomatized either in terms of the welfare rank of the person among the poor (as in Axiom R) or in terms of that among the entire population (see Axiom R^* in the sixth section below). Both lead to essentially the same result if correspondingly normalized (see Axiom N).

[8] The poverty index P to emerge in Theorem 1 is completely insensitive to the way we rank people with the same income. See equation (15) below.

CRUDE INDICATORS AND NORMALIZATION

In the first section, references were made to two measures of poverty currently in use. The 'headcount ratio' is the ratio of the number of people with income $y_i \leq z$, to the total population size n:

$$H = \frac{q}{n}. \tag{5}$$

The other measure — the poverty gap — is silent on the number of people who share this gap, but can be easily normalized into a per-person percentage gap I, which we shall call the 'income-gap ratio':[9]

$$I = \sum_{i \varepsilon\, S(z)} g_i / qz. \tag{6}$$

While the headcount ratio tells us the percentage of people below the poverty line, the income-gap ratio tells us the percentage of their mean shortfall from the poverty level. The headcount ratio is completely insensitive to the *extent* of the poverty shortfall per person, the income-gap ratio is completely insensitive to the *numbers* involved. Both should have some role in the index of poverty. But H and I together are not sufficiently informative either, since neither gives adequate information on the exact income distribution among the poor. Further, neither measure satisfies the transfer axiom, or the requirement of putting a greater weight on the income gap of the poorer person (axiomatized in Axiom E given Axiom M).

However, in the special case in which all the poor have exactly the *same* income level $y^* < z$, it can be argued that H and I together should give us adequate information on the level of poverty, since in this special case the two together can tell us all about the proportion of people who are below the poverty line and the extent of the income shortfall of each. To obtain a simple normalization, we make P equal HI in this case.

Axiom N (Normalized Poverty Value). *If the poor have the same income, then $P = HI$.*

---

[9] Another measure — let us call it I^* — is obtained by normalizing the 'poverty gap' on the total income of the community:

$$I^* = Iqz/nm^*, \tag{6*}$$

where m^* is the mean income of the entire population.

THE POVERTY INDEX DERIVED

The axioms stated determine one poverty index uniquely. It is easier to state that index if we number the persons in a non-decreasing order of income,[10] that is satisfying:

$$y_1 \le y_2 \le \ldots y_n. \tag{7}$$

Theorem 1. *For large numbers of the poor, the only poverty index satisfying Axioms R, M, and N is given by*:

$$P = H[I + (1 - I)G], \tag{8}$$

where G is the Gini coefficient of the income distribution of the poor.

Proof. By Axiom M, there is a way of numbering the individuals satisfying (7), such that:

$$W_1(y) < W_2(y) \ldots < W_n(y). \tag{9}$$

For any person $i \le q$, there are exactly $(q + 1 - i)$ people among the poor with at least as high a welfare level as person i. Hence by Axiom R:

$$v_i(z, y) = q + 1 - i. \tag{10}$$

Therefore, from (2) and (4):

$$P = A(z, q, n) \sum_{i=1}^{q} g_i(q + 1 - i). \tag{11}$$

In the special case in which all the poor have the same income y^* and the same income gap $g^* = z - y^*$, we must have:

$$P = A(z, q, n)g^* q(q + 1)/2. \tag{12}$$

But according to Axiom N:

$$P = \left(\frac{q}{n}\right)\left(\frac{g^*}{z}\right). \tag{13}$$

---

[10] If there is more than one person having the same income, (7) does not of course determine the numbering uniquely. But the formula for the poverty index specified in Theorem 1 yields the same P no matter which numbering convention is chosen satisfying (7).

Therefore from (12) and (13):

$$A(z, q, n) = 2/(q + 1)nz . \qquad (14)$$

From (11) and (14), it follows that:

$$P = \frac{2}{(q+1)nz} \sum_{i=1}^{q} (z - y_i)(q + 1 - i) . \qquad (15)$$

The Gini coefficient G of the Lorenz distribution of incomes of the poor is given by (see Gini 1912 and Theil 1967):

$$G = \frac{1}{2q^2 m} \sum_{i=1}^{q} \sum_{j=1}^{q} |y_i - y_j| , \qquad (16)$$

where m is the mean income of the poor.

Since $|y_i - y_j| = y_i + y_j - 2 \min (y_i, y_j)$, clearly

$$G = 1 - \frac{1}{q^2 m} \sum_{i=1}^{q} \sum_{j=1}^{q} \min (y_i, y_j)$$

$$= 1 + \frac{1}{q} - \frac{2}{q^2 m} \sum_{i=1}^{q} y_i (q + 1 - i) . \qquad (17)$$

From (15) and (17), it follows that:

$$P = \frac{1}{(q+1)nz} \left[zq(q + 1) + q^2 m \left(G - \frac{q+1}{q} \right) \right]$$

which in view of (5) and (6) reduces to:

$$P = H \left[1 - (1 - I) \left(1 - G \left(\frac{q}{q+1} \right) \right) \right] . \qquad (18)$$

For large q, (18) yields (8). This establishes the necessity part of Theorem 1, and the sufficiency part is easily established by checking that P given by (18), and for large q by (8), does indeed satisfy Axioms R, M, and N.

POVERTY AND INEQUALITY

The role of the Gini coefficient of the Lorenz distribution of the incomes of the poor is worth clarifying. This is best done by posing the question:

what measure of inequality would follow from the same approach as used here in deriving the poverty measure?

The poverty index was derived by making use of the more primitive concept of the aggregate gap $Q(x)$. It should be noticed that given the weighting system precipitated by Axioms R and M, the value of $Q(x)$ is the same for all $x \geq z$, so that P defined by (3) as $\max_x Q(x)$ can be taken to be $Q(x)$ for any $x \geq z$ and not merely $x = z$. This is because Axiom R makes the weight on the income gap g_i of person i equal to the number of people *among the poor* who are at least as well off as person i. The inclusion of people above the poverty line z does not affect the value of Q since the weight on their income gap g_i is zero in view of Axiom M.

This is reasonable enough in measuring poverty, but if we now shift our attention to the measurement of inequality, we would like to consider the income gaps of people above the poverty line as well. Furthermore, the income gaps should be calculated not from the exogenously given poverty line z, but from some internal characteristic of the income configuration y, possibly the mean income. Variations in these lines will transform an absolute poverty measure into a relative measure of inequality.

To do this, we replace z by the mean income m^* of y. Further, the weighting given by Axiom R is modified to include all the people whether poor or not.

Axiom R*. *The weight $v_i(z, y)$ on the income gap of person i equals the number of people in S who are at least as well off as person i.*

Axiom R* will require that the weight v_i on the income gap of person i should be $(n + 1 - i)$.

The problem of measurement of inequality and that of poverty can be seen to be two intertwined exercises. The measure of inequality corresponding to the measure of poverty P can be defined in the following way.

Definition. The measure of inequality η corresponding to the poverty measure P as specified in Theorem 1 is the value obtained in place of P by replacing q (the number of poor) by n (the total number of people in the community), and replacing z (the poverty level) by m^* (the mean income of the community).

Theorem 2. *The measure of inequality η corresponding to the poverty index approximates the Gini coefficient for large n.*

The proof is obvious from (15) and (17) replacing q by n, and z and m by m^*, in the formulations of P and the Gini coefficient (now redefined for the whole community). This is also checked by putting $H = 1$ and $I = 0$ in P as given by Theorem 1.

Thus the poverty measure P obtained in Theorem 1 is essentially a translation of the Gini coefficient from the measurement of inequality to that of poverty.[11]

A diagrammatic representation of G and P is provided in Figure 8.1. Line OGB is the Lorenz curve, while OB is the line of equal division. The Gini coefficient G is given by area OGB divided by area OAB.

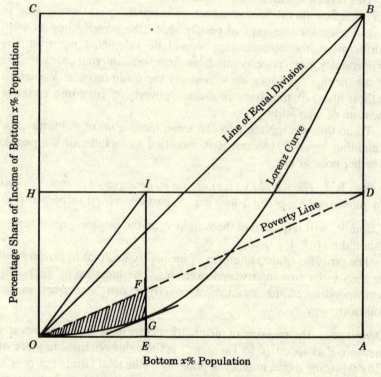

Figure 8.1

[11] An axiomatization of the Gini coefficient as a measure of inequality can be found in Sen (1974). The more primitive axiom system used there leads to R^* as a theorem without being taken as an axiom in itself.

The slope of the line OD gives 'the poverty line' in these normalized units, and OE is the number of the poor. The poverty measure P can be seen to correspond to area OGF divided by area OEI. The difference between the two lies in (i) the slope of line OD ('the poverty line') being different from the slope of line OB (the normalized mean income), and (ii) counting only the poor, that is OE, in the poverty measure, as opposed to all, that is OA.

The rank-order weighting form of the Gini coefficient G and the poverty measure P can be understood intuitively by considering the area under the curve OGB, which the Gini numerator leaves out, that is what $(1 - G)$ includes. The poorest man's income is included at every point and if there are n persons his income comes in n times. On the other hand, the highest income is included in the area under OGB exactly once at the point A when everyone is counted in, that is the richest man makes it exactly once more than the camel can get through the eye of a needle. The ith poorest man comes in at the ith point of observation and has his income included for the remaining $(n - i)$ observations as well, thereby having his income counting in $(n + 1 - i)$ times. This produces the rank-order weighting through the mechanism of the Lorenz curve, and it is this remarkable coincidence that makes the Gini coefficient give expression to the normative value judgement of weighting according to ordinal ranks satisfying Axiom R^* (and Axiom E) given Axiom M. The same way of intuitively understanding the result regarding the poverty measure can be easily suggested by considering the number of times the gap between the slope of OD (the poverty line) and the slope of OGB (the income of the poor) gets counted in.

INTERPRETATION AND VARIATIONS

The poverty index proposed here turns out to have quite an easy interpretation. The measure is made up of the headcount ratio H multiplied by the income-gap ratio I augmented by the Gini coefficient G of the distribution of income among the poor weighted by $(1 - I)$, that is weighted by the ratio of the mean income of the poor to the poverty line income level. One way of understanding its rationale is the following: I represents poverty as measured by the proportionate gap between the mean income of the poor and the poverty line income. It ignores distribution *among* the poor, and G provides this information. In addition to the poverty gap of the mean income of the poor reflected in I, there is the 'gap' arising from the unequal distribution of the mean income, which is reflected by the Gini coefficient G of that distribution multiplied by the mean income ratio. The income-gap measure thus augmented to take note of inequality among the poor, that is $I + (1 - I)G$, is normalized per poor person, and does not take note of the number of people below the poverty line, which could be minute or large. Multiplying $[I + (1 - I)G]$ by the headcount ratio H now produces the composite measure P.

While this is perhaps the easiest way of interpreting the poverty index P, it must be borne in mind that its justification lies in the axioms used to derive it. The multiplicative form chosen in Axiom N, though simple, is arbitrary. Axiom M, perhaps justifiable in the absence of detailed information on the poor, is objectionable when much is known about individual members of the group, for example that cripple Mr A while richer than robust Mr B is less well off in some sense (see Sen 1973a, pp. 17–20). Finally, Axiom R follows Borda's procedure of cardinalizing an ordering by treating rank numbers as weights. This is, of course, also arbitrary, though frequently used in other contexts as the popularity of several variants of the rank-order procedures of voting indicates. The justification can be either in terms of intensity of preference being surmised from rankings only by using a version of 'insufficient reason' (following Borda), or in terms of an essentially relativist conception of poverty. Axiom R may not be acceptable to many since there is arbitrariness in making the weight on person i's income gap equal his poverty rank. Even with a *given* level of income, a person's poverty weight will go down if a richer poor becomes poorer than him. The advantages and defects of the rank-order system are clear enough.

A few properties of P may be worth pointing out. It lies in the closed interval [0, 1], with $P = 0$ if everyone has an income greater than z, and $P = 1$ if everyone has zero income. In practice, of course, P will never equal unity, both because there are subsistence requirements (so that for each i: $y_i > 0$) as well as because even in very poor economies the class system ensures the prosperity of some (so that for some i:$y_i > z$).

Note also that when all the poor have the same income, that is $G = 0$, the lower the income of the poor, the closer will P approach the headcount measure H, and the larger the proportion of the poor, the closer will P approach the income-gap measure I.

Some variations of the normalization procedures may be worth considering. First, if the weights on income gaps are all reduced by one-half, that is the income gap g_i of the ith poorest is taken to be $(q - i + \frac{1}{2})$, then (8) holds not only for large q but for any q. However, for measuring poverty of any sizeable community, the two procedures do not make any real difference.

Second, even retaining the weighting procedure, the normalization reflected in Axiom N can be changed. In particular, the poverty measure can be made to depend also on the *ratio* of the mean income of the poor to the mean income of the entire community (Sen 1973b, equations (8) and (9)). This would give the poverty measure wider coverage. For example exactly the same number and income distribution of the poor will have a *higher* poverty index if the income of some people above the poverty line falls even without taking them below the poverty line.[12] In contrast, the measure P is completely invariant with respect to changes in the income of people *above* the poverty line and depends only on the incomes of the poor. This does not, of course, prevent us from defining the poverty line z taking note of the entire distribution of income (for example a higher z for the United States than for India), but once the poverty line has been specified, the poverty measure P depends only on the incomes of the poor.

CONCLUDING REMARKS

(i) The measure of poverty P presented here uses an ordinal approach to welfare comparisons. The need for placing a greater weight on the income of a poorer person is derived from equity considerations (Axiom E) without necessarily using interpersonally comparable *cardinal* utility functions. Ordinal-level comparability is used to obtain rank-order weighting systems (Axiom R) given a monotonic relation between income and welfare (Axiom M).

(ii) The poverty measure P obtained axiomatically in Theorem 1 corresponds to the Gini measure of inequality in the sense that replacing the poor by the entire population and replacing the poverty threshold of income by the mean income would transform P into G. This poverty measure P contrasts sharply with the crude measures of poverty used in the statistical literature on the subject and in policy discussions. Unlike H (the percentage of people below the poverty line), P is not insensitive to the extent of the shortfall of income of the poor from the poverty line. Unlike I (the percentage average shortfall of the income of the poor from the poverty line), P is not insensitive to the number below the poverty line.[13] And unlike any conceivable function

---

[12] Consider the 'mean-dependent measure' $P^* = Pz/m^*$.

[13] The alternative definition of the income-gap measure I^* is sensitive to the number

$\Psi(H, I)$ of these crude measures, P *is* sensitive to the exact pattern of distribution of the incomes of the poor.

(iii) Throughout this chapter income has been taken to be a homogeneous magnitude represented by a real number. The framework developed here can be extended to multicommodity cases as well, evaluating the consumption of commodity j by person i in terms both of the price of j and the income rank of i, basing the calculation on Fisher's (Fisher 1956; and Kenen and Fisher 1957) 'commodity matrices'.[14]

(iv) If one accepts the ordinal welfare interpretation of the rationale of the Gini coefficient (Axiom R^*), then one might wonder about the significance of the debate on the non-existence of any 'additive utility function which ranks income distributions in the same order as the Gini coefficient' (see Newbery 1970, p. 264; Sheshinski 1972; Dasgupta, Sen and Starrett 1973; and Rothschild and Stiglitz 1973). Evidently G is not an additive function of individual incomes, nor is it strictly concave or strictly quasi-concave (as is obvious from equation (17)). Axiom E and specifically Axiom R^* precipitate the equality-preferring result noted in Dasgupta, Sen and Starrett (1973) and Rothschild and Stiglitz (1973); but the ordinal weighting of the Gini coefficient cannot be cast into the strictly concave utilitarian framework, or into any other social welfare function that makes marginal weights sensitive to the exact values of income (as opposed to their ordinal ranks). The same applies to the poverty measure P proposed here.

(v) Finally, it should be pointed out that any system of measurement that takes note only of *ordinal* welfare information must be recognized to be deficient by an observer who is convinced that he has access to cardinal interpersonally comparable welfare functions. If such cardinal information did obtain, the fact that P should throw away a part of it and use only the ordering information must be judged to be wasteful. On the other hand, it is much more difficult to agree on interpersonally comparable cardinal welfare functions than to find agreement on welfare rankings only. The approach proposed here, while deficient in the sense described, also demands less. It is a compromise in much the same way as the Borda method of voting is, in making do with rankings

---

below the poverty line, but it is also sensitive to the incomes of people *above* the poverty line. Furthermore, I^* is insensitive to the *distribution* of income among the poor.

[14] The use of such an approach has been explored, as an illustration of a general system of real income comparisons with explicit treatment of distribution, in Sen (1976).

only and in slipping in an assumption of equidistance to get numerical weights. The data requirement in estimating the poverty measure P is, as a consequence, quite limited.

Acknowledgements: For helpful comments I am very grateful to Sudhir Anand, Tony Atkinson, Idrak Bhatty, Frank Fisher, Richard Layard, Suresh Tendulkar, and to an anonymous referee of *Econometrica*.

REFERENCES

Atkinson, A.B. (1970a). *Poverty in Britain and the Reform of Social Security*. Cambridge: Cambridge University Press.

—— (1970b). 'On the Measurement of Inequality', *Journal of Economic Theory*, 2, pp. 244–63.

Bardhan, P. (1970). 'On the Minimum Level of Living and the Rural Poor', *Indian Economic Review*, 5.

—— (1971). 'On the Minimum Level of Living and the Rural Poor: A Further Note', *Indian Economic Review*, 6.

Batchelder, A.B. (1971). *The Economics of Poverty*. New York: Wiley.

Black, D. (1958). *The Theory of Committees and Elections*. Cambridge: Cambridge University Press.

Borda, J.C. de (1781). 'Memoire sur les Élections au Scrutin', in *Histoire de l'Académie Royale des Sciences*. Paris; extracts translated in English in D. Black (1958). *The Theory of Committees and Elections*. Cambridge: Cambridge University Press, ch. XVIII.

Dandekar, V.M. and N. Rath (1971). *Poverty in India*. Poona: Indian School of Political Economy.

Dasgupta, P., A.K. Sen and D. Starrett (1973). 'Notes on the Measurement of Inequality', *Journal of Economic Theory*, 6, pp. 180–7.

Engels, F. (1969 [1892]). *The Condition of the Working Class in England*. London: Panther.

Fine, B. and K. Fine (1974). 'Social Choice and Individual Ranking', *Review of Economic Studies*, 41, pp. 303–22, 459–75.

Fishburn, P.C. (1973). *The Theory of Social Choice*. Princeton, NJ: Princeton University Press.

Fisher, F.M. (1956). 'Income Distribution, Value Judgements, and Welfare', *Quarterly Journal of Economics*, 70, pp. 380–424.

Gärdenfors, P. (1973). 'Positional Voting Functions', *Theory and Decision*, 4, pp. 1–24.

Gini, C. (1912). *Variabilità e Mutabilità*. Bologna.

Graaff, J. de V. (1967). *Theoretical Welfare Economics*. Cambridge: Cambridge University Press.

Hansson, B. (1973). 'The Independence Condition in the Theory of Social Choice', *Theory and Decision*, 4, pp. 25–50.

Kenen, P.B. and F.M. Fisher (1957). 'Income Distribution, Value Judgements and Welfare: A Correction', *Quarterly Journal of Economics*, 71, pp. 322–4.

Kolm, S. Ch. (1969). 'The Optimal Production of Social Justice', in J. Margolis and H. Guitton (eds), *Public Economics*. London: Macmillan.

Minhas, B.S. (1970). 'Rural Poverty, Land Redistribution, and Development, *Indian Economic Review*, 5.

—— (1971). 'Rural Poverty and the Minimum Level of Living', *Indian Economic Review*, 6.

Mukherjee, M., N. Bhattacharya and G.S. Chatterjee (1972). 'Poverty in India: Measurement and Amelioration', *Commerce*, 125.

Newbery, D.M.G. (1970). 'A Theorem on the Measurement of Inequality', *Journal of Economic Theory*, 2, pp. 264–6.

Ojha, P.D. (1970). 'A Configuration of Indian Poverty', *Reserve Bank of India Bulletin*, 24.

Pattanaik, P.K. (1971). *Voting and Collective Choice*. Cambridge: Cambridge University Press.

Rothschild, M. and J.E. Stiglitz (1973). 'Some Further Results on the Measurement of Inequality', *Journal of Economic Theory*, 6, pp. 188–204.

Rowntree, B.S. (1901). *Poverty: A Study of Town Life*. London: Macmillan.

Runciman, W.G. (1966). *Relative Deprivation and Social Justice*. London: Routledge.

Sen, A.K. (1970a). 'Interpersonal Aggregation and Partial Comparability', *Econometrica*, 38, pp. 393–409.

—— (1970b). *Collective Choice and Social Welfare*. San Francisco: Holden-Day.

—— (1972). 'Interpersonal Aggregation and Partial Comparability: A Correction', *Econometrica*, 40, p. 959.

—— (1973a). *On Economic Inequality*. Oxford: Clarendon Press.

—— (1973b). 'Poverty, Inequality, and Unemployment: Some Conceptual Issues in Measurement', *Economic and Political Weekly*, 8, pp. 1457–64.

—— (1974). 'Informational Bases of Alternative Welfare Approaches: Aggregation and Income Distribution', *Journal of Public Economics*, 4, pp. 387–403.

Sen, A.K. (1976). 'Real National Income', *Review of Economic Studies*, 43, pp. 19–39.

Sheshinski, E. (1972). 'Relation between a Social Welfare Function and the Gini Index of Inequality', *Journal of Economic Theory*, 4, pp. 98–100.

Srinivasan, T.N. and A. Vaidyanathan (1971). 'Data on Distribution of Consumption Expenditure in India: An Evaluation', mimeographed, ISI Seminar on Income Distribution, New Delhi.

Theil, H. (1967). *Economics and Information Theory*. Chicago: Rand McNally.

Townsend, P. (1954). 'Measuring Poverty', *British Journal of Sociology*, 5, pp. 130–7.

Vaidyanathan, A. (1971). 'Some Aspects of Inequalities in Living Standards in Rural India', mimeographed, ISI Seminar on Income Distribution, New Delhi.

Weisbrod, B.A. (ed.) (1965). *The Economics of Poverty*. Englewood Cliffs, NJ: Prentice-Hall.

A Class of Decomposable Poverty Measures

JAMES FOSTER, JOEL GREER AND ERIK THORBECKE

Several recent studies of poverty have demonstrated the usefulness of breaking down a population into subgroups defined along ethnic, geographical, or other lines (for example Anand 1977; Van Ginneken 1980). Such an approach to poverty analysis places requirements on the poverty measure in addition to those proposed by Sen (1976, 1979). In particular, the question of how the measure relates subgroup poverty to total poverty is crucial to its applicability in this form of analysis. At the very least, one would expect that a decrease in the poverty level of one subgroup *ceteris paribus* should lead to less poverty for the population as a whole. At best, one might hope to obtain a quantitative estimate of the effect of a change in subgroup poverty on total poverty, or to give a subgroup's contribution to total poverty.

One way to satisfy the above criteria is to use a poverty measure that is additively decomposable in the sense that total poverty is a weighted average of the subgroup poverty levels.[1] However, the existing decomposable poverty measures are inadequate in that they violate one or more of the basic properties proposed by Sen.[2] Stated another way, of all the measures (Anand 1977; Blackorby and Donaldson 1980; Kakwani 1980; Shorrocks 1980) that are acceptable by the Sen criteria, none is decomposable. In fact, the Sen measure and its variants that rely on rank-order weighting fail to satisfy the basic condition that an increase in subgroup poverty must increase

---

[1] See (Anand 1977; Van Ginneken 1980). In contrast, decomposability as applied to inequality measures involves a 'between-group' term to account for differences among subgroup mean incomes (Bourguignon 1979; Shorrocks 1980). Here one poverty level is postulated to apply to all subgroups; hence a 'between-group' poverty term would appear to be unnecessary.

[2] In their empirical work, Anand (1977), Kakwani (1977) and Van Ginneken (1980) use decomposable measures that violate the transfer axioms.

total poverty (see footnote 5). This chapter is a first step towards resolving these inadequacies.

In what follows we present a simple, new poverty measure[3] that (i) is additively decomposable with population-share weights, (ii) satisfies the basic properties proposed by Sen, and (iii) is justified by a relative deprivation concept of poverty. The inequality measure associated with our poverty measure is shown to be the squared coefficient of variation and indeed the poverty measure may be expressed as a combination of this inequality measure, the headcount ratio, and the income-gap ratio in a fashion similar to Sen (1976). We generalize the new poverty measure to a parametric family of measures where the parameter can be interpreted as an indicator of 'aversion to poverty'. A brief empirical application demonstrates the usefulness of the decomposability property.

A DECOMPOSABLE POVERTY MEASURE

Let $y = (y_1, y_2, \ldots, y_n)$ be a vector of household incomes in increasing order, and suppose that $z > 0$ is the predetermined poverty line. Where $g_i = z - y_i$ is the income shortfall of the ith household, $q = q(y; z)$ is the number of poor households (having income no greater than z), and $n = n(y)$ is the total number of households, consider the poverty measure P defined by

$$P(y; z) = \frac{1}{nz^2} \sum_{i=1}^{q} g_i^2 . \qquad (1)$$

Following Sen (1979), poverty is a (normalized) weighted sum of the income shortfalls of the poor. In contrast to the Sen measure, which adopts a 'rank-order' weighting scheme, P takes the weights to be the shortfalls themselves; deprivation depends on the distance between a poor household's actual income and the poverty line, not the number of households that lie between a given household and the poverty line.

Despite this basic difference in weighting, several of the arguments advanced in support of the Sen measure also justify P. For instance Sen has proposed that poorer households should have higher weights (1976, Axioms E and M). Clearly P satisfies this requirement. Further, Sen argues that the weights should be based on a notion of relative

---

[3] While revising the initial submitted version, we became aware of independent work by Kundu (1981) which also gives P_2 and indicates some of its properties. However, Kundu's paper addresses quite different issues and, in particular, decomposability is not mentioned.

deprivation experienced by the poor households. In his seminal work on the subject, Runciman considers several different aspects of relative deprivation including the magnitude of relative deprivation, or 'the extent of the difference between the desired situation and that of the person desiring it (as he sees it)' (1966, p. 10). Where the 'desired situation' is to receive enough income to be able to 'meet the accepted conventions of minimum needs' (Sen 1979, p. 29) and the 'existing situation' is given by the poor household's income, the magnitude of relative deprivation is precisely the income shortfall of that household. Clearly, the weighting scheme behind P is closely related to this aspect of relative deprivation.

Sen (1976, 1979) has formulated two axioms for a poverty measure to satisfy:

Monotonicity Axiom.   *Given other things, a reduction in the income of a poor household must increase the poverty measure.*

Transfer Axiom.   *Given other things, a pure transfer of income from a poor household to any other household that is richer must increase the poverty measure.*[4]

It can be shown that P satisfies these two axioms (see Proposition 1, below). Further, P is associated with a well-known inequality measure, the squared coefficient of variation. Let $H = q/n$ be the headcount ratio, $I = \Sigma_{i=1}^{q} g_i/(qz)$ be the income-gap ratio, and $C_p^2 = \Sigma_{i=1}^{q} (\bar{y}_p - y_i)^2/(q\,\bar{y}_p^2)$, where $\bar{y}_p = \Sigma_{i=1}^{q} y_i/q$. Then

$$P(y; z) = H\left[I^2 + (1 - I)^2\,C_p^2\right], \tag{2}$$

as shown in (Foster, Greer and Thorbecke 1981). Finally, the squared coefficient of variation C^2 is the measure of inequality 'corresponding' to P in the sense that C^2 is obtained when n and $\bar{y}$ (the mean of y) are substituted for q and z in the definition of P (see Sen 1976, p. 224).

A CLASS OF DECOMPOSABLE MEASURES

It can be seen from (2) and the properties of C_p^2 (see Atkinson 1980) that a given transfer has the same effect on P at low or high income levels. Kakwani has proposed a property that stresses transfers among the poorest poor:

Transfer Sensitivity Axiom.   *If a transfer $t > 0$ of income takes place*

---

[4] See also Thon (1979); Kundu and Smith (1981) question on the desirability of the Transfer Axiom.

from a poor household with income y_i to a poor household with income $y_i + d$ ($d > 0$), then the magnitude of the increase in poverty must be smaller for larger y_i (Kakwani 1980, p. 439).

While P does not satisfy this axiom, it can be generalized to a class which contains poverty measures that do. For each $\alpha \geq 0$, let P_α be defined by

$$P_\alpha(y; z) = \frac{1}{n} \sum_{i=1}^{q} \left(\frac{g_i}{z} \right)^\alpha. \tag{3}$$

The measure P_0 is simply the headcount ratio H, while P_1 is $H \cdot I$, a renormalization of the income-gap measure. The measure P is obtained by setting $\alpha = 2$. The parameter α can be viewed as a measure of poverty aversion: a larger α gives greater emphasis to the poorest poor. As α becomes very large P_α approaches a 'Rawlsian' measure which considers only the position of the poorest household. The properties of this family of measures are summarized in the following proposition.

Proposition 1. *The poverty measure P_α satisfies the Monotonicity Axiom for $\alpha > 0$, the Transfer Axiom for $\alpha > 1$, and the Transfer Sensitivity Axiom for $\alpha > 2$.*

Proof. The Monotonicity Axiom holds for $\alpha > 0$ by the fact that g_i increases as y_i falls. To verify the Transfer Axiom, note that any transfer from a poor household to a richer one may be viewed as some combination of the following two types of 'regressive' transfers: (i) from a poor household to another poor household that stays poor, or (ii) from a poor household to a household at or above the poverty line. The strict convexity of P_α in the vector of poor incomes for $\alpha > 1$ covers (i), while a transfer of the form (ii) increases P_α by inspection. That P_α satisfies the Transfer Sensitivity Axiom for $\alpha > 2$ follows from Kolm (1976, p. 88).

DECOMPOSABILITY

Suppose that the population is divided into m collections of households $j = 1, \ldots, m$ with ordered income vectors $y^{(j)}$ and population sizes n_j. In analysing poverty by population subgroups, the following axiom may be taken as a basic consistency requirement.

Subgroup Monotonicity Axiom. *Let $\hat{y}$ be a vector of incomes obtained from y by changing the incomes in subgroup j from $y^{(j)}$ to $\hat{y}^{(j)}$, where*

n_j is unchanged. If $\hat{y}^{(j)}$ has more poverty than $y^{(j)}$, then $\hat{y}$ must also have a higher level of poverty than y.

When incomes in a given subgroup change (the rest remaining fixed), this axiom requires subgroup and total poverty to move in the same direction. By this criterion the Sen measure and its variants (Anand 1977; Kakwani 1977, 1980; Takayama 1979; Thon 1979) are not well suited for poverty analysis by subgroup, since they violate this consistency requirement in certain cases.[5] On the other hand it can be shown that P_α satisfies subgroup monotonicity, and an even stronger decomposability property:

Proposition 2. *For any income vector y broken down into subgroup income vectors $y^{(1)}, \ldots, y^{(m)}$,*

$$P_\alpha(y; z) = \sum_{j=1}^{m} \frac{n_j}{n} P_\alpha(y^{(j)}; z). \tag{4}$$

P_α *is additively decomposable with population share weights.*

The decomposition in (4) allows a quantitative, as well as qualitative, assessment of the effect of changes in subgroup poverty on total poverty. In fact, increased poverty in a subgroup will increase total poverty at a rate given by the population share n_j/n; the larger the population share, the greater the impact. The quantity $T_j = (n_j/n)P_\alpha(y^{(j)}; z)$ may be interpreted as the total contribution of a subgroup to overall poverty while $100\, T_j/P_\alpha(y; z)$ is the percentage contribution of subgroup j.

AN ILLUSTRATIVE EXAMPLE

In this section, the poverty measure P_2 is applied to data from the 1970 Nairobi Household Survey to illustrate the usefulness of decomposability.

The Nairobi Household Survey was conducted by the Institute for Development Studies. A total of 1416 families were interviewed and information obtained regarding income, education, occupation, marital status, and other characteristics of all adult household members. To

---

[5] For instance, where $y = (1, 6, 6, 7, 8, 12)$, $\hat{y} = (3, 3, 6, 7, 8, 13)$, and $y^{(1)} = (1, 6, 12)$, $y^{(2)} = (6, 7, 8)$, $\hat{y}^{(1)} = (3, 3, 13)$, and $y^{(2)} = \hat{y}^{(2)}$, we have more poverty in $y^{(1)}$ than $\hat{y}^{(1)}$ by the Sen measure as long as $z \geq 13$ and yet $\hat{y}$ has more poverty than y using the same measure. Note that the mean incomes of $y^{(1)}$ and $\hat{y}^{(1)}$ are the same in this example. This example can be found in Cowell (1984) who applied it to the Gini inequality measure.

analyse poverty, a poverty line of 515 Kenya Shillings/year/adult was derived from the one calculated by Crawford and Thorbecke (1978). The overall results of the analysis contain few surprises. The very tentative estimates by previous authors (Collier and Lal 1977; Crawford and Thorbecke 1978) that poverty is not a major problem in Nairobi were confirmed. Only 13 per cent of the survey sample live in poor households and P_2 is equal to 0.056 (see Table 9.1).

Table 9.1
Decomposition of Poverty (P_2) by Number
of Years Household Head Has Lived in Nairobi[a]

Years in Nairobi	Number of individuals n_j	Level of poverty $P_2(y^{(j)}; z)$[b]	Percentage contribution to total poverty[c]	Average income of poor[d]	Proportion of poor in each group
0	29	.4267	5.6	93.3	.55
.01–1	117	.1237	6.5	221.9	.30
2	116	.1264	6.6	140.0	.20
3–5	438	.0257	5.1	295.1	.09
6–10	793	.0343	12.1	273.8	.11
11–15	719	.0291	9.4	286.6	.10
16–20	565	.0260	6.6	329.3	.11
21–70	954	.0555	23.8	198.8	.12
Permanent Residents	116	.1659	8.7	203.3	.35
Don't Know	140	.2461	15.5	93.0	.34
Total	3987	.0558	99.9		

a   The poverty line z is 515 Kenya Shillings per adult equivalent per year, or roughly $72 (US) per year (See Crawford and Thorbecke 1970).
b $P_2(y^{(j)}; z) = 1/n_j z^2 \sum_{i=1}^{q} g_i^2$ where q_j is the number of individuals below the poverty line in group j.
c   i.e. $100(n_j/n)(P_2(y^j; z)/P_2(y; z))$. (This column does not sum to 100 due to rounding errors.)
d   In Kenya shillings per adult equivalent per year.

The relation between poverty and certain specific household characteristics may be analysed with the aid of a collection of tables called a poverty profile. Table 9.1 shows one such relation, describing poverty for subgroups differentiated by the number of years since the household head moved to Nairobi. The first column gives the total number of household members in the subgroup. The second gives the level of poverty for each subgroup as measured by P_2. The poverty level is then weighted by the population share to determine the contribution of the subgroup to total poverty, which is given as a percentage of total poverty in column 3. Complete elimination of poverty within a subgroup would lower total poverty precisely by this percentage.

As can be seen in Table 9.1, of all those answering the question, poverty is worst among short-term residents (that is those in Nairobi less than two years). However, these recently arrived subgroups do not contribute much to total poverty due to their relatively small population. Rather, it is the group of households whose heads migrated to Nairobi twenty or more years ago which contributes most prominently to total poverty: 23.8 per cent of total poverty is accounted for by this subgroup. This cannot be seen from their level of poverty, which is far below the level for the recently arrived subgroups.

Acknowledgements: We would like to thank the participants of the Cornell Development Seminar, Gary Fields, and the anonymous referees for helpful comments. In addition, we owe a special debt of gratitude to Amartya Sen for his thoughtful remarks and encouragement. This chapter is based on a longer working paper (Foster, Greer and Thorbecke 1981) and on dissertation research by J. Greer.

REFERENCES

Anand, S. (1977). 'Aspects of Poverty in Malaysia', *Review of Income and Wealth*, 23, pp. 1–16.

Atkinson, A.B. (1970). 'On the Measurement of Inequality', *Journal of Economic Theory*, 2, pp. 244–63.

Blackorby, C. and D. Donaldson (1980). 'Ethical Indices for the Measurement of Poverty', *Econometrica*, 48, pp. 1053–60.

Bourguignon, F. (1979). 'Decomposable Income Inequality Measures', *Econometrica*, 47, pp. 901–20.

Collier, P. and D. Lal (1977). 'Poverty and Growth in Kenya — A Preliminary Note', International Bank for Reconstruction and Development, December.

Cowell, F.A. (1984). 'The Structure of American Income Inequality', *Review of Income and Wealth*, 30.

Crawford, E. and E. Thorbecke (1978). 'Employment, Income Distribution,

Poverty Alleviation and Basic Needs in Kenya: Report of an ILO Consulting Mission', Cornell University, April.

Foster, J., J. Greer and E. Thorbecke (1981). *A Class of Decomposable Poverty Measures*, Working Paper No. 243, Department of Economics, Cornell University.

Kakwani, N.C. (1977). 'Measurement of Poverty and the Negative Income Tax', *Australian Economic Papers*, 16, pp. 237–48.

—— (1980). 'On a Class of Poverty Measures', *Econometrica*, 48, pp. 437–46.

Kolm, S. Ch. (1976). 'Unequal Inequalities', *Journal of Economic Theory*, 13, pp. 82–111.

Kundu, A. (1981). 'Measurement of Poverty — Some Conceptual Issues', *Anvesak*, 11, pp. 80–96.

Kundu, A. and T.E. Smith (1983). 'An Impossibility Theorem on Poverty Indices', *International Economic Review*, 24, pp. 423–34.

Runciman, W.G. (1966). *Relative Deprivation and Social Justice, Berkeley*, CA: University of California Press.

Sen, A. 'Poverty: An Ordinal Approach to Measurement', *Econometrica*, 44(1976), pp. 219–41.

—— (1979). 'Issues in the Measurement of Poverty', *Scandinavian Journal of Economics*, 81, pp. 285–307.

Shorrocks, A.F. (1980). 'The Class of Additively Decomposable Inequality Measures', *Econometrica*, 48, pp. 613–25.

Takayama, N. (1979). 'Poverty, Income Inequality, and Their Measures: Professor Sen's Axiomatic Approach Reconsidered', *Econometrica*, 47, pp. 747–59.

Thon, D. (1979). 'On Measuring Poverty', *Review of Income and Wealth*, 25, pp. 429–40.

Van Ginneken, W. (1980). 'Some Methods of Poverty Analysis: An Application to Iranian Data, 1975–76', *World Development*, 8, pp. 639–46.

The Definition and Measurement of Poverty[*]

Sudhir Anand

The redress of poverty, it can be argued, is the most efficient method of redressing inequality. The eradication of poverty irrespective of race is, in fact, one of the two objectives of the government's New Economic Policy. In the present chapter I explore the extent and nature of poverty in Malaysia, so that policy measures for its alleviation might be considered.

This chapter is specifically concerned with the definition and measurement of poverty in Malaysia. A poverty line is estimated after considering both the absolute and relative approaches to the definition. Various indices of poverty are then discussed, ranging from the simple incidence-of-poverty measure (that is the percentage of the population in poverty) to others that take account of the poverty gap. A new index proposed by Sen (1976a) is derived, and alternative normalizations are suggested for it. Estimates of all these measures are presented for Malaysia. Finally, the simple incidence-of-poverty measure, which is decomposable, is used to construct a profile of the poor in Malaysia.

The profile adumbrates the poor in terms of variables that can provide a basis for policy action, describing the poor by such characteristics as race, location, employment status, occupation, and education. Such information should help not only to trace the correlates of poverty, but also to identify areas of government intervention for the redress of poverty.

PREVIOUS ATTEMPTS AT DEFINING POVERTY

One of the earliest recorded discussions of poverty in Malaysia was written fifty years ago by the literary figure Za'ba. In an article entitled

[*] This chapter was presented as a paper (Anand 1975) to the Fourteenth General Conference of the International Association for Research in Income and Wealth, Aulanko, Finland, August 1975.

'The Poverty of the Malays' in the *Malay Mail* of 1 December 1923, Za'ba drew attention to the fact of Malay poverty, but made no attempt to define or measure poverty.[1]

More recent explorations of the nature and causes of poverty in Malaysia have been made by Ungku A. Aziz. In a couple of stimulating contributions to the *Kajian Ekonomi Malaysia*, he has discussed various aspects of the problem (Aziz 1964 and 1965). Although his approach is somewhat different from mine, Aziz recognizes the need to define and measure poverty.[2] Indeed, he has proposed the so-called sarong index of poverty, which is based on the long cloths that are traditionally worn by Malaysian men and women.

There is one index that I have found to be convenient for purposes of measuring the extent of poverty among Malays in any kampong. This is the per capita sarong index. If we take the number of sarongs in a household and divide it by the number of persons above the age of one living in the household, then we can obtain a ratio of sarongs per capita. Any figure below one sarong per capita would indicate a condition of extreme poverty. Wealthy kampong dwellers like landlords, boatlords or the better-off Government employees generally have rates of 7–15 sarongs per capita. The index can be refined by taking a valuation of the sarongs and by differentiating between the types of sarongs. To measure the effect of a rural development programme on a particular kampong we could compare the per capita sarong indices before and after implementation of the programme. This index is a fairly good measure of any reduction in poverty (Aziz 1964, pp. 79–80).

The sarong index of poverty, albeit ingenious, is too susceptible to the vagaries of fashion to be of much practical use!

In any case, poverty has to do with *incomes* that are low in some sense, rather than the amounts consumed or held of a single commodity. It can, of course, happen that some commodity has a perfect, or near-perfect, correlation with income. A definition of poverty could then be based on the consumption of this commodity. But since there do not seem to be any obvious advantages in this approach — not even easier data collection — attention might as well be focused on income itself, rather than on some commodity which is supposed to be a proxy

[1] Za'ba wrote: 'The Malays, as a whole, are a particularly poor people. Poverty is their most outstanding characteristic and their greatest handicap' (as cited in Aziz 1975a, p. 9). His 1923 article is described by Ungku A. Aziz in *Jejak–Jejak di Pantai Zaman* (1975a).

[2] Aziz asserts that there are three basic causes of poverty: 'neglect, low productivity and exploitation' (via has 'MM', now modified to 'OO', system). He also develops an intriguing 'MV scale' to explain the phenomenon (Aziz 1964).

for it. Even Aziz himself appears to have abandoned the sarong index and now favours the position that 'if we adopt the income gap approach, we can minimize the quantum of nebulous quiddities and think more effectively' (Aziz 1975b, p. 6).

THE DEFINITION OF A POVERTY LINE

My analysis of poverty is based on an examination of the lower end of the Malaysian income distribution. The precise truncation point depends on the definition of poverty, to which there are essentially two approaches, an *absolute* and a *relative* one. In the absolute approach a certain minimal living standard is specified in terms of nutritional level, clothing and the like, and the income required to support it is calculated. The relative approach interprets poverty in relation to the prevailing living standards of the society, recognizing explicitly the interdependence between the poverty line and the entire income distribution. My estimate of a poverty line is a compromise between these two considerations. It should elicit agreement about a definition of the poor in Malaysia.

The crudest definition of a relative poverty line is that income level which cuts off the lowest p per cent of the population in the national income distribution. There are two objections to this method of defining the poor. First, the method prejudges the *extent* of poverty (it is p per cent by definition!). Second, it implies that 'the poor are always with us'. In a trivial statistical sense there is always a bottom p per cent in the income distribution, and thus one could never actually eradicate poverty. Even so, it could still be perfectly reasonable for a government to be continually concerned with the lowest p per cent of the population. Indeed, with a Rawlsian criterion of justice, one is concerned precisely with improving the welfare levels of the worst-off group — defined in this case as the lowest p per cent.[3]

The choice of percentile p in the distribution is, of course, somewhat arbitrary. In the context of developing countries, the figure of 40 per cent has sometimes been suggested.[4] For Malaysia, the per capita household income level which cuts off the bottom 40 per cent of the

[3] See Rawls (1971) for the now famous 'maximin' criterion of social welfare. Strictly speaking, the Rawlsian welfare function as interpreted by economists is concerned with increasing the income level of the worst-off *individual*.

[4] The popularity of this particular figure seems to stem from Robert McNamara's plea that special policies be initiated to increase the income growth of the lowest 40 per cent in developing countries (McNamara 1972).

population from the rest is very slightly under M$25 per month. I have rounded this off to an income level of M$25 per month. The percentage of individuals who fall below this level of per capita household income is thus a little higher, at 40.2 per cent. The percentage of *households* falling below such a poverty line is 36.5 per cent, however, because the poor have larger households on average than the non-poor (see the later section entitled 'A Profile of Poverty in Malaysia').

Another method, which does not make it a matter of definition that the poor are always with us, is to define poverty in relation to contemporary living standards by drawing the poverty line at, say, half the average income level of society.[5] In this case, although the poverty line rises with the general level of incomes, it is no longer true that poverty cannot be eliminated. In fact, it is 'quite possible to imagine a society in which no one has less than half the average income — in which there is no poverty according to this definition' (Atkinson 1975, p. 189). The per capita income in Malaysia has been estimated at M$50 per month, so the relative poverty line according to this definition is also M$25 per month.

An absolute poverty line has been estimated by the Ministry of Welfare Services (Department of Social Welfare) in Malaysia. The ministry is considering a public assistance programme, a major objective of which is to institute 'a scheme of social assistance based on principles of social justice whereby all those in poverty through circumstances beyond their control should be eligible for assistance in the quantum related to their needs' (Department of Social Welfare 1975, p. 105).[6] For this purpose, the ministry identified a poverty line in terms of the income required to maintain a family in 'good nutritional health' as well as to satisfy 'minimum conventional needs in respect of clothing, household management, transport and communication'. The minimum basket of food to maintain good nutritional health was devised with assistance from the Institute of Medical Research in Malaysia. The items of food chosen were costed at prices prevailing in August 1974, and a minimum food budget was thus obtained.

The minimum food budget was estimated separately for adults (male

5 See Atkinson (1975). This suggestion has the merit that perceptions of poverty are tied up with perceptions of inequality.

6 Other objectives of the scheme are to 'suggest various formulae and structures for the sharing of financial and technical responsibility by State and Federal Governments', and eventually to 'integrate this social assistance with social insurance to form a nationwide social security scheme in the full sense of the term'.

and female) by ethnic group,[7] and for children (divided into two age groups), both according to rural and urban location. It was found, however, that there was very little difference in cost between the food baskets of the three ethnic groups. There was also 'very little variation between urban and rural prices for the items considered' (Department of Social Welfare 1975, para. 16, p. 119).[8] Accordingly, the average cost was taken of the food baskets for the three ethnic groups in rural and urban areas.[9]

Table 10.1

Cost of Nutritionally Adequate Diet at 1970 Prices
(M$ per month)

Location	Malay		Chinese		Indian		Children	
	Male	Female	Male	Female	Male	Female	0–6 years	7–11 years
Rural	25.39	24.13	24.56	23.29	25.67	24.41	14.95	21.04
Urban	25.85	24.59	25.00	23.74	26.41	25.15	15.29	21.46
Average	25.62	24.36	24.78	23.51	26.04	24.78	15.09	21.25

Source: Department of Social Welfare (1975), app. V.

A food price index provided by the Department of Statistics was used to deflate the food budgets back to 1970, the year to which the

[7] The breakdown by ethnic group allows for the different dietary habits and conventions of the three major communities in Malaysia.

[8] Details of urban and rural market prices for individual food items are set out in Department of Social Welfare (1975, app. II). Rural market prices, however, do not necessarily apply to the food baskets of peasant farmers, whose income from own consumption of produce is valued at farm-gate prices.

[9] Details of the monthly food basket for each racial group are shown in Department of Social Welfare (1975), app. II (males) and app. III (females). There are separate food baskets in app. IV for children of 0–6 years and 7–11 years, which are not broken down by racial group. In choosing items for the food basket,

the cheapest items were chosen, particularly for vegetables. In the case of fish, the two varieties of fish chosen, i.e. ikan cincaru and ikan kembong, may not be the cheapest available in the market but they are the two most common types, which are consumed by the people in the low income group. In the case of milk, sweetened condensed milk was chosen for adults, as it is used as sweetener in coffee or tea; and for children, powdered milk, as recommended by the nutritionist. For meat, a combination of pork and chicken for Chinese, beef and chicken for Malays, and mutton and chicken for Indians was adopted (Department of Social Welfare 1975, pp. 118–19).

survey data refer. Table 10.1 shows the estimates obtained of the monthly cost of food at 1970 prices for Malays, Chinese, and Indians in rural and urban areas.

The average monthly cost in 1970 of a nutritionally adequate diet for a male was M$25.37, for a female M$24.21, for a child M$18.17, and the average for an individual in the population at large was M$22.58. The food budget for a household thus depends on its composition as well as its size. The ministry, however, assumes a fixed relation between size and composition,[10] so that, for instance, the average-size five-member household is assumed to consist of two adults and three children. The minimum food budget for such a household in 1970 was thus M$104.09 per month.

An estimate of non-food expenditure is also required to calculate the total poverty budget. Three different methods have been used for this purpose, all based on expenditure data obtained from the 1973 Household Expenditure Survey (HES). In the first method, the proportion of total expenditure on food was estimated for families in the 1973 HES with monthly incomes less than M$200. The poverty line for each household size class was then calculated by multiplying the reciprocal of this proportion by the minimum food budget for that household size class.[11]

In the second method, the non-food budget was restricted to four essential items: clothing and footwear; rent, fuel and power; household equipment and operation; and transport and communications. The ratio of expenditure on each of these items to food expenditure was then estimated from the 1973 HES for families with less than M$200 monthly income. These ratios were applied to the minimum food budget for each household size class to calculate the non-food portion of its poverty budget. This method is thus similar to the first except that all non-food items other than the above four are excluded from the poverty budget.[12] Naturally, it leads to a lower poverty line.

The third method estimates the non-food part of the poverty line budget by taking the absolute expenditure incurred on the four items by households in the 1973 HES with monthly incomes less than M$200.

[10] See Department of Social Welfare (1975), app. VI.

[11] This method of blowing up minimum food expenditure to get the total poverty budget is due to Orshansky (1965).

[12] Excluded, for example, are the following categories of expenditure: beverages and tobacco; medical care and health needs; education and cultural services; recreation and entertainment.

These were adjusted upward for price increases between July 1973 and August 1974 to obtain the non-food component corresponding to the (August 1974) minimum food budget. The adjusted value was divided by the average household size in the less than M$200 monthly income class to yield the non-food cost per person. Finally, the poverty line for each household size class was calculated by adding the minimum food budget for that size class to the product of non-food cost per person and household size. Thus the non-food budget of a household was assumed to be shared equally among its members.

The non-food budget has been estimated at 1970 prices for each of the three methods. Different price indices provided by the Department of Statistics have been applied to deflate the different non-food items. A breakdown of the non-food cost per person in 1970 arrived at by the third method is:

	Cost per person (M$ per month)
Clothing and footwear	0.98
Rent, fuel, and power	4.74
Household equipment and operation	0.58
Transport and communications	1.44
Total non-food cost per person for essential items	7.74

For a five-member household in 1970, therefore, the poverty line according to the third method is M$104.09 + (5 × M$7.74) = M$142.79 per month. The 1970 poverty line for a household of five persons according to the first method has been estimated at M$207.70 per month, and according to the second method at M$163.24 per month.

It is difficult to defend the first method on the basis of an absolute subsistence definition of poverty. The non-food budget includes many items which might be considered inessential for subsistence. The second and third methods come closer to the subsistence notion of poverty in as much as they specify only certain non-food items deemed to be essential. Even for these methods, however, the food basket chosen is obviously not a nutritional minimum.[13] The food budget

[13] The diet for the minimum food budget was obtained 'basically from the diet provided in government hospitals for a "normal average adult" ' (Department of Social Welfare 1975, p. 118). For children it was the 'diet required for normal growth and maintenance of good nutritional health'.

estimated by the ministry appears to be based more on general consumption patterns in the society than on an absolute minimum required for subsistence. It is likely, therefore, to be higher than is strictly implied by the latter definition.

In fact, the concept of 'minimum' is itself difficult to fix, since minimum requirements, in terms of the intake of calories and proteins, vary with the amount of physical activity of an individual. There are also large inter-individual variations in requirements stemming from physiological factors such as age, sex, body weight and size, and metabolism. Taking an average of minimum requirements for all individuals in society as the per capita subsistence level (or poverty line) leads to familiar problems of misclassification. Individuals above their own minimum requirement may be below the per capita subsistence level and therefore misclassified as poor; conversely, individuals below their own minimum requirement may be above the per capita subsistence level and therefore misclassified as non-poor.[14] These classification errors are reduced by taking the household as the survey unit — because of the averaging of individual requirements when persons are considered as part of a household.

The eventual choice of a poverty line must to some extent remain arbitrary. Per person, the absolute poverty line under the second method is M$32.6 per month, and under the third method it is M$28.6 per month (dividing by five the household poverty line for the average five-member household). The estimates suggested by this absolute approach turn out to be fairly close to the M$25 poverty line of the relative approach considered earlier. In view of this, and for computational convenience. I choose a poverty line of M$25 per month household income per capita.[15] Later in the chapter, I conduct some sensitivity analysis around this poverty line.

THE SEN POVERTY MEASURE

Two types of indices have hitherto been used to measure the extent of poverty after the poverty line has been defined. The commonest index is the percentage of the population in poverty, also referred to as the incidence of poverty. The other index is the poverty gap, which is the total income needed to bring all the poor up to the poverty line. (In the United States, the poverty gap is sometimes expressed as a fraction of

[14] Note the analogy with Type I and Type II errors in statistical inference.
[15] In 1970 US dollars, this is equivalent to a poverty line of about US$110 a year.

GNP). The former index ignores the amounts by which the incomes of the poor fall short of the poverty line, while the latter index ignores the number actually in poverty. Both, moreover, are insensitive to a transfer of income from the poor to the very poor. In other words, neither measure is sensitive to the income distribution among the poor. A new measure of poverty has recently been proposed by Sen (1976a) which incorporates all three of these concerns into a single index.

The index is axiomatically derived after the general form for the poverty measure is taken to be a 'normalized weighted sum of the income gaps of the poor'. Two axioms then suffice to derive the index. The first specifies the income-weighting scheme, and the second stipulates the normalization procedure. Sen chooses the rank-order-weighting scheme, in which the weight on the income gap of a poor person is simply his or her rank in the income ordering below the poverty line. It should come as no surprise that this weighting scheme will yield the Gini coefficient of the income distribution among the poor. Sen's normalization axiom requires that when all the poor have the same income, the index takes a value equal to the proportion of persons in poverty multiplied by the proportionate average shortfall of their income from the poverty line.

The following notation is introduced to set up the Sen index and relate it to other poverty measures:

n = total population size
μ = mean income of the population
π = poverty line
q = number of people in poverty (that is with income less than or equal to π)
ν = mean income of the poor
G_p = Gini coefficient of the income distribution among the poor.

Relabel the population (if necessary) in non-descending order of income so that

$$y_1 \leq y_2 \leq \ldots \leq y_n.$$

Then $y_q \leq \pi$, but $y_{q+1} > \pi$. The proportion of the population in poverty is (q/n), and the poverty gap is

$$\sum_{i=1}^{q} g_i$$

where $g_i = (\pi - y_i)$ is the income gap of person i. Thus the poverty gap is equal to

$$\sum_{i=1}^{q} (\pi - y_i) = q\,(\pi - v).$$

Therefore, the average poverty gap is $(\pi - v)$; the proportionate average income shortfall from the poverty line is $(\pi - v)/\pi$; and the normalized value of the Sen index is $(q/n)\,(\pi - v)/\pi$.

The rank-order-weighting scheme implies a weight of $(q + 1 - i)$ on the income gap g_i of person i, since there are $(q + 1 - i)$ persons among the poor with incomes at least as large as that of person i. The Sen index P is then

$$A \sum_{i=1}^{q} (q + 1 - i)\,(\pi - y_i)$$

where A is a parameter depending on the normalization selected. The normalized value of the index, when each $y_i = v$, is

$$\frac{q}{n} \cdot \frac{\pi - v}{\pi} = A\,(\pi - v)\,\frac{q\,(q+1)}{2}, \text{ since } \sum_{i=1}^{q} (q + 1 - i) = \frac{q\,(q+1)}{2}.$$

Thus $A = 2/[(q + 1)\,n\pi]$. Now the Gini coefficient G_p of the income distribution among the poor can be written as:[16]

$$G_p = \frac{q+1}{q} - \frac{2}{q^2 v} \sum_{i=1}^{q} (q + 1 - i)\,y_i$$

Therefore,

$$P = \frac{q}{n} \cdot \frac{1}{\pi} \left[\pi - v + \frac{q}{q+1}\, v G_p \right].$$

For large q, $q/(q + 1) \simeq 1$, and the index P reduces to

$$P = \frac{q}{n} \cdot \frac{1}{\pi} \left[\pi - v(1 - G_p) \right].$$

---

[16] If G is the Gini coefficient for the whole population, and G_{np} the Gini coefficient of the income distribution among the non-poor, the following relation holds:

$$G = \left(\frac{q}{n} \right)\left(\frac{qv}{n\mu} \right) G_p + \left(\frac{n-q}{n} \right)\left(\frac{n\mu - qv}{n\mu} \right) G_{np} + \left(\frac{q}{n} \right)\left(\frac{\mu - v}{\mu} \right)$$

Thus the Gini coefficient for the non-poor G_{np} can be inferred from a knowledge of G and G_p.

The effect of the weighting scheme is to *augment* the average poverty gap by the Gini coefficient times mean income of the poor. Thus an additional income 'loss' arises when inequality in the income distribution among the poor is taken into account. The correction for this loss involves deflating the mean income v of the poor by $(1 - G_p)$, which yields the familiar equally distributed equivalent income (see Atkinson 1970) corresponding to the rank-order welfare function. Hence the weighted income gap is calculated by taking the difference, not between the poverty line and the mean income of the poor, but between the poverty line and the equally distributed equivalent income of the poor.

The index P lies between 0 and 1. It assumes the value 0 when everyone's income is above the poverty line π (that is when $q = 0$), and the value 1 when everyone has zero income (implying $v = 0$ and $q = n$).

The rank-order welfare function is rather special in that the relative weight on a person's income depends only on the rank of the person in the income ordering and not on the amount of the person's income as such. Other welfare functions with relative weights that do depend directly on the size of a person's income may be found more acceptable. The weighting schemes implied by them produce different expressions for equally distributed equivalent income and, by the same token, different indices of inequality. It is evident that the weighted income gap under any welfare function is simply the difference between the poverty line and the corresponding equally distributed equivalent income. Hence for each different welfare function there corresponds by this approach a different *index of poverty*.

An obvious consequence of using such income-weighting schemes should be mentioned. In the Sen index P, for example, there is clearly a trade-off between the mean income (v) of the poor and equality $(1 - G_p)$ in their income distribution, the trade-off being given by $v(1 - G_p)$. Thus it is perfectly possible for the Sen index to register a decline in poverty when the poor have become poorer in absolute terms (that is v has decreased) so long as equality in their income distribution $(1 - G_p)$ has increased more than proportionately. Put another way, the index implies a reduction in poverty even if there are transfers of income from the poor to the non-poor (or the amount taken from the poor is simply thrown away) so long as the remaining incomes of the poor are sufficiently better distributed. A maximum reduction of $(1 - G_p)$ per cent can be made in the total income of the poor, yet an improvement in distribution can still neutralize the effect of this income loss on the Sen index. These implications, while acceptable when weighting the incomes of the entire population as in the Atkinson inequality index, may be more difficult to swallow when applied only to those below the poverty line, especially if this is interpreted as an absolute minimum. In this case, one may not wish to weight the incomes of poor people differently, preferring instead the value judgement of equal or unit weights on all their income gaps. Treating the incomes of the poor similarly yields a poverty measure which is simply the normalized value of the Sen index.

It was noted earlier that a commonly used index of poverty is the percentage of GNP needed to close the poverty gap. A slightly different normalization from the one used by Sen produces a poverty measure which generalizes this index to correct for income inequality among the poor. The normalization can be modified so that when incomes below the poverty line are equal the measure reduces to the poverty gap expressed as a fraction of the total income of society; that is $(q/n)(\pi - v)/\mu$. With this normalization, A takes the value: $A = 2/[(q + 1) n\mu]$.[17] The rank-order weighting procedure now yields the modified Sen measure given by

$$M = \frac{q}{n} \cdot \frac{1}{\mu} [\pi - v(1 - G_p)].$$

The relation between P and M is $M = (\pi/\mu) P$, and the measure M lies between the limits 0 and π/μ.[18]

The measure M reduces to the proportion of total income needed to close the poverty gap in either of two circumstances: (1) incomes below the poverty line are equally distributed (implying $G_p = 0$), or (2) the same weight of unity attaches to the income gap of every person below the poverty line.

Instead of expressing the income required to close the poverty gap as a fraction of total income, define an index F (after Fishlow 1972, 1973) which expresses the gap as a fraction of the income of the non-poor:

[17] Sen himself (1973b) alludes to this kind of normalization, but his equations (8) and (9) imply a different value for A, namely, $A = 2/n^2 \mu$.

[18] If one adopts Atkinson's suggestion for defining a relative poverty line (discussed earlier in this chapter), π and μ stand in constant relation to each other, namely $\pi/\mu = 1/2$. In this case, M and P are related as $M = P/2$, and M lies between the limits of 0 and 1/2.

$$F = \frac{q}{n\mu - qv}[\pi - v(1 - G_p)]$$

$$= \frac{\pi}{\mu - \frac{q}{n}v}P.$$

The idea behind this index is the elimination of poverty through a direct transfer of income from the non-poor to the poor.[19] The ratio reflects the burden on the non-poor since it represents the proportionate reduction in their income if the poverty gap is to be closed through redistribution alone.

Three comments are appropriate about these indices M and F. First, they are not so much measures of poverty as indicators of the economy's capacity for its alleviation. Failure to distinguish the measurement of poverty from the prospects for its alleviation can lead to the following anomalous consequence. With no change in the number or the incomes of the poor, an increase in the incomes of people above the poverty line will lead to a fall in both the indices M and F. Yet no reduction in poverty has actually occurred since the position of the poor remains unchanged.[20] What has happened is that a smaller fraction of society's income is now required to eliminate poverty, and to that extent the task may be regarded as potentially easier. The measurement of poverty thus needs to be conceptually separated from the possibilities for its alleviation.

Second, the values of F and M could exceed unity if the poverty

---

[19] If poverty is to be eliminated by transfers alone, the income of the non-poor must be large enough not to drag the non-poor themselves into poverty in the course of income transfers. This motivates yet another normalization for the Sen index, in which the poverty gap is expressed as a fraction of the income of the non-poor *in excess of* the poverty level. This measure is easily seen to reduce to

$$\frac{\pi}{\mu - \frac{q}{n}v - \pi\left(1 - \frac{q}{n}\right)}P$$

where P is the Sen index.

[20] There might even be an increase in poverty if one takes a relative view of poverty. The Sen poverty measure P is unchanged in this case since the income gap of the poor is normalized on the poverty line π and not on the mean income μ of the entire community. Only an actual reduction in the number of poor, or an increase in their incomes, or an improvement in their income distribution, or an increase in the number of non-poor can lead to a fall in the Sen poverty index.

line happens to be drawn at a level higher than the mean income of society. Then the augmented poverty gap could exceed the income of the non-poor (or even the total income of society), implying a value of F (or of M) larger than unity. A sufficient condition for the poverty problem to be tractable through transfers is that the mean income of society exceed the poverty-line income. There is then enough income to bring everyone in the population above the poverty line. With this condition satisfied, both the indices M and F are bounded above by unity.

Third, the assumption implicit in the indices M and F is that the redistribution of income to close the poverty gap does not affect the size of total income in the economy. Yet any transfer scheme based on the taxation system is likely to influence both the (pre-transfer) poverty gap and the (pre-transfer) income of the non-poor through its disincentive effects. A full income support programme implies a 100 per cent marginal rate of taxation at and below the poverty line, as well as changes in taxation at higher income levels (to raise the required revenue). The work disincentive effects of such changes in the tax schedule could substantially increase the pre-transfer poverty gap and reduce the size of pre-transfer income of the non-poor. This, of course, would alter the values of the indices M and F. Indeed, for each different tax schedule/transfer scheme that is contemplated to eliminate poverty, there will correspond different values for M and F. To calculate these and the optimum tax schedule requires information on individual labour supply functions, the distribution of skills, and so on.[21]

ESTIMATES OF POVERTY IN MALAYSIA

The indices discussed above have been estimated for the Malaysian population in poverty. It is assumed first that the weights attaching to each person's income gap are unity. The indices then reduce to the poverty gap expressed as a fraction of various income aggregates. Estimates of these measures, as well as the proportion in poverty and the average poverty gap, are presented in Table 10.2 for Peninsular Malaysia and each ethnic group separately.

The percentage of the population in poverty was calculated as 40.2 per cent, and the average poverty gap as M\$9.05 per month. The

[21] See Mirrlees (1971) for the pioneering contribution in the theory of optimum income taxation. The optimum tax schedule mentioned here is different from that of Mirrlees because of the additional constraint that no one's post-tax income should fall below an exogenously chosen poverty line.

Table 10.2
Estimates of Poverty by Racial Group

Racial group	Proportion of persons in poverty (q/n)	Average poverty gap per person (M$ per month) (π − μ)	Weights of unity on income gaps of the poor			Gini coefficient of income distribution among the poor	Rank-order weights on income gaps of the poor		
			Index P	Index M	Index F		Index P	Index M	Index F
Peninsular Malaysia	0.402	9.05	0.145	0.073	0.083	0.2126	0.200	0.100	0.115
Malay	0.562	9.74	0.219	0.161	0.215	0.2200	0.294	0.216	0.290
Chinese	0.183	6.80	0.050	0.018	0.019	0.1677	0.072	0.026	0.028
Indian	0.334	7.28	0.097	0.043	0.048	0.1658	0.137	0.060	0.067
Other	0.433	12.44	0.215	0.029	0.030	0.3328	0.288	0.039	0.040

poverty gap as a fraction of the total income needed to support everyone in the population at the poverty level is 14.5 per cent. The index M for the country was estimated as 0.073, which implies that the poverty gap in Malaysia stands at 7.3 per cent of total personal income. If poverty were to be eliminated by transfers from the non-poor to the poor, the non-poor would need to sacrifice 8.3 per cent of their income (or 12.7 per cent of their income in excess of the poverty level).[22]

These indices have also been computed separately for each ethnic group. The average income gap is largest for the small and hetero-geneous community of 'others' (Europeans, Thais, other Asians and so forth), while the incidence of poverty is highest among Malays. The product of these two measures divided by poverty-line income gives the Sen index in the case of unit weights, which shows that poverty is more acute among Malays than among 'others'.

The values of M and F for the communities show the poverty gap of each racial group as a fraction of various income aggregates for that group. For policy purposes, however, it is probably more useful to express the poverty gap of each racial group as a fraction of the *overall* poverty gap. Of the overall income shortfall, the Malays account for 79.0 per cent, the Chinese for 11.9 per cent, the Indians for 8.0 per cent, and other races for 1.1 per cent.[23] Of the overall number in poverty, however, the Malays account for 73.5 per cent, the Chinese for 15.8 per cent, the Indians for 9.9 per cent, and other races for 0.8 per cent. The difference between these two sets of figures obviously reflects the difference between races in their average poverty gaps.

Assume now that rank-order weights attach to the income gaps of poor persons. The average poverty gap then needs to be augmented by the mean income times the Gini coefficient of the income distribution among the poor. This adjustment yields values for P, M and F shown in the last three columns of Table 10.2. The Sen poverty measure takes the value 0.200 for Peninsular Malaysia. It is difficult to judge whether the degree of poverty which this represents is large or small in the absence of estimates for other countries.[24] In fact, one of the main

[22] See note 19 above.

[23] In a poverty relief programme, allocation to communities in these percentages will reduce their income gaps equiproportionately.

[24] Like most indices of inequality, the Sen poverty measure is useful mainly for comparisons across countries or over time. Unlike indices of inequality, which are relative, however, indices of poverty (including the one by Sen) are sensitive to the choice of poverty line. This needs to be borne in mind when making intercountry

258 MEASUREMENT OF INEQUALITY AND POVERTY

reasons for evaluating the Sen measure in the unit weights (or distribution free) case is that it has a straightforward interpretation there. Its value under rank-order weighting indicates the magnitude of the correction to the unit weights case, which arises from the inequality in incomes among the poor.

According to the Sen index, poverty is greatest among Malays, followed by 'others', Indians, and Chinese, respectively. Although the Sen index points to the severity of the problem within each racial group, it cannot be used to indicate the contribution of a group to overall poverty. Yet in the design of policies to redress poverty, it would seem important to be informed of the extent to which a particular group accounts for overall poverty. An index which does permit poverty to be 'decomposed' as a weighted average of poverty in each group is the simple incidence-of-poverty measure (unlike the case for an inequality index, there is obviously no between-group component for a poverty index).[25] In the next section, this index is adopted to characterize the nature of poverty in Malaysia.

A PROFILE OF POVERTY IN MALAYSIA

A characterization of poverty requires answers to questions such as: Who are the poor? Where are they located? In which sectors do they work? What are the characteristics of the poor that are different from those of the non-poor? The profile of poverty in this section identifies the poor in terms of socio-economic variables such as race, location, employment status, occupation, sector of employment, and education. It also indicates the extent of poverty accounted for by separate values of each variable (or characteristic) — made possible by the decomposability of the incidence-of-poverty measure.

Since the household is the basic income-sharing unit, it appears more appropriate for policy purposes to describe the population in poverty

comparisons of poverty. So far I have seen an estimate of the Sen index for only one other country: from National Sample Survey data on consumption in 1970–1, Ahluwalia (1977) estimates the Sen index for rural India as 0.176 and the incidence of rural poverty as 47.5 per cent.

[25] The overall incidence of poverty can be written as a weighted average of the poverty incidence in each group, where the weights are the population shares of the groups. The income gap measures (aggregate and proportionate) are similarly decomposable (with income share weights), but the Sen index, which uses the Gini coefficient to correct for inequality among the poor, is not. Because the Gini coefficient is not decomposable, the Sen index cannot indicate the proportion of poverty accounted for by a particular group.

in terms of *households*, rather than *individuals*. Accordingly, the population unit in the poverty profile is chosen to be the household, and poor households are those with per capita household incomes below M$25 per month. While the percentage of persons in poverty is 40.2 per cent (Table 10.2), the percentage of households in poverty is 36.5 per cent (Table 10.3). This is because the poor have a larger average household size than the non-poor (see point 8[3] below).[26]

Table 10.3
Profile of Poverty at a Poverty Line of M$25

Selected characteristic of household	Percentage distribution among:			Incidence of poverty (per cent)	Relative incidence of poverty (2)/(1)
	All house-holds	Poverty house-holds	Non-poverty house-holds		
	(1)	*(2)*	*(3)*	*(4)*	*(5)*
Race					
Malay	55.4	78.1	42.4	51.4	1.41
Chinese	32.0	12.9	42.9	14.7	0.40
Indian	11.7	8.0	13.9	24.8	0.68
Other	0.9	1.0	0.8	40.3	1.11
Total	100.0	100.0	100.0		
Location					
Urban	28.4	12.3	37.6	15.8	0.43
Rural	71.6	87.7	62.4	44.6	1.22
Total	100.0	100.0	100.0		
State					
Johore	13.4	12.1	14.1	32.9	0.90
Kedah	11.3	15.1	9.2	48.6	1.34
Kelantan	9.5	17.0	5.2	65.2	1.79
Malacca	4.6	4.1	4.9	32.0	0.89

Table 10.3 (cont.)

[26] Whereas there is a negative correlation between average household size and per capita household income, there is a positive correlation between average household size and household income.

Table 10.3 (cont.)

Selected characteristic of household	Percentage distribution among:			Incidence of poverty (per cent)	Relative incidence of poverty (2)/(1)
	All households	Poverty households	Non-poverty households		
	(1)	(2)	(3)	(4)	(5)
Negri Sembilan	4.7	4.2	5.1	32.1	0.89
Pahang	5.8	4.9	6.3	30.7	0.84
Penang	8.5	6.9	9.4	29.7	0.81
Perak	17.8	16.8	18.3	34.5	0.94
Perlis	1.5	2.4	1.0	58.9	1.60
Selangor	18.2	9.5	23.2	19.1	0.52
Trengganu	4.7	7.0	3.3	54.6	1.49
Total	100.0	100.0	100.0		
Employment status of head					
Employer	2.7	0.4	4.0	5.1	0.51
Employee	51.8	38.2	59.3	26.3	0.74
Own-account worker	39.3	55.3	30.4	50.1	1.41
Housewife or houseworker	2.6	2.2	2.8	30.5	0.85
Unemployed	3.6	3.9	3.5	38.0	1.08
Total	100.0	100.0	100.0		
Occupation of head					
Professional and technical	5.7	1.1	8.2	6.7	0.19
Administrative and managerial	3.3	0.4	4.9	4.4	0.12
Clerical and related	4.0	0.3	6.1	2.7	0.08
Sales	11.5	6.4	14.3	20.0	0.56
Service	8.3	3.4	10.9	14.9	0.41
Farmers	27.6	47.9	16.4	61.9	1.74
Farm labourers	21.6	29.5	17.3	48.6	1.37
Production	18.0	11.0	21.9	21.9	0.61
Total	100.0	100.0	100.0		

Table 10.3 (cont.)

Selected characteristic of household	Percentage distribution among:			Incidence of poverty (per cent)	Relative incidence of poverty (2)/(1)
	All house-holds	Poverty house-holds	Non-poverty house-holds		
	(1)	(2)	(3)	(4)	(5)
Sector of employment of head					
Agriculture	24.1	41.7	14.4	61.5	1.73
Agricultural products	25.7	33.4	21.4	46.2	1.30
Mining and quarrying	1.8	0.9	2.3	18.1	0.50
Manufacturing	8.6	5.2	10.4	21.8	0.60
Construction	3.2	2.0	4.0	21.5	0.63
Public utilities	1.6	1.0	2.0	21.0	0.63
Commerce	12.6	7.2	15.6	20.2	0.57
Transport and communications	5.5	3.3	6.7	21.2	0.60
Services	16.9	5.3	23.2	11.1	0.31
Total	100.0	100.0	100.0		
Education of head					
None	32.1	43.2	25.7	49.0	1.35
Some primary	33.1	35.6	31.7	39.1	1.08
Completed primary	20.4	18.4	21.6	32.8	0.90
Lower secondary (forms I–III)	6.7	2.1	9.3	11.7	0.31
Some upper secondary (forms IV–V)	3.0	0.4	4.4	5.2	0.13
School certificate or higher	4.7	0.3	7.3	2.1	0.06
Total	100.0	100.0	100.0		

Table 10.3 (cont.)

Table 10.3 (cont.)

Selected characteristic of household	Percentage distribution among:			Incidence of poverty (per cent)	Relative incidence of poverty (2)/(1)
	All house-holds	Poverty house-holds	Non-poverty house-holds		
	(1)	*(2)*	*(3)*	*(4)*	*(5)*
Sex of head					
Male	81.7	77.5	84.2	34.6	0.95
Female	18.3	22.5	15.8	44.9	1.23
Total	100.0	100.0	100.0		
Age of head					
Under 20	1.5	1.3	1.6	31.5	0.87
20–9	15.3	11.5	17.5	27.4	0.75
30–9	25.2	26.7	24.4	38.5	1.06
40–9	22.9	25.4	21.5	40.4	1.11
50–9	19.1	18.0	19.7	34.3	0.94
60 +	16.0	17.1	15.3	39.0	1.07
Total	100.0	100.0	100.0		
Household size					
1	8.9	5.7	10.7	23.5	0.64
2	9.5	6.1	11.6	23.2	0.64
3	11.7	9.4	12.9	29.5	0.80
4	13.1	11.4	14.0	31.8	0.87
5	12.6	13.8	11.9	40.0	1.10
6	12.0	13.8	11.0	41.8	1.15
7	9.8	12.5	8.2	46.7	1.28
8	7.9	9.9	6.8	45.6	1.25
9	5.5	6.1	5.2	40.3	1.11
10 +	9.0	11.3	7.7	45.7	1.26
Total	100.0	100.0	100.0		
Number of children under age 15					
0	24.7	14.0	30.9	20.7	0.57
1	17.0	14.3	18.5	30.7	0.84
2	15.5	14.9	15.8	35.2	0.96

Table 10.3 (cont.)

Selected characteristic of household	Percentage distribution among:			Incidence of poverty (per cent)	Relative incidence of poverty (2)/(1)
	All house-holds	Poverty house-holds	Non-poverty house-holds		
	(1)	(2)	(3)	(4)	(5)
3	13.6	15.5	12.5	41.5	1.14
4	11.5	15.3	9.3	48.4	1.33
5 +	17.7	26.0	13.0	53.5	1.47
Total	100.0	100.0	100.0		
Number of income recipients					
0	1.3	3.4	0.0	99.0	2.62
1	57.8	66.5	52.9	41.9	1.15
2	26.4	22.5	28.6	31.1	0.85
3	9.1	5.6	11.1	22.4	0.62
4 +	5.4	2.0	7.4	13.3	0.37
Total	100.0	100.0	100.0		

Note: The poverty line is defined at a per capita household income of M$25 per
month; 36.5 per cent of all households fall below this line.

Table 10.3 shows two distinct aspects of poverty. In column 2 the
percentage distribution of poverty among the values of each variable
is shown, which indicates concentrations of poverty. Column 4 shows
which groups suffer from a particularly high incidence of poverty; these
are so-called high risk groups which may, in fact, account for only a
small proportion of overall poverty. Clearly, both types of information
are important in the design of policies to redress poverty.

The following picture of the poor emerges from an examination of
the characteristics of households and their heads in Table 10.3.

1. The problem is overwhelmingly a Malay one, with 78.1 per cent
of poor households being Malay. There are six Malay households in
poverty for every one Chinese. Malays, who constitute 55.4 per cent
of all households, are over-represented among poor households by a
factor of 1.41 (see column 5 on the relative incidence of poverty). More
than half (51.4 per cent) of Malay households suffer from poverty,
while the incidence among Chinese is 14.7 per cent, and among Indians,
24.8 per cent.

2. Poverty is also overwhelmingly a rural phenomenon, with 87.7 per cent of poor households living in rural areas.[27]

3. The four northern states of Kedah, Kelantan, Perlis and Trengganu stand out as having above average incidences of poverty. Together they account for 41.5 per cent of poverty households, but for only 27.0 per cent of all households.

4. Of poor households, 93.5 per cent are headed by employees or own-account (self-employed) workers. The incidence of poverty among households whose heads are own-account workers is 50.1 per cent, which is higher than that among households whose heads are employees (26.3 per cent). The unemployment rate among heads of poverty households is a mere 3.9 per cent, and the rate of poverty among households with unemployed heads is 38.0 per cent.[28]

5. Farmers head 47.9 per cent of poor households and farm labourers, 29.5 per cent. The incidence of poverty among households headed by farmers and farm labourers is 61.9 per cent and 48.6 per cent, respectively. The higher incidence of poverty among households headed by farmers reflects something of a dual economy in the rural sector. The category of farm labourers includes both relatively well-paid estate workers, who form a significant proportion of the rural labour force, as well as casual and other labourers. The category of farmers includes all peasants and smallholders.

6. The incidence of poverty is well above average among households with heads in the agricultural sector (61.5 per cent) and in the agricultural products sector (46:2 per cent). These two sectors account for three-quarters (75.1 per cent) of poverty households but less than half (49.8 per cent) of all households.[29]

[27] Separate profiles of the urban and rural poor reveal that the ethnic distribution of urban poverty is quite different from that of rural poverty. The Chinese form the most numerous group among the urban poor, but the incidence of urban poverty among Malays is almost twice that among Chinese.

[28] Thus the problem of poverty needs to be distinguished from the problem of unemployment. A policy of absorbing unemployed heads of households into the labour market will not make a significant dent in poverty. Of course, a general expansion of formal sector employment, which also absorbs subsistence sector own-account and family workers, could contribute appreciably to a reduction in poverty.

[29] This is in accordance with the finding of 77.4 per cent of poverty households headed by farmers or farm labourers. The breakdown by employment status of head of household includes categories (own-account workers and employees) that overlap with the occupations of farmer and farm labourer. The overlap or *joint* distribution of categories must obviously be borne in mind when policy interpretations are attempted.

7. Persons whose schooling does not extend beyond primary school head 97.2 per cent of all poverty households. Of these, 43.2 per cent have had no education at all. There is a strong negative correlation between education and poverty incidence, and the decline in incidence is particularly marked for households whose heads have acquired even *some* secondary education. Of households whose heads have received some upper secondary education, only 5.2 per cent are poor, and of those whose heads have received the school certificate, only 2.1 per cent are poor.

8. The distribution and incidence of poverty as a function of household composition show the following features: (i) Households headed by females are somewhat more poverty prone (44.9 per cent) than those headed by males (34.6 per cent). (ii) The incidence of poverty does not show wide variation according to age of household head, but it is lowest for the 20–9 age group. (iii) The incidence of poverty increases with household size up to seven-member households, after which the relation is unclear (owing to the effect of additional income recipients); but the incidence is above average for all size classes above five and below average for all lower size classes. A comparison of the percentage distribution of household size among poverty and non-poverty households shows a larger average household size for the poor. (iv) The incidence of household poverty increases steadily with the number of children under age 15 (who are unlikely to be income recipients).[30] (v) Almost all (99 per cent) of the households with no income recipients are in poverty, and the incidence rate falls with the number of recipients. Among poor households, 66.5 per cent have just one income recipient, and 22.5 per cent have two.

When several of the characteristics associated with high degrees of poverty are taken together, the chances of being poor can become extremely high. Thus, for example, a Malay farmer in rural Kelantan has a worse than three-fourths probability of being poor. In order to design policies and projects to help the poor selectively and with minimal leakage, it is necessary to identify smaller, more homogeneous groups such as these, with particularly high incidences of poverty.

---

[30] This relation might weaken if the per equivalent adult household income had been used instead of per capita household income to measure living standards. But the relation between poverty incidence and household size need not be affected by this very much. Because of the prevalence of the joint family system in Malaysia, larger households do not necessarily have a larger proportion of children.

Table 10.4
Household Percentages in Four Per Capita
Household Income Classes by Racial Group and Location

Per capita household income class (M$ per month)	Percentage of households in income class	Percentage distribution among racial groups					Percentage of households in income class	
		Malay	Chinese	Indian	Other	Total	Urban	Rural
0–15	15.5	85.3	7.8	5.4	1.5	100.0	5.0	19.6
Urban	1.4	42.6	34.7	21.6	1.1	100.0		
Rural	14.1	89.6	5.1	3.8	1.5	100.0		
0–25	36.5	78.1	12.9	8.0	1.0	100.0	15.8	44.6
Urban	4.5	37.4	41.9	19.6	1.1	100.0		
Rural	32.0	83.9	8.8	6.3	1.0	100.0		
0–33	49.3	73.0	16.9	9.3	0.8	100.0	25.5	58.6
Urban	7.3	34.5	47.0	17.7	0.8	100.0		
Rural	42.0	79.6	11.7	7.9	0.8	100.0		
185 +	5.0	21.5	55.8	16.9	5.8	100.0	11.4	2.6
Urban	3.2	14.9	61.9	17.3	5.9	100.0		
Rural	1.8	33.2	44.9	16.3	5.6	100.0		
All income classes (0 +)	100.0	55.4	32.0	11.7	0.9	100.0	100.0	100.0
Urban	28.4	25.9	57.9	14.9	1.3	100.0		
Rural	71.6	67.1	21.7	10.5	0.7	100.0		

SENSITIVITY OF THE POVERTY PROFILE

Before zeroing in on subgroups in poverty, it should be established that the picture of poverty in Table 10.3 does not hinge crucially on the chosen poverty line of M$25 per capita household income per month. Accordingly, I consider two further poverty lines, at M$15 and M$33 per month, and conduct sensitivity analysis on the profile of poverty.[31] This is partially possible through Table 10.4, which shows the percentage of households falling below these poverty lines with a breakdown by location and racial group.

The M$15 poverty line cuts off roughly the bottom 20 per cent of the population, and may be said to identify the 'very poor' in Malaysia. Since the redress of poverty rule requires filling the poverty gap from the bottom upward, this poorest group may be of special interest. Some 15.5 per cent of households, containing 17.3 per cent of individuals, receive a per capita household income of less than M$15 per month. The average per capita income of these individuals is slightly less than M$10 per month, while that of the other 82.7 per cent is M$58 per month. A transfer of just 1.8 per cent of the income of this upper group can bring all the very poor up to the income level of M$15 per month.

The M$33 poverty line corresponds to that of the second method used earlier in this chapter to define an absolute poverty line. The proportion of households falling below M$33 per month is 49.3 per cent.[32] Thus when the poverty line is raised from M$25 to M$33, the incidence of poverty rises from 36.5 to 49.3 per cent, and when it is lowered from M$25 to M$15, the incidence of poverty falls from 36.5 to 15.5 per cent. Hence the incidence of poverty is fairly sensitive to changes in the poverty line, showing an elasticity of 1.1 for upward movement from M$25 and an elasticity of 1.4 for downward movement from M$25.

The profile of poverty is much less sensitive to variations in the

[31] This is an obvious but somewhat neglected exercise in the growing empirical literature on poverty. As attempts to estimate poverty in developing countries get under way and cross-country comparisons begin to be made, it becomes important to establish the robustness of estimates through sensitivity analysis. In some countries it is possible that the estimates are highly sensitive to small variations in the poverty threshold.

[32] This is the figure for poverty incidence mentioned in the Third Malaysia Plan (TMP) (see Government of Malaysia 1976, p. 160). In addition to this, the TMP (Tables 9.1, 9.2, 9.3 and 9.6) quotes detailed poverty incidence figures from my M$33 poverty profile (see Anand 1974, or Table 10.6 below). The plan document, however, does not mention that these figures correspond to a poverty line of M$33 income per month.

poverty line than is the incidence of poverty.[33] As the poverty line is lowered from M$33 to M$25 and then to M$15, Malays account for 75.3, 78.1, and 85.3 per cent, respectively, of poverty households, while the reverse trend is in evidence for the Chinese, who account for a decreasing percentage of poverty households. As the poverty line is lowered, the rural concentration of poverty also increases a little: 85.2 per cent of M$33 poverty households reside in rural areas, compared with 87.7 and 91.0 per cent, respectively, of M$25 and M$15 poverty households. It seems that racial and rural–urban features of poverty are not very sensitive to the choice of poverty line within a reasonably wide range, although they are accentuated as the poverty line is dropped.

The distribution of poverty according to other characteristics also remains relatively stable as the poverty line rises from M$15 to M$33 (see Tables 10.5 and 10.6).[34] Kedah, Kelantan, Perlis, and Trengganu remain the states worst affected by poverty. As the poverty line rises, the relative incidence of poverty in these states drops slightly but remains well above unity. Households whose heads are own-account workers continue to be overrepresented among the poor as the poverty line is raised, with the relative incidence dropping a little from 1.61 to 1.32. The relative incidence of poverty among households whose heads are employees increases (from 0.61 to 0.81) but remains well below unity. With respect to sectors of employment, the relative incidence among households with heads in agriculture declines from 2.12 to 1.56, while for those in agricultural products it remains virtually stationary around 1.30. By occupational category, the relative incidence of poverty for households headed by farmers declines from 2.07 to 1.58 as the poverty line is raised, while for those headed by farm labourers it oscillates from 1.34 to 1.37 to 1.32. Finally, the educational and demographic characteristics of poverty households display similarly small variations as the poverty line is altered.

Thus the picture of poverty in Table 10.3 does not seem very sensitive to the variations considered in the poverty line. One can remain fairly confident about the profile it depicts, and in subsequent discussion on

[33] It is the presence of bunching, or excessive inequality, in the lower portions of the income distribution that could cause profile characteristics and the incidence of poverty to move discontinuously as a function of the poverty line. Since the Sen index specifically incorporates inequality among the poor, it may be relatively immune to such jumps.

[34] Separate rural and urban poverty profiles for the M$15 and M$33 poverty lines were presented in Anand (1974).

poverty I adhere to the original line of M$25 per month. Such changes in emphasis as there are in the poverty profile suggest that households headed by farmers and those in agriculture form the hard core of the poor. This highlights the need to study rural poverty in greater detail.

Table 10.5
Profile of Poverty at a Poverty Line of M$15

Selected characteristic of household	Percentage distribution among:			Incidence of poverty (per cent)	Relative incidence of poverty (2)/(1)
	All house-holds	Poverty house-holds	Non-poverty house-holds		
	(1)	(2)	(3)	(4)	(5)
Race					
Malay	55.4	85.3	49.9	23.9	1.54
Chinese	32.0	7.8	36.4	3.8	0.24
Indian	11.7	5.4	12.9	7.2	0.46
Other	0.9	1.5	0.8	25.3	1.67
Total	100.0	100.0	100.0		
Location					
Urban	28.4	9.0	32.0	5.0	0.32
Rural	71.6	91.0	68.0	19.6	1.27
Total	100.0	100.0	100.0		
State					
Johore	13.4	11.7	13.7	13.5	0.87
Kedah	11.3	15.8	10.5	21.7	1.40
Kelantan	9.5	21.4	7.4	34.8	2.25
Malacca	4.6	3.4	4.8	11.4	0.74
Negri Sembilan	4.7	3.9	4.9	12.7	0.83
Pahang	5.8	4.6	6.0	12.4	0.79
Penang	8.5	5.1	9.1	9.3	0.60
Perak	17.8	15.5	18.2	13.6	0.87
Perlis	1.5	3.0	1.2	31.1	2.00
Selangor	18.2	7.1	20.2	6.0	0.39
Trengganu	4.7	8.5	4.0	28.2	1.31
Total	100.0	100.0	100.0	100.0	

Table 10.5 (cont.)

Table 10.5 (cont.)

Selected characteristic of household	Percentage distribution among:			Incidence of poverty (per cent)	Relative incidence of poverty (2)/(1)
	All house-holds	Poverty house-holds	Non-poverty house-holds		
	(1)	*(2)*	*(3)*	*(4)*	*(5)*
Employment status of head					
Employer	2.7	0.3	3.1	1.8	0.11
Employee	51.8	31.6	55.2	8.7	0.61
Own-account worker	39.3	63.1	35.3	23.1	1.61
Housewife or houseworker	2.6	1.7	2.8	9.1	0.65
Unemployed	3.6	3.3	3.6	13.2	0.92
Total	100.0	100.0	100.0		
Occupation of head					
Professional and technical	5.7	0.6	6.5	1.6	0.11
Administrative and managerial	3.3	0.1	3.9	0.5	0.03
Clerical and related	4.0	0.1	4.7	0.2	0.03
Sales	11.5	4.6	12.7	6.0	0.40
Service	8.3	2.3	9.3	4.0	0.28
Farmers	27.6	57.0	22.5	30.6	2.07
Farm labourers	21.6	28.9	20.4	19.8	1.34
Production	18.0	6.4	20.0	5.3	0.36
Total	100.0	100.0	100.0		
Sector of employment of head					
Agriculture	24.1	51.1	19.5	30.9	2.12
Agricultural products	25.7	33.5	24.4	18.9	1.30
Mining and quarrying	1.8	0.3	2.1	2.4	0.17
Manufacturing	8.6	3.5	9.4	6.0	0.41
Construction	3.2	1.0	3.6	4.3	0.31
Public utilities	1.6	0.2	1.9	1.5	0.13
Commerce	12.6	5.1	13.9	5.9	0.41

Selected characteristic of household	Percentage distribution among:			Incidence of poverty (per cent)	Relative incidence of poverty (2)/(1)
	All house-holds (1)	Poverty house-holds (2)	Non-poverty house-holds (3)	(4)	(5)
Transport and communications	5.5	2.2	6.0	5.7	0.40
Services	16.9	3.1	19.2	2.7	0.18
Total	100.0	100.0	100.0		
Education of head					
None	32.1	48.2	29.1	23.2	1.50
Some primary	33.1	34.0	33.0	15.8	1.03
Completed primary	20.4	15.1	21.4	11.4	0.74
Lower secondary (forms I–III)	6.7	1.9	7.5	4.5	0.28
Some upper secondary (forms IV–V)	3.0	0.4	3.5	2.0	0.13
School certificate or higher	4.7	0.4	5.5	1.2	0.09
Total	100.0	100.0	100.0		
Sex of head					
Male	81.7	73.5	83.2	13.9	0.90
Female 18.3	26.5	16.8	22.5	1.45	
Total	100.0	100.0	100.0		
Age of head					
Under 20	1.5	1.4	1.5	14.9	0.93
20–9	15.3	11.6	16.0	11.6	0.76
30–9	25.2	28.4	24.7	17.4	1.13
40–9	22.9	25.2	22.5	17.0	1.10
50–9	19.1	17.7	19.3	14.3	0.93
60 +	16.0	15.7	16.0	15.2	0.98
Total	100.0	100.0	100.0		

Table 10.5 (cont.)

Selected characteristic of household	Percentage distribution among:			Incidence of poverty (per cent)	Relative incidence of poverty (2)/(1)
	All house-holds	Poverty house-holds	Non-poverty house-holds		
	(1)	(2)	(3)	(4)	(5)
Household size					
1	8.9	0.7	10.4	1.3	0.08
2	9.5	10.5	9.4	17.0	1.11
3	11.7	9.6	12.1	12.7	0.82
4	13.1	7.1	14.2	8.4	0.54
5	12.6	15.5	12.0	19.1	1.23
6	12.0	17.0	11.1	21.9	1.42
7	9.8	11.8	9.4	18.7	1.20
8	7.9	11.0	7.3	21.7	1.39
9	5.5	6.6	5.3	19.6	1.20
10 +	9.0	10.2	8.8	17.6	1.13
Total	100.0	100.0	100.0		
Number of children under age 15					
0	24.7	10.5	27.3	6.6	0.43
1	17.0	14.3	17.5	13.1	0.84
2	15.5	13.2	15.9	13.2	0.85
3	13.6	18.4	12.7	21.0	1.35
4	11.5	17.0	10.5	22.8	1.40
5 +	17.7	26.6	16.1	23.3	1.50
Total	100.0	100.0	100.0		
Number of income recipients					
0	1.3	8.0	0.0	98.7	6.15
1	57.8	67.7	56.1	18.1	1.17
2	26.4	18.9	27.8	11.1	0.72
3	9.1	4.0	10.0	6.7	0.44
4 +	5.4	1.4	6.1	4.1	0.26
Total	100.0	100.0	100.0		

Note: The poverty line is defined at a per capita household income of M$15 per month; 15.5 per cent of all households fall below this line.

Table 10.6
Profile of Poverty at a Poverty Line of M$33

Selected characteristic of household	Percentage distribution among:			Incidence of poverty (per cent)	Relative incidence of poverty (2)/(1)
	All house-holds	Poverty house-holds	Non-poverty house-holds		
	(1)	*(2)*	*(3)*	*(4)*	*(5)*
Race					
Malay	55.4	73.0	38.4	64.8	1.32
Chinese	32.0	16.9	46.6	26.0	0.53
Indian	11.7	9.3	14.0	39.2	0.79
Other	0.9	0.8	1.0	44.8	0.89
Total	100.0	100.0	100.0		
Location					
Urban	28.4	14.8	41.6	25.5	0.52
Rural	71.6	85.2	58.4	58.6	1.19
Total	100.0	100.0	100.0		
State					
Johore	13.4	12.4	14.3	45.7	0.93
Kedah	11.3	14.6	8.2	63.2	1.29
Kelantan	9.5	14.8	4.5	76.1	1.56
Malacca	4.6	4.2	5.0	44.9	0.91
Negri Sembilan	4.7	4.3	5.1	44.8	0.91
Pahang	5.8	5.1	6.5	43.2	0.88
Penang	8.5	7.5	9.4	43.7	0.88
Perak	17.8	17.5	18.0	48.6	0.98
Perlis	1.5	2.3	0.8	73.9	1.53
Selangor	18.2	10.8	25.4	29.2	0.59
Trengganu	4.7	6.5	2.8	68.9	1.38
Total	100.0	100.0	100.0		
Employment status of head					
Employer	2.7	0.5	4.8	8.8	0.19
Employee	51.8	41.8	61.2	39.1	0.81
Own-account worker	39.3	51.9	27.4	64.0	1.32

Table 10.6 (cont.)

Table 10.6 (cont.)

Selected characteristic of household	Percentage distribution among:			Incidence of poverty (per cent)	Relative incidence of poverty (2)/(1)
	All households	Poverty households	Non-poverty households		
	(1)	(2)	(3)	(4)	(5)
Housewife or houseworker	2.6	2.3	2.9	42.8	0.88
Unemployed	3.6	3.5	3.7	47.2	0.97
Total	100.0	100.0	100.0		
Occupation of head					
Professional and technical	5.7	1.2	9.8	10.6	0.21
Administrative and managerial	3.3	0.7	5.8	9.5	0.21
Clerical and related	4.0	0.9	6.9	10.7	0.23
Sales	11.5	7.2	15.5	30.5	0.63
Service	8.3	4.6	11.7	27.0	0.55
Farmers	27.6	43.5	12.7	76.4	1.58
Farm labourers	21.6	28.5	15.2	63.8	1.32
Production	18.0	13.4	22.4	36.0	0.74
Total	100.0	100.0	100.0		
Sector of employment of head					
Agriculture	24.1	37.5	11.5	75.4	1.56
Agricultural products	25.7	32.7	19.1	61.7	1.27
Mining and quarrying	1.8	1.3	2.3	34.0	0.72
Manufacturing	8.6	5.7	11.2	32.3	0.66
Construction	3.2	2.4	4.0	36.6	0.75
Public utilities	1.6	1.3	2.0	37.0	0.81
Commerce	12.6	7.9	17.1	30.3	0.63
Transport and communications	5.5	4.2	6.8	36.6	0.76
Services	16.9	7.0	26.0	20.3	0.41
Total	100.0	100.0	100.0		

Selected characteristic of household	Percentage distribution among:			Incidence of poverty (per cent)	Relative incidence of poverty (2)/(1)
	All house- holds	Poverty house- holds	Non-poverty house- holds		
	(1)	*(2)*	*(3)*	*(4)*	*(5)*
Education of head					
None	32.1	40.6	23.8	62.3	1.26
Some primary	33.1	36.2	30.2	53.7	1.09
Completed primary	20.4	19.8	21.0	47.7	0.97
Lower secondary (forms I–III)	6.7	2.6	10.6	19.0	0.39
Some upper secondary (forms IV–V)	3.0	0.5	5.4	7.6	0.17
School certifi- cate or higher	4.7	0.3	9.0	3.3	0.06
Total	100.0	100.0	100.0		
Sex of head					
Male	81.7	79.2	84.2	47.7	0.97
Female	18.3	20.8	15.8	56.1	1.14
Total	100.0	100.0	100.0		
Age of head					
Under 20	1.5	1.2	1.8	38.3	0.80
20–9	15.3	11.8	18.7	37.9	0.77
30–9	25.2	26.6	23.9	51.9	1.06
40–9	22.9	25.4	20.5	54.5	1.11
50–9	19.1	18.1	19.9	46.9	0.95
60 +	16.0	16.9	15.2	51.9	1.06
Total	100.0	100.0	100.0		
Household size					
1	8.9	4.3	13.4	23.5	0.48
2	9.5	7.8	11.3	40.2	0.82

Table 10.6 (cont.)

Table 10.6 (cont.)

Selected characteristic of household	Percentage distribution among:			Incidence of poverty (per cent)	Relative incidence of poverty (2)/(1)
	All house-holds	Poverty house-holds	Non-poverty house-holds		
	(1)	*(2)*	*(3)*	*(4)*	*(5)*
3	11.7	9.3	13.9	39.3	0.79
4	13.1	11.6	14.5	43.8	0.89
5	12.6	14.5	10.7	56.7	1.15
6	12.0	13.8	10.3	56.5	1.15
7	9.8	10.4	9.2	52.3	1.06
8	7.9	10.4	5.5	65.0	1.32
9	5.5	7.3	3.7	65.5	1.33
10 +	9.0	10.6	7.5	57.8	1.18
Total	100.0	100.0	100.0		
Number of children under age 15					
0	24.7	14.4	34.8	28.6	0.58
1	17.0	14.8	19.1	43.0	0.87
2	15.5	15.2	15.3	40.2	0.99
3	13.6	15.8	11.4	57.3	1.16
4	11.5	14.5	8.6	62.2	1.26
5 +	17.7	25.3	10.3	70.4	1.43
Total	100.0	100.0	100.0		
Number of income recipients					
0	1.3	2.5	0.0	99.0	1.92
1	57.8	64.0	51.9	54.4	1.11
2	26.4	24.2	28.6	45.1	0.92
3	9.1	6.7	11.4	36.0	0.74
4 +	5.4	2.6	8.1	23.9	0.48
Total	100.0	100.0	100.0		

Note: The poverty line is defined at a per capita household income of M$33 per month; 49.3 per cent of all households fall below this line.

APPENDIX: A PROFILE OF THE RICH

For comparative purposes, it is interesting to look briefly at the top end of the per capita household income distribution. Defining rich households as those belonging in the top 5 per cent of this distribution, that is those with per capita household income above M$185 per month, certain characteristics of 'richness' are apparent from Table 10.4. Of the 5.0 per cent rich households, 3.2 per cent reside in urban areas and 1.8 per cent in rural areas. As many as 11.4 per cent of urban households, but only 2.6 per cent of rural households, are rich. Only 2.0 per cent of Malay households are rich, compared with 8.8 per cent of Chinese, 7.3 per cent of Indian, and 33.5 per cent of other races.[35] Of rich households 55.8 per cent are Chinese, compared with 21.5 per cent Malay, 16.9 per cent Indian, and 5.8 per cent others. Further characteristics (not shown in Table 10.4) of the top 5 per cent of households are:[36]

1. Almost three-quarters (73.8 per cent) of the rich are concentrated in the four states of Johore, Penang, Perak and Selangor, with Selangor itself accounting for 37.7 per cent.

2. Households whose heads are employers are overrepresented among the rich by a factor of 4.26 (that is they show a relative incidence of richness of 4.26), and those whose heads are own-account workers are underrepresented (with a relative incidence of 0.33). Among rich households 2.3 per cent have heads who are unemployed, and 3.4 per cent of households with unemployed heads are rich.

3. With respect to sector of employment, heads of rich households are highly concentrated in services (46.7 per cent), commerce (20.3 per cent) and manufacturing (12.0 per cent). Few of them are to be found in agriculture (3.1 per cent) or agricultural products (5.4 per cent), which also accords with the occupational finding that few are farmers (2.3 per cent) or farm labourers (1.2 per cent). Indeed, an extremely small percentage of households whose heads are farmers (0.5 per cent) or farm labourers (0.3 per cent) are rich.[37] In contrast, the professional and technical and the administrative and managerial categories each have an incidence of richness above 30 per cent.

[35] This last fact, together with 40.3 per cent of 'others' being poor (Table 10.3), confirms the wide income inequality within this racial group.

[36] A detailed profile of the rich is contained in Anand (1974), pp. 29–37, which also has a disaggregation according to separate urban and rural profiles.

[37] The incidence of richness among urban households whose heads are farmers is 2.8 per cent, whereas that among rural households whose heads are farmers is 0.4 per cent. This is to some extent explained by different cropping patterns in urban and rural areas, with urban farmers probably growing high-value perishables such as fruits and vegetables for nearby markets.

4. Education of the household head seems positively correlated with the household's being rich. Only 1.2 per cent of households whose heads have no education belong to the M$185 + group, compared with 45.5 per cent of those whose heads have a school certificate (form V) or more.[38] The chances of being rich improve significantly for households whose heads have completed even some secondary education.

5. Other, demographic features of richness stand in mirror image to those associated with poverty.

REFERENCES

Ahluwalia, Montek S. (1974). 'Income Inequality: Some Dimensions of the Problem', in Chenery, et al. (1974).

Anand, Sudhir (1974). 'Addendum to the Size Distribution of Income in Malaysia, Part I', Development Research Center, World Bank, Washington, D.C.

—— (1975). 'Aspects of Poverty in Malaysia', Paper presented to the Fourteenth General Conference of the International Association for Research on Income and Wealth, Aulanko, Finland.

Atkinson, Anthony B. (1970). 'On the Measurement of Inequality', *Journal of Economic Theory*, 2(3), September.

—— (1975). *The Economics of Inequality*. Oxford: Clarendon Press.

Aziz, Ungku A. (1964). 'Poverty and Rural Development in Malaysia', *Kajian Ekonomi Malaysia*, 1(1), June.

—— (1965). 'Poverty, Proteins and Disguised Starvation', *Kajian Ekonomi Malaysia*, 1(1), June.

—— (1975a). *Jejak–Jejak di Pantai Zaman*. Kuala Lumpur: University of Malaya Press.

—— (1975b). 'Recent Thoughts on Poverty', Paper presented at the Second Malaysian Economic Convention, Kuala Lumpur.

Chenery, Hollis B., Montek S. Ahluwalia, C.L.G. Bell, John H. Duloy and Richard Jolly (1974). *Redistribution with Growth*. London: Oxford University Press.

Department of Social Welfare (1975). *A Joint State and Federal Government Public Assistance Programme*. Kuala Lumpur: Ministry of Welfare Services.

---

[38] The strong relation persists even when rural areas are considered separately from urban areas: 36.9 per cent of rural households whose heads have a school certificate or higher education are rich (51.1 per cent of urban households). While I have partially tested for the effect of education on income in urban areas, no such test has been conducted for rural areas. The evidence here, however, suggests that even in rural areas living standards are positively correlated with education.

Department of Social Welfare (1976). 'Public Assistance as a State/Federal Responsibility', Kuala Lumpur: Ministry of Welfare Services.

Fishlow, Albert (1972). 'Brazilian Size Distribution of Income', *American Economic Review*, 62, May.

—— (1973). 'Brazilian Income Size Distribution — Another Look'. Berkeley: University of California.

Government of Malaysia (1976). *Third Malaysia Plan, 1976–1980.* Kuala Lumpur: Government Press. Referred to as TMP in text.

McNamara, Robert S. (1972). *Address to the Board of Governors.* Washington, D.C.: World Bank. Reprinted in *The McNamara Years at the World Bank: Major Policy Addresses of Robert S. McNamara, 1968–1981.* Baltimore, Md.: Johns Hopkins University Press, 1981.

Mirrlees, James A. (1971). 'An Exploration in the Theory of Optimum Income Taxation', *Review of Economic Studies*, 38, April.

Orshansky, M. (1965). 'Counting the Poor: Another Look at the Poverty Profile', *Social Security Bulletin*, 28.

Rawls, John (1971). *A Theory of Justice.* Cambridge, Mass.: Harvard University Press.

Sen, Amartya K. (1973a). *On Economic Inequality.* Oxford: Clarendon Press.

—— (1973b). 'Poverty, Inequality and Unemployment: Some Conceptual Issues in Measurement', *Economic and Political Weekly*, Special Number, August.

—— (1976a). 'Poverty: An Ordinal Approach to Measurement', *Econometrica*, 44(2), March.

On the Coverage of Public Employment Schemes for Poverty Alleviation

MARTIN RAVALLION

INTRODUCTION

The provision of employment on public works has been advocated as a means of relieving poverty and famines in South Asia for at least a century; for example the Indian famine codes of the late nineteenth century strongly recommended this form of relief (Bhatia 1967, Aykroyd 1974). Probably the most well-known example is the 'Employment Guarantee Scheme' run by Maharashtra state in India since the early 1970s. National public employment schemes have now also been introduced in India, namely the 'Rural Landless Employment Guarantee Programme' and the 'National Rural Employment Programme'.[1] By these and other means, the Government of India is explicitly aiming to achieve a very substantial contraction in the number of people in rural areas whose incomes fall below the country's poverty line. India's public employment schemes (and particularly that of Maharashtra) have been praised by a number of observers and advocated as a model for poverty alleviation programmes throughout South Asia and, indeed, elsewhere.[2]

Direct interventions aimed at alleviating poverty in the short run may involve costs against other policy objectives, including intertemporal trade-offs in alleviating poverty now, versus later. For example direct intervention may deplete resources available for future economic growth, thus restricting a potentially important *indirect* channel for

---

[1] For useful discussions of recent poverty alleviation schemes in India see Sundaram and Tendulkar (1985), Bagchee (1987) and Narayana et al. (1988).

[2] For example see Lieberman (1985), Basu (1987), Drèze (1988), Lele (1988), Narayana et al. (1988).

future poverty alleviation. The *cost-effectiveness* of such schemes then emerges as an important policy issue. There may well be alternative policies or alternative ways of designing the scheme which can achieve a greater reduction in poverty, for the same budgetary outlay, or which can achieve the same reduction in poverty at lower cost.

The cost-effectiveness of a relief work scheme can depend quite crucially on details of its design, such as the wage rate offered to participants. And yet, with the exception of Basu (1981), there has been little effort by economists to probe these issues analytically. The lack of systematic investigations of programme design issues has been identified as an important reason for some of the past failures of such schemes (see, for example, Bagchee 1987).

This chapter addresses some of the issues which arise in designing cost-effective relief work schemes, focusing on two closely related aspects: the choice of *coverage* for the scheme, and the choice of the *benefit level* to participants. The aim is to look at these issues within an analytically tractable theoretical framework, in the hope of both illuminating the policy trade-offs and of identifying key empirical questions which will need to be answered when designing specific programmes. The following section gives a non-technical overview of the issues involved. The third section outlines a simple theoretical model of the stylized policy choice to be considered. The fourth section discusses how poverty is likely to be affected by that choice, identifying circumstances under which a policy ranking is possible. Drawing on these results, calculations are presented in the fifth section of the effects on poverty in Bangladesh of a number of hypothetical relief work schemes. A few concluding comments are given in the final section.

AN OVERVIEW OF THE ISSUES

The most obvious reason for incomplete coverage in a poverty alleviation scheme is the need for targeting a limited budget. Leakage of benefits to the non-poor is now recognized as a serious problem with such schemes.[3] This is particularly so of programmes which aim to provide universal coverage. More limited coverage targeted at the poor will generally enable a greater impact on poverty for a given budget.

The case for restricting coverage is less obvious for *self-targeting* schemes which are designed such that only the poor (or at least very

---

[3] For further discussion, see Reutlinger and Selowsky (1976), World Bank (1986), Kanbur (1987), Ravallion and Chao (1988), Besley and Kanbur (1988).

few of the non-poor) will *want* to participate. Public employment schemes are an example. The government offers work at some wage rate and only those who are currently earning less than this amount in similar activities will turn up. Thus the policy can automatically target relief towards workers with low reservation wage rates. And such workers are often (though not always) amongst the poorest persons. Queueing for rationed food is another example of a self-targeting poverty alleviation scheme. Only those persons who value their queueing time less than some critical amount will participate. And it may be assumed (though it *is* an assumption) that the non-poor will have prohibitively high time values.[4] Accepting that poverty alleviation is their objective, the attraction of such self-targeting schemes is plain enough; leakage to the non-poor is a deadweight loss from the point of view of this objective.

However, even if *only* the poor want to participate in such a scheme (so that it is *perfectly* self-targeting), this need not mean that the poverty alleviation objective is best served by allowing *all* of the poor to participate. Incomplete coverage may also be desirable for self-targeting poverty alleviation schemes.

The case in point here concerns the setting of the wage rate for relief work. This has been a source of considerable debate in policy-oriented discussions.[5] One option is to employ all workers who want work at a wage consistent with the available budget, as advocated by Basu (1981, 1987). Such a scheme guarantees employment, but the budget available need not be sufficient to bring all participants up to a socially acceptable income level. Indeed, the wage rate on such a scheme may be very low. For example in a study of Maharashtra's 'Employment Guarantee Scheme', Dandekar and Sathe (1980) found that 90 per cent of those employed under the scheme continued to have incomes below a widely accepted poverty line. Unless the budget happens to be generous enough to bring all workers up to the poverty line, such a scheme will leave the same number of persons amongst any homogeneous set of workers in poverty as before the policy existed, though ameliorating some of the worst extremes.

An alternative policy is to set the wage rate at a higher level, which is considered socially acceptable. But, unless the budget is very generous, this policy will leave some workers unable to obtain relief

[4] See Alderman (1987) for further discussion of such schemes.
[5] See, for example, Abraham (1980), Dandekar and Sathe (1980), Basu (1981, 1987), Ravallion (1987b) and World Bank (1986).

work, though they would like it at that wage rate. A 'poverty line' wage rate for relief work will often be too high to *guarantee* employment on relief work for a given budget. The poverty of a subset of the poor can be dramatically reduced by such a policy, but the rest may be left destitute.

Thus the design of public works schemes for poverty alleviation raises a fundamental question: is it better to guarantee employment at potentially low wages for all of the poor, or to guarantee that at least some of the poor are deemed to have adequate incomes?

Similar questions arise for other poverty alleviation schemes. Concerns have often been expressed about the poverty impact of subsidized credit programmes such as India's large 'Integrated Rural Development Programme'. Monitoring studies of the latter scheme have generally found that only a small proportion of beneficiaries have actually crossed the poverty line.[6] Disappointed by this outcome, the Public Accounts Committee of the Indian parliament has recently recommended that, unless the scheme's budget can be substantially increased, future coverage should be limited so as to enable more beneficiaries to exit poverty (Hirway 1988).[7]

These policy issues raise long-standing questions concerning the measurement of poverty. The existence of a *poverty line* is one such issue, with bearing on the policy choice over coverage. If one accepts the view that there is a well-defined critical income level needed to escape poverty in a given society and that attaining this income is qualitatively significant then, under otherwise identical conditions, one would tend to favour schemes which allow at least some poor people to obtain that income, over schemes which allow only small gains to the very poor.

In support of this view, it can be argued that, unless an individual can afford some critical bundle of goods, his or her basic functionings in a society will be impeded. And this may persist over time. For example to obtain a job, it is often essential that a worker is *already*

[6] For example, an (unpublished) evaluation of that scheme by the Ministry of Rural Development found that, despite very wide coverage (27 million households), only 13 per cent of beneficiaries had crossed the poverty line. Also see Kurian (1987) and Bandyopadhyay (1988).

[7] A similar question arises in food-rationing schemes which use desired waiting time as the indicator for self-targeting: is it better to give a small amount of food to everyone who is willing to wait for it, or to give a more adequate amount to as many people in the queue as the available supply permits?

adequately clothed and fed. Similarly, an impoverished farmer who is regularly obliged to consume past savings and has little access to credit can have little hope of making lumpy investments needed to permanently escape poverty some time in the future. A poverty alleviation scheme which guaranteed this outcome *now* for at least some of the poor may then be expected to have a greater impact on poverty for a given budget, both immediately and in the longer term, than a scheme which spread its resources thinly.

I shall assume here that a poverty line does exist. Furthermore, I shall identify this as a unique income level which is deemed to be socially acceptable for participants in a poverty alleviation scheme. (The relationship between the wage paid to participating workers and their final welfare level will be discussed further below.) Note that the proportion of a population which would like to participate in a perfectly self-targeting scheme which offers that income level also measures the prevalence of poverty in the population; indeed it is simply the popular *headcount index* of poverty.

Other aspects of poverty measurement also have bearing on the policy choice over coverage and benefit level. If one relies solely on the headcount index, then limitations on coverage will typically be deemed desirable from the point of view of poverty alleviation. For this poverty measure, it would obviously be much better to guarantee a benefit level which is sufficient to escape poverty to as many persons as possible, recognizing that some will simply have to go without. However, the drawbacks of the headcount index as a measure of poverty are now well recognized, particularly following Sen's (1976, 1981) criticisms. The headcount index gives equal weight to all poor persons, irrespective of how poor they are. It can be argued that a better poverty measure would attach highest weight to the poorest of the poor, and least weight to those who are just at the margin of poverty. One would expect such a measure to put wide coverage schemes in a more favourable light, but it is far from clear whether such schemes would then dominate over the alternatives. For example would a 'poverty-gap' measure (which weights the poor by their distance from the poverty line) favour wide coverage?

A further question begging here concerns the welfare relevance of the reservation wage rate. In particular, two workers willing to work for the same wage need not be deemed to be equally well-off; for example one of them may have a far more benevolent friend. Similarly, there may be poor persons who have high reservation wage rates for relief work, because, for example, they find it physically demanding. However, while such heterogeneity has bearing on the effectiveness of relief work as a scheme for alleviating poverty defined in terms of welfare (and hence the need for some form of supplementary income support), it is not obviously relevant to the aforementioned policy choice over wage rate and coverage. For the purpose of focusing on that choice, it does not seem unreasonable to ignore welfare differences between potential relief work participants which are not reducible to a difference in their reservation wage rate.

Furthermore, such homogeneity may not be an unrealistic assumption in many circumstances in which public employment is used to alleviate poverty. For example Basu (1987) suggests two reasons why non-poor persons with high non-labour income would be unlikely to want to participate in such programmes: first, that manual labour is considered too demeaning, and, second, that the reservation wage to relief work will tend to be positively correlated with non-labour income; thus, generally better-off persons will also tend to have higher reservation wages and so be less likely to participate.

It is likely that many potential participants in a public works scheme have positive reservation wage rates; they will only participate if they are adequately compensated for foregone activities. Thus there will generally be a *participation cost* to the poor. Their participation may also be costly to the budget and, hence, net disbursements; for example tools may have to be supplied. The existence of such costs will tend to enhance any case for limitations on coverage; for a given gross outlay, the *net* income gain to the poor from increasing the wage paid to an existing poor worker will exceed that from employing an extra worker. It remains unclear whether such costs are sufficient to justify coverage restrictions when assessments are sensitive to the depth of poverty.

A potentially important aspect of the design of a relief work scheme not discussed here is its effect on existing labour markets. The supply of relief work is often restricted to places and seasons in which it does not compete with alternative employment opportunities. While the social opportunity cost of such a restriction may be low, in discussing effects on poverty alleviation one must also consider the *transfer benefit* to the poor. This will include any secondary effects on earnings from alternative employment. And if labour demand is fairly wage inelastic (as some recent empirical evidence has suggested), then these secondary effects will be far from negligible (Ravallion 1987a, 1987b). A more cost-effective poverty alleviation scheme will generally be possible by exploiting such effects in policy design. However, to simplify the present analysis, secondary earnings effects will be ignored; for further discussion of this issue, see Ravallion (1987b).

A MODEL OF THE POLICY OPTIONS

This and the following section examine further the main issues raised above, within a simple analytical framework, aiming to characterize the circumstances under which a policy ranking over coverage can be established. In keeping with the frequently stated objectives of governments and other agencies funding these schemes, the sole criterion for choice in their design will be the extent to which poverty is reduced for any given budget (or, equivalently, the budgetary cost of achieving a given reduction in poverty).

To make a fair comparison between the policy alternatives over coverage, certain things will be held constant. The initial distribution of reservation wages is the same, as are the characteristics of the activities performed by participants (such as the type of job on a relief work scheme). Thus, for any given benefit level, the same number of persons will be willing to participate in either scheme. Nor does one policy alternative have advantages over the other in terms of the set of information available to the policy-maker. Both will be modelled as pure self-targeting schemes in that they rely solely on voluntary participation in attempting to reach the poor.

Such a scheme can be characterized as follows. Anyone who participates receives a known *benefit* level, but must incur a *cost* in doing so. In a relief work scheme, the benefit to participants is the wage offered on that scheme. But to participate, a relief worker must forego any income from other activities while working on the relief work project. The disutility of relief work at any given wage may also differ from that of alternative activities. Combining these considerations, one can postulate the existence of a *reservation wage rate for relief work*, being the minimum wage rate for such work which would induce participation for a particular worker.

In general, the potential clients for a relief work scheme will be heterogeneous in terms of, for example, the numbers of their dependents, the type of work they do and their unearned income. In such circumstances, the reservation wage rate for relief work need not be a good indicator of welfare, as noted earlier. However, for present purposes, I shall ignore such heterogeneity, and treat the reservation wage as a suitable scalar and interpersonally comparable welfare measure on which poverty comparisons can be based. Similarly, the socially determined minimum wage rate will be interpreted as a welfare relevant poverty line; an individual is deemed to be 'poor' if and only if he or she is willing to work at less than that wage.[8]

The proportion of the population with reservation wage at or below w is denoted $F(w)$ with corresponding density function $f(w)$ over $w \geq w_0 \geq 0$. The distribution is allowed to have a mass point at w_0 (so that $F[w_0]$ is positive). This captures the possibility that there is more than a negligible number of persons who have the lowest reservation wage which might be interpreted as the minimum needed for survival; this is not implausible for many rural areas of South Asia and elsewhere. The population size is normalized at unity.

The poverty relief agency has a given budget b. The agency incurs an administrative cost of c per participant, in addition to the benefit paid out. For example in a relief work scheme, this covers supervision and all materials and tools used, net of the value of the relief worker's output. It would be unreasonable to assume that such a scheme is particularly profitable, though it may be able to cover average cost. I shall generally assume that even at the subsistence wage rate, the value of the scheme's output is at most sufficient to cover unit costs (that is $w_0 + c \geq 0$), though this can be relaxed somewhat. (Note that c may be negative if the output of the scheme is sufficiently valuable to the non-poor.)

As an aside, it may be noted that one can also set up the following model in terms of a distribution of total income rather than reservation wage rates (and, indeed, the empirical example will be based on the former interpretation). Total income can then be taken to include the 'displaced component' which must be given up in order to participate in relief work, and a 'fixed component' which remains constant and (given the above homogeneity assumption) is also constant across households. The 'benefit level' for relief work is then the *gross* income of a participant, and the 'administration cost' is then net of a participant's unearned income component. And, of course, the relevant 'poverty line' is then the income needed to escape poverty, rather than the wage needed to do so (given the size of the unearned income component).

By definition, a person will only want to join the scheme if his or her reservation wage rate does not exceed the offered wage. So the

---

[8] In other words, it is assumed that the reservation wage rate for relief work is a monotonic increasing function of the welfare measure (such as income) used in measuring poverty and, furthermore, it is the same function for all persons.

proportion of the population who are willing to join is simply the point on the reservation wage distribution function F, corresponding to the benefit level for relief work.

The agency need not, however, offer participation to all persons who are willing to take up the scheme at the offered wage. Two stylized policy options are considered here:

Option 1: Wide coverage with a flexible wage rate (WIDCOV). In this case, the agency allows all persons who want to join to do so. When the scheme offers the wage η, the proportion of the population actually participating will be $F(\eta)$. For any given budget b at which WIDCOV participation is positive, the WIDCOV benefit level η can then be found from the agency's budget constraint:[9]

$$F(\eta)(\eta + c) = b. \tag{1}$$

Notice that there exists a critical budget,

$$b_0 = F(w_0)(w_0 + c) \geq 0, \tag{2}$$

below which participation in WIDCOV is zero. Also let

$$b_z = F(z)(z + c) \tag{3}$$

denote the minimum budget level needed to bring all persons up to the poverty wage $z > w_0$. I shall refer to any budget less than b_z as a *limited budget*. Note that this also depends on the cost of administration; any given budget will be insufficient to eliminate poverty if the cost of administering the scheme is high enough. For budgets within the interval (b_0, b_z), the final distribution function of wages under WIDCOV is given by

$$F_w(w) = 0 \qquad \text{for } w < \eta$$

$$= F(w) \qquad \text{for } w > \eta.$$

Figure 11.1(b) illustrates the effect of WIDCOV on the wage distribution.

[9] The agency will generally have to determine η by trial and error; for example an initial wage rate is set for relief work, but adjusted later according to the revealed demand for work at that wage rate and the available budget. Of course, the agency may adjust employment independently of the wage rate, but then the scheme ceases to provide universal coverage (it is not an 'employment guarantee scheme'). I am here focusing on the 'pure' form of a wide coverage scheme to be contrasted with a scheme which provides a guaranteed wage but limited coverage.

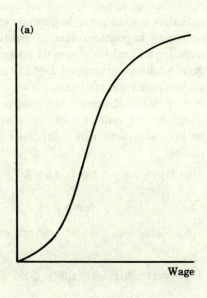

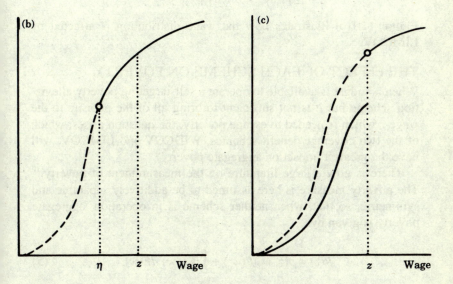

Figure 11.1

Option 2: Limited coverage at a socially determined minimum wage (LIMCOV).   Alternatively, the policy-maker may set the benefit level at a socially determined minimum wage. Participants are then allowed to join until the budget is exhausted. In general, some of the poor will have to be refused entry. In practice, other information may be available to permit the targeting of positions towards poorer persons. Here it is assumed that the available positions on LIMCOV are rationed randomly. I shall comment further on this later.

The proportion of the population participating in LIMCOV is simply the budget divided by the unit cost of the scheme, $b/(z + c)$. The proportion of the poor who participate is denoted h and this is a function of b, c and z, namely

$$h = b/(F(z)(z + c)) \quad \text{for } 0 \le b < b_z \tag{4a}$$

$$= 1 \quad \text{for } b \ge b_z. \tag{4b}$$

For budgets in (b_0, b_z) the wage distribution achieved by LIMCOV is simply

$$F_L(w) = (1 - h)F(w) \quad \text{for } w \le z$$

$$= F(w) \quad \text{for } w > z$$

Figure 11.1(c) illustrates how the wage distribution is affected by LIMCOV.

THE EFFECT OF EACH SCHEME ON POVERTY

When a budget is available to operate a self-targeting poverty alleviation scheme but it is not sufficient to bring all of the poor up to the wage z which is needed to escape poverty, the question arises: which of the two coverage/benefit schemes, WIDCOV and LIMCOV, will have the greatest impact on aggregate poverty?

There is now a large literature on the measurement of poverty.[10] The poverty measure is here assumed to be additively separable and symmetric, so that, when neither scheme is in operation, aggregate poverty is given by

$$P(z) = p(z, w_0)F(w_0) + \int_{w_0}^{z} p(z, w) \, dF(w), \tag{5}$$

[10] For recent surveys, see Foster (1984) and Atkinson (1987).

where $p(z, w)$ can be interpreted as the 'individual' poverty measure for a person with wage w when the wage needed to escape poverty is z. Note that, by the homogeneity assumption discussed above, the poverty wage z is unique. It is assumed that $p(z, w) = 0$ for all $w \geq z$ and that the function p is non-increasing in w elsewhere. When $p(z, w)$ is independent of w in the interval $[w_0, z]$ the measure (5) is (ordinally) equivalent to the headcount index, while when $p(z, w)$ is strictly decreasing in w over that interval, the contribution to aggregate poverty of any poor person depends on how poor that person is, with the poorest of the poor recording the highest weight. When $p(z, w)$ is strictly decreasing in w for all wages up to the poverty level, the poverty measure is said to be *monotonic*.

Though a monotonic poverty measure gives higher weight to poorer persons, it need not register a decrease in poverty when income is transferred from a poor person to someone who is poorer.[11] This also requires that p is strictly convex below the poverty line, and when this holds, the resulting measure can be said to be *distributionally sensitive*. The poverty measure is said to be *smooth* if the function p is twice differentiable throughout. This precludes 'kinks' in either p or its wage derivative.

There are a number of examples of this general class of poverty measures; one is the Foster, Greer and Thorbecke (FGT) (1984) measure, for which $p(z, w) = ((z - w)/z)^{\alpha}$ for a non-negative parameter α. This is a smooth distributionally sensitive measure for $\alpha > 1$. The FGT measure for $\alpha = 2$ has been popular in recent analyses of poverty alleviation policy issues (Greer and Thorbecke 1986, Kanbur 1987, Besley and Kanbur 1988, Ravallion and Chao 1988, Thorbecke and Berrian 1988). Figure 11.2 illustrates the shape of the FGT function $p(z, w)$ for $\alpha = 0$, 1 and 2. Other examples from the literature on poverty measurement can be found in Atkinson (1987).

The level of poverty under WIDCOV depends, in part, on the budget and the cost of administration. For any budget less than b_0 the scheme will not be able to attract any participants. For all budgets in excess of b_z the scheme will eliminate poverty. Between these extremes, the scheme guarantees all participants a wage η at which point their individual poverty measure becomes $p(z, \eta)$. The value of η is implicitly a function of b and c, as given by equation (1). Thus the level of poverty under WIDCOV is given by

---

[11] As required by Sen's (1976) Weak Transfer Axiom.

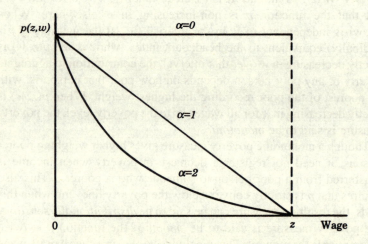

Figure 11.2

$$P_w(b, c, z) = P(z) \qquad \text{for } b \in [0, b_0] \qquad (6a)$$

$$= p(z, \eta)F(\eta) + \int_\eta^z p(z, w) \, dF(w) \quad \text{for } b \in (b_0, b_z) \qquad (6b)$$

$$= 0 \qquad \text{for } b \geq b_z \qquad (6c)$$

Under LIMCOV, aggregate poverty declines in direct proportion to the number of persons participating in the scheme. The final level of poverty achieved by the policy is then the product of the proportion of applicants who are not admitted and the initial poverty level, namely

$$P_L(b, c, z) = (1 - h)P(z). \qquad (7)$$

In comparing the induced poverty levels under the two schemes, it is convenient to define the function

$$D(b, c, z) = P_w(b, c, z) - P_L(b, c, z). \qquad (8)$$

If D is positive (negative) then the LIMCOV (WIDCOV) scheme is to be preferred as a poverty alleviation policy. By straightforward manipulations of (6) and (7), it is evident that

$$D(b, c, z) = hP(z) \qquad \text{for } b \in [0, b_0] \qquad (9a)$$

$$= hP(z) + p(z, \eta)F(\eta) - p(z, w_0)F(w_0)$$
$$= \int_{w0}^{\eta} p(z, w) \, dF(w) \qquad \text{for } b \in (b_0, b_z) \qquad (9b)$$

$$= 0 \qquad \text{for } b \geq b_z. \qquad (9c)$$

Plainly, the LIMCOV scheme dominates WIDCOV at low positive budgets less than b_0, for then WIDCOV participation falls to zero. LIMCOV also achieves lower poverty for all budgets up to b_z whenever the poverty measure is the headcount index; for then $p(z, w)$ is invariant to w and so (9) simplifies to

$$D(b, c, z) = hP(z) \qquad \text{for } b \in [0, b_z]$$

$$= 0 \qquad \text{for } b \geq b_z$$

However, the more interesting cases are for monotonic poverty measures and budgets in the interval (b_0, b_z).

As long as $b_0 > 0$, there clearly exist budgets exceeding b_0 by at least some small amount for which $D > 0$ according to any monotonic poverty measure.[12] Thus small budgets beyond b_0 will continue to favour LIMCOV within some interval when WIDCOV participation is positive.

Consider, instead, budgets approaching b_z. On differentiating (9b) and noting that η is implicitly a function of b with slope $1/(F(\eta) + (\eta + c)f(\eta))$, one finds that

$$D_b(b, c, z) = \frac{P(z)}{F(z)(z + c)} + \frac{P_w(z, \eta)F(\eta)}{F(\eta) + (\eta + c)f(\eta)} \text{ for } b \in (b_0, b_z). \quad (10)$$

For smooth poverty measures, the second term on the right hand side vanishes as b approaches b_z in which case the left derivative at b_z is positive.[13] Thus while poverty vanishes at b_z under both schemes,

---

[12] Noting that D is continuous at b_0 and the right derivative is not infinitely negative. The argument breaks down if $b_0 = 0$, since then $D(b_0, c, z) = 0$. Hence the existence of a lower mass point in the wage distribution is crucial to this result.

[13] Noting that $p_w(z, z) = 0$ for any smooth measure.

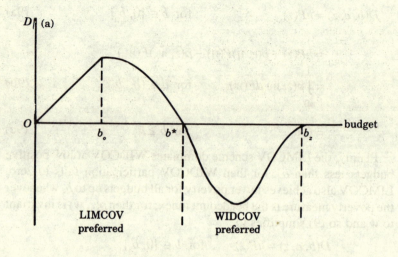

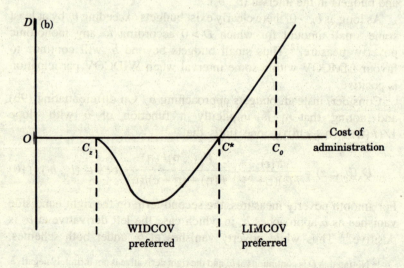

Figure 11.3

budgets slightly less than this amount must favour WIDCOV according to such poverty measures. By continuity of D there must also exist at least one switch point at which $D = 0$. Figure 11.3(a) illustrates the relationship for the special case of a unique switch point at b^*.

By similar reasoning, it can be readily verified that an analogous result holds when one considers alternative costs of administration. Consider first a 'high' administrative cost $c_0 = -w_0 + b/F(w_0)$ such that WIDCOV participation falls to zero at all $c \geq c_0$ (since the WIDCOV benefit level will be driven down below w_0). LIMCOV then achieves lower poverty and, by continuity, this also holds for some interval of smaller budgets less than c_0. Next, consider the lower administrative cost $c_z = -z + b/F(z)$. Poverty vanishes at this point for both schemes. But it is readily verified that the right derivative of D with respect to c at c_z is negative for smooth distributionally sensitive poverty measures, implying that low administrative costs above c_z will favour WIDCOV. Figure 11.3(b) illustrates the relationship, again assuming a unique switch point, though this is not necessary.

A special case of pedagogic interest is when the administrative cost incurred by the government and the opportunity cost to the poor of participation are both zero. So let $c = 0$ and $F(w) = 1$ for all $w \geq w_0 = 0$. (The latter conditions entail that all of the poor are willing to work at *any* positive wage rate.) Then it is readily verified that $D = p(z, \eta) - p(z, 0)(z - \eta)/z$ which is negative (for $0 < b < z$) if and only if $p(z, w)$ is strictly convex in w. Thus the necessary and sufficient condition for WIDCOV to be preferred when there are no participation costs is simply that the poverty measure is distributionally sensitive. This is intuitive.

These observations can be summarized as follows: for all monotonic poverty measures and initial income distributions which have a mass point at the subsistence wage, LIMCOV will result in lower poverty levels than WIDCOV when the budget is low and/or administrative cost is high, and this also holds for situations in which the WIDCOV benefit level is sufficient to attract participants. However, when the assessment is based on monotonic measures which are also smooth and distributionally sensitive, WIDCOV is the preferred policy for higher budgets and/or lower costs of administration approaching the critical values needed to eliminate poverty. There will be at least one intermediate budget level and one administrative cost at which the policy choice should switch. In the special case in which no participation costs are incurred (either by the government or the poor),

WIDCOV is the preferred option as long as the poverty measure is distributionally sensitive.

It is of interest to explore further the sufficient conditions for an unambiguous policy ranking at intermediate budgets in the interval (b_0, b_z). The following results hold for all monotonic poverty measures and also when $b_0 = 0$. From (9b), it is evident that a sufficient condition for $D > 0$ at any point in the interval (b_0, b_z) is that

$$p(z, \eta)/p(z, w) > (1 - h)/h \text{ for all } w \text{ in } [w_0, \eta], \qquad (11)$$

that is the proportionate drop in the poverty level of all participants in WIDCOV exceeds the rate of non-participation by the poor in LIMCOV.

There are two alternative ways of stating the condition in (11) which may be more revealing. Consider first the number w_0^* defined implicitly by

$$p(z, \eta)/p(z, w_0^*) = 1 - h. \qquad (12)$$

Then (11) will hold if and only if $w_0 > w_0^*$. One can also view the case for limited coverage in terms of the level of poverty aversion, as parameterized by α in the FGT class poverty measures discussed above. Consider, in particular, the value of $\alpha = \alpha^*$ such that

$$\left(\frac{z - \eta}{z - w_0}\right)^{\alpha^*} = 1 - h. \qquad (13)$$

Since $z > \eta \geq w_0$, the inequality in (11) must hold for all (positive) values of $\alpha < \alpha^*$.

The question then arises as to whether the value of α^* accords with prior value judgments on poverty aversion. Recall that for $\alpha > 1$ the FGT measure is distributionally sensitive. Clearly $\alpha^* > 0$ (since $\eta > w_0$ and $h > 0$). If α^* also exceeds unity then there exist distributionally sensitive poverty measures for which LIMCOV is the preferred policy option. Of course, the condition that $\alpha < \alpha^*$ is only sufficient for this outcome; in general, there will exist situations in which LIMCOV dominates even though the policy-maker's poverty aversion exceeds α^*.

The value of α^* can be calculated from data on the distribution of wages amongst potential participants in a public employment scheme of known budget and administrative costs. In the following section I shall illustrate such calculations using some readily available (though less than ideal) data for Bangladesh.

If one confines attention to smooth distributionally sensitive poverty measures, then a simple second-order dominance condition can also be used to quickly establish at least a partial ordering of the two schemes. In particular, poverty will be higher under WIDCOV for all such poverty measures and all poverty lines up to z_1 (say) if and only if

$$G(z) = \int_0^z (F_w(w) - F_1(w))\, dw = h \int_\eta^z F(w)\, dw - (1-h) \int_0^\eta F(w)\, dw \geq 0$$

for all $z < z_1$, and with strict inequality for at least one value of z. This result is a straightforward application of Atkinson's (1987) Condition IIA for ranking distributions in terms of separable, symmetric and smooth distributionally sensitive poverty measures. One can estimate the expected rate of participation by the poor in LIMCOV from wage distribution data for a given budget and administrative cost. One can also calculate the areas under the cumulative distribution to the left and right of the WIDCOV benefit level from the same data. Thus the second-order dominance test can be applied. The test then entails comparing the odds of LIMCOV participation $(h/(1-h))$ with the ratio of these two areas under the wage distribution at all values of z (with corresponding values of η and h) up to the stipulated maximum poverty line; WIDCOV will be the unambiguously preferred option if and only if the odds of LIMCOV participation are less than the ratio of these areas, at all such values of z. The following section gives illustrative calculations.

AN EMPIRICAL ILLUSTRATION

The previous section has suggested a number of tests which may be useful in illuminating the policy choice over coverage. Some of these can be readily implemented for specific schemes (with given budget and known cost of administration) if one has data on the distribution of reservation wages amongst potential participants. This section gives calculations for Bangladesh; the data used are far from ideal, but are adequate for illustrative purposes.

Bangladesh is of particular interest as a country where the prevalence and severity of poverty amongst the rural landless is a major problem, and where rural public employment schemes have been widely advocated and used as a poverty alleviation scheme.[14]

---

[14] On Bangladesh's food-for-work programme see the special issue of *Bangladesh Development Studies*, 1983, including Osmani and Chowdhury (1983).

As noted earlier, one can base the analysis on either a distribution of household income, or one of reservation wages, as in the above formulation. This is really only a matter of how one interprets the variables describing benefit levels and costs of administration. (Though it should be recalled that this does assume that potential relief workers and the households from which they come are suitably homogeneous.) The following calculations are based on a household income distribution for rural Bangladesh.

Table 11.1
Distribution of Income, Rural Bangladesh

	Upper bound of income class							
	300	400	500	750	1000	1250	1500	2000
Cumulative frequency $F(y)(\%)$	8.72	19.3	30.6	55.2	72.1	82.5	88.7	94.8
Mean income of income class	233	350	448	618	863	1113	1364	1709

Source: BBS (1984), from the 1978–1979 Household Expenditure Survey. All monetary units are Taka per household per month.

Table 11.1 gives the frequency distribution of household income in rural areas from the 1978–1979 Household Expenditure Survey of Bangladesh. Table 11.2 gives calculations based on a wide range of hypothetical public employment schemes. The subsistence income is assumed to be Tk300 per month, though the calculations were repeated for a lower subsistence income (Tk200); the main qualitative results concerning the poverty ordering of the coverage options were unaffected by this change. The poverty line is assumed to be Tk1000 per month, which seems to accord reasonably well with past poverty lines for rural Bangladesh (Ravallion 1988b). The dominance tests will allow a wide range of poverty lines, up to Tk2000.

Note that since we are now working from a *household* income distribution, the 'benefit levels' are *gross*, in that they comprise both the relief work wage and the household's residual 'unearned' income. Similarly, the 'administrative cost' is *net*, being the unit cost actually incurred by the relief work agency, less the same residual income component of participating workers.

Table 11.2
Illustrative WIDCOV and LIMCOV schemes[a]

WIDCOV benefit level (gross) η	Cost of admin- istration (net) (c)	Budget cost (b)	Participation rates (% of poor)		Critical poverty aversion (α*)	2 Dominance: lower poverty for:
			WIDCOV $F(\eta)/F(z))$	LIMCOV (h)		
(1)	(2)	(3)	(4)	(5)	(6)	(7)
400	−200	39	27	6.7	0.45	WIDCOV
400	0	77	27	11	0.73	Ambiguous
400	200	116	27	13	0.93	Ambiguous
400	400	154	27	15	1.1	Ambiguous
500	−200	92	42	16	0.52	WIDCOV
500	0	153	42	21	0.71	WIDCOV
500	200	214	42	25	0.85	WIDCOV
500	400	275	42	27	0.95	WIDCOV
750	−200	304	77	53	0.73	WIDCOV
750	0	414	77	57	0.83	WIDCOV
750	200	524	77	61	0.91	Ambiguous[b]
750	400	635	77	63	0.96	LIMCOV

[a] All monetary units are Taka per household per month, Bangladesh, 1978–1979.
[b] WIDCOV dominates for a maximum poverty line of $z_1 = 1000$.

The budgetary and cost characteristics of each scheme are given in columns (1) to (3) of Table 11.2. The schemes range from relatively 'profitable' (in that the value of output is more than sufficient to cover non-labour costs) to relatively 'costly' (with net administration cost as high as the benefit level to WIDCOV participants). Budgets per head (of the rural population) range from about 4 per cent of the poverty line to nearly two-thirds of the poverty line. Columns (4) and (5) then give the percentages of the poor who can be expected to participate in each scheme.

Columns (6) and (7) of Table 11.2 give two of the tests discussed above, namely the critical poverty aversion parameter (α^*) of the FGT index and the second-order dominance condition for all separable, symmetric and distributionally sensitive measures.

The values of α^* are generally less than one. Recall that LIMCOV will be the preferred option whenever $\alpha < \alpha^*$, though this is only a sufficient condition in that LIMCOV may also dominate at some

$\alpha > \alpha^*$. Thus the results in column (6) are quite inconclusive on the question of whether there exist distributionally sensitive FGT measures for which LIMCOV is the preferred option for these data.

The second-order dominance test in column (7) is more powerful for this purpose. I have allowed poverty lines up to Tk2000 per month. One finds that an unambiguous ordering is possible in two-thirds of the cases, with WIDCOV being the preferred option in all except one of these. In one of the undecided cases, WIDCOV is found to yield unambiguously lower poverty for all poverty lines up to $z_1 = 1000$ (that is the intersection point occurs between 1000 and 2000). However, the other ambiguous cases remain so in spite of such a contraction in the range of admissible poverty lines.

Table 11.3

Effects of WIDCOV and LIMCOV on FGT Poverty Measures

η	c	WIDCOV; $\alpha =$			LIMCOV; $\alpha =$		
		1	2	3	1	2	3
400	−200	0.295	0.143	0.0748	0.294	0.158	0.0949
400	0	0.295	0.143	0.0748	0.281	0.151	0.0905
400	200	0.295	0.143	0.0748	0.274	0.147	0.0885
400	400	0.295	0.143	0.0748	0.268	0.144[a]	0.0864
500	−200	0.270	0.116	0.0524	0.265	0.143	0.0854
500	0	0.270	0.116	0.0524	0.249	0.134	0.0803
500	200	0.270	0.116	0.0524	0.237	0.127	0.0763
500	400	0.270	0.116	0.0524	0.239	0.124	0.0742
750	−200	0.161	0.0377	0.00906	0.148	0.0797	0.0478
750	0	0.161	0.0377	0.00906	0.136	0.0729	0.0437
750	200	0.161	0.0377	0.00906	0.123	0.0661	0.0498
750	400	0.161	0.0377	0.00906	0.117	0.0797	0.0376
Original		0.315	0.170	0.102			

[a] The poverty measure is 0.142 for $c = 500$, so that LIMCOV then dominates WIDCOV.

Table 11.3 gives specific cardinal poverty measures in the FGT class for $\alpha = 1$, 2 and 3, for each of these stylized schemes. The bottom row of the table also gives the values of the poverty measures for the pre-reform distribution. One finds that LIMCOV achieves lower poverty than WIDCOV in all cases for the poverty-gap measure ($\alpha = 1$), while the ranking is uniformly reversed in favour of WIDCOV for the distributionally sensitive measures ($\alpha > 1$). Notice though that for $\alpha = 2$, the measures come close to converging at the highest cost of administration when $\eta = 400$; indeed, if one considers a somewhat higher administrative cost, $c = 500$, LIMCOV achieves lower poverty by this measure. Thus the critical value of administrative cost for a policy switch (c^* in figure 11.3[b]) is found in the interval (400, 500).

CONCLUSIONS

When the budget for poverty alleviation is limited, flexible benefit levels and universal coverage of even a perfectly self-targeting public employment scheme need not be the best policy, in the sense that lower poverty levels may be achieved at the same cost by imposing limitations on coverage at benefit levels sufficient to escape poverty. The point is made most evident by considering an alternative scheme which guarantees the poverty level of income to only a subset of the poor. It is plain that, for a limited budget, this scheme will always have greater impact on the headcount index of poverty than a scheme which guarantees entry to all, at whatever wage is possible with that budget. Maharashtra's 'Employment Guarantee Scheme' is an example of the latter policy, and it has been advocated as a model for poverty alleviation schemes elsewhere. And yet, unless the budget happens to be particularly generous, such a scheme will have little or no impact on the *number* of people who are poor.

The potential poverty alleviation gains from limitations on coverage are not, however, confined to the headcount index as Basu (1981) has suggested. Limitations on coverage will be desirable for monotonic poverty measures (which attach greater weight to poorer persons) when the budget is low and/or the cost of administration is high. This also holds irrespective of the budget (within limits) as long as the initial distribution of wages is suitably bounded below, or the policy-maker's aversion to poverty is not too high. Distributionally sensitive poverty measures can support restrictions on coverage when a worker's participation in the scheme is costly to either the worker or to the government's budget.

However, for all such measures, high budgets and/or low administrative costs near the levels needed to eliminate poverty will tend to favour universal coverage and flexible benefit levels. For example this will be the case when the policy alternatives are evaluated using any smooth distributionally sensitive poverty measure, and the available budget is only slightly below the amount necessary to eliminate poverty. There will be one or more intermediate budgets between the lowest and highest levels at which policy rankings change.

I have offered some simple empirical illustrations of the policy issue over coverage for a number of hypothetical relief work schemes using a household income distribution for rural Bangladesh. The use of a distribution of household income is only strictly valid for this purpose if households are homogeneous in certain respects; for example the tests used here assume that one can stipulate a single gross benefit level (actual payout to relief workers, *plus* a fixed allowance for other income sources) and that all households with incomes less than this amount (and only those households) will then want to participate in the scheme. In practice, households will be heterogeneous in terms of their other income sources, their welfare relevant needs, and their work preferences. In principle, one could reconstruct the distributional data to control for the relevant heterogeneity. However, this would require access to suitable unit record data, which would have to be quite rich in its detail on, for example, income sources, labour supply allocations and wage rates. In lieu of such data, the present calculations do at least offer us a rough indication of which way the policy choice should go.

Over the (very wide) range of schemes considered here, wide coverage at low wages turns out to be generally the preferred means of reducing distributionally sensitive poverty measures. On the other hand, rationed coverage at a 'poverty level' wages is more effective for the monotonic but distributionally neutral poverty-gap measure and, of course, the headcount index.

Thus these results clearly illustrate the policy relevance of the poverty measurement issue. Though exceptions can be expected, these data do suggest that Sen's (1976) persuasive arguments in favour of distributionally sensitive poverty measures are likely to reinforce the case for wide coverage in poverty alleviation schemes.

This analysis has been based on a stylized representation of the policy options over coverage. Probably one of the most important restrictions is that I have assumed that limited coverage schemes ration participation randomly amongst their applicants. Some might claim that it is more likely that 'the more privileged among prospective participants would get the lion's share' (to quote an anonymous referee). Such a bias would further strengthen the argument in favour of universal coverage amongst desired participants at a correspondingly low wage. Of course, one must also note that limited coverage schemes do give a poverty alleviation agency the *option* of attempting to target benefits towards the poorest of the poor. A crucial issue begging is then whether or not the agent's targeting performance can be monitored or if appropriate incentives can be devised to encourage better performance.

Acknowledgements: I have had useful discussions on this topic with Gaurav Datt, Jean Drèze, Stephen Coate and Dominique van de Walle. I am also grateful to the referees of the *Journal of Development Economics* (where this chapter was originally published) for their helpful comments. The views expressed here are those of the author, and should not be associated with the World Bank.

REFERENCES

Abraham, A. (1980). 'Maharashtra's Employment Guarantee Scheme', *Economic and Political Weekly*, 15, pp. 1339–42.

Alderman, H. (1987). 'Allocation of Goods through Non-price Mechanisms: Evidence on Distribution by Willingness to Wait', *Journal of Development Economics*, 25, pp. 105–24.

Atkinson, A.B. (1987). 'On the Measurement of Poverty', *Econometrica*, 55, pp. 749–64.

Aykroyd, W.R. (1974). *The Conquest of Famine*. London: Chatto and Windus.

Bagchee, S. (1987). 'Poverty Alleviation Programmes in Seventh Plan: An Appraisal', *Economic and Political Weekly*, 22, pp. 139–48.

Bandyopadhyay, D. (1988). 'Direct Intervention Programmes for Poverty Alleviation', *Economic and Political Weekly*, 23, pp. A77–A88.

Bangladesh Bureau of Statistics (BBS) (1984). *Statistical Yearbook of Bangladesh 1983–1984*. Dhaka: Bangladesh Bureau of Statistics.

Basu, K. (1981). 'Food for Work Programmes: Beyond Roads that Get Washed Away', *Economic and Political Weekly*, 16, pp. 37–40.

—— (1987). 'The Elimination of Persistent Hunger in South Asia: Policy Options', in J.P. Drèze and A.K. Sen (eds), *The Political Economy of Hunger*. Oxford: Oxford University Press.

Besley, T. and R. Kanbur (1988). 'The Principles of Targeting', Discussion paper 85 (Development Economic Research Centre, Coventry: University of Warwick).

Bhatia, B.M. (1967). *Famines in India: A Study of Some Aspects of the Economic History of India (1860–1965)*. London: Asia Publishing House.

Dandekar, K. (1983). *Employment Guarantee Scheme: An Employment Opportunity for Women*. Pune: Gokhale Institute of Politics and Economics.

Dandekar, K. and M. Sathe (1980). 'Employment Guarantee Scheme and Food for Work Programme', *Economic and Political Weekly*, 15.

Drèze, J.P. (1988). 'Famine Prevention in India', in Drèze and Sen (eds), *The Political Economy of Hunger*.

Drèze, J.P. and A.K. Sen (1988). *Hunger and Public Action*, mimeo. (Department of Economics, Cambridge, MA: Harvard University).

Foster, J.E. (1984). 'On Economic Poverty: A Survey of Aggregate Measures', *Advances in Econometrics*, 3, pp. 215–51.

Foster, J.E. and A.F. Shorrocks (1988). 'Poverty Orderings', *Econometrica*, 56, pp. 173–7.

Foster, J.E., J. Greer and E. Thorbecke (1984). 'A Class of Decomposable Poverty Measures', *Econometrica*, 52, pp. 761–6.

Greer, J. and E. Thorbecke (1986). 'A Methodology for Measuring Food Poverty Applied to Kenya', *Journal of Development Economics*, 24, pp. 59–74.

Hirway, I. (1988). 'Reshaping IRDI', *Economic and Political Weekly*, 23, pp. A89–A96.

Kanbur, R. (1987). 'Measurement and Alleviation of Poverty', IMF Staff papers 34. Washington, D.C.: IMF, pp. 60–85.

Kurian, N.J. (1987). 'IRDP: How Relevant Is It?', *Economic and Political Weekly*, 26 December.

Lieberman, S.S. (1985). 'Field-level Perspectives on Maharashtra's Employment Guarantee Scheme', *Public Administration and Development*, 5, pp. 109–27.

Lele, U. (1988). 'Poverty, Hunger and Food Security: A Perspective on Domestic Policies and Implications for External Assistance to South Asia', Paper presented at the World Food Colloquium (Washington, D.C.).

Narayana, N.S.S., K.S. Parikh and T.N. Srinivasan (1988). 'Rural Works Programs in India: Costs and Benefits', *Journal of Development Economics*, 29, pp. 131–56.

Osmani, S.R. and O.H. Chowdhury (1983). 'Short Run Impacts of Food for Work Programme in Bangladesh', *Bangladesh Development Studies*, 11, pp. 135–90.

Ravallion, M. (1987a). *Markets and Famines*. Oxford: Oxford University Press.

—— (1987b). 'Market Responses to Anti-hunger Policies: Effects of Wages, Prices and Employment', Working paper 28, World Institute for Development Economics Research, Helsinki, in Drèze and Sen, *The Political Economy of Hunger.*

Ravallion, M. and K. Chao (1988). 'Targeted Policies for Poverty Alleviation under Imperfect Information: Algorithms and Applications', *The Journal of Policy Modeling*, 11, pp. 213–24.

Reutlinger, S. and M. Selowsky (1976). *Malnutrition and Poverty, Magnitude and Policy Options.* Baltimore, MD: Johns Hopkins University Press.

Sen, A.K. (1976). 'Poverty: An Ordinal Approach to Measurement', *Econometrica*, 48, pp. 437–46.

—— (1981). *Poverty and Famines: An Essay on Entitlement and Deprivation.* Oxford: Oxford University Press.

—— (1985). *Commodities and Capabilities.* Amsterdam: North-Holland.

Sundaram, K. and S.D. Tendulkar (1985). 'Anti-poverty Programmes in India: An Assessment', in S. Mukhopadhyay (ed.), *The Poor in Asia: Productivity-raising Programmes and Strategies.* Kuala Lumpur: Asian and Pacific Development Centre.

Thorbecke, E. and D. Berrian (1988). Budgetary rules to minimize societal poverty, mimeo.

World Bank (1986). *Poverty and Hunger: Issues and Options for Food Security in Developing Countries.* Washington, D.C.: World Bank.

Social Security Options
for Developing Countries[*]

S. GUHAN

The debate on social security in developing countries has emerged largely since the 1980s, prompted by several factors. One was the acknowledgement of the glaring dichotomy in the availability of social security between the industrial and developing countries; and, not unrelated to this, the dichotomy between the access to social security in the developing countries themselves for labour in the organized sectors of public and industrial employment *vis-à-vis* the vast majority in the unorganized rural and urban sectors. The second was the realization that even the portfolio of direct poverty alleviation measures cannot be depended upon to provide adequate, timely or guaranteed protection to insure the poor against identifiable forms of deprivation. The third, and more proximate, factor has been the recognition of the role of social safety nets in cushioning the poor during the structural adjustment which many developing countries initiated in the 1980s in response to the debt crisis or as part of domestic economic reform processes. Parallel with these trends, the literature on poverty in the 1980s has paid much greater attention to its relationship with risk and vulnerability. The decade has also seen an extensive appraisal of country experiences in poverty alleviation. These trends appear to strike chords with one another at different pitches. Policy and need call for the location of specific social security entitlements within the anti-poverty framework, while theorizing relates anti-poverty measures to an overarching notion of social security.

[*] This is an abridged version of a paper with the same title presented at the symposium on 'Poverty: New Approaches to Analysis and Policy', organized by the International Institute for Labour Studies, Geneva, 22–24 November 1993.

Drawing from conceptual insights and from empirical lessons provided by country experiences, it is necessary to formulate working definitions for social security in developing countries and to translate them into an agenda for practical action. This is necessary for informing national policies, for providing the basis for normative recommendations from international agencies, and for guiding international co-operation in the relief of deprivation.

This chapter is an exploration of the possible contents of such an agenda. Organized in five sections, it first discusses the limitations of the formal security model to developing countries and then the elements of what could constitute appropriate social security for poor countries. Third, the cost effectiveness of the principal approaches is reviewed. The fourth section is devoted to three generic issues: targeting, resources and administration. Finally, an agenda based on the earlier discussion is set out.

FORMAL SOCIAL SECURITY AND DEVELOPING COUNTRIES

The term 'formal social security' used here is based on ILO Convention No. 102 (1952) which covers the nine branches of social security: medical care and benefits addressed to sickness, unemployment, old age, employment injury, family size, maternity, invalidity and widowhood.[1] The extent and coverage of formal social security in developing countries suffer from a number of shortcomings. In the first instance, their mere availability varies considerably across contingencies. Work injury benefits are available in most developing countries. Benefits for old age, disability and to survivors are also prevalent in fair measure. Availability of schemes covering sickness or maternity is more restricted; even more so are family allowance schemes. Few developing countries provide unemployment benefits. Second, most of the schemes cover only workers in the government and quasi-government sectors and workers in organized employment in mining, manufacturing or plantations where the workforce is stable, employment is regular and a clear employer–employee nexus exists. Large segments of workers in the agricultural sector, in rural non-farm employment, and in the

---

[1] Related ILO Conventions are the Medical Care and Sickness Benefits Convention, 1969 (No. 130); the Invalidity; Old Age and Survivors' Benefits Convention, 1967 (No. 128); the Employment Injury Benefits Convention, 1964 (No. 121); the Maternity Protection (Revised) Convention, 1952 (No. 103); the Occupational Safety and Health Convention, 1981 (No. 155).

urban informal sector are excluded. Third, the regional dispersion of formal social security is very uneven in the Third World. It is relatively well developed in the highly urbanized, middle-income countries of Latin America and the Caribbean (LAC), while outside the LAC region (with few exceptions) its availability is very restricted. Fourth, formal social security systems are malfunctional in several ways. Evasion of employer liabilities is widespread (for example for work injury and maternity). The regular and timely collection of contributions from the insured and their employers is not easy. Provident funds do not provide adequate retirement benefits. Administrative overheads are high. Disbursement is delayed and is subject to cumbersome procedures. Many schemes have also run into actuarial and fiscal imbalances (ILO 1993, pp. 57–61; Mesa–Lago 1991).

Limitations of the Formal Model

Clearly an exclusive reliance on formal systems would be inappropriate in developing countries for several reasons stemming both from their levels of economic development and the structures of their economies. Fundamentally, the diagnosis of poverty in industrial countries from which formal systems are derived is not applicable to low-income developing countries since in their case the incidence of poverty is high, has been persistent over time and is rooted in several structural features of their economies.

Moreover, while the nature and magnitude of deprivation in the poor countries indicate a massive need for intervention of some sort, several limitations render the conventional formal model of social security inapplicable. Credit and insurance markets are underdeveloped, restricting the scope for private insurance. The scope for social insurance is limited because the labour market is characterized by high proportions of self-employment and unstable and irregular wage employment. While this implies a predominant role for social assistance provided through the budget, tax resources (especially from direct taxes on incomes) are limited. At the same time, competing demands on budgetary resources — for capital outlays on infrastructure and on primary education and primary health care, for example — insistently use up resources that would otherwise be available for social transfers. The resource constraint combined with the objective of covering all the needy entails targeting through income testing. However, given the irregularity of incomes and the diversity of their sources characterizing the populations concerned, the measurement of incomes is a daunting task in developing countries.

Two other features which render formal models inappropriate in this context are the intractability of the problems represented by the needy themselves and of unemployment as a cause of loss or interruption of income. Rural populations are spatially scattered, occupationally diffuse and difficult to reach administratively. High occupational diversity and employment instability occur in the urban informal sector as well. Much unemployment is underemployment (irregular employment of short duration, diverse jobs) rather than the frictional and cyclical 'open' unemployment normally experienced in industrial economies. Nor are unemployment and poverty congruent: the poor in developing countries are poor not because they lack employment (in fact, they are overworked) but because they are employed irregularly at low wages or derive low incomes from self-employment based on low assets. All in all, in the words of two leading authorities on the subject, it does not make sense to regard the social programmes of France, the United Kingdom, and the United States as presenting a shop window from which a developing country can select the goods it prefers. Neither Beveridge nor Bismarck nor Roosevelt can provide a model for social security in developing countries (Atkinson and Hills 1991, p. 103).

SOCIAL SECURITY APPROPRIATE TO DEVELOPING COUNTRIES

The negative conclusion that developing countries cannot rely on the formal model *alone* for social security provision implies in essence that social security in poor countries will have to be viewed as part of and fully integrated with anti-poverty policies, with such policies themselves being broadly conceived in view of the complex, multi-dimensional nature of poverty and deprivation. In a context of massive and persistent poverty, the concept of social security has to extend considerably beyond the conventional social insurance model and encompass a large measure of social assistance. The conceptual problem is to situate an operationally useful notion of social security — one that is neither excessively specific (as in the formal model) nor excessively general — *within* a comprehensive anti-poverty approach.[2] From this standpoint, a categorization of the instruments I consider relevant for poverty alleviation may be useful. There are three broad categories: *promotional* measures that aim to improve endowments, exchange entitlements, real incomes and social consumption; *preventive* measures that seek more directly to

[2] For comprehensive approaches to social security, see Sen (1981, 1983, 1985); Drèze and Sen (1989, 1991); and Burgess and Stern (1991).

avert deprivation in specific ways; and *protective* (or safety net) measures that are yet more specific in their objective of guaranteeing relief from deprivatiqn.

This is a taxonomy with overlapping categories. Works programmes, for instance, promote employment; they can also be seen as preventing unemployment. Health care promotes well-being; it may also prevent sickness. The value of these categories does not, therefore, lie in their being clear cut or mutually exclusive. My purpose is rather to suggest a gradation of measures that proceed, like a set of concentric circles, from wider to narrower domains of specificity, while recognizing that all three types of measures are called for. The outer circle of promotional measures would include the whole array of macroeconomic, sectoral and institutional measures of major importance for poverty reduction, operating at the macro and meso levels. Though oriented towards the poor, they may not be confined to them or addressed specifically to the prevention of actual types of deprivation (for example primary education, primary health care, child nutrition, slum improvement). The middle circle would consist of what have come to be known as direct measures for poverty alleviation such as asset redistribution, employment creation and food security. The inner circle would contain specific measures for the relief from or protection against deprivation to the extent that the latter is not — or cannot be — averted through promotional and preventive approaches.

This visualization helps clarify several questions. The first is that social security provision in developing countries requires a multiple approach. The second arises from the residual nature of safety nets: poverty must be alleviated as much as possible by the outer circles of promotional and preventive measures so that the burden on safety nets can be lessened. Third, safety nets must indeed act as the last resort as regards any entitlements.

RELEVANT PREVENTIVE AND PROTECTIVE MEASURES

Scope and Limitations of the Discussion

Using this frame, one can appropriately limit the following discussion to the set of preventive and protective measures most relevant for social security provision in developing countries. Broadly these include (a) measures to provide assets; (b) measures to improve exchange entitlements; and (c) specifically protective, safety net measures.

As well as identifying the programmes involved, it is necessary to assess their effectiveness in terms of quantifiable indicators. The limitations of data being what they are, any such attempt will be crude but it can be useful in broadly differentiating between the sheep and the goats. In this spirit, I have used five broad indicators wherever, and to the extent, possible. The first is the *coverage ratio*, which is simply the coverage in a specific programme of the contingency or need to which it is purportedly addressed (for exmple poverty alleviation, employment, old-age relief, etc.). The coverage depends both on the budgetary outlay and the take-up by intended beneficiaries. Second, the *transfer efficiency*, which is the proportion of the likely net benefit to one unit of gross expenditure, after allowing for programme and administrative overheads, administrative leakages, and any other offsets. Third, the *targeting efficiency*, which is the proportion of the transfer that reaches its target group after allowing for the share going to those outside the target group either explicitly (as in universal schemes) or because of leakages. This is equivalent to the concept of vertical targeting efficiency.[3] Fourth is the *benefit–cost ratio*, which is the product of transfer efficiency and targeting efficiency. It seeks to indicate how much the target group is likely to benefit in the final outcome from one unit of expenditure. Fifth is the *impact efficiency*, which is the product of the coverage ratio and the benefit–cost ratio. As the broadest indicator, it gives an idea of the overall impact of any specific programme after taking into account outlay and take-up, vertical and horizontal efficiencies, and overheads and leakages.

Two caveats are necessary in respect of the scope of this chapter. The more important schemes are discussed at some length in preference to comprehensive coverage. Several important aspects of social security have been omitted. Famine prevention and famine relief — because the subject has been definitively dealt with by Drèze and Sen (1989, part II). Another type of extraordinary deprivation is that caused by wars, a subject on which not much light has been cast.[4] The meeting of basic needs, especially in health care and education, is vital to social security; the literature on this is extensive and easily accessible (ILO 1976, Streeten, et al. 1981, Stewart 1985, Ron, et al. 1990, UNDP 1993 and earlier, World Bank 1993). Besides, as far as the poor are concerned, the measures involved are largely promotional, while the focus of this

---

[3] Vertical efficiency involves covering *only* those in the target group and horizontal efficiency involves covering *all* those in the target group. See Weisbrod (1969).

[4] Stewart (1993) contains an excellent discussion of magnitudes and issues.

article is on protection. Social security under conditions of structural adjustment has been the subject of much recent discussion; here again, there is adequate and accessible literature (Cornia, et al. 1987, Burgess, et al. 1993). Furthermore, structural adjustment only accentuates the need for social security and does not basically alter the types of protection required. Finally, there is traditional, informal and familial social security, on which again the literature is good though mostly anthropological.[5]

The second caveat relates to the fact that for reasons of space much of the empirical material relied upon comes from India. India has a very large weight among developing countries in both population (about 20 per cent) and in rural poverty (about 30 per cent). Second, Indian programmes for social security provision have operated on a fairly large scale and over a fairly long period, have encompassed a variety of interventions, and have attracted a considerable evaluative literature. As such, they can potentially provide models for other low-income countries.

With this clarification of the scope and with these caveats in mind, we turn to the examination of the most salient programmes for social security provision in developing countries.

Access to Land

In the agricultural economy, land is the primary asset from a subsistence point of view: it provides food security, enables utilization of family labour, and reduces vulnerability to labour and food markets. Land redistribution is important not only for providing the rural poor with a primary asset but also from the point of view of deconcentrating the economic and political power of large landlords which enables them to reduce wages, increase rents, operate in interlocked credit markets, and exercise diverse forms of extra-economic oppression over the poor (Bell 1990). In India and Bangladesh land reform has been prominent on the agenda but actual implementation has fallen far short of original promises and objectives, reflecting the difficulty of reformist redistribution by autonomous and stable governments (Osmani 1991).

The example of China shows how access to land can provide the fundamental basis for social security in an agrarian economy. As Ahmad and Hussain point out.

---

[5] See Platteau (1991) for a survey.

Land reform has been the most fundamental of the transformations. . . . The shift back to family farming since 1979 has reversed collective farming but not the essential feature of the land reform: guaranteeing all rural households access to land. . . . [Land reform] eliminated landlessness as a cause of destitution. Herein lies a crucial difference between the attributes of the rural poor in China and those in most other developing countries, where rural poverty and landlessness often go together [Ahmad and Hussain 1991, pp. 263–4.]

This example illustrates why land reform must continue to have a high priority in the social security agenda; it cannot be dismissed as a lost cause. To maintain political pressure for land reform and circumvent opposition, the credit mechanism is one means of facilitating land transfers from rich to poor. As landowning households tend to convert landed assets into urban property and financial assets, tenants, small farmers and rural craftsmen tend to accumulate savings which could be supplemented with credit for land purchase, and natural market processes could be made redistributive.[6] Availability of credit can also prevent divestiture of land and other assets (livestock, implements), thus playing an important safety net function. Concurrently, preservation and expansion of common property resources (land, forests, grazing areas, fisheries) are important aspects of social security which thus should not be neglected (Jodha 1986, Agarwal 1991).

Asset Creation

The example of India's Integrated Rural Development Programme (IRDP) shows a large-scale, country-wide intervention designed to create assets for the poor so as to generate incomes via self-employment. In operation since 1978, this scheme finances a variety of investments through a combination of loans and subsidies for households whose incomes fall under a stipulated poverty line: irrigation wells, milch cattle, draught animals, other livestock, poultry, carts and facilities for small-scale production, trade and services. Currently, 3 to 4 million rural households are targeted annually for benefits under the IRDP with cumulative coverage being some 30 million households.

More than a decade of experience and numerous evaluations have drawn attention to a variety of shortcomings in the IRDP,[7] which can be summarized as follows:

6 For an interesting proposal in this connection see Bell (1990, p. 158). Also, Guhan (1988, p. 201).

7 For a collection of evaluations see Krishnaswamy (1990, part III).

1. Targeting to poor households is weak, with the result that a substantial proportion of actual beneficiaries are the ineligible non-poor.

2. Beneficiaries below the poverty line tend to cluster just below it, with only a small proportion of them being the poorest of the poor.

3. Incomes that the assets might generate are mostly used for current consumption, especially in emergencies such as droughts, sickness or death, with the result that beneficiaries either fall into a debt trap or are forced to default on repayments.

4. External, complementary support services are inadequate for dependable streams of income to be derived from the assets provided to the poor. Nilakantha Rath estimates that, altogether, after the first seven years of the operation (1978–85), only 'about 3 per cent of the poor households in rural India would have been helped to live above poverty, even if for a while only' (Rath 1985). The impact ratio in the IRDP is thus very low.

Each of these findings illustrates important issues in social security provision: (1) and (2) show that means-tested targeting through administrative mechanisms is not likely to be efficient, either vertically or horizontally; (3) indicates that anti-poverty programmes need protective safety nets if they are to succeed; and (4) draws attention to the importance of externalities and the futility, in their absence, of micro household approaches to poverty alleviation.

Employment

Direct employment generation for the rural poor is sometimes viewed as a prime instrument of poverty alleviation and social security provision. Large schemes for providing employment for rural unskilled labour have been in operation in India and in Bangladesh for nearly two decades. India has had a nation-wide scheme since 1977 but an earlier, more intensive and widely reported example is the Employment Guarantee Scheme (EGS) in the state of Maharashtra which has been in operation since 1972. The Food for Work Programme (FFWP) in Bangladesh was started soon after the 1974 famine and has expanded since then. In the late 1980s each of these schemes provided about 100 million persondays of employment annually. Both use labour for the creation of a variety of communal assets: irrigation works, roads, soil conservation, afforestation, small buildings. Wages are paid in cash in the EGS and mostly in kind (imported wheat from food aid) in the FFWP.[8]

[8] For an account of the South Asian schemes see Osmani (1991, pp. 330–8). On employment schemes in other countries see ILO (1992).

Rural employment schemes have a great deal in their favour. They link the creation of rural assets to providing supplementary employment for unskilled labour. In social security terms, their most important contribution is the stabilization and ensuring of incomes in lean seasons, droughts and famines, providing immediate relief as well as protection against costlier adjustments such as the sale of land and assets. By way of poverty alleviation, they improve exchange entitlements for small farmers and the landless who constitute 70 to 80 per cent of the rural poor in most developing countries and whose only endowment is labour power.

Employment schemes have been advocated not only as a useful form of social security intervention but also on the ground that they have an outstanding characteristic making them preferable to other modalities.[9] This lies in the property of self-selection, the importance of which as a desideratum in poverty alleviation is based on the savings in administrative costs and the difficulty in obtaining accurate information. Given these information and agency problems, there is no satisfactory alternative to shifting the costs of selection on to the participants themselves by imposing on them the costs of any income forgone through their participation, of travel to and residence at work sites, and of extra nutrition. In as much as such costs are likely to be lower for the poor, a works programme is self-selecting.[10]

The *a priori* appeal of employment schemes is, however, seriously undermined by empirical evidence relating to the Maharashtra EGS, a prime example of this form of intervention. The overall impact of the EGS has been estimated to affect only 2.5 per cent of unemployment among all rural workers (Mahendra Dev 1992, pp. 46–7). This is despite budgetary outlays for the scheme amounting to as much as 10 per cent of Maharashtra's total developmental expenditure. In other words, the EGS is far from providing an employment guarantee, despite entailing a relatively high budgetary outlay.

Benefits to the poor from one personday of employment will be a function of the targeting efficiency under the scheme and the wage income actually transferred less the forgone income. Available studies suggest that the EGS performs well in terms of its targeting efficiency: 80 to 90 per cent of participants are likely to be under the poverty line. The nominal wage component in the total cost involved in creating a

---

[9] For a vigorous advocacy of employment programmes, especially in the famine prevention context, see Drèze and Sen (1989, pp. 113–18).

[10] For an exposition of these arguments see Ravallion (1990, pp. 7–13).

personday of employment was about 50 per cent in the late 1980s, but there is evidence that wages actually received by workers were less on account of corruption and manipulation in the piece-rate wage system. Allowing for this factor, the ratio of the actual transfer via wages to the total cost may turn out to be 30 to 40 per cent. Ravallion (1990, p. 27) estimates forgone incomes alone in the range of 40 to 50 per cent of wages received. Assuming the best estimates for all three parameters (90 per cent coverage of the poor, 40 per cent for the wage component and 40 per cent for forgone incomes) the benefit–cost ratio turns out to be 21.6 per cent ($0.9 \times 0.4 \times 0.6$), that is overheads (administrative and material costs), leakages, forgone incomes and the targeting factor consume about 80 per cent of the gross outlay. Thus, despite self-selection having a high targeting efficiency, any other mode of transfer in which the information, agency and other dead-weight losses are likely to be less than about 80 per cent can, in principle, be more cost-effective.

The poor can derive indirect benefits from the assets created under the EGS but only on two conditions: the assets must be durable (not just roads that are washed away in the next rains) and they should be such as to benefit the poor (at least along with the non-poor). Available studies indicate that non-durable rather than more permanent works tend to be preferred for a variety of reasons: the dispersion of the works, the tendency to economize on materials in order to increase the wage content, and local political pressures. In many cases, works are abandoned incomplete and new ones started elsewhere: the maintenance is sorely neglected (Mahendra Dev 1992, pp. 52–3). Furthermore, assets such as irrigation, soil conservation, and roads are likely, by their very nature, to benefit the landowning and trading non-poor rather than those who have laboured to create them. Second-run benefits can also occur if the EGS wages have the effect of raising normal agricultural wages by providing a bargaining threat to EGS participants. For this to happen, EGS works need to be undertaken during normal agricultural operations but if they are, the dilemma is that they will not be able to ensure incomes in the lean season of peak unemployment. A further dilemma is that if, in order to provide the bargaining strength, EGS wages are kept above normal agricultural wages, this will conflict with the objective of maximizing employment from a given budgetary outlay.

Some broad conclusions can be drawn from employment schemes. One is that they may have a small impact on rural unemployment and poverty despite large budgetary outlays; they leave out, in any case, the unemployable such as the old and the handicapped and do not have an urban equivalent. Second, it becomes necessary to keep wages low so as to be able to capture the neediest and to maximize employment; this could, however, erode the extent of relief. Third, the assets to be created need to be durable and of a kind that can be expected to benefit the poor through growth, rural–urban linkages or more directly. This involves local-level prioritization, planning and the sequencing of public works.[11] Fourth, the need for administrative efficiency and to reduce corruption and leakages is as strong in works programmes as it is in other forms of transfer which entail administrative selection. Fifth, while self-selection may result in a high targeting efficiency in employment schemes, their benefit–cost ratio is not so attractive as to exclude serious consideration of direct transfers.

Minimum Wages

If enforced, minimum wages can offer vastly greater potential for transfers than employment schemes such as the EGS, which pay an equivalent of less than a minimum wage.

Received wisdom would discourage faith in minimum wages, with excess labour supply, labour substitution through mechanization and/or changes in the cropping pattern, enforcement problems, opposition from rural oligarchies and so on. Yet there is no reason why the room for manoeuvre in wage upgradation should not be probed through such measures as: (i) making widely available information on minimum wages and on penalties for non-compliance; (ii) specific emphasis on enforcing minimum wages for time-bound activities such as harvesting, sowing, transplanting, etc. in which both the bargaining strength of labour is relatively strong and wages earned amount to a sizeable proportion of annual wage incomes; (iii) adequate and motivated enforcement machinery; (iv) the establishment of local wage-monitoring committees with representation from male and female agricultural labourers; (v) encouragement to NGOs working in this field; (vi) in-season public works in low-wage pockets (see also Shaheed 1993).

Food Subsidies

Many developing countries have intervened in the food market through public distribution systems (PDS) and food subsidies linked to them

---

[11] This aspect is stressed in a number of contributions in ILO (1992) and by Osmani (1991). In the Indian context see Dantwala (1985).

and there is an extensive literature on country experiences in food security, PDS and food subsidies.[12] The discussion here will be limited to reviewing experience with the PDS and related food subsidies in India.

Table 12.1

Comparison of Cost-effectiveness in the Employment Guarantee Schemes (EGS) and Public Distribution Systems (PDS) in India

		EGS	PDS
1.	Budgetary cost	100[a]	100[b]
2.	Overheads	50[c]	37[d]
3.	Leakage	10[e]	35[f]
4.	Gross benefit (1–2–3)	40	28
5.	Participation cost	16[g]	Neg[h]
6.	Net benefit (4–5) i.e. transfer efficiency	24	28
7.	Targeting efficiency (coverage of poor)	0.9	0.4
8.	Final transfer to poor (6 × 7) (benefit–cost ratio)	21.6	11.2

[a] Aggregate cost for creating one personday of employment.
[b] Cost of food subsidy.
[c] Administrative overheads and non-labour expenditures.
[d] Distribution overheads such as freight, storage costs, interest, etc. being 57 per cent of 65 per cent reaching consumers.
[e] Underpayment of wages.
[f] In transit and at points of sale.
[g] Foregone earnings.
[h] Negligible, assuming that forgone earnings due to waiting time and transport costs to retail shops are not significant.

The Indian PDS handles 10 to 15 per cent of foodgrain availability in the country and is almost wholly based on domestically procured stocks. There are wide variations in its functioning in different states in India. In addition to the food subsidy provided by central government, some of the states also subsidize grain. In general, entitlement to a ration card is universal, that is not targeted on the poor. Leakages occur at different points in the distribution chain and are estimated at up to 35 per cent of the gross amount of grain distributed (World Bank

[12] For an overview see World Bank (1986). For China, Ahmad and Hussain (1991); India and Bangladesh, Osmani (1991); Sri Lanka, Edirisinghe (1987).

1992, p. 83). At the central level alone, overheads currently amount to 57 per cent of the value of subsidy. Based on these estimates, Table 12.1 compares the benefit–cost ratio in the PDS with that in the Maharashtra EGS and indicates that this ratio in the PDS is probably only half of that in the employment programme, although the transfer efficiency in the PDS is somewhat higher. This is because targeting efficiency in the PDS is less than half as good as in self-targeting employment. However, the PDS has a much wider coverage than the EGS: even if its effective coverage is taken as being confined to the urban population in India (27 per cent), its impact ratio (11.2 per cent of 27 per cent, or 3 per cent) will be twice that in the EGS (21.6 per cent of 7 per cent, or 1.5 per cent).

School meal and child nutrition schemes can be viewed both as food security and as forms of family allowance which ease the burden of child rearing. They can also improve school enrolment and attendance.

Social Assistance

The main elements of social assistance are: targeting of the poor; need-based minimal assistance; tax financing; and protection as a matter of entitlement.[13] In the light of the relative neglect of social assistance, it may be useful to begin with a few general considerations that underline its importance and necessity. First, a large proportion of the poor in developing countries are immiserized in long-run poverty. Such 'chronic poverty' both exacerbates and is explained by contingent poverty arising from large family size, unemployment, old age, sickness, disability, maternity and widowhood. Second, it is not true that promotional measures, if implemented on a sufficiently large scale and over a sufficiently long time, will reduce the need for protection in the case of *all* contingencies. While, for instance, unemployment and sickness can be ameliorated through the provision of employment and health care measures, old age and death, to take two extreme examples, cannot be prevented through measures promoting, respectively, eternal youth and immortality. Poverty in such contingencies, if it is to be tackled at all, has to be tackled through direct relief. Third, while budgetary constraints are important, they have to be looked at in the overall framework of fiscal management:

---

[13] The ILO (1942) defines social assistance as 'a service or scheme which provides benefits to persons of small means as of right in amounts sufficient to meet minimum standards of need and financed from taxation'.

raising resources, curtailing inessential expenditures, greater equity in the mobilization and use of resources, and so on. Fourth, promotion measures share almost all of the problems associated with protective measures since these problems are inherent to all direct anti-poverty programmes: low coverage, lax targeting, high overheads, leakage, low benefit–cost ratios. Furthermore, information and agency problems occur in any form of social provision. There is no reason to assume that such problems in social assistance schemes will be so serious as to disqualify direct transfers altogether. On the other hand, social assistance could have a reasonably high targeting efficiency precisely because it is contingency related.

Candidates for Social Assistance

Against this background, it is useful to recall the nine main branches of social security covered in ILO Convention No. 102 and to consider how efforts can be made to provide them to the poor not covered by formal security. Clearly unemployment, family support and sickness have to be tackled largely through promotional measures, namely employment schemes, child nutrition and health care. The five other contingencies (old age, widowhood, maternity, disability and employment injury) need to be tackled, if at all, through social assistance.

There is sufficient empirical evidence to argue confidently that these five contingencies can be feasibly covered by social assistance in terms of meeting minimum standards of need, even in India. Means-tested old age pensions for the poor were first introduced in India at the state level in 1957. In subsequent decades, almost all the states in India have introduced old age pension schemes for the poor above the age of 60 or 65. In addition to general old age pension schemes, many states have more liberal schemes for agricultural labourers who are likely to be the poorest in the elderly population. Pensions are also available in most states for widows and for the physically handicapped in the form of survivor and disability benefits. Some states provide survivor, disability and employment injury benefits to families or victims involved in specified hazardous occupations such as fishing, construction work, tree tapping, well digging, pesticide spraying, tractor driving, loading and so on.

There is wide variation in the coverage, benefits and eligibility conditions among the states and also in implementation efficiency and take-up.[14] However, two states in India — Kerala and Tamil Nadu —

---

[14] On Indian social assistance schemes see Guhan (1992c, p. 287).

have demonstrated the viability and potential of such schemes. The Kerala pension scheme has been estimated to cover almost all of the target group of the elderly poor and some form of social assistance is available to half the workers in the unorganized sector (United Nations 1992). The current social assistance package in Tamil Nadu includes pensions for old age, agricultural labours, widows and the physically handicapped, survivor benefits, maternity assistance and accident relief. All households below the poverty level are eligible under these schemes except in the case of pensions where means-testing is more stringent. In both states, pensions are likely to meet 50 per cent or more of subsistence requirements; the survivor benefit in Tamil Nadu may amount to about six months' earnings or more for a poor household and maternity assistance may equal three months' wages for a female agricultural labourer. It has been estimated that about 17 per cent of poor households in Tamil Nadu are protected from contingencies which, without these schemes, might have immiserized them in extreme poverty, if not in absolute destitution. A very high proportion of beneficiaries are women (nearly 60 per cent) (Guhan 1992a).

A detailed evaluation suggests that, despite stringent means-testing, about a third of the elderly poor proved eligible for old age pensions in Tamil Nadu in 1990. The coverage was 60 to 70 per cent in the case of maternity assistance and survivor benefits.[15] The targeting efficiency was high for three reasons. The benefits are small enough for the non-poor to desist from infiltrating into the eligible group, risking stigma at the local level. Second, no ceilings were placed on the number of eligible beneficiaries; accordingly, infiltration by the non-poor does not displace the poor from benefits. Third, income status is, more reliably, verified on the basis of local inquiries while deciding on claims and not on a prior wholesale basis for large populations, as in the case of the Indian IRDP. The transfer efficiency is also high. Moral hazard — the incentive to induce the contingency

---

[15] Guhan (1992a). It is interesting that the proportions of the aged poor covered by pensions in Kerala and Tamil Nadu are much higher than the 3 per cent reported for China in Ahmad and Hussain (1991, p. 274). The very low coverage in China can perhaps be explained by stringent means-testing and the stigma associated with *wubao* relief to some extent but the major explanation could be that access to land and grain relief in China have greatly reduced the demand on *wubao* relief. Ahmad and Hussain are not, however, right in asserting that 'in most developing economies, public provisions for the indigent elderly in rural areas simply do not exist and that the coverage in China is exceptional for a developing economy'.

involved — does not pose a serious problem here: it is impossible in the case of old age; maternity assistance is limited to the first two births; and the survivor benefit provides no special incentive for spouse murder. Overheads are low (3–5 per cent) because claims are verified by the regular government staff. Disbursements are made through the post office in order to prevent corruption at this stage. Thus on all accounts, contingency-related social assistance in this model fares much better in terms of its cost–benefit ratio than even 'self-targeted' employment schemes.

Extrapolating the Tamil Nadu package to the all-India level, I have demonstrated elsewhere that a nation-wide 'minimum relevant' social assistance package of old age pensions, survivor benefits, accident relief and maternity assistance for poor households is likely to cost no more than 0.3 per cent of India's GDP and about 1 per cent of the combined revenues of the central and state governments in India (Guhan 1992b). Even with an increasing proportion of the elderly in the process of demographic change, the cost-to-GDP ratio in real terms will remain at about the same level in future decades. The minimum package can thus be both affordable and sustainable.

THREE GENERIC ISSUES

Targeting

The issue of targeting is central to budget-financed social assistance transfers. The search is for mechanisms that can achieve the widest coverage of the target group (maximizing horizontal efficiency) by concentrating benefits on them (maximizing vertical efficiency). Although the two types of efficiency will generally move in the same direction, this may not always happen since, within a given budgetary ceiling, there are two kinds of trade-off. One is between the administrative costs involved in targeting and the outlay available for benefits (programme costs). The other is between such administrative costs and vertical targeting efficiency. Although reducing administrative costs may lower vertical efficiency, it will increase programme outlays for a given budgetary allocation; and larger programme outlays can conceivably improve horizontal efficiency. Thus a trade-off between vertical and horizontal targeting efficiencies can emerge. Furthermore, political economy considerations call for a wide spread of benefits, which requires (near-)universal schemes with low overheads, large programme outlays and a sacrifice of vertical efficiency. Horizontal efficiency in such schemes may be less than in more closely targeted schemes but not proportionately so, because of the large programme outlays available. In other words, the price to be paid in efficiency for political sustainability may not be excessive.[16]

The ideal in targeting is to achieve both efficiency and equity by both minimizing administrative overheads *and* maximizing vertical efficiency. The quest for this optimum implies two broad approaches. One is to bypass administrative selection through resort to self-targeting schemes (for example employment schemes). The other is to tackle directly the information and agency problems involved in administrative selection so as to reduce their costs and/or improve their efficiency. The proposals made from this point of view include resort to indicator targeting using a variety of surrogates for income testing: landlessness or marginal land ownership; residence in disadvantaged locations; consumption of foods generally eaten by the poor; age (pensions for the old and nutrition for the very young); sex (support for maternity, post-natal assistance and widowhood); and so on. Means-testing itself can be improved by excluding the obviously non-poor on the basis of easily identifiable characteristics such as ownership of land and property, liability to taxes, salaries and so on, rather than aiming at a precise identification of the poor. In the case of contingency-related social assistance, incomes can be more reliably verified since relief is sanctioned on a case-by-case basis after the event. Furthermore, a reduction in agency problems can be sought through administrative and participatory decentralization.

Finally, it must be remembered that the different types of social assistance scheme, are not fungible. It is not meaningful to choose the most cost-effective among them for application across the board: each type of need calls for a specific form of relief. It is the optimal mix of schemes in terms of feasibility and appropriateness in meeting the spectrum of needs that will determine cost-effectiveness in the social security system as a whole. What is important, therefore, is not so much fine-tuned comparisons between alternatives but rather every attempt to reduce administrative overheads, leakage, corruption and other factors which undermine the targeting *and* transfer efficiencies in *all* major schemes. Good governance, alas, is inescapable.

---

[16] There is an extensive literature on targeting. For discussion and further references see Kanbur and Besley (1990); Kumar and Stewart (1992, pp. 269–74); and Lipton and Ravallion (1993, pp. 58–60).

Financing

There is no better maxim than 'where there's a will, there's a way' to guide discussion of financing the fight against deprivation. Apart from the reduction of expenditure on other outlays (notably military expenditures and subsidies for the non-poor) and the reallocation of resources saved thereby for social security, it is also possible to raise additional resources for social security. Typically, social security payments (about 10 per cent of GDP) explain the major part of the difference between tax-to-GDP ratios in the developed countries (about 30 per cent of GDP) and in the developing ones (15–20 per cent). This indicates that if resources are not available for social security, it may be largely because the opportunity for mobilizing *and* spending *additional* resources that social security offers is being missed. Of course, every effort must be made towards containing costs and improving benefits in social assistance transfers, as this chapter has argued.

The Indian experience could suggest a broad indicative target for expenditures on social assistance. India's current outlay on the set of schemes referred to above adds up to about 1.5 per cent of its (1993) GDP.[17] *Prima facie*, a doubling of this level of outlay, that is 3 per cent of GDP, would appear to be necessary as well as feasible.

Administration

The importance of decentralized delivery systems operating through local institutions in which the poor are not only enfranchised but empowered emerges from everything that has been discussed so far: reducing information and agency costs in targeting, micro-level planning for employment programmes, localized provision of credit, checking fraud and corruption at the root, quick settlement of claims, mobilizing local revenues. Most importantly, locally provided social security can be of fundamental importance in generating and sustaining 'solidarity' which is the essence of social security.[18]

[17] My rough estimate.

[18] As Keith Griffin and Terry McKinley (1993, p. 72) eloquently point out:

Empowerment . . . is not only democratic, it may also be efficient. It calls for a streamlined central administration which devolves authority as much as possible to the local level. By enlisting the active participation of the people instead of relying on a cumbersome bureaucracy to 'deliver' services to beneficiaries who have little voice in what is delivered and how it is delivered, empowerment may actually be more cost-effective than the alternatives. . . . Where this does occur, empowerment, human development and economic efficiency are inextricably intertwined. They are the principal components of a strategy that puts people first.

See also UNDP (1993, chs 2, 4 and 5).

A PROPOSED AGENDA

The agenda for 'appropriate social security for developing countries' that emerges from this review can be summarized quite simply.

While formal social security systems cannot be exclusively relied upon in developing countries, it is necessary to reform them and to extend their application where and when appropriate.

Land redistribution must be placed and maintained at the forefront of the social security agenda. Even under reformist regimes, it may be possible to stimulate and facilitate land transfers from the rich to the poor, through the credit mechanism.

Credit can be of fundamental importance for preventing asset depletion, enabling the acquisition by the poor of land and other assets, and for providing working capital to the self-employed poor in rural and urban areas.

Rural employment schemes, wage upgrading for rural labour, food subsidies linked to public distribution systems, child nutrition and contingency-related support for old age, maternity, survivors and the disabled could constitute a minimal social assistance package. An optimal mix of these programmes focusing on both needs and cost-effectiveness would be necessary, though decision-makers must recognize that cost-effectiveness is a function not only of targeting efficiency but also of the transfer efficiency in specific schemes.

Prima facie, a target of 3 per cent GDP for such basic minimum social assistance appears to be reasonable and affordable in most developing countries. Decentralized, participatory institutional arrangements would be essential.

REFERENCES

Agarwal, B. (1991). 'Social Security and the Family: Coping with Seasonality and Calamity in Rural India', in E. Ahmed, J. Drèze, J. Hills and E. Sen (eds) (1991). *Social Security in Developing Countries*. Oxford: Clarendon.

Ahmad, E. and A. Hussain (1991). 'Social Security in China: A Historical Perspective', in Ahmed, et al. (1991).

Atkinson, A.B. and G. Hills (1991). 'Social Security in Developed Countries: Are There Lessons for Developing Countries?', in Ahmed, et al. (1991).

Bell, C. (1990). 'Reforming Property Rights in Land and Tenancy', *The World Bank Research Observer*, 5(2), July, pp. 143–66.

Burgess, R. and N. Stern (1991). 'Social Security in Developing Countries: What, Why, Who and How?', in Ahmed, et al. (1991).

Burgess, R., J. Drèze, F. Ferreira, A. Hussain and J. Thomas (1993). Social Protection and Structural Adjustment (mimeo.). London: London School of Economics.

Cornia, G.A., R. Jolly and F. Stewart (eds) (1987). Adjustment with a Human Face. Oxford: Clarendon Press.

Dantwala, M.L. (1985). ' "Garibi Hatao": Strategy Options', in Economic and Political Weekly, 20(11), pp. 475–6.

Drèze, J. and A. Sen (1989). Hunger and Public Action. Oxford: Clarendon Press.

—— (1991). 'Public Action for Social Security: Foundations and Strategy', in Ahmed, et al. (1991).

Edirisinghe, N. (1987). The Food Stamp Scheme in Sri Lanka: Costs, Benefits and Options for Modification. Washington, D.C.: International Food Policy Research Institute.

Griffin, K. and T. McKinley (1993). Towards a Human Development Strategy. New York: UNDP.

Guhan, S. (1988). 'Aid for the Poor: Performance and Possibilities in India', in John P. Lewis and Contributors: Strengthening the Poor: What have We Learned? New Brunswick: Transaction Books.

—— (1992a). 'Social Security Initiatives in Tamil Nadu, 1989', in S. Subramanian (ed.), Themes in Development Economics: Essays in Honour of Malcolm S. Adiseshiah. Delhi: Oxford University Press.

—— (1992b). Social Security for the Unorganized Poor: A Feasible Blueprint for India (mimeo.). Madras: Madras Institute of Development Studies.

—— (1992c). 'Social Security in India: Looking One Step Ahead', in Harriss, Guhan and Cassen (1992).

Harriss, B., S. Guhan and R.H. Cassen (eds) (1992). Poverty in India, Research and Policy. Bombay: Oxford University Press.

ILO (1942). Approaches to Social Security: An International Survey. Montreal.

—— (1976). Employment, Growth and Basic Needs: A One-world Problem. Geneva.

—— (1992). International Labour Review, 131(1), Special issue on 'Productive Employment for the Poor'.

—— (1993). World Labour Report. Geneva.

Jodha, N.S. (1986). 'Common Property Resources and Rural Poor', in Economic and Political Weekly, 21, 5 July.

Kanbur, R. and T. Besley (1990). *The Principles of Targeting*, WPS No. 85. Washington, D.C.: World Bank.

Krishnaswamy, K.S. (ed.) (1990). *Poverty and Income Distribution*. Bombay: Oxford University Press.

Kumar, G. and F. Stewart (1992). 'Tackling Malnutrition: What Can Targeted Nutritional Interventions Achieve?', in Harris, Guhan and Cassen (1992).

Lipton, M. and M. Ravallion (1993). *Poverty and Policy*, WPS No. 1130. Washington, D.C.: World Bank.

Mahendra Dev, S. (1992). 'Poverty Alleviation Programmes: A Case Study of Maharashtra with Emphasis on Employment Guarantee Scheme', Discussion Paper No. 7. Bombay: Indira Gandhi Institute of Development Research.

Mesa–Lago, C. (1991). 'Social Security in Latin America and the Caribbean: A Comparative Assessment', in Ahmed, et al. (1991).

Osmani, S.R. (1991). 'Social Security in South Asia', in Ahmed, et al. (1991).

Parikh, K.S. (1993). *Who Gets How Much from PDS: How Effectively Does it Reach the Poor?* Bombay: Indira Gandhi Institute of Development Research.

Platteau, J.-P. (1991). 'Traditional Systems of Social Security and Hunger Insurance: Past Achievements and Modern Challenges', in Ahmed, et al. (1991).

Rath, N. (1985). ' "Garibi Hatao": Can IRDP Do It?', *Economic and Political Weekly*, 20(6), pp. 238–46.

Ravallion, M. (1990). 'Reaching the Poor through Rural Public Employment: A Survey of Theory and Evidence', World Bank Discussion Paper No. 94. Washington, D.C.: World Bank.

Ron, A., B. Abel-Smith and G. Tamburi (1990). *Health Insurance in Developing Countries: The Social Security Approach*. Geneva: ILO.

Sen, A. (1981). *Poverty and Famines: An Essay on Entitlement and Deprivation*. Oxford: Clarendon Press.

—— (1983). 'Development: Which Way Now?', *The Economic Journal*, (Cambridge), 93, December, pp. 745–62.

—— (1985). *Commodities and Capabilities*. Amsterdam: North Holland.

Shaheed, Z. (1993). Minimum Wages and Their Impact on Poverty (mimeo.). Geneva: ILO.

Stewart, F. (1985). *Planning to Meet Basic Needs*. London: Macmillan.

—— (1993). 'War and Underdevelopment: Can Economic Analysis Help Reduce the Costs?' Development Studies Working Paper No. 56. Oxford: International Development Centre.

Streeten, P. with S.J. Burki, M. Ul Haq, N. Hicks and F. Stewart (1981). *First Things First: Meeting Basic Needs in Developing Countries.* New York: Oxford University Press.

United Nations Development Programme (1993). *Human Development Report 1993.* New York: United Nations.

Weisbrod, B.A. 1969. 'Collective Action and the Distribution of Income: A Collective Approach', in US Congress, Joint Economic Committee, *The Analysis and Evaluation of Public Expenditures*, Washington, D.C.

World Bank (1986). *Poverty and Hunger: Issues and Options for Food Security in Developing Countries.* Washington, D.C.

—— (1992). *India: Stabilizing and Reforming the Economy.* Washington, D.C.

—— (1993). *World Development Report 1993 (Investing in Health).* Washington, D.C.

Human Development in India

BHASKAR DUTTA, MANOJ PANDA AND WILIMA WADHWA

INTRODUCTION

Until the mid-1960s, the main thrust of development policies all over the world was to accelerate the growth process since the 'trickle down' mechanism was supposed to take care of distributional objectives.[1] Unfortunately, the development experience of many countries during the two decades after World War II raised questions about the relevance and efficiency of the 'trickle down' hypothesis since a large fraction of the population of underdeveloped countries continued to live in abject poverty. A qualitative change in development policies was discernible in the 1970s. The reduction of poverty became an explicit goal of development and programmes were designed so as to increase income and employment opportunities of target groups of the population. Of course, the redistributional objective still remained an *income-oriented* goal, in the sense that income was viewed as the only concept of value to individuals.

A very different perspective on development is provided by the UNDP's *Human Development Report* (*HDR*). The essence of the UNDP's perspective is that while income is an important objective, development must encompass improvements in other non-income indicators as well, because human well-being cannot be equated with wealth or income.[2] In particular, the *HDR* advocates the use of the

[1] Of course, even in the early 1960s, some doubts were expressed about the efficacy of the trickle-down mechanism. See, for instance, the Perspective Planning Division (1962).

[2] The conceptual basis of the human development approach is due to Sen (1985, 1987), who argues persuasively against the *opulence* approach which places undue emphasis on command over commodities (or more simply income) in the assessment of well-being.

Human Development Index (HDI), which is a composite of three basic components of human development: longevity, knowledge and income, as a more comprehensive measure of socio-economic progress.

It is, therefore, important to evaluate a country's performance in the areas of health and education, as well examine the role of government expenditures in promoting these non-income objectives. This is the underlying motivation of this paper, which has two principal objectives. First, we describe the development experience of India during the last two decades from the human development perspective. Following the *HDR* as far as possible, we concentrate on health, education, and income as the essential components of well-being. We use time series data on infant and child mortality from the Sample Registration System to measure achievements in health of seventeen major states. As far as education is concerned, we use gross school enrolment data reported by the Ministry of Human Resource Development, Government of India. The state gross domestic product data, published by the Central Statistical Organization, constitute our income data.

Second, we explore the implications of the human development experience in India for its development policy. We examine whether the Indian experience throws any light on the issue of the need to radically restructure development policies because of possible conflicts between the various ends. Our description of the human development experience in India suggests that the correlation between per capita incomes and performance levels in health or education is not very high. We, therefore, turn to regression analysis to see whether per capita incomes or public expenditure in the social sectors is the major determinant of performance levels in these sectors.

The plan of this chapter is as follows. In the second section we review the UNDP methodology and suggest modifications. Next we describe the human development experience of seventeen states in our sample. In the fourth section, we describe the regression results. The final section sums up our conclusions.

METHODOLOGICAL ISSUES

The basic premise underlying the UNDP's approach to evaluation of alternative paths of development is that the main concern of development *should be* the provision of basic *capabilities* which enhance the quality of people's lives. The UNDP's construction of the Human Development Index reflects these views. We will first describe the procedure recommended in several versions of the *HDR*, and then comment on some features of their construction. This will be followed by a discussion of the procedure that we have followed in this chapter.

Human development is defined to be a process of enlarging people's opportunities and expanding capabilities. Ideally, any index of development should incorporate all the capabilities that enhance individual well-being. Obviously, this cannot lead to an index which is operational from an empirical standpoint. So, there is a need to *select* the most important capabilities affecting well-being, and the *HDR* selects longevity, knowledge and income.

The *HDR* measures longevity by life expectancy at birth. Knowledge is represented by two educational variables: adult literacy and mean years of schooling, the weights assigned being two-thirds and one-third, respectively. For income, the HDI is based on the premise of diminishing returns from income for development. One interpretation is that what is important is not the level of *income per se*, but the *utility* derived from income. The general form used to incorporate diminishing returns to income is the well-known Atkinson formulation for the utility of income.

$$W(y) = \frac{1}{(1-e)} y^{(1-e)}, e < 1. \tag{1}$$

Here, the parameter e is the elasticity of the marginal utility of income and measures the extent of diminishing returns. When $e = 1$, W takes the logarithmic form.

The first step in the construction of the HDI is to calculate a country's extent of deprivation for each of the three indicators, life expectancy (X_1), literacy (X_2) and adjusted per capita income (X_3). The notion of deprivation used by the *HRD* is one of *absolute* deprivation. So a particular country feels deprived because its achievement for, say, literacy, is below that attained by the top performer in literacy. The *HDR* also assumes that the extent of deprivation is *linear* in the difference between a country's attainment and the global maximum for any particular indicator. In order to get an index of deprivation, this measure of a country's deprivation is divided by the difference between the global maximum and minimum. Letting I_{ij} denote country j's index of deprivation for the i-th social indicator, we have:

$$I_{ij} = \frac{(M_i - X_{ij})}{(M_i - m_i)} \tag{2}$$

where M_i and m_i are the global maximum and minimum values for indicator i respectively.

The second step is to define the overall index of deprivation for country j as the simple average of the deprivation indices for the three indicators. Finally, human development is defined as the absence of deprivation. Hence

$$(HDI)_j = \left(1 - \frac{1}{3} \sum I_{ij} \right)$$ (3)

There is a need to modify[3] the basic index if comparisons are to be made across time. Such comparisons are essential because the issue of how countries have performed over time is often as interesting as their performance at a point in time. The basic HDI cannot be used to measure a country's performance across time because the global maximum and minimum values will naturally change. This is because an *absolute* improvement in an indicator may still be associated with an increase in the deprivation index if the country's *relative* position deteriorates. The *HDR* suggests that in order to correct for these anomalies, the global minimum and maximum values should be defined over a period of time and not for each point of time. Suppose $[t^1, t^2]$ is the time period over which the comparison is to be made. Let M_{it} and m_{it} denote the global maximum and minimum values of indicator i. Then, the deprivation index for country j with respect to indicator i for the time period $[t^1, t^2]$ is given by

$$\bar{I}_{ij} = \frac{(M_{it} - X_{ijt})}{(M_{it} - m_{it})}$$ (4)

So the index of human development is

$$(HDI)_j = \left(1 - \frac{1}{3} \sum \bar{I}_{ij} \right)$$ (5)

The *HDR's* procedure for measuring deprivation is not without problems. For any indicator, a country's index of deprivation is measured by the difference between the global maximum and the actual value relative to the range of values recorded by the different countries. (When comparisons are being made over time, then the maximum and

---

[3] The *HDR* also discusses other modifications of the basic index. See Dutta, et al. (1994) for a discussion.

minimum values are defined for the entire period.) Hence the country which records the highest value does not experience any deprivation according to this formula! Suppose, now, that each country wants to maximize the value of its human development index. Then the leading country in, say, health has no incentive to improve achievements in health, since that does not give it any extra benefits.

A more important problem is that deprivation is defined to be linear in the difference between the maximum and actual value. Kakwani (1993) points out that as far as the non-income indicators are concerned, there are biological and physical limits to the maximum achievements possible. Consider two countries A and B with literacy levels of, say, 40 and 60, respectively. Obviously, it is more difficult for country B to record incremental improvements. Alternatively, the same country with varying levels of performance (relative to the biological or physical maximum) would find it more difficult to achieve improvements in the indicator for which its current performance is better. A linear measure of deprivation does not take this into account. This represents a serious flaw in the construction of the HDI and makes it inappropriate for measuring *changes* or *improvements* in performance. Also, the policy implications in so far as investment in the different sectors is concerned may be strange. Kakwani (1993) suggests an axiomatic procedure for deriving indices of achievement[4] for indicators which have asymptotic limits. This is outlined below.

Let x denote some non-income indicator such that higher levels are desirable. For example x could represent literacy.[5] Let the asymptotic upper bound for this indicator be M. M is an asymptotic limit in the sense that x never reaches this value, although it may come arbitrarily close to M. Let m be the lower bound for x. The problem considered by Kakwani is to define an appropriate index $Q(x_1, x_2, M, m)$ to measure a country's improvement when the value of the indicator x moves from x_1 to x_2. Notice that the index has been defined so as to take into account the upper and lower bounds. Kakwani's improvement index is defined as:

$$Q(x_1, x_2, M, m) = f(x_2, M, m) - f(x_1, M, m) \qquad (6)$$

where $f(x_2, M, m)$ and $f(x_1, M, m)$ are the values of an *achievement*

[4] An index of achievement is the obverse of an index of deprivation.

[5] If x represents an indicator such as infant mortality, then it is socially optimal to reduce the level of x. In this case, the role of M and m need to be interchanged.

index. In order to ensure that the achievement index lies between 0 and 1, Kakwani specifies:

$$f(x, M, m) = 1 - \frac{g(M - x)}{g(M - m)} \qquad (7)$$

where $g(.)$ is a positive, increasing function with $\lim g(x) = 0$ as x approaches 0.

The higher the value of x, the more difficult is it to record a further increase. In order to incorporate this into the achievement index, it is sufficient to make g a *concave* function. Kakwani uses the class of constant elasticity (Atkinson) functions defined in equation (2). So

$$g(x) = \frac{1}{(1 - e)} x^{(1 - e)}, \ 0 \le e \le 1 \qquad (8)$$

This also gives a class of improvement indices with the property that an equal increase is translated into a bigger improvement if it is achieved at a higher level.[6] Also notice that the *HDR's* deprivation index is a special case in that it assumes that g is linear. In other words, e is set equal to-zero.

Of course, the maximum value, M, has to be chosen carefully. The logic of the procedure dictates that it should be set at a level which is higher than the maximum recorded value. One interpretation of M is that it represents an unattainable target, something like a bliss point which can never actually be achieved. Similarly, the minimum can be the actual minimum value attained historically, or some smaller number. These modifications will remove one source of 'externality' in the HDI which has bothered some critics. They have pointed out that an improvement in the performance level of the lowest performing country will cause the index for all other countries to drop. A similar effect is present if the top performing country improves its performance. And one can legitimately question why the level of human development of country j should be affected by country i's performance. However, once the maximum and minimum values are chosen in the manner suggested above, this sort of externality will no longer be present.

The advantage of using achievement and improvement indices of the class given by equations (6–8) is that even the highest performing

---

[6] Kakwani chooses the form $g(x) = Ln(x)$, and claims that the corresponding improvement index lies between 0 and 1. This claim is based on the intriguing assertion that 'it is customary to define $Ln(x)$ approaching zero as x approaches zero'!

country in any given indicator has an incentive to improve its performance, because any increase will show up as an increase in achievement in that indicator.[7] This procedure will also correct for the other biases that we have referred to earlier in connection with linear measures of deprivation.

HUMAN DEVELOPMENT IN INDIA

As we have remarked earlier, a major objective of this study is to describe the human development experience in India. In order to do this, we have taken seventeen major states as the 'units' of analysis. Deprivation and achievement levels have been derived through comparisons amongst these states. In order to follow the UNDP's perspective as far as possible, we have concentrated on health, education and income as the three essential components of well-being. Considerations of data availability have influenced our choice of variables to measure these indicators.

Indicators and Data Sources

The major exercise is the analysis of time series data from the 1970s onwards. The only health-related variables for which time series data are available are infant and child mortality rates reported by the Sample Registration System (SRS), which is supervized by the office of the Registrar General of India. The SRS is the main source of information on fertility and mortality indicators in India. These data are available at the state and national levels, and are further subclassified by gender as well as by location (rural or urban). As far as education is concerned, we have used gross school enrolment data, published by the Ministry of Human Resource Development, Government of India, in *Education in India*. Enrolment statistics by various stages of school education — primary, middle and high school — are published on an annual basis. Gross enrolment is calculated as the ratio of the total number of students enrolled in the relevant stage by the *estimated* population in a specified age group. Thus the primary section is defined as Classes 1–5, while the corresponding age group is 6–11 years. Classes 6–8 constitute the middle school with associated age group being 11–14 years, while high school is Classes 9–11 with associated age group 14–17.[8]

---

[7] As we have remarked earlier, this is not the case with the *HDR* procedure, where the top performer has zero deprivation.

[8] In later years, this has become Classes 9–12 with associated age group being 14–18 years.

There are some problems with the enrolment data. First, several researchers have raised doubts about the reliability of the data. It is often said that there is over-reporting in order to show fulfilment of targets (see, for instance, Kurien 1983). Second, the enrolment ratio does not take into account drop-out rates which may be as high as 60 per cent in the terminal stages of primary education (see Mehta 1993). Third, the gross enrolment ratios can be misleading because children outside the age group of, say, 6–11 years may also be enrolled in the primary section. Despite these problems, we have been forced to use this data source simply because nothing else is available on a time series basis. However, there is strong anecdotal evidence to suggest that the primary school enrolment data are particularly unreliable. We have taken this into consideration by carrying out two parallel exercises with the enrolment data, one exercise *omitting* primary school data. However, it turns out that the results are not affected significantly when the primary school data are omitted. We, therefore, only report results with the full set of data.[9]

As far as income is concerned, we have used the State Gross Domestic Product (SGDP) data published by the Central Statistical Organization. These data in real terms are available for some years of the time period covered here at 1970–1 prices and for other years at 1980–1 prices. We have converted the SGDP at 1980–1 prices into SGDP at 1970–1 prices, using conversion factors for 1980–1 for which SGDP data are available at both prices. For comparability across states, the SGDP at 1970–1 prices have to be corrected for interstate price variations because the cost of living across states is known to differ substantially at a point in time. The SGDP at 1970–1 prices have been converted to a common base over space by using state specific price indices (SSPI) with base All-India = 100. The SSPI series for 1970–1 for the middle income group of the population in rural and urban areas have been reported by Minhas, et al. (1991). We have taken a weighted average of the rural and urban series using rural–urban *consumption* weights for 1970–1 (in the absence of the income data by rural–urban areas) in order to obtain an aggregate interstate price differential series. The per capita SGDP at 1970–1 prices are divided by this series to obtain comparable state income figures. Thus all SGDPs in different years are evaluated at a common All-India base year price.

We have argued earlier against the use of linear deprivation or

---

[9] The results omitting primary school data are reported in Dutta, et al. (1994).

achievement indices. In this chapter, we use different functional forms. In one exercise, we mimic the UNDP procedure for health and education by using linear deprivation indices, with the maximum and minimum values being the actual extreme points across states during the reference period. As far as income, or more correctly, the utility of income is concerned, we use the logarithmic specification, with state income being measured by the per capita state domestic product adjusted for interstate price differentials.[10]

As far as the health indicator, measured by either infant mortality or child mortality, is concerned, the (UNDP) deprivation indices have been obtained in a straightforward manner. We have followed a slightly different procedure for obtaining deprivation indices for education. Deprivation indices have been obtained separately for each stage of school education. The overall index of deprivation in education is defined as a weighted average of the deprivation indices for primary, middle and high school enrolment, the weights of 0.4, 0.3 and 0.3, respectively being the proportions of estimated population in the associated age groups.

We have divided the period 1970–90 into four subperiods.[11] The annual deprivation indices for each indicator have been averaged to obtain indices for each subperiod. In conformity with the UNDP approach, we have constructed human development indices for each subperiod by taking simple averages of the (linear) achievement indices.

We have also constructed *non-linear* achievement indices for health and education using the formulation described in equations (6–8). Keeping in mind the observations we have made in the second section, the maximum and minimum values have been taken to be larger and smaller, respectively than the actual extreme points observed during the reference period. Also, for each indicator we have used *two* functional forms. Again, the results are not sensitive to the choice of functional form, and we will only report with one specification. The achievement index for infant mortality in a state whose *IMR* equals X is:

$$AIMR\,(X) = 1 - \left(\frac{X-10}{220}\right)^{0.5} \qquad (9)$$

[10] The Atkinson form with $e = 0.5$ was also used. However, none of the results are sensitive to this alternative specification of the utility function.

[11] See Appendix A to this chapter for a description of these subperiods.

Similarly, the index for child mortality (*CMR*) is:

$$ACMR\,(X) = 1 - \left(\frac{X - 1.5}{118.5}\right)^{0.5} \tag{10}$$

Non-linear achievement indices for education have first been computed separately for each level of education, using the same functional form as in the case of health indicators. These separate indices have been combined into an overall index of achievement in primary to high school (AEPH), using weights of 0.4, 0.3, 0.3.

In order to present the achievements of states in a comprehensible form, we have again divided the period 1970–90 into four subperiods, and have taken subperiod averages of the annual indices. The four subperiod achievement indices have been combined to obtain the achievement indices for each decade. The difference between the achievement indices for each decade yields the *improvement* index between two decades.

Empirical Results

We start with a discussion of the results in child mortality. Except in Jammu and Kashmir, the child mortality rates generally decline over time. As is to be expected, the decline in rates is low in some of the states where the initial rates were low. Time trends in *achievement* are more revealing. These show significantly increasing trends at the 5 per cent level of significance for all states except Jammu and Kashmir. Table 13.1 presents the achievement indices in child mortality for the four subperiods. The table reveals a rise in the achievement index over the four subperiods for different states as well as for the country as a whole. For most of the states, the rise occurs in every period over the previous one. There are, however, three states — Haryana, Jammu and Kashmir, and Madhya Pradesh — which witnessed a fall in the achievement index in period II over period I. Assam is the only state where there has been a fall in the index in period III. As is to be expected, Kerala occupies the top position throughout this period among the Indian states. The other notable feature of the table is that the ranks of the states in general do not reveal large variations over the subperiod. Some exceptions to this general pattern are Karnataka and Tamil Nadu, which interchange their ranks of 3 and 8 in subperiods III and IV, and Haryana which slips quite sharply from position 6 to 10 after the first subperiod.

Table 13.1
Child Mortality Achievement Index

	Levels				Rankings			
	I	II	III	IV	I	II	III	IV
AP	0.375	0.419	0.523	0.561	9	9	7	9
AS	0.354	0.439	0.430	0.477	10	7	12	13
BI			0.398	0.481			14	12
GU	0.317	0.360	0.437	0.511	11	12	11	11
HA	0.440	0.416	0.496	0.547	6	10	10	10
HP	0.432	0.490	0.549	0.589	7	5	5	5
JK	0.541	0.511	0.537	0.571	2	2	6	7
KA	0.489	0.507	0.551	0.564	3	3	3	8
KE	0.589	0.664	0.721	0.799	1	1	1	1
MP	0.317	0.294	0.337	0.386	12	14	16	17
MH	0.441	0.498	0.550	0.615	5	4	4	2
OR	0.314	0.375	0.401	0.427	13	11	13	15
PU	0.446	0.472	0.558	0.600	4	6	2	4
RA	0.296	0.347	0.382	0.439	14	13	15	14
TN	0.418	0.431	0.505	0.600	8	8	8	3
UP	0.162	0.229	0.314	0.400	15	15	17	16
WB			0.498	0.580			9	6
AI	0.339	0.377	0.434	0.500				

Note: $ACMR = 1 - ((X - 1.5)/(120 - 1.5)^0.5)$.

Broadly similar patterns emerge in the case of infant mortality. Achievement levels in infant mortality show an increasing trend at the 5 per cent level of significance for all states except Jammu and Kashmir. The achievement indices for infant mortality for the four subperiods are shown in Table 13.2. The list of states doing consistently better than All-India turns out to be the same as before. Kerala's achievement is again way ahead of other states. Jammu and Kashmir stands next to Kerala in the 1970s, though its position deteriorates over time. Similarly, Haryana also drops in the state rankings.

We now describe the pattern of *improvement* in the health sector. The improvement indices and the rankings of states according to these indices are presented in Table 13.3. Perhaps the most striking features of this table are the performances of Kerala and Uttar Pradesh. The

Table 13.2
Infant Mortality Achievement Index

	Levels				Rankings			
	I	II	III	IV	I	II	III	IV
AP	0.319	0.319	0.434	0.444	9	10	7	9
AS	0.237	0.317	0.352	0.387	11	11	11	13
BI			0.340	0.403			12	12
GU	0.236	0.267	0.335	0.411	12	12	13	11
HA	0.373	0.335	0.382	0.436	4	9	10	10
HP	0.341	0.361	0.443	0.445	6	5	6	8
JK	0.478	0.477	0.458	0.470	2	2	5	6
KA	0.400	0.430	0.480	0.457	3	3	2	7
KE	0.536	0.599	0.684	0.764	1	1	1	1
MP	0.218	0.223	0.266	0.302	14	14	15	16
MH	0.359	0.411	0.459	0.513	5	4	3	3
OR	0.231	0.232	0.258	0.283	13	13	16	17
PU	0.339	0.354	0.459	0.516	7	6	4	2
RA	0.251	0.351	0.330	0.379	10	8	14	14
TN	0.319	0.353	0.420	0.484	8	7	9	4
UP	0.114	0.151	0.203	0.307	15	15	17	15
WB			0.423	0.477			8	5
AI	0.251	0.280	0.346	0.400				

Note: $AIMR = 1 - ((X - 10)/(230 - 10)^0.5)$.

impressive *levels* of achievements of Kerala in health and education will not come as a surprise to anyone. What is not so universally known is that even in terms of *change*, Kerala does remarkably well. Kerala records the highest rate of improvement for infant mortality. In the case of child mortality, it occupies the fourth position. At the other end of the scale in terms of achievement is Uttar Pradesh. However, Uttar Pradesh records the highest rate of improvement in child mortality, while in terms of improvement in infant mortality, it occupies the third position. In contrast, some of the other poor performers in achievement such as Madhya Pradesh, Orissa and Rajasthan continue to be at the bottom even in terms of improvement indices. Apart from Uttar Pradesh, and to a lesser extent Andhra Pradesh, the rankings of states according to achievement and improvement do not show any great divergence. One may therefore conclude that the disparity in health achievement levels among Indian states in general does not seem to have narrowed down over the last two decades.

Table 13.3
Infant and Child Mortality Improvement Indices

	Indices		Rankings	
	ICMR	*IAMR*	*ICMR*	*IAMR*
AP	0.146	0.121	2	5
AS	0.059	0.095	13	8
GU	0.139	0.125	3	4
HA	0.095	0.058	9	11
HP	0.110	0.093	8	15
JK	0.026	−0.014	15	13
KA	0.060	0.052	12	11
KE	0.137	0.160	4	1
MP	0.059	0.065	14	10
MH	0.116	0.103	7	7
OR	0.071	0.040	11	14
PU	0.122	0.143	6	2
RA	0.092	0.056	10	12
TN	0.132	0.118	5	6
UP	0.165	0.127	1	3
AI	0.112	0.109		

Note: $ICMR_{t+1} = ACMR_{t+1} - ACMR_t$.
$IAMR_{t+1} = IAMR_{t+1} - IAMR_t$.

We will now comment on performances in achievement and improvement in education. Even a cursory examination of the data makes it clear that in almost all states, the gross enrolment ratios have been much higher in the primary stage. Moreover, even the growth rate in the primary stage has been appreciably higher.

Tables 13.4 and 13.5 show levels of achievement and improvements in education, respectively. Just as in the case of health indicators, Kerala ranks at the top in education, with Tamil Nadu and Himachal Pradesh close at its heels. Andhra Pradesh is near the bottom of the rankings in terms of achievement in education, though it was in the middle of

Table 13.4
Achievement in Education — Primary to High School

	Levels				Rankings			
	I	II	III	IV	I	II	III	IV
AP	0.094	0.110	0.163	0.250	15	14	12	9
AS	0.159	0.135	0.169	0.234	11	13	11	12
BI	0.078	0.098	0.109	0.149	16	15	17	17
GU	0.210	0.253	0.275	0.342	5	6	5	5
HA	0.180	0.145	0.184	0.243	8	11	9	10
HP	0.242	0.289	0.326	0.431	3	4	3	3
JK	0.137	0.146	0.134	0.162	12	10	15	16
KA	0.170	0.191	0.205	0.285	9	7	8	7
KE	0.420	0.453	0.475	0.501	1	1	1	1
MP	0.096	0.092	0.153	0.237	14	16	13	11
MH	0.236	0.277	0.321	0.396	4	5	4	4
OR	0.102	0.136	0.174	0.225	13	12	10	13
PU	0.204	0.305	0.263	0.286	7	3	7	6
RA	0.064	0.086	0.121	0.166	17	17	16	15
TN	0.285	0.308	0.366	0.496	2	2	2	2
UP	0.205	0.165	0.143	0.169	6	9	14	14
WB	0.169	0.166	0.274	0.264	10	8	6	8
AI	0.170	0.179	0.206	0.254				

Table 13.5
Improvement in Education

	Index IEPH	Rankings IEPH
AP	0.100	4
AS	0.051	11
BI	0.039	14
GU	0.073	8
HA	0.048	13
HP	0.107	2
JK	0.005	16
KA	0.060	10

	Index IEPH	Rankings IEPH
KE	0.050	12
MP	0.096	6
MH	0.098	5
OR	0.077	7
PU	0.018	15
RA	0.066	9
TN	0.127	1
UP	–0.031	17
WB	0.102	3
AI	0.053	

Note: Improvement is in 1980–8 over 1970–9

the rankings in achievement in health. By and large, there is no spectacular change from one extreme to the other in terms of achievement and improvement ranks. States with high achievement levels like Tamil Nadu and Himachal Pradesh maintain a lead in terms of improvement too. However, the most surprising feature of Table 13.5 is the performance of Kerala, which is near the bottom of the rankings in terms of improvement. There are also cases of 'low-achievement' states recording high improvements. The most striking case here is Andhra Pradesh.

Table 13.6 shows the (UNDP) deprivation index for income, along with rankings of the states. In order to make the ranks here easily comparable with those in earlier tables, the ranking in Table 13.6 is in ascending order, whereas those in the earlier tables were in descending order. As far as the income ranking is concerned, Punjab and Haryana top the list of states in all the subperiods. Maharashtra and Gujarat take the next two positions, though they change positions amongst themselves in the different subperiods. Bihar, Madhya Pradesh and Uttar Pradesh, which were often among the worst performers in health or education achievements, belong to the bottom rung by per capita income too. Note that Kerala, the star performer in health and education, does not perform well in terms of income in any of the subperiods. Its income rank goes down from 12 in the 1970s to 15 in the 1980s, when it is the third poorest state in terms of per capita state domestic

Table 13.6
UNDP Deprivation Index — Income

| | Levels | | | | Rankings | | | |
	I	II	III	IV	I	II	III	IV
AP	0.623	0.598	0.514	0.454	6	9	5	6
AS	0.800	0.807	0.716	0.632	15	15	14	14
BI	0.978	0.941	0.878	0.796	17	17	17	17
GU	0.547	0.450	0.372	0.318	4	4	3	4
HA	0.484	0.392	0.330	0.216	2	2	2	2
HP	0.644	0.599	0.595	0.505	8	10	9	8
JK	0.648	0.597	0.552	0.576	9	8	7	11
KA	0.610	0.556	0.520	0.432	5	5	6	5
KE	0.740	0.743	0.744	0.712	12	12	15	15
MP	0.789	0.807	0.706	0.596	14	14	13	12
MH	0.526	0.416	0.394	0.279	3	3	4	3
OR	0.860	0.832	0.829	0.728	16	16	16	16
PU	0.323	0.219	0.153	0.047	1	1	1	1
RA	0.688	0.647	0.657	0.569	11	11	11	10
TN	0.655	0.593	0.607	0.512	10	7	10	9
UP	0.776	0.746	0.674	0.600	13	13	12	13
WB	0.629	0.590	0.569	0.487	7	6	8	7

Note: Deprivation index for income = $Ln\ Y$

product. However, it has to be pointed out that the SGDP in Kerala may underestimate the state income because of large remittances into the state. Unfortunately, we have not been able to correct for this.

Table 13.7
Rank Correlation Coefficients

| | Decade 1 | | Decade 2 | |
	Education	Health	Education	Health
Income	0.429	0.429	0.449	0.473
Health	0.507		0.843	
	Excluding Kerala		*Excluding Kerala*	
Income	0.540	0.556	0.629	0.694

It is interesting to compare the strength of the association between achievements in income and in the non-income indicators. In order to analyse this, we have computed the interstate rankings in income, health and education for the decades of the 1970s and 1980s, and then computed the rank correlation coefficients, which are reported in Table 13.7. For health, only one indicator, child mortality, has been considered since the rankings according to child and infant mortality almost coincide when decadal averages are considered. Also, note that the interstate rankings are *invariant* to the functional form of the deprivation index as long as they are ordinal transforms of one another.

The rank correlation coefficients between income and education or health variables are not at all high and range between 0.43 and 0.47. The coefficients indicate a slight tendency to rise over time. The relationship between health and educational achievements turns out to be somewhat stronger than the relationship between income and any of the non-income indicators. In fact, health and education are becoming more closely related over time. The corresponding coefficients ranged between 0.51 and 0.57 in the 1970s, but increased to 0.80 and above in the 1980s.

Since Kerala's achievements in education and health in spite of its low income level are often viewed as an exception, it may be thought that Kerala alone is responsible for the low observed correlation between income and the non-income indicators. We have therefore worked out the correlation of income with education and health excluding Kerala. The exclusion of Kerala certainly increases the value of the correlation coefficient. Without Kerala, these lie between 0.54 and 0.56 in the 1970s to between 0.63 and 0.69 in the 1980s, indicating a rise in the strength of the relationship over time. Nevertheless, the degree of association amongst the non-income indicators (including Kerala) is higher than the association between income and the non-income indicators excluding Kerala.

The pattern of rank correlation coefficients has a significant bearing on the debate about the nature of the 'right' development policy. Should policies be geared to growth alone in the hope that higher growth itself will lead to greater achievements in the social sectors? Or do we need to target government expenditure to the social sectors? The Indian experience suggests that higher incomes *alone* will not necessarily lead to significant improvements in the levels of education and health.

Having discussed the behaviour of individual components, we now turn to an overall index of human development, which is computed following the UNDP procedure. The specific indicators chosen are infant mortality rates for health, enrolment rates in primary to high schools for education and logarithm of income.[12] Table 13.8 shows the ranks of the states by such an overall index for the four subperiods selected earlier. We comment on some of the more interesting features of the table.

Table 13.8
Human Development Index — Interstate Ranking

	I	II	III	IV
AP	10	10	10	10
AS	11	12	12	12
BI			17	17
GU	9	7	6	5
HA	4	9	7	7
HP	6	5	5	6
JK	7	8	11	11
KA	8	6	9	8
KE	1	2	2	3
MP	14	15	14	14
MH	3	3	3	2
OR	15	13	15	16
PU	2	1	1	1
RA	12	11	13	13
TN	5	4	4	4
UP	13	14	16	15
WB			8	9

Note: This ranking is based on an overall index, giving equal weight to deprivation in education (EPH), infant mortality and income (Ln Y).

First, Kerala tops the list of states in terms of the overall index for the first subperiod, but loses this position to Punjab in later years. In fact, Kerala gets only the third position in the last subperiod, the first and second being Punjab and Maharashtra, respectively. The declining

[12] We have constructed indices using other combinations of deprivation indices. But these do not change the rankings in any significant way.

position of Kerala in the overall index is due not only to its low income ranking, but also because Punjab and Maharashtra have reasonable achievements in both health and education. Second, Haryana, which remains the second highest in terms of income, is reduced to the middle rung in the overall index because of its relative neglect of health and education. A similar point emerges for Gujarat too, though it has improved its position over time. Third, Bihar, Madhya Pradesh, Orissa and Uttar Pradesh remain at the bottom in the overall index, despite some improvements in their ranks in individual components as discussed earlier.

Perhaps the most important conclusion which emerges from this table is the relatively stagnant pattern of human development in the country. The relative positions of the states have hardly changed over the two decades. As far as regional patterns are concerned, the eastern states (Assam, Bihar, Orissa) are at the bottom, with West Bengal somewhere in the middle. The north-western states of Punjab, Gujarat and Maharashtra are clearly in a dominant position, closely followed by the southern states.

REGRESSION ANALYSIS

The debate on the relationship between the growth of national income and social indicators is not merely of academic interest but also has important implications for public policy. To the extent that growth in incomes is instrumental in raising levels of achievement in social indicators such as literacy and life expectancy, there is less of a need for public provisioning of social services. If, however, only a weak causal link exists between growth in per capita incomes and achievements in social indicators, then development policies cannot be centred on incomes alone. There would then be a need for more 'activist' government policies in so far as the social sectors are concerned.

To a large extent, the effectiveness of income growth in promoting achievements in social sectors is an empirical issue. Unfortunately, despite a substantial volume of work involving both cross-country studies as well as time series studies of specific countries, the evidence is inconclusive. *Ceteris paribus*, countries with higher income levels can naturally be expected to have higher levels of achievement is basic capabilities such as longevity and knowledge simply because these countries have more resources to spend on health care and education.[13]

[13] For example Anand and Ravallion (1993) find a statistically significant positive relationship between a non-linear transformation of life expectancy and log mean

However, the *ceteris paribus* assumption is inappropriate in this context because it does not take into account the possible impact of public spending on social services. In particular, it leaves open the possibility that poorer countries with significantly greater social sector spending may well outperform richer countries which follow income-centred objectives in terms of human development.

The case of Sri Lanka is often cited as an example in this context. Sri Lanka has extremely high achievements in longevity with life expectancy at birth being 71 years, as well as education with a literacy rate of 88 per cent. These figures compare very well with those of developed countries, though its real GDP per capita is far lower. Isenman (1980) and Sen (1981) attribute Sri Lanka's performance in the social sectors to active government intervention in the areas of health, education, food subsidies and other social welfare measures. These claims have been challenged by Bhalla (1988) and Bhalla and Glewwe (1986), who have questioned the effectiveness of the Sri Lankan government's welfare programmes. Nearer home, the performance of Kerala in social sector achievements is a close parallel. As we have seen in the previous section, Kerala is consistently at the top in health and education indicators, although in terms of per capita state domestic product, it performs rather poorly.[14] Indeed the rank correlation coefficients between the ranking of states according to income and either of the non-income indicators are not at all high. All this suggests the need for closer investigation of the effects of real per capita incomes and public expenditure on indicators of education and health. In this section, we report some results of a preliminary exercise on this issue.

Notice that separate regressions with income and public expenditure as explanatory variables may be misleading. For instance while income may turn out to be a significant explanatory variable according to such an exercise, this may be because income is correlated with other variables which are the *real* causes of high achievement levels in the social sectors (see Anand and Ravallion 1993). The correct procedure therefore is to use a *single* regression with both real per capita income and real per capita public expenditure as explanatory variables.

Since we have time series data on income and public expenditure for

income adjusted for purchasing power parity for a sample of twenty-two countries. A similar result is reported for income and infant mortality by Kakwani (1993).

[14] However, as we have pointed out earlier, Kerala's SGDP figures may underestimate its income because of large inward remittances.

individual states, we have investigated the relationship between education and health, and income and public expenditure separately for each state, instead of pooling the data. In the field of education, since data for high school enrolment are not comparable after 1988, our regressions are for the period 1970–88. For income, we have used real per capita state GDP at 1970–1 prices (RPCY) as reported by the CSO. The details of constructing this series have been given in the third section. Since we have one regression equation for *each* state, we have not adjusted for interstate price differentials. Public expenditure figures are available at the state level in RBI bulletins. However, the categories which are reported change over time, with recent years giving more disaggregated data. When disaggregated data are available, we have clubbed categories trying to maintain consistency as far as possible. For 1970–1 and 1971–2, just the broad heading of 'education' is available. From 1972–3 to 1984–5, the expenditure on education, art and culture, scientific services and research has been treated as expenditure on education. This category has again been revised from 1985–6 onwards to education, sports, and art and culture. The public expenditure series is available at current prices. We have deflated this series by the state GDP deflator (1970–1 = 100), to get public expenditure at 1970–1 prices. This was then divided by state population figures to get a series of real per capita public expenditure on education (RPCEX).

As far as the health sector is concerned, we concentrated on achievement in infant (AIMR) and child (ACMR) mortality rates.[15] As in the case of achievement in education, we look at the effects of real per capita income and real per capita public expenditure in health (RPCHX). The data for mortality rates are available for 1971–91, while those for income and public expenditure on health for 1970–90. The regressions were therefore run for the period 1971–90. Public expenditure on health is collected from various RBI bulletins. Here the problem is two-fold. First, over time, reported categories change. Second, greater disaggregation of expenditure is available in recent years. Since we are considering the wider issue of health, we have clubbed categories of expenditure which would affect general 'health' levels of the population. For 1970–1 and 1971–2, public expenditure data relating to health are available for only one category — medical and public health. For 1972–3 to 1984–5 we added two categories: (a) medical, family planning, public health,

---

[15] There have been several studies in India on the determinants of the infant mortality rate. See, for instance, Nag (1983), Visaria (1985), Tulasidhar and Sarma (1993), Reddy and Selvaraju (1993).

sanitation and water supply; and (b) food and nutrition. The data for 1985–6 to 1990–1 are more disaggregated and we had to club four categories to get the aggregate public expenditure on health. These categories were: (a) medical, public health and family planning; (b) water supply and sanitation; (c) nutrition; and (d) food storage and warehousing. Public expenditure data on health thus constructed are at current prices. To get real per capita public expenditure on health we deflated by the state GDP deflator (1970–1 = 100) and then divided it by population figures.

The other data issue is one of frequency of measurement of the variables. Public expenditure and income data relate to the fiscal year. However, enrolment figures are available for the school year, which also changes across states. Similarly, mortality rates relate to the calendar. Since, we only have annual data, there is no way to adjust for this.

Tables 13.9–13.11 describe the main regression results. Here we comment on the more important aspects. Table 13.9 shows the regression results of controlling for effects of both income and public expenditure on achievement indices. In most states the coefficient of income is either perverse or insignificantly different from zero. In contrast, public expenditure has a significant positive effect on AEPH after controlling for income in thirteen out of seventeen states. The fit of the equation is reasonably good, as indicated by the adjusted (for degrees of freedom) R^2, except in the case of Kerala, Orissa, Punjab and Uttar Pradesh. This regression exercise therefore suggests that public expenditure plays a significant role in increasing levels of education and that growth in income alone is not sufficient to explain increases in AEPH. Growth in income is important in so far as it facilitates greater public expenditure on education.

We also checked for the effect of lagged per capita real public expenditure on education on achievement indices. Lagged expenditure could have an effect due to the delayed effect of capital expenditure like building schools. To control for any lagged effect of public expenditure, the achievement index was regressed on current period per capita real income and public expenditure as well as real per capita public expenditure lagged by one period. The explanatory power of the equation went down in most cases, and the coefficient of lagged public expenditure was insignificantly different from zero in most cases. It therefore seems that lagged public expenditure has no power in explaining achievement indices of education in primary to high school.

Table 13.9
Regression Results — Achievement in Primary to High School
AEPH = a + b RPCY + c RPCEX

States	Coefficients			Adjusted R^2
	Constant	*RPCY*	*RPCEX*	
AP	−0.08	0.07	0.88	0.83
	(1.08)	(0.43)	(4.24)*	
AS	−0.13	0.50	0.02	0.70
	(−2.12)*	(3.37)*	(0.12)	
BI	−0.14	0.57	0.08	0.79
	(−4.48)*	(7.27)*	(1.23)	
GU	0.12	0.01	0.51	0.81
	(3.14)*	(0.21)	(5.22)*	
HA	0.22	−0.23	0.79	0.60
	(3.41)*	(−2.08)	(3.65)*	
HP	−0.09	0.33	0.41	0.66
	(−0.51)	(1.09)	(2.92)*	
JK	0.16	−0.14	0.28	0.55
	(5.14)*	(−2.36)*	(4.73)*	
KA	−0.03	0.12	0.69	0.86
	(0.61)	(0.90)	(3.26)*	
KE	0.87	−1.14	0.81	0.41
	(3.18)*	(−2.38)*	(3.62)*	
MP	−0.06	−0.05	1.42	0.92
	(−1.35)	(−0.36)	(5.69)*	
MH	0.01	0.08	0.83	0.93
	(0.29)	(1.01)	(5.22)*	
OR	−0.002	0.01	0.95	0.48
	(−0.02)	(0.03)	(3.21)*	
PU	−0.07	0.42	−0.66	0.43
	(−0.77)	(2.84)*	(−2.05)	
RA	0.04	−0.17	0.83	0.88
	(1.08)	(−2.59)*	(10.55)*	
TN	0.01	−0.22	2.16	0.74
	(0.09)	(−0.50)	(3.42)*	
UP	0.42	−0.65	0.61	0.21
	(3.93)*	(−2.00)	(1.24)	
WB	0.12	−0.09	0.74	0.52
	(0.71)	(−0.32)	(2.73)*	

Notes: The coefficient of RPCY is to be multiplied by E–03 and that of RPCEX by E–02.
t-statistics in parentheses below coefficients.
* significant at 5 per cent.
Time period of regression: 1970–88.

Table 13.10

Regression Results — Achievement in Infant Mortality Rate

AIMR = a + b RPCY + c RPCHX

States	Coefficients			Adjusted R^2
	Constant	RPCY	RPCHX	
AP	0.05	0.36	0.77	0.70
	(0.73)	(2.43)*	(1.99)	
AS	0.06	0.38	0.27	0.50
	(0.37)	(1.22)	(0.59)	
GU	0.06	0.16	0.79	0.61
	(0.86)	(1.67)	(2.50)*	
HA	0.23	0.13	0.02	0.23
	(3.71)*	(1.50)	(0.06)	
HP	0.36	−0.08	0.46	0.44
	(2.21)*	(−0.29)	(2.42)*	
JK	0.70	−0.34	−0.08	0.17
	(6.60)*	(−2.28)*	(−0.82)	
KA	0.31	0.15	0.17	0.25
	(4.06)*	(1.05)	(0.51)	
KE	0.91	−1.12	3.70	0.59
	(2.34)*	(−1.48)	(4.30)*	
MP	0.11	0.18	0.45	0.76
	(3.05)*	(1.91)	(2.33)*	
MH	0.16	0.16	0.85	0.79
	(3.59)*	(2.33)*	(3.12)*	
OR	0.15	0.09	0.60	0.40
	(2.89)*	(0.65)	(2.04)*	
PU	0.04	0.22	0.29	0.78
	(0.62)	(2.51)*	(0.66)	
RA	0.18	0.06	0.91	0.08
	(1.05)	(0.15)	(1.10)	
TN	0.09	0.32	0.73	0.79
	(1.08)	(2.20)	(4.26)*	
UP	−0.13	0.41	1.51	0.77
	(−0.98)	(1.12)	(1.58)	

Notes: The coefficient of RPCY is to be multiplied by E–03 and that of RPCHX by
E–02.

t-statistics in parentheses below coefficients.

* significant at 5 per cent.

Time period of regression: 1971–90.

Table 13.11
Regression Results — Achievement in Child Mortality Rate
ACMR = a + b RPCY + c RPCHX

States	Coefficients			Adjusted R^2
	Constant	RPCY	RPCHX	
AP	0.05	0.45	1.06	0.84
	(0.75)	(3.40)*	(3.07)*	
AS	0.35	0.02	0.59	0.35
	(2.40)*	(0.07)	(1.30)	
GU	0.12	0.18	0.86	0.72
	(2.12)*	(2.16)*	(3.14)*	
HA	0.26	0.15	0.38	0.53
	(4.19)*	(1.71)	(1.12)	
HP	0.40	−0.07	0.63	0.73
	(3.14)*	(−0.32)	(3.95)*	
JK	0.67	−0.20	−0.03	−0.09
	(3.37)*	(−0.72)	(0.13)	
KA	0.37	0.16	0.35	0.45
	(5.21)*	(1.18)	(1.10)	
KE	1.12	−1.39	3.75	0.67
	(3.57)*	(−2.28)*	(5.40)*	
MP	0.13	0.36	0.03	0.42
	(1.94)	(2.00)	(0.07)	
MH	0.20	0.21	0.82	0.87
	(5.48)*	(3.66)*	(3.60)*	
OR	0.20	0.13	1.24	0.65
	(3.22)*	(0.75)	(3.47)*	
PU	0.17	0.25	−0.03	0.74
	(2.61)*	(2.89)*	(−0.08)	
RA	0.29	−0.18	1.48	0.48
	(3.31)*	(−0.90)	(3.45)*	
TN	0.06	0.51	0.66	0.75
	(0.64)	(2.78)*	(3.01)*	
UP	−0.11	0.45	2.10	0.790
	(−0.68)	(1.01)	(1.81)	

Notes: The coefficient of RPCY is to be multiplied by E–03 and that of RPCHX by E–02.

t-statistics in parentheses below coefficients.

* significant at 5 per cent.

Time period of regression 1971–90.

Tables 13.10 and 13.11 present the results of controlling for the effects of both real per capita income and public expenditure on health on infant and child mortality rates.[16] Unlike in the case of education, the results are not so clear-cut. The coefficient of public expenditure on health is significant and positive in some states for both regression equations. This is also the case with the income variable, although for a smaller number of states. Also, in Kerala, the sign of per capita income was significant and *negative: In many states, neither variable turned out to be significant. Moreover, the adjusted R^2 in almost all equations for the health indicators was low.* We also controlled for the effect of lagged public expenditure on health. In almost all cases, the explanatory power of the equation went down, and the coefficient of the lagged expenditure variable was insignificant.

We are forced to conclude that our regression exercise is inconclusive so far as achievements in health indicators are concerned. There can be at least two reasons for this. First, factors such as the mother's level of education as a proxy for awareness about the importance of general hygiene, the number of other children in the family, and natal and post natal care facilities are likely to be important in influencing mortality rates amongst infants and young children. Second, the public expenditure variable that we have used is a 'catch-all' variable and includes expenditure on categories that are unlikely to have any significant impact on mortality rates.

Our results are at variance with those of Tulasidhar and Sarma (1993), who find a significant impact of real public expenditure on mortality rates. However, they distinguish between neonatal and perinatal mortality rates and pool time series and cross-section data. They also find significant state and time effects, which we account for by running separate state regressions. Finally, we have concentrated on achievement indices which are non-linear transforms of the mortality rates.

CONCLUSION

This study pursues the UNDP's perspective on human development by describing the human development experience in India during the decades of the 1970s and 1980s. The major empirical finding is that

---

[16] It should be noted that achievement indices of infant and child mortality exhibit significant rising trends in almost all states, and that in most states, a time trend alone explains a large fraction of the variation in these indices.

achievement levels in health and education have increased significantly during the last two decades. As far as the individual states are concerned, Kerala occupies the predominant position in achievement in health and education, though it is amongst the poorest in terms of income. This is, of course, part of traditional wisdom. Our results, however, strengthen this fact by pointing out that Kerala does remarkably well even in terms of *change*, particularly in health. The relative position of the various states indicates an almost stagnant pattern of human development at the interstate level.

The interstate experience also indicates that the correlation between per capita incomes and achievements in health and education is low. The time series regression analysis also indicates that expenditure in the health and education sectors is an important determinant of levels of achievement in these sectors. This suggests a reorientation of development policies in India, where social sector spending is low in comparison to that of many other countries at a similar stage of development.

Acknowledgements: We are most grateful to Jean Drèze and T.N. Srinivasan for detailed comments on an earlier version of the chapter, which is based on a study commissioned by the UNDP.

REFERENCES

Anand, S. and M. Ravallion (1993). 'Human Development in Poor Countries: On the Role of Private Incomes and Public Services', *Journal of Economic Perspectives*, 7(1), pp. 133–50.

Bhalla, S.S. (1988). 'Is Sri Lanka an Exception? A Comparative Study of Living Standards', in P.K. Bardhan and T.N. Srinivasan (eds), *Rural Poverty in South Asia*. New York: Columbia University Press.

Bhalla, S.S. and P. Glewwe (1986). 'Growth and Equity in Developing Countries: A Reinterpretation of Sri Lanka's Experience', *The World Bank Economic Review*, 1, pp. 35–63.

Dutta, B., M. Panda and W. Wadhwa (1994). 'Human Development in India: An Inter-State Analysis', mimeo.

Human Development Report (1990). New York: Oxford University Press.

—— (1991). New York: Oxford University Press.

—— (1992). New York: Oxford University Press.

—— (1993). New York: Oxford University Press.

Isenman, P. (1980). 'Basic Needs: The Case of Sri Lanka', *World Development*, 8.

Kakwani, N. (1993). 'Performance in Living Standards: An International Comparison', *Journal of Development Economics*, 41, pp. 307–36.

Kurien, J. (1983). *Elementary Education in India.* New Delhi: Vikas Publishing House.

Mehta, A.C. (1993). 'A Note on Educational Statistics in India', *Journal of Educational Planning and Administration*, 7, pp. 105–17.

Minhas, B.S. (1992). 'Educational Deprivation and Its Role as a Spoiler of Access to Better Life in India', in A. Dutta and M.M. Agrawal (eds), *The Quality of Life.* Shimla: Indian Institute of Advanced Study.

Minhas, B.S., L.R. Jain and S.D. Tendulkar (1991). 'Declining Incidence of Poverty in the 1980s: Evidence versus Artefacts', *Economic and Political Weekly*, 6–13 July.

Morris, Morris D. (1979). *Measuring the Condition of the World's Poor: The Physical Quality of Life Index.* New York: Pergamon Press.

Reddy, K.N. and V. Selvaraju (1993). 'Determinants of Health Status in India: An Empirical Verification', mimeo., National Institute of Public Finance and Policy, New Delhi.

Sen, A.K. (1981). 'Public Action and the Quality of Life in Developing Countries', *Oxford Bulletin of Economics and Statistics*, 43, pp. 287–319.

—— (1985). *Commodities and Capabilities.* Amsterdam: North Holland.

—— (1987). *The Standard of Living.* The Tanner Lectures, New York: Cambridge University Press.

Tulasidhar, V.B. and J.V.M. Sarma (1993). 'Public Expenditure, Medical Care at Birth and Infant Mortality: A Comparative Study of States in India', in P. Berman and M.E. Khan (eds), *Paying for India's Health Care.* New Delhi: Sage Publications.

APPENDIX   A

EXPLANATORY NOTE ON PERIODS

We have divided the time series analysis into four periods. The periods are:

	Health	*Education*	*Income*
Period I	1971–5	1970–1 to 1974–5	1970–1 to 1974–5
Period II	1976–80	1975–6 to 1979–80	1975–6 to 1979–80
Period III	1981–5	1980–1 to 1984–5	1980–1 to 1984–5
Period IV	1986–91	1985–6 to 1988–9	1985–6 to 1990–1

Health data (IMR and CMR) for two states — Bihar and West Bengal — are available only from 1981 onwards covering periods III and IV only. Enrolment data for high school after 1988–9 are not available and hence period IV for EPH and EMH variables covers only the period up to 1988–9. A few more gaps in data availability are: (i) IMR by male and female categories for 1973 to 1976 and for 1978; (ii) for Jammu and Kashmir, CMR and IMR data for 1971 and 1991 and enrolment data for 1973.

APPENDIX   B

LIST OF STATES

Andhra Pradesh	AP	Madhya Pradesh	MP
Assam	AS	Maharashtra	MA
Bihar	BI	Orissa	OR
Gujarat	GU	Punjab	PU
Haryana	HA	Rajasthan	RA
Himachal Pradesh	HP	Tamil Nadu	TN
Jammu & Kashmir	JK	Uttar Pradesh	UP
Karnataka	KA	West Bengal	WB
Kerala	KE	All-India	AI

Annotated Bibliography

Note: This bibliography is not intended to be anything like exhaustive. To the contrary, it is a select and restricted list of readings, designed to provide the interested reader with references which will afford him/her a broad overview of certain crucial issues thrown up by the literature. Those interested in deeper explorations may find some useful guidelines in the fairly extensive References at the end of the editor's Introduction.

1. INEQUALITY: GENERAL CONCEPTUAL ISSUES

Sen, A.K. (1973). *On Economic Inequality*. Oxford: Clarendon. A remarkably lucid account of the conceptual, philosophical and measurement issues underlying the notion of economic inequality. Essential and indispensable.

—— (1992). *Inequality Reexamined*. New York: Russel Sage Foundation/ Oxford: Clarendon. An essay on the place of inequality in alternative ethical systems, and a critical evaluation of the philosophical foundations of inequality as a concept.

2. AGGREGATION ISSUES IN INEQUALITY MEASUREMENT

Foster, J. (1985). 'Inequality Measurement', in H.P. Young (ed.), *Fair Allocation*. Providence, RI: American Mathematical Society. A fine survey of alternative approaches to the measurement of inequality, with the technical aspects of the exercise treated with both care and clarity.

Sen, A.K. (1978). 'Ethical Measurement of Inequality: Some Difficulties', in W. Krelle and A.F. Shorrocks (eds), *Personal Income Distribution*. Amsterdam: North Holland. A critical assessment of the class of 'ethical' inequality indices which have their basis in an explicitly social welfare approach to the measurement of inequality.

Shorrocks, A.F. (1988). 'Aggregation Issues in Inequality Measurement', in W. Eichhorn (ed.), *Measurement in Economics: Theory and Applications in Economic Indices*. Heidelberg: Physica–Verlag. Again a survey of inequality measurement, with specific reference to the important issue of decomposability of inequality measures.

Research and Policy. Bombay: Oxford University Press. A collection of essays dealing with various aspects of poverty — from prevalence to policy — in contemporary India.

Srinivasan, T.N. and P.K. Bardhan (eds) (1988). *Rural Poverty in South Asia.* New York: Columbia University Press. A subcontinental perspective of country experiences, from different authors.

8. THE REDRESSAL OF POVERTY

Ahmed, E., J. Drèze, J. Hills and A. Sen (eds) (1991). *Social Security in Developing Countries.* Oxford: Clarendon Press. A collection of essays reviewing diverse country experiences in the matter of the performance and potential of social security measures as an ingredient of anti-poverty policy in the developing world.

Besley, T. and R. Kanbur (1993): 'The Principles of Targeting', in M. Lipton and J. van der Gaag (eds) (1993). *Including the Poor.* Washington, D.C.: The World Bank. A remarkably lucid and non- technical treatment of several issues associated with the problem of 'targeting' in anti-poverty policy.

Drèze, J. and A. Sen (1989). *Hunger and Public Action.* Oxford: Clarendon Press. A consideration of the conceptual and practical problems of implementing anti-poverty policy, including under conditions of famine.

9. POVERTY AND INEQUALITY: CONNECTED TREATMENTS

Foster, J. and A.F. Shorrocks (1988). 'Inequality and Poverty Orderings', *European Economic Review*, 32, pp. 654–62. A brief but illuminating statement of issues and results dealing with the conditions under which unambiguous rankings of income distributions, in terms of inequality and poverty judgments, are possible.

Kakwani, N.C. (1980). *Income Inequality and Poverty.* New York: Oxford University Press. An extremely useful handbook for practitioners, especially in terms of providing guidelines on computational and estimation techniques involved in handling data-sets.

Lewis, G.W. and D.T. Ulph (1988). 'Poverty, Inequality and Welfare', *Economic Journal*, 98, pp. 117–31. An instructive analysis of the points of convergence and divergence between the notions of poverty and inequality, located within a framework of social welfare.

Author Index